ROOM ACOUSTICS

Third Edition

ROOM ACOUSTICS

THIRD EDITION

HEINRICH KUTTRUFF

Institut für Technische Akustik, Technischen Hochschule, Aachen, Germany

ELSEVIER APPLIED SCIENCE
LONDON and NEW YORK

ELSEVIER SCIENCE PUBLISHERS LTD
Crown House, Linton Road, Barking, Essex IG11 8JU, England

Sole distributor in the USA and Canada
ELSEVIER SCIENCE PUBLISHING CO., INC.
655 Avenue of the Americas, New York, NY 10010, USA

First Edition 1973
Second Edition 1979
Third Edition 1991

WITH 13 TABLES AND 125 ILLUSTRATIONS

© 1991 ELSEVIER SCIENCE PUBLISHERS LTD

British Library Cataloguing in Publication Data

Kuttruff, Heinrich
  Room Acoustics—3rd ed.
  1. Buildings. Interiors. Acoustics.
  I. Title.
  729.29

ISBN 1-85166-576-5

Library of Congress Cataloging-in-Publication Data

Kuttruff, Heinrich.
  Room Acoustics/Heinrich Kuttruff.—3rd ed,
    p.   cm.
  Includes bibliographical references and index.
  ISBN 1-85166-576-5
  1. Architectural acoustics. I. Title.
  NA2800.K87 1991   90-28296
  729'.29—dc290   CIP

Printed in Great Britain by Galliard (Printers) Ltd, Great Yarmouth

Preface to the Third Edition

Since the second edition of this book was published more than a decade has elapsed, and in this period many new ideas and methods have been introduced into room acoustics. Therefore, I welcome the opportunity to prepare a new edition of this book and to include those developments which are considered more important.

In room acoustics, as in many other technical fields, the digital computer has continued its triumphal march; nowadays hardly any acoustical measurement is carried out without employing some kind of computer, allowing previously inconceivable improvements in accuracy and rapidity. Therefore, a thorough revision of the chapter on measuring techniques was mandatory (Chapter VIII). Furthermore, the increased availability of digital computers has opened new ways for the computation and simulation of sound fields in enclosures. These have led to better and more reliable methods in the practical design of halls; indeed, due to its flexibility and low cost, sound field simulation will probably replace the conventional scale model in the near future. Moreover, whilst a new concert hall is still on the drawing board, it demonstrates what the hall will sound like when completed. Such methods have been included in Chapter IX of the new edition.

Also included in the new edition are the developments of diffusors based on pseudostochastic sequences or on number-theoretical schemes (so-called 'Schroeder' diffusors), the modulation transfer function and quality criteria derived from the aforementioned, and the prediction of noise levels in enclosures, including those in which diffuse sound field conditions cannot be expected.

Finally, the preparation of a new edition offered the chance to improve numerous text passages and formulae, and to eliminate errors and mistakes which inevitably crept into the previous editions. I appreciate the suggestions of many critical readers; in particular, I am indebted to the late Professor L. Cremer (Berlin/Miesbach) and Professor J. Makita (Tokyo) for drawing my attention to any weak, misleading or incorrect material in the book.

As in the earlier editions, no attempt is made to list all relevant publications on room acoustics; references are made only when the author adopted results from a particular publication, or to enable the reader to obtain more detailed information on a topic dealt within the book. I apologise for leaving many important and interesting publications unmentioned.

Finally, I would like to express my most sincere thanks to Professor Peter Lord of the University of Salford, who translated the author's manuscript into 'real' English, as he did in such a marvellous way in the earlier editions.

HEINRICH KUTTRUFF
Aachen

Preface to the Second Edition

The need for a second edition of this book has provided the author with the opportunity to eliminate errors in text and formulae, and—even more important—to add recent developments which were not available at the time the first edition was written. Furthermore, certain sections and passages have been revised in order to make the text more complete and comprehensible. However, it was possible to retain the approximate length of the original book by omitting less important or obsolete material.

The author is indebted to all those readers who have pointed out incorrect formulae or symbols and who have helped, by their constructive criticism, to improve the substance of the book. Special thanks are again due to Professor P. Lord of the University of Salford for critically reviewing the manuscript of the second edition.

HEINRICH KUTTRUFF
Aachen

Preface to the Second Edition

Preface to the First Edition

This book is intended to present the fundamentals of room acoustics in a systematic and comprehensive way so that the information thus provided may be used for the acoustical design of rooms and as a guide to the techniques of associated measurement.

These fundamentals are twofold in nature: the generation and propagation of sound in an enclosure, which are physical processes which can be described without ambiguity in the language of the physicist and engineer; and the physiological and psychological factors, of prime importance but not capable of exact description even within our present state of knowledge. It is the interdependence and the equality of importance of both these aspects of acoustics which are characteristic of room acoustics, whether we are discussing questions of measuring techniques, acoustical design, or the installation of a public address system.

In the earlier part of the book ample space is devoted to the objective description of sound fields in enclosures, but, even at this stage, taking into account, as far as possible, the limitations imposed by the properties of our hearing. Equal weight is given to both the wave and geometrical description of sound fields, the former serving to provide a more basic understanding, the latter lending itself to practical application. In both instances, full use is made of statistical methods; therefore, a separate treatment of what is generally known as 'statistical room acoustics' has been dispensed with.

The treatment of absorption mechanisms is based upon the concept that a thorough understanding of the various absorbers is indispensable for the acoustician. However, in designing a room he will not, in all probability, attempt to calculate the absorptivity of a particular arrangement but instead will rely on collected measurements and data based on experience. It is for this reason that in the chapter on measuring techniques the methods of determining absorption are discussed in some detail.

Some difficulties were encountered in attempting to describe the factors which are important in the perception of sound in rooms, primarily because of the fragmentary nature of the present state of knowledge, which seems to

ix

consist of results of isolated experiments which are strongly influenced by the conditions under which they were performed.

We have refrained from giving examples of completed rooms to illustrate how the techniques of room acoustics can be applied. These are already in print, for example Beranek,[1] Bruckmayer,[2] and Furrer and Lauber.[3] Instead, we have chosen to show how one can progress in designing a room and which parameters need to be considered. Furthermore, because model investigations have proved helpful these are described in detail.

Finally, there is a whole chapter devoted to the design of loudspeaker installations in rooms. This is to take account of the fact that nowadays electroacoustic installations are more than a mere crutch in that they frequently present, even in the most acoustically faultless room, the only means of transmitting the spoken word in an intelligible way. Actually, the installations and their performance play a more important role in determining the acoustical quality of what is heard than certain design details of the room itself.

The book should be understood in its entirety by readers with a reasonable mathematical background and some elementary knowledge of wave propagation. Certain hypotheses may be omitted without detriment by readers with more limited mathematical training.

The literature on room acoustics is so extensive that the author has made no attempt to provide an exhaustive list of references. References have only been given in those cases where the work has been directly mentioned in the text or in order to satisfy possible demand for more detailed information.

The author is greatly indebted to Professor Peter Lord of the University of Salford and Mrs Evelyn Robinson of Prestbury, Cheshire, for their painstaking translation of the German manuscript, and for their efforts to present some ideas expressed in my native language into colloquial English. Furthermore, the author wishes to express his appreciation to the publishers for this carefully prepared edition. Last, but not least, he wishes to thank his wife most sincerely for her patience in the face of numerous evenings and weekends which he has devoted to his manuscript.

HEINRICH KUTTRUFF
Aachen

1. Beranek, L. L. (1962). *Music, Acoustics and Architecture.* John Wiley, New York/London.
2. Bruckmayer, F. (1962). *Schalltechnik im Hochbau.* Franz Deuticke, Wien.
3. Furrer, W. & Lauber, A. (1972). *Raum und Bauakustik, Lärmabwehr,* 3rd edn. Birkhäuser, Basel.

Contents

Contents xiii

Introduction

We all know that a concert hall, theatre, lecture room or a church may have
good or poor 'acoustics'. As far as speech in these rooms is concerned, it is
relatively simple to make some sort of judgement on their quality by
rating the ease with which the spoken word is understood. However,
judging the acoustics of a concert hall or an opera house is generally more
difficult, since it requires considerable experience, the opportunity for
comparisons and a critical ear. Even so the inexperienced cannot fail to
learn about the acoustical reputation of a certain concert hall if they wish,
for instance by listening to the comments of others, or by reading the
critical reviews of concerts in the press.

An everyday experience (although most people are not consciously
aware of it) is that living rooms, offices, restaurants and all kinds of rooms
for work can be acoustically satisfactory or unsatisfactory. Even rooms
which are generally considered insignificant or spaces such as staircases,
factories, passenger concourses in railway stations and airports may exhibit
different acoustical properties; they may be especially noisy or exception-
ally quiet, or they may differ in the ease with which announcements over the
public address system can be understood. That is to say, even these spaces
have 'acoustics' which may be satisfactory or less than satisfactory.

Despite the fact that people are subconsciously aware of the acoustics to
which they are daily subjected, there are only a few who can explain what
they really mean by 'good or poor acoustics' and who understand factors
which influence or give rise to certain acoustic properties. Even fewer
people know that the acoustics of a room is governed by principles which
are amenable to scientific treatment. It is frequently thought that the
acoustical design of a room is a matter of chance, and that good acoustics
cannot be designed into a room with the same precision as an atomic
reactor or space vehicle is designed. This idea is supported by the fact that

1

opinions on the acoustics of a certain room or hall frequently differ as widely as the opinions on the literary qualities of a new book or on the architectural design of a new building. Furthermore, it is well known that sensational failures in this field do occur from time to time. These and similar anomalies add even more weight to the general belief that the acoustics of a room is beyond the scope of calculation or prediction, at least with any reliability, and hence the study of room acoustics is an art rather than an exact science.

In order to shed more light on the nature of room acoustics, let us first compare it with a related field: the design and construction of musical instruments. This comparison is not as senseless as it may appear at first sight, since a concert hall too may be regarded as a large musical instrument, the shape and material of which determine to a considerable extent what the listener will hear. Musical instruments—string instruments for instance—are, as is well known, not designed or built by scientifically trained acousticians but, fortunately, by people who have acquired the necessary experience through long and systematic practical training. Designing or building musical instruments is therefore not a technical or scientific discipline but a sort of craft, or an 'art' in the classical meaning of this word.

Nevertheless, there is no doubt that the way in which a musical instrument functions, i.e. the mechanism of sound generation, the determining of the pitch of the tones generated and their timbre through certain resonances, as well as their radiation into the surrounding air, are all purely physical processes and can therefore be understood rationally, at least in principle. Similarly, there is no mystery in the choice of materials; their mechanical and acoustical properties can be defined by measurements to any required degree of accuracy. (How well these properties can be reproduced is another problem) Thus, there is nothing intangible nor is there any magic in the construction of a musical instrument: many particular problems which are still unsolved will be understood in the not too distant future. Then one will doubtless be in a position to design a musical instrument according to scientific methods, i.e. not only to predict its timbre but also to give, with scientific accuracy, details for its construction, all of which are necessary to obtain prescribed or desired acoustical qualities.

Room acoustics is in a different position from musical instrument acoustics in that the end product is usually more costly by orders of magnitude. Furthermore, rooms are produced in much smaller numbers and have by no means geometrical shapes which remain unmodified through the centuries. On the contrary, every architect, by the very nature of his professsion, strives to create something which is entirely new and original. The materials used are also subject to the rapid development of building technology. Therefore, it is impossible to collect in a purely empirical manner sufficient know-how from which reliable rules for the acoustical design of rooms or halls can be distilled. An acoustical consultant is confronted with quite a new situation with each task, each theatre, concert hall or lecture room to be designed, and it is of little value simply to transfer the experience of former cases to the new project if nothing is known about the conditions under which the transfer may be safely made.

This is in contrast to the making of a musical instrument where the use of unconventional materials as well as the application of new shapes is firmly rejected either as an offence against sacred traditions or dismissed as a whim. As a consequence, time has been sufficient to develop well established empirical rules. And if their application happens to fail in one case or another, the faulty product is abandoned or withdrawn from service—which is not true for large rooms in an analogous situation.

For the above reasons, the acoustician has been compelled to study sound propagation in closed spaces with increasing thoroughness and to develop the knowledge in this field much further than is the case with musical instruments, even though the acoustical behaviour of a large hall is considerably more complex and involved. Thus, room acoustics has become a science during the past seven decades and those who practise it on a purely empirical basis will fail sooner or later, like a bridge builder who waives calculations and relies on experience or empiricism.

On the other hand, we are not stating that the present level of reliable knowledge in our field is particularly advanced. Many important factors influencing the acoustical qualities of large rooms are understood only incompletely or even not at all. As will be explained below in more detail, this is due to the complexity of sound fields in closed spaces—or, as we may say equally well—to the large number of 'degrees of freedom' which we have to deal with. Another difficulty is that the acoustical quality of a room ultimately has to be proved by subjective judgements.

In order to gain more understanding about the sort of questions which can be answered eventually by scientific room acoustics, let us look over the procedures for designing the acoustics of a large room. If this room is to be newly built, some ideas will exist as to its intended use. It will have been established, for example, whether it is to be used for the reproduction of ciné films, for sports events, for concerts or as an open-plan office. One of the first tasks of the consultant is to translate these ideas concerning the practical use into the language of objective sound field parameters and to fix values for them which he thinks will best meet the requirements. During this step he has to keep in mind the limitations and peculiarities of our subjective listening abilities. (It does not make sense, for instance, to fix the duration of sound decay with an accuracy of 1% if no one can subjectively distinguish such small differences.) Ideally, the next step would be to determine the shape of the hall, to choose the materials to be used, to plan the arrangement of audience, of the orchestra and other sound sources, and to do all this in such a way that the sound field configuration will develop which has previously been found to be the optimum for the intended purpose. In practice, however, the architect will have worked out already a preliminary design, certain features of which he considers imperative. In this case the acoustical consultant has to examine the objective acoustical properties of the design by calculation, by geometric ray considerations, by model investigations or even by computer simulation, and he will eventually have to submit proposals for suitable adjustments. As a general rule there will have to be some compromise in order to obtain a reasonable result.

Frequently the problem is refurbishment of an existing hall, either to remove architectural, acoustical or other technical defects or to adapt it to a new purpose which was not intended when the hall was originally planned. In this case an acoustical diagnosis has to be made first on the basis of appropriate measurement. A reliable measuring technique which yields objective quantities, which are subjectively meaningful at the same time, is an indispensable tool of the acoustician. The subsequent therapeutic step is essentially the same as described above: the acoustical consultant has to propose measures which would result in the intended objective changes in the sound field and consequently in the subjective impressions of the listeners.

In any case, the acoustician is faced with a two-fold problem: on the one hand he has to find and to apply the relations between the structural features of a room—such as shape, materials and so on—with the sound field which will occur in it, and on the other hand he has to take into consideration as far as possible the interrelations between the objective and measurable sound field parameters and the specific subjective hearing impressions effected by them. Whereas the first problem lies completely in the realm of technical reasoning, it is the latter problem which makes room acoustics different from many other technical disciplines in that the success or failure of an acoustical design has finally to be decided by the collective judgement of all 'consumers', i.e. by some sort of average, taken over the comments of individuals with widely varying intellectual, educational and aesthetic backgrounds. The measurement of sound field parameters can replace to a certain extent systematic or sporadic questioning of listeners. But, in the final analysis, it is the average opinion of listeners which decides whether the acoustics of a room is favourable or poor. If the majority of the audience (or that part which is vocal) cannot understand what a speaker is saying, or thinks that the sound of an orchestra in a certain hall is too dry, too weak or indistinct, then even though the measured reverberation time is appropriate, or the local or directional distribution of sound is uniform, the listener is always right; the hall does have acoustical deficiencies.

Therefore, acoustical measuring techniques can only be a substitute for the investigation of public opinion on the acoustical qualities of a room and it will serve its purpose better the closer the measured sound field parameters are related to subjective listening categories.

Not only must the measuring techniques take into account the hearing response of the listeners but the acoustical theory too will only provide meaningful information if it takes regard of the consumer's particular listening abilities. It should be mentioned at this point that the sound field in a real room is so complicated that it is not open to exact mathematical treatment. The reason for this is the large number of components which make up the sound field in a closed space regardless of whether we describe it in terms of vibrational modes or, if we prefer, in terms of sound rays which have undergone one or more reflections from boundaries. Each of these components depends on the sound source, the shape of the room and on the materials from which it is made; accordingly, the exact computation of the sound field is usually quite involved. Supposing this procedure were possible with reasonable expenditure, the results would be so confusing that such a treatment would not provide a comprehensive survey and hence would not be of any practical use. For this reason, approximations and simplifications are inevitable; the totality of possible sound field data has to be reduced to averages or average functions which are more tractable and condensed to provide a clearer picture. This is why we have to resort so frequently to statistical methods and models in room acoustics, whichever way we attempt to describe sound fields. The problem is to perform these reductions and simplifications once again in accordance with the properties of human hearing, i.e. in such a way that the remaining average parameters correspond as closely as possible to particular subjective sensations.

From this it follows that essential progress in room acoustics depends to a large extent on the advances in psychological acoustics. As long as the physiological and psychological processes which are involved in hearing are not completely understood, the relevant relations between objective stimuli and subjective sensations must be investigated empirically—and should be taken into account when designing the acoustics of a room.

Many interesting relations of this kind have been detected and successfully investigated during the past few decades. But other questions which are no less important for room acoustics are unanswered so far, and much work remains to be carried out in this field.

It is, of course, the purpose of all efforts in room acoustics to avoid acoustical deficiencies and mistakes. It should be mentioned, on the other hand, that it is neither desirable nor possible to create the 'ideal acoustical environment' for concerts and theatres. It is a fact that the enjoyment when listening to music is a matter not only of the measurable sound waves hitting the ear but also of the listener's personal attitude and his individual taste, and these vary from one person to another. For this reason there will always be varying shades of opinion concerning the acoustics of even the most marvellous concert hall. For the same reason, one can easily imagine a wide variety of concert halls with excellent, but nevertheless different, acoustics. It is this 'lack of uniformity' which is characteristic of the subject of room acoustics, and which is responsible for many of its difficulties, but it also accounts for the continuous power of attraction it exerts on many acousticians.

I

Some Facts on Sound Waves, Sources and Hearing

In principle, any complex sound field can be considered as a superposition of numerous simple sound waves, e.g. plane waves. This is especially true of the very involved sound fields which we have to deal with in room acoustics. So it is useful to describe first the properties of a simple plane or a spherical sound wave, or, more basically, the general features of sound propagation. We can, however, restrict our attention to sound propagation in gases, because in room acoustics we are only concerned with air as the medium.

In this chapter we assume the sound propagation to be free of losses and ignore the effect of any obstacles such as walls, i.e. we suppose the medium to be unbounded in all directions. Furthermore, we assume our medium to be homogeneous and at rest. In this case the velocity of sound is constant with reference to space and time. For air, its magnitude is

$$c = (331 \cdot 4 + 0 \cdot 6\Theta) \quad \text{m/s} \tag{I.1}$$

Θ being the temperature in centigrade.

In large halls, variations of temperature and hence of the sound velocity with time and position cannot be entirely avoided. Likewise, because of temperature differences and air conditioning, the air is not completely at rest, and so our assumptions are not fully realised. But the effects which are caused by these inhomogeneities are so small that they can be neglected.

I.1 ACOUSTICAL QUANTITIES

In any sound wave, the particles of the medium undergo vibrations about their mean positions. Therefore, a wave can be described completely by indicating the instantaneous displacements of these particles. It is more

7

customary, however, to consider the velocity of particle displacement as a basic acoustical quantity rather than the displacement itself.

The vibrations in a sound wave do not take place at all points with the same phase. We can, in fact, find points in a sound field where the particles vibrate in opposite phase. This means that in certain regions the particles are pushed together or compressed and in other regions they are pulled apart or rarefied. Therefore, under the influence of a sound wave, variations of gas density and pressure occur, both of which are functions of time and space. The difference between the instantaneous pressure and the static pressure is called the sound pressure.

The changes of gas pressure caused by a sound wave in general occur so rapidly that heat cannot be exchanged between adjacent volume elements. Consequently, a sound wave causes adiabatic variations of the temperature, and so the temperature too can be considered as a quantity characterising a sound wave.

The various acoustical quantities are connected by a number of basic laws which enable us to set up a general differential equation governing sound propagation. Firstly, conservation of momentum is expressed by the relation

$$\operatorname{grad} p = -\rho_0 \frac{\partial \mathbf{v}}{\partial t} \tag{I.2}$$

where p denotes the sound pressure, $\mathbf{v}$ the vector particle velocity, t the time and ρ_0 the static value of the gas density.

Furthermore, conservation of mass leads to

$$\rho_0 \operatorname{div} \mathbf{v} = -\frac{\partial \rho}{\partial t} \tag{I.3}$$

ρ being the time-dependent part of the gas density. In these equations, it is tacitly assumed that the changes of p and ρ are small compared with the static values p_0 and ρ_0 of these quantities; furthermore, the absolute value of the particle velocity $\mathbf{v}$ should be much smaller than the sound velocity c.

Under the further supposition that we are dealing with an ideal gas, the following relations hold between the sound pressure, the density variations and the temperature changes $\delta\Theta$:

$$\frac{p}{p_0} = \kappa \frac{\rho}{\rho_0} = \frac{\kappa}{\kappa - 1} \frac{\delta\Theta}{\Theta + 273} \tag{I.4}$$

Here κ is the adiabatic exponent (for air $\kappa = 1\cdot4$).

The particle velocity $\mathbf{v}$ and the variable part ρ of the density can be eliminated from eqns (I.2) to (I.4). This yields the differential equation

$$c^2 \, \overset{\frown}{\Delta p} = \frac{\partial^2 p}{\partial t^2}$$

(I.5)

where

$$c^2 = \kappa \frac{p_0}{\rho_0}$$

(I.5a)

This differential equation governs the propagation of sound waves in any lossless fluid and is therefore of central importance for all acoustical phenomena. We shall refer to it as the 'wave equation'. It holds not only for sound pressure but also for density variations and temperature variations as well.

I.2 PLANE WAVES, ENERGY DENSITY AND SOUND INTENSITY

Now we assume that the acoustical quantities depend only on the time and on one single direction, which may be chosen as the x-direction of a cartesian coordinate system. Then eqn (I.5) reads

$$c^2 \frac{\partial^2 p}{\partial x^2} = \frac{\partial^2 p}{\partial t^2}$$

(I.6)

The general solution of this differential equation is

$$p(x, t) = F(ct - x) + G(ct + x)$$

(I.7)

where F and G are arbitrary functions, the second derivatives of which exist. The first term on the right represents a pressure wave travelling in the positive x-direction with a velocity c, because the value of F remains unaltered if a time increase δt is associated with an increase in the coordinate $\delta x = c \delta t$. For the same reason the second term describes a pressure wave propagated in the negative x-direction. Therefore the constant c is the sound velocity.

Solutions of special importance are obtained by specifying F and G as exponential functions with imaginary arguments. Then the component propagated in the positive x-direction is

$$p(x, t) = \hat{p} \exp\left[ik(ct - x)\right] = \hat{p} \exp\left[i(\omega t - kx)\right]$$

(I.8)

with arbitrary real constants $\hat{p}$ and k. Here we have introduced

$$k = \frac{\omega}{c} \tag{I.9}$$

Since any observable physical quantity is always real, only the real part (or the imaginary part) of eqn (I.8) has a physical meaning. Therefore, we consider eqn (I.8) as a shorthand notation of

$$p(x, t) = \hat{p}\cos(\omega t - kx) \quad \text{or} \quad \hat{p}\sin(\omega t - kx)$$

So eqn (I.8) represents a temporal and spatial harmonic vibration of amplitude $\hat{p}$. The constant ω denotes the angular frequency, so $2\pi/\omega$ is the temporal period of the vibration. Corresponding values of the sound pressure are separated by a distance

$$\lambda = \frac{2\pi}{k} \tag{I.10}$$

or multiples of it. This is the spatial period of the wave, called 'wavelength'. According to eqn (I.9) it is related to the angular frequency by

$$\lambda = \frac{2\pi c}{\omega} = \frac{c}{f} \tag{I.11}$$

where $f = \omega/2\pi$ is the frequency of the vibration. It is measured in Hertz and has the dimension second^{-1}. (Abbreviations: Hz, kHz, etc.) The constant k is the propagation constant or the wave number of the wave. If the frequency is fixed, the wavelength and the wave number are also determined.

The complex representation of a vibration has several advantages compared with the real notation. Any differentiation or integration with respect to time, for instance, is equivalent to multiplication or division by $i\omega$. Furthermore, only the complex notation makes the concept of impedance reasonable (see Section II.1). It fails, however, in all cases where complex quantities are to be multiplied or squared. If doubts arise concerning the physical meaning of an expression, it is always advisable to take the real part of it.

Equation (I.8) describes a plane wave. In any plane perpendicular to the x-axis the exponent and hence the phase of vibration is constant. According to eqn (I.2), the particle velocity has only one non-vanishing component parallel to the x-axis:

$$v = v_x = -\frac{1}{i\omega}\frac{1}{\rho_0}\frac{\partial p}{\partial x} = \frac{k}{\rho_0\omega}p = \frac{p}{\rho_0 c} \tag{I.12}$$

This means sound waves are longitudinal waves. The ratio of sound pressure and particle velocity in a plane wave is frequency independent and real, i.e. pressure and particle velocity have the same phase. This ratio is called the 'characteristic impedance' of the medium. For air at normal conditions its value is

$$\rho_0 c = 414 \, \text{kgm}^{-2} \, \text{s}^{-1} \tag{I.13}$$

If the wave is travelling in the negative x-direction, the ratio of sound pressure and velocity has a negative sign.

We imagine a surface with unit area perpendicular to the wave direction. The sound energy flowing per second across this surface is called the 'intensity' of the wave. It equals the time average of the product of pressure and particle velocity:

$$I = \overline{pv} = \frac{\overline{p^2}}{\rho_0 c} \tag{I.14}$$

(the bars indicate averaging with respect to time).

Since the wave travels a distance c per second and in this time transports energy I, the energy per unit volume is

$$w = \frac{I}{c} = \frac{\overline{p^2}}{\rho_0 c^2} \tag{I.15}$$

This quantity is called the 'energy density' in a sound wave.

For harmonic vibrations, i.e. for $p = \hat{p} \cos \omega t$, the time average of the squared trigonometric function is $\frac{1}{2}$ and so

$$I = \frac{\hat{p}^2}{2\rho_0 c} \qquad w = \frac{\hat{p}^2}{2\rho_0 c^2} \tag{I.16}$$

where $\hat{p}$ is the sound pressure amplitude from eqn (I.8).

Experimentally, a plane wave can only be raised approximately. Thus a sufficiently narrow section of a spherical wave (*see* Section I.3) or a sound wave excited in a tube with hard walls, the lateral dimensions of which are much smaller than a wavelength, approximate to plane waves.

I.3 SPHERICAL WAVES, SOUND RADIATION

Another simple wave type is obtained by writing the wave equation (I.5) in spherical polar coordinates and by assuming that all acoustical quantities, especially the sound pressure, depend only on the distance r from the origin, but not on direction. In this case the differential equation (I.5) reads

$$\frac{\partial^2 p}{\partial r^2} + \frac{2}{r}\frac{\partial p}{\partial r} = \frac{1}{c^2}\frac{\partial^2 p}{\partial t^2} \qquad (I.17)$$

or, if we again assume a harmonic law for the time dependence $[p \sim \exp(i\omega t)]$ and remember that $\omega = kc$,

$$\frac{d^2 p}{dr^2} + \frac{2}{r}\frac{dp}{dr} + k^2 p = 0 \qquad (I.18)$$

One solution of this equation is given by

$$p(r, t) = C\frac{\exp[i(\omega t - kr)]}{r} \qquad (I.19)$$

with the arbitrary constant C. This expression represents a spherical wave since the surfaces of constant phase are concentric spheres, the centres of which coincide with the origin of the coordinate system $r = 0$. According to the sign in the exponent, the wave is propagated in the direction of increasing distance; its amplitude decreases as $1/r$. (The less significant case of an in-going wave would be obtained by reversing the sign in the bracket of eqn (I.19).)

Inserting eqn (I.19) into eqn (I.2) yields the radial component of the particle velocity (the only non-vanishing component):

$$v_r = -\frac{1}{\rho_0}\frac{1}{i\omega}\frac{dp}{dr} = \frac{p}{\rho_0 c}\left(1 + \frac{1}{ikr}\right) \qquad (I.20)$$

This formula indicates that the ratio of sound pressure and particle velocity in a spherical sound wave depends on the distance r and the frequency $\omega = kc$. Furthermore, it is complex, i.e. between both quantities there is a phase difference. For $kr \gg 1$, i.e. for distances which are large compared with the wavelength, the ratio p/v_r tends asymptotically to $\rho_0 c$, the characteristic impedance. In this region, the relations (I.16) for the intensity and energy density in a plane wave can be applied. By multiplying the former with the area of the sphere of radius r we obtain the energy, which is carried away by the wave in 1 s:

$$P = 4\pi r^2 I = \frac{2\pi |C|^2}{\rho_0 c} \qquad (I.21)$$

This energy has to be supplied by a sound source in the origin, so P is the acoustical power of a sound source, which produces a spherical wave of the type described.

On the other hand, we obtain from eqn (I.20) for $kr \ll 1$, i.e. for distances small compared with the wavelength:

$$v_r \approx \frac{p}{ikr\rho_0 c} = \frac{C}{ikr^2\rho_0 c} \exp(i\omega t) \tag{I.22}$$

If this limiting value of the particle velocity is multiplied by the surface area of the sphere with radius r ($\ll 1/k$), the volume velocity of the sound source is obtained, i.e. the volume which is expelled in 1 s from the origin:

$$Q(t) = \frac{4\pi C}{ik\rho_0 c} \exp(i\omega t) \tag{I.23}$$

A sound source with these properties is called a 'point source', but because of its vanishing dimensions it cannot be realised physically. However, any simple sound source, the only effect of which is to expel and to take in air periodically, has approximately the properties of a point source provided it has a substantial net volume velocity.

The amplitude of the volume velocity according to eqn (I.23) is $\hat{Q} = 4\pi|C|/k\rho_0 c$. By introducing this into eqn (I.21), the power of the point source turns out to be

$$P = \frac{\rho_0 c k^2 \hat{Q}^2}{8\pi} = \rho_0 \frac{\hat{Q}^2 \omega^2}{8\pi c} \tag{I.24}$$

Most man-made and natural sound sources are not small compared with the wavelength, or there are reflecting obstacles in their vicinity which disturb their sound field. For these reasons, they do not behave as point sources. The sound pressure as well as the intensity in these cases depend not only on the distance r but also on the direction, which can be characterised by a polar angle ϑ and an azimuth angle φ. For distances exceeding a characteristic range, which depends on the sort of the sound source and the frequency, the sound pressure is given by

$$p(r, \vartheta, \varphi, t) = \frac{A}{r} \Gamma(\vartheta, \varphi) \exp[i(\omega t - kr)] \tag{I.25}$$

where the 'directivity function' $\Gamma(\vartheta, \varphi)$ is normalised so as to make $\Gamma = 1$ for its absolute maximum. Another useful quantity is the 'gain' or 'directivity factor' of a sound source, i.e. the ratio of its maximum intensity in a certain distance r to the average intensity $P/4\pi r^2$:

$$G = \frac{I_{max}}{P} 4\pi r^2 \qquad (I.26)$$

Evidently G is always larger than or equal to unity, the latter being the case for uniform radiation in all directions. Therefore, the frequently used 'directivity index' (DI) can be derived from it:

$$DI = 10 \log G \qquad (I.27)$$

measured in decibels (dB) (*see also* Section I.5).

I.4 NON-HARMONIC SOUND SIGNALS

So far we have dealt almost exclusively with harmonic sound signals. We have assumed that acoustical quantities such as sound pressure or particle velocity depend on time according to a sine or cosine law, mathematically expressed by an exponential function with imaginary argument. In what follows we shall use the same mathematical expression of acoustical quantities although most signals of practical interest are much more complicated. The link between the latter and the simple harmonic signals we have so far considered is the Fourier theorem, the application of which is especially useful where signals are applied to linear transmission systems. A room is such a linear system; if the volume velocity of a sound source is doubled, the sound pressure produced by the sound source at some distant point doubles its value. This important property of any room has its mathematical analogue in the linearity of the wave equation (I.6).

The Fourier theorem states that any signal, provided it can be realised physically, may be considered as the superposition of harmonic signals. If the transmitting properties of a room are known with respect to harmonic signals of all possible frequencies, its transmitting properties with respect to any signal can be evaluated by superposing the harmonic output signals in a manner which is prescribed by the structure of the original input signal.

More exactly, the Fourier theorem can be formulated as follows: let $s(t)$ be a real time function describing, for example, the time dependence of the sound pressure or the volume velocity, this function being sufficiently steady (a requirement which is fulfilled in all practical cases), and the integral $\int_{-\infty}^{+\infty} [s(t)]^2 \, dt$ have a finite value. Then

$$s(t) = \int_{-\infty}^{+\infty} S(f) \exp (2\pi i f t) \, df \qquad (\text{I}.28a)$$

with

$$S(f) = \int_{-\infty}^{+\infty} s(t) \exp (-2\pi i f t) \, dt \qquad (\text{I}.28b)$$

Because of the symmetry of these formulae (with the exception of the physically meaningless change of sign in the exponent) $S(f)$ is not only the Fourier transform of $s(t)$ but $s(t)$ is the Fourier transform of $S(f)$ as well. The complex function $S(f)$ is called the 'spectral function' or the 'complex amplitude spectrum', or simply the 'spectrum' of the signal $s(t)$. It can easily be shown that $S(-f) = S^*(f)$, where the asterisk denotes the transition to the complex conjugate function. $S(f)$ and $s(t)$ are completely equivalent representations of the same process.

According to eqn (I.28a), the signal $s(t)$ is composed of harmonic time functions with continuously varying frequencies f. The absolute value of the spectral function, which can be written as

$$S(f) = |S(f)| \exp [i\psi(f)] \qquad (\text{I}.29)$$

is the amplitude of the harmonic vibration with frequency f; the argument $\psi(f)$ is the phase angle of this particular vibration.

The Fourier theorem assumes a slightly different form if $s(t)$ is a periodic function with period T, i.e. if $s(t) = s(t + T)$. Then the integral in eqn (I.28a) has to be replaced by a series:

$$s(t) = \sum_{n=-\infty}^{+\infty} S_n \exp \left(\frac{2\pi i n t}{T} \right) \qquad (\text{I}.30a)$$

with

$$S_n = \frac{1}{T} \int_0^T s(t) \exp \left(\frac{-2\pi i n t}{T} \right) dt \qquad (\text{I}.30b)$$

The steady spectral function has changed now into discrete 'Fourier coefficients', for which $S_{-n} = S_n^*$ as before. Hence a periodic signal consists of discrete harmonic vibrations, the frequencies of which are multiples of a fundamental frequency $1/T$. These components are called 'partial vibrations' or 'harmonics', the first harmonic being identical with the fundamental vibration.

Of course all the formulae above can be written with the angular frequency $\omega = 2\pi f$ instead of the frequency f. Furthermore, a real notation is possible. It can be obtained simply by separating the real parts from the imaginary parts of eqns (I.28) and (I.30) respectively. Equations (I.28) cannot be applied in this form to stationary non-periodic signals, i.e. to signals which are not limited in time and the average properties of which are not time dependent. In this case the integrals do not converge. Therefore, firstly a 'window' of width T_0 is cut out of the signal. For this section the spectral function $S_{T_0}(f)$ is well defined and can be evaluated numerically or experimentally. The 'power spectrum' of the whole signal is then given by

$$W(f) = \lim_{T_0 \to \infty} \left[\frac{1}{T_0} S_{T_0}(f) S_{T_0}^*(f) \right] \tag{I.31}$$

The determination of the complex spectrum $S(f)$ or of the power spectrum $W(f)$, known as 'spectral analysis' is of great theoretical and practical importance. It can be achieved by means of a set of bandpass filters, analogue spectral analysers or, most conveniently and precisely, by digital computers. A particularly efficient procedure for computing spectral functions is the 'fast Fourier transform' (FFT) algorithm. Since the description of this method is beyond the scope of this book, the reader is referred to the extensive literature on this subject (see, for instance, Ref. 1).

The power spectrum, which is an even function of the frequency, does not contain all the information on the original signal $s(t)$, because it is based on the absolute value of the spectral function only, whereas its phase has been eliminated. Inserted into eqn (I.28a), it does not restore the original function $s(t)$ but instead yields another important time function, called the 'autocorrelation function' of $s(t)$:

$$\phi_{ss}(\tau) = \int_{-\infty}^{+\infty} W(f) \exp(2\pi i f \tau) \, df = 2 \int_{0}^{+\infty} W(f) \cos(2\pi f \tau) \, df \tag{I.32}$$

The time variable has been denoted by τ in order to indicate that it is not identical with the real time. In the usual definition of the autocorrelation function it occurs as a delay time:

$$\phi_{ss}(\tau) = \lim_{T_0 \to \infty} \frac{1}{T_0} \int_{-T_0/2}^{+T_0/2} s(t) s(t + \tau) \, dt \tag{I.33}$$

Since ϕ_{ss} is the Fourier transform of the power spectrum, the latter is also obtained by Fourier transformation of the autocorrelation function:

$$W(f) = 2 \int_{0}^{+\infty} \phi_{ss}(\tau) \cos(2\pi f \tau) \, d\tau \tag{I.34}$$

Equations (I.32) and (I.34) are the mathematical expressions of the theorem of Wiener and Khinchine. Power spectrum and autocorrelation function are Fourier transforms of each other.

If $s(t + \tau)$ in eqn (I.33) is replaced with $s'(t + \tau)$, where s' denotes a time function different from s, one obtains the 'cross-correlation function' of the two signals $s(t)$ and $s'(t)$:

$$\phi_{ss'}(\tau) = \lim_{T_0 \to \infty} \frac{1}{T_0} \int_{-T_0/2}^{+T_0/2} s(t)s'(t + \tau)\,dt \qquad (I.33a)$$

In a certain sense a sine or cosine signal can be considered as an elementary signal; it is unlimited in time and steady in all its derivatives, and its spectrum consists of a single line. The counterpart of it is Dirac's delta function: it has one single line in the time domain, so to speak, whereas its amplitude spectrum is constant for all frequencies, i.e. $S(f) = 1$ for the delta function. This leads to the following representation:

$$\delta(t) = \lim_{f_0 \to \infty} \int_{-f_0}^{+f_0} \exp{(2\pi i f t)}\,df \qquad (I.35)$$

It can easily be shown that the delta function has the following fundamental property:

$$s(t) = \int_{-\infty}^{+\infty} s(\tau)\delta(t - \tau)\,d\tau \qquad (I.36)$$

where $s(t)$ is any function of time. Especially, for $s(t) \equiv 1$ we obtain

$$\int_{-\infty}^{+\infty} \delta(t)\,dt = 1 \qquad (I.36a)$$

The delta function $\delta(t)$ is zero for all $t \neq 0$; the relation (I.36a) indicates that its value at $t = 0$ must be infinite.

According to eqn (I.36), any signal can be considered as being built up of a close succession of very short pulses, each of which is represented by a delta function. If a linear transmission system, e.g. a room, is excited by one of these pulses, the corresponding output signal of the system (for instance the resulting sound pressure at some point in the room) is the 'impulse response', denoted by $g(t)$. If the impulse response of the system is known, its output signal $s'(t)$ with respect to any exciting input signal $s(t)$ can be

built up by a close succession of impulse responses, i.e. it is given by analogy
with eqn (I.36) by

$$s'(t) = \int_{-\infty}^{+\infty} s(\tau)g(t-\tau)\,d\tau \tag{I.37}$$

This important relation shows that the properties of a linear system are
known completely, if its impulse response is known.

Equation (I.37) has its analogue in the frequency domain, which looks
even simpler: let $S(f)$ be the complex spectrum of the input signal $s(t)$ of our
linear system, then the spectrum of the resulting output signal $s'(t)$ is

$$S'(f) = G(f)S(f) \tag{I.38}$$

The complex function $G(f)$ is the 'transmission function' or 'transfer
function' of the system; it is related to the impulse response by the Fourier
transformation:

$$G(f) = \int_{-\infty}^{+\infty} g(t)\exp(-2\pi i f t)\,dt \tag{I.39a}$$

$$g(t) = \int_{-\infty}^{+\infty} G(f)\exp(2\pi i f t)\,df \tag{I.39b}$$

Experimentally the absolute value of the transfer function is obtained by
applying a harmonic signal of frequency f to the input of the system, and by
dividing the amplitude of the resulting output signal by the amplitude of the
input signal. The phase angle of the transfer function can be measured by
comparing the phase angles of the output and input signals.

I.5 SOUND PRESSURE LEVEL AND SOUND POWER LEVEL

In the frequency range in which our hearing is most sensitive (1000–
3000 Hz) the threshold sensation and the threshold of pain in hearing are
separated by about 13 orders or magnitude of intensity. For this reason it
would be impractical to characterise the strength of a sound signal by its
sound pressure or its intensity. Instead, the so-called 'sound pressure level'
is generally used for this purpose, defined by

$$SPL = 20\log_{10}\left(\frac{\tilde{p}}{\tilde{p}_0}\right) \quad \text{decibels} \tag{I.40}$$

In this definition, $\tilde{p}$ denotes the 'root mean square' pressure, i.e. the square root of $\overline{p^2}$. $\tilde{p}_0$ is an internationally standardised reference pressure and its value is 2×10^{-5} N/m², which corresponds roughly to the normal hearing threshold at 1000 Hz. The 'decibel' (abbreviated dB) is not a unit in a physical sense but is used rather to recall the above level definition. Strictly speaking, $\tilde{p}$ as well as the *SPL* are defined only for stationary sound signals since they both imply an averaging process.

According to eqn (I.40), two different sound fields or signals may be compared by their level difference:

$$\Delta SPL = 20 \log\left(\frac{\tilde{p}_1}{\tilde{p}_2}\right) \quad \text{decibels} \tag{I.40a}$$

It is often convenient to express the sound power delivered by a sound source in terms of the 'sound power level', defined by

$$PL = 10 \log\left(\frac{P}{P_0}\right) \quad \text{decibels} \tag{I.41}$$

where P_0 denotes a reference power of 10^{-12} W. Using this quantity, the sound pressure level in a spherical wave field (Section I.3) can be expressed as follows:

$$SPL = PL - 20 \log\left(\frac{r}{r_0}\right) - 11 \, \text{dB} \quad \text{with } r_0 = 1 \, \text{m}$$

I.6 SOME PROPERTIES OF HUMAN HEARING

Since the ultimate consumer of all room acoustics is the listener, it is important to consider at least a few facts relating to the performance of the human hearing organ.

The sound pressure level as defined in eqn (I.40) is a purely objective quantity; although the subjective loudness sensation of a sound signal is related to it, it is not the only factor which determines the loudness. For instance, a sinusoidal signal with a *SPL* of 120 dB is heard very loud at a frequency of 1000 Hz; at 30 kHz it is completely inaudible. That means the subjective loudness of a sinusoidal tone depends on its frequency as well as on its physical strength. Or conversely: tones of equal loudness, but of different frequencies, generally have different levels. If these levels are plotted as a function of the frequency, the so-called 'contours of equal loudness' are obtained. These contours, measured for frontal incidence of the sound waves and averaged over many subjects, are shown in Fig. I.1.

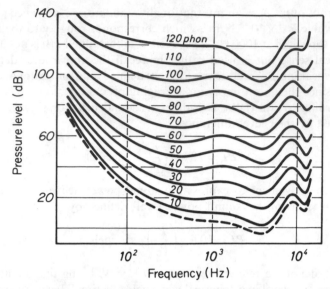

Fig. I.1.   Curves of equal loudness level for frontal sound incidence. The dashed
curve corresponds to the average hearing threshold.

Every curve is denoted by a number, the value of which agrees with the
sound pressure level at 1000 Hz. This number is the 'loudness level' of the
sound, the unit of which is the 'phon'.

Using these curves, the loudness level of any pure tone can be evaluated,
provided its frequency and its sound pressure or intensity level is known. In
order to simplify this somewhat tedious procedure, meters have been
constructed which measure the sound pressure level. The 'curves of equal
loudness' are taken into account by electrical networks, the frequency-
dependent attenuation of which approximate to the shape of these curves.
Several attenuation functions are in use and have been standardised
internationally; the measured loudness levels are accordingly expressed in
dB(A), dB(B), etc. Strictly speaking, these instruments ought to be used only
for loudness measurements of pure tones since they neglect an effect which
takes place in our hearing when perceiving a complex tone, namely the
mutual masking of different spectral components.

The neglect of masking effects is not the only weak point in our definition
of loudness level; another is that doubling the subjective loudness sensation
is not equal to doubling the number of phons or decibels but is equal to an
approximate increase of 10 phons only. This disadvantage is avoided by the

loudness scale with the 'sone' as a unit. The sone scale is defined in such a way that 40 phons correspond to 1 sone and that every increase of the loudness level by 10 phons corresponds to doubling the number of sones. Nowadays instruments as well as computer programs are available which are able to measure or to calculate the loudness of almost any type of sound signal, taking into account the above-mentioned masking effect.

Another important property of our hearing is its ability to detect the direction from which a sound wave is arriving, and thus to localise the direction of sound sources. For sound incidence from a lateral direction it is easy to understand how this effect is brought about: the sound signal does not reach both ears simultaneously, the more remote ear receives a somewhat delayed signal, and this delay, which corresponds to a phase difference when the signal is sinusoidal, depends on the direction of sound incidence. Furthermore, the amplitudes of both ear signals exhibit differences depending on frequency and direction. They are caused by the fact that the sound wave is diffracted by the head, including the pinnae, and that both ears probe different points of the diffraction field. Or, put in a simpler way: at lateral sound incidence one ear is within the shadow produced by the head but the other is not.

Quantitatively, the changes a sound signal undergoes on its way to the entrance of the ear canal can be characterised by transfer functions which depend on the direction of sound incidence and which also show individual differences, and it is the difference between these transfer functions of both ears which enable us to localise sound sources outside the vertical symmetry plane of the head. As an example, Fig. I.2(a) shows the transfer functions for both ears for sound incident from one side (90°); the shadowing effect of the head, especially at higher frequencies, is evident. However, if the sound source is situated within the vertical symmetry plane, this explanation fails since then the source produces equal sound signals at both ear canals. But even then the ear transfer functions show characteristic differences for various elevation angles of the source (see Fig. I.2(b)), and it is commonly believed that the way in which they modify a sound signal enables us to distinguish whether a sound source is behind, above or in front of our head.

These considerations are valid only for the localisation of sound sources in a free sound field. In a closed room, however, the sound field is made up of many sound waves propagating in different directions, accordingly matters are more complicated. We shall discuss the subjective effects of more complex sound fields as they are encountered in room acoustics in Chapter VII.

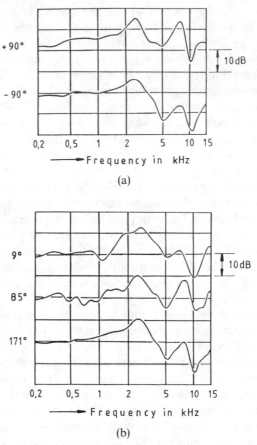

Fig. I.2. Magnitude of ear transfer functions: (a) horizontal plane, the sound source is at $+90°$ azimuth; (b) vertical plane (median plane), various elevation angles (after Mehrgardt and Mellert[2]).

I.7 PROPERTIES OF NATURAL SOUND SOURCES

In room acoustics there are two kinds of sound sources of particular importance: the human voice and musical instruments. Here we refer to them as 'natural sound sources', although, strictly speaking, all musical instruments are technical devices. Nowadays, however, traditional instruments are—as pointed out in the Introduction—no longer subject to significant technical development. Therefore we have to accept them, like the human voice, as given sound sources with more or less fixed acoustical properties. (This is not true for electronic musical instruments, which do not fall into this category since they make use of electroacoustical sound sources, i.e. of loudspeakers.)

Let us first of all consider the range of frequencies which are emitted by sound sources. Generally all natural sound sources generate tones which usually contain a large number of overtones or higher harmonics, provided these are at all periodic. For normal speech the fundamental frequency lies between 50 and 350 Hz, and is identical to the frequency of the vibrations of the vocal chords. In speech sounds, however, the overtones are much more characteristic than the fundamental tone; they are especially strong in certain specific frequency ranges called 'formants' and extend up to about 3500 Hz. This is true for vowels and for voiced consonants. Voiced consonants, in addition, also have continuous spectral components at frequencies up to 10 kHz and higher whereas the spectrum of voiceless consonants is purely continuous. Since consonants are of particular importance for the intelligibility of speech, a room or hall intended for speech, as well as a public address system, should transmit the high frequencies with great fidelity. The transmission of the fundamental vibration, on the other hand, is less important since our hearing is able to reconstruct it if the periodic sound signal is rich in higher harmonics.

Among musical instruments, large pipe organs have the widest frequency range, reaching from 16 Hz to about 9 kHz. (There are some instruments, especially percussion instruments, which produce sounds with even higher frequencies.) The piano follows, having a frequency range which is smaller by about three octaves, i.e. by nearly a decade. The frequencies of the remaining instruments lie somewhere within this range. This is true, however, only for the fundamental frequencies. Since almost all instruments produce higher harmonics, the actual range of frequencies occurring in music extends still further, up to about 15 kHz. In music, unlike speech, all frequencies are of almost equal importance, so it is not permissible deliberately to suppress or to neglect certain frequency ranges. On the other hand, the entire frequency range is not the responsibility of the acoustical engineer. At 10 kHz and above the attenuation in air is so large that the influence of a room on the propagation of high-frequency sound components can safely be neglected. At frequencies lower than 50 Hz geometrical considerations are almost useless because of the large wavelengths of the sounds; furthermore, at these frequencies it is almost impossible to assess correctly the sound absorption by vibrating panels or walls which influences the reverberation, especially at low frequencies. This means that, in this frequency range too, room acoustical design possibilities are very limited. On the whole, it can be stated that the frequency range relevant to room acoustics reaches from 50 to 10 000 Hz, the most important part being between 100 and 5000 Hz.

Another remarkable property of natural sound sources is their directionality, i.e. the fact that they do not emit sound with equal intensity in all directions. In speech this is because of the 'sound shadow' cast by the head. The lower the sound frequency, the less pronounced is the reduction of sound intensity by the head, because with decreasing frequencies the sound waves are increasingly diffracted around the head. In Figs I.3a and I.3b the distribution of the relative pressure level for different frequency bands is plotted on a horizontal plane and a vertical plane respectively. These curves are obtained by filtering out the respective frequency bands from natural speech; the direction denoted by 0° is the frontal direction.

Musical instruments usually exhibit a pronounced directionality because of the linear dimensions of their sound-radiating surfaces, which, in the interest of high efficiency, are often large compared with the wavelengths. Unfortunately general statements are almost impossible, since the

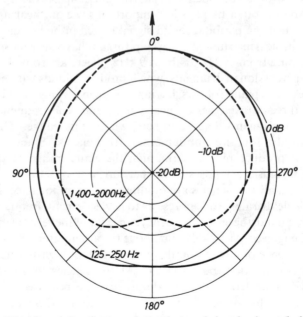

Fig. I.3a. Directional distribution of speech sounds in a horizontal plane for two different frequency bands. The arrow points in the viewing direction.

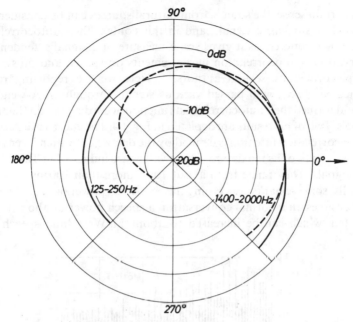

Fig. I.3b. Directional distribution of speech sounds in a vertical plane for two different frequency bands. The arrow points in the viewing direction.

directional distribution of the radiated sound changes very rapidly, not only from one frequency to the other, but can be quite different for instruments of the same sort but different manufacture. This is true especially for string instruments, the bodies of which exhibit very complicated vibration patterns, particularly at higher frequencies. The radiation from a violin takes place in a fairly uniform way at frequencies lower than about 450 Hz; at higher frequencies, however, matters become quite involved. For wind instruments the directional distributions exhibit common features to a much higher degree, since here the sound is not radiated from a curved anisotropic plate with complicated vibration patterns but from a fixed opening which is very often the end of a horn. The 'directional characteristics of an orchestra' are highly involved and space is too limited here to discuss this in detail. For the room acoustician, however, it is important to know that strong components, particularly from the strings but likewise from the piano, the woodwinds and of course from the tuba, are radiated upwards. For further details we refer to the exhaustive account of J. Meyer.[3]

In a certain sense, the sounds from natural sources can be considered as statistical or stochastic signals, and in this context their autocorrelation function is of interest as it gives some measure of a signal's 'tendency of conservation'. Autocorrelation measurements on speech and music have been performed by several authors.[4,5] Here we are reporting results obtained by Ando, who passed various signals through an A-weighting filter and formed their autocorrelation function according to eqn (I.33) with $T_0 = 35$ s. Two of his results are depicted in Fig. I.4. The effective duration of the autocorrelation function is defined by the delay τ_e, at which its envelope is just one-tenth of its maximum. These values are indicated in Table I.1 for a few signals. They range from about 10 to more than 100 ms.

Finally, some remarks concerning the acoustical power output of natural sound sources: in a normal conversation a speech power of about 1 μW is generated, which can be increased to about 1 mW in loud speech. The

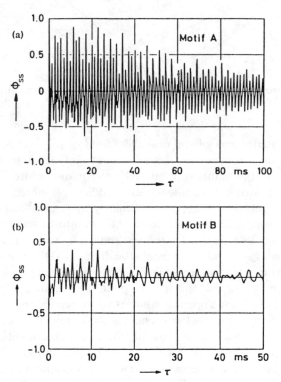

Fig. I.4. Examples of measured autocorrelation functions: (a) music motif A; (b) music motif B (both from Table I.1) (after Ando[5]).

Table I.1
Duration of Autocorrelation Functions of Various Sound Signals
(after Ando[5])

Motif	Name of piece	Composer	Duration τ_e in ms
A	Royal Pavane	Gibbons	127
B	Sinfonietta opus 48, 4th movement (Allegro con brio)	Arnold	43
C	Symphony No. 102 in B flat major, 2nd movement (Adagio)	Haydn	65
D	Siegfried Idyll; bar 322	Wagner	40
E	Symphony KV551 in C major (Jupiter), 4th movement (Molto allegro)	Mozart	38
F	Poem read by a female	Kunikita	10

power of a single musical instrument may lie in the range from 10 μW to 100 mW. A large orchestra can easily generate a power of 10 W in fortissimo passages. In this context we must add that the dynamic range of most musical instruments is about 30 dB (woodwind) to 50 dB (string instruments). A large orchestra can cover a dynamic range of 100 dB.

REFERENCES

1. Papoulis, A., *Signal Analysis*, International Student Edition. McGraw-Hill, Kogagusha, 1982.
2. Mehrgardt, S. & Mellert, V., *J. Acoust. Soc. America*, **61** (1977) 1567.
3. Meyer, J., *Akustik und musikalische Aufführungspraxis*. Verlag Das Musik-instrument, Frankfurt/M, 1980.
4. Furdujev, V., Proceedings of the Fifth International Congress on Acoustics, Liège, 1965, p. 41.
5. Ando, Y., *J. Acoust. Soc. America*, **62** (1977) 1436. Proc. Vancouver Symposium, p. 112 (12th Int. Congr. on Acoustics, Toronto, 1986).

II

The Sound Field in Front of a Wall

Up to now we have dealt with sound propagation in a medium which was unbounded in every direction. In contrast to this simple situation, room acoustics is concerned with sound propagation in enclosures where the sound conducting medium is bounded on all sides by walls, ceiling and floor. These room boundaries usually reflect a certain fraction of the sound energy impinging on them. Another fraction of the energy is 'absorbed', i.e. it is extracted from the sound field inside the room, either by conversion into heat or by being transmitted to the outside by the walls. It is just this combination of the numerous reflected components which is responsible for what is known as 'the acoustics of a room' and also for the complexity of the sound field in a room.

Before we discuss the properties of such involved sound fields we shall consider in this chapter the process which is fundamental for their occurrence: the reflection of a plane sound wave by a single wall or surface. In this context we shall encounter the concepts of wall impedance and absorption coefficient, which are of special importance in room acoustics. The sound absorption by a wall will be dealt with mainly from a formal point of view, whereas the discussion of the physical causes of sound absorption and of the functional principles of various absorbent arrangements will be postponed to a subsequent chapter.

Throughout this chapter the sound-reflecting wall will be assumed to be plane, unbounded and smooth. The latter condition means that any surface irregularities are much smaller than the wavelength and hence will not influence the sound wave. (The case of an acoustically rough surface will be dealt with in Section IV.1.) If, however, the surface shows a slight and regular curvature, the condition of planeness can be relaxed provided the wall is only slightly curved; indeed, the quantities introduced in the following, such as the reflection factor, the absorption coefficient and the

28

wall impedance as well as the laws of sound reflection, can be applied without much error to walls whose radius of curvature is very large compared with the acoustic wavelength.

Finally, we must add a remark concerning the shape of the incident wave. Strictly speaking, plane waves do not exist anywhere. In reality we are dealing with spherical waves or sections of a spherical wave. If the reflecting wall is far enough from the sound source, then the curvature of the wave fronts can be neglected with the same degree of approximation as the curvature of a non-plane wall. In practice the error produced by replacing a spherical wave by a plane one will usually be very small.

II.1 REFLECTION FACTOR, ABSORPTION COEFFICIENT AND WALL IMPEDANCE

If a plane wave strikes a wall, in general a part of the sound energy will be reflected from it in the form of a reflected wave originating from the wall, the amplitude and the phase of which differ from those of the incident wave. Both waves interfere with each other and form a 'standing wave', at least partially.

The changes in amplitude and phase which take place during the reflection of a wave are expressed by the complex reflection factor

$$R = |R| \exp(i\chi)$$

which is a property of the wall. Its absolute value as well as its phase angle depend on the frequency and on the angle between the wave normal (its direction of propagation) and the wall normal.

According to eqn (I.16), the intensity of a plane wave is proportional to the square of the pressure amplitude. Therefore, the intensity of the reflected wave is smaller by a factor $|R|^2$ than that of the incident wave and the fraction $1 - |R|^2$ of the incident energy is lost during reflection. This quantity is called the 'absorption coefficient' of the wall:

$$\alpha = 1 - |R|^2 \qquad (II.1)$$

For a wall with zero reflectivity $R = 0$ and the absorption coefficient has its maximum value 1. The wall is said to be totally absorbent or sometimes 'matched to the sound field'. If $R = 1$ (in-phase reflection, $\chi = 0$), the wall is 'rigid' or 'hard'; in the case of $R = -1$ (phase reversal, $\chi = \pi$), we speak of a 'soft' wall. In both cases there is no sound absorption ($\alpha = 0$). The latter case, however, very rarely occurs in room acoustics and only in limited frequency ranges.

The acoustical properties of a wall surface—as far as they are of interest in room acoustics—are completely described by the reflection factor for all angles of incidence and for all frequencies. Another quantity which is even more closely related to the physical behaviour of the wall and to its construction is based on the particle velocity normal to the wall which is generated by a given sound pressure at the surface. It is called the wall impedance and is defined by

WALL IMPEDANCE

$$Z = \left(\frac{p}{v_n}\right)_{surface} \tag{II.2}$$

where v_n denotes the velocity component normal to the wall. For non-porous walls which are excited into vibration by the sound field, the normal component of the particle velocity is identical to the velocity of the wall vibration. Like the reflection factor, the wall impedance is generally complex and a function of the angle of sound incidence.

Frequently the wall impedance is divided by the characteristic impedance of the air. The resulting quantity is called the 'specific acoustic impedance':

SPECIFIC ACOUSTIC IMPEDANCE
$$\zeta = \frac{Z}{\rho_0 c} \tag{II.3}$$

The reciprocal of the wall impedance is the 'acoustic admittance'; the reciprocal of ζ is called the 'specific acoustic admittance' of the wall.

Of special interest is the case where the impedance of a wall is independent of the direction of the incident sound. This applies if the normal component of the particle velocity at the wall surface depends only on the sound pressure in front of the wall element under consideration and not on the pressure in front of neighbouring elements. Walls or surfaces with this property are referred to as 'locally reacting' surfaces.

Since the reflection factor as well as the impedance contains the complete acoustical behaviour of a wall, a certain relation must hold between these two quantities. This relation for normal and for oblique sound incidence will be derived in the following two sections.

II.2 SOUND REFLECTION AT NORMAL INCIDENCE

First we assume the wall to be normal to the direction in which the incident wave is travelling, which is chosen as the x-axis of a rectangular coordinate

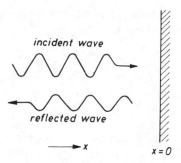

incident wave

reflected wave

x

$x = 0$

Fig. II.1. Reflection of a normally incident sound wave from a plane wall.

system. The wall intersects the x-axis at $x = 0$ (Fig. II.1). The wave is coming from the negative x-direction and its sound pressure is

$$p_i(x, t) = \hat{p}_0 \exp[i(\omega t - kx)] \tag{II.4a}$$

The particle velocity in the incident wave is according to eqn (I.12):

$$v_i(x, t) = \frac{\hat{p}_0}{\rho_0 c} \exp[i(\omega t - kx)] \tag{II.4b}$$

The reflected wave has a smaller amplitude and has undergone a phase change; both changes are described by the reflection factor R. Furthermore, we must reverse the sign of k because of the reversed direction of travel. The sign of the particle velocity is also changed according to eqn (I.12) ($\partial p/\partial x$ has opposite signs for positive and negative travelling waves). So we obtain for the reflected wave:

$$p_r(x, t) = R\hat{p}_0 \exp[i(\omega t + kx)] \tag{II.5a}$$

$$v_r(x, t) = -R\frac{\hat{p}_0}{\rho_0 c} \exp[i(\omega t + kx)] \tag{II.5b}$$

The total sound pressure and particle velocity in the plane of the wall are obtained simply by adding the above expressions and by setting $x = 0$:

$$p(0, t) = \hat{p}_0(1 + R) \exp(i\omega t)$$

and

$$v(0, t) = \frac{\hat{p}_0}{\rho_0 c}(1 - R) \exp(i\omega t)$$

Since the only component of particle velocity is normal to the wall, dividing $p(0, t)$ by $v(0, t)$ gives

$$Z = \rho_0 c \frac{1+R}{1-R} \tag{II.6}$$

and from this

$$R = \frac{Z - \rho_0 c}{Z + \rho_0 c} = \frac{\zeta - 1}{\zeta + 1} \tag{II.7}$$

A rigid wall ($R = 1$) has impedance $Z = \infty$; for a soft wall ($R = -1$) the impedance will vanish. For a completely absorbent wall the impedance equals the characteristic impedance of the medium.

Inserting eqn (II.7) into the definition (II.1) gives

ABSORPTION COEFFICIENT $\zeta = SPECIFIC\ ACOUSTIC\ IMPEDANCE$

$$\alpha = \frac{4 \operatorname{Re}(\zeta)}{|\zeta|^2 + 2 \operatorname{Re}(\zeta) + 1} = \frac{Z}{\rho c} \tag{II.8}$$

In Fig. II.2 this relation is represented graphically. The diagram shows the circles of constant absorption coefficient in the complex ζ-plane, i.e. abscissa and ordinate in this figure are the real and imaginary part of the specific wall impedance, respectively. As α increases the circles contract towards the point $\zeta = 1$, which corresponds to complete matching of the wall to the medium.

The distribution of sound pressure in the standing wave in front of the wall is found by adding eqns (II.4a) and (II.5a), and evaluating the absolute value

$$\hat{p}(x) = \hat{p}_0 [1 + |R|^2 + 2|R| \cos(2kx + \chi)]^{1/2} \tag{II.9}$$

Similarly, for the particle velocity we find

$$\hat{v}(x) = \frac{\hat{p}_0}{\rho_0 c} [1 + |R|^2 - 2|R| \cos(2kx + \chi)]^{1/2} \tag{II.10}$$

The time dependence of the pressure and the velocity is taken into account simply by multiplying these expressions by $\exp(i\omega t)$. According to eqns (II.9) and (II.10), the pressure amplitude and the velocity amplitude in the standing wave vary periodically between the maximum values

$$p_{max} = \hat{p}_0(1 + |R|) \quad \text{and} \quad v_{max} = \frac{\hat{p}_0}{\rho_0 c}(1 + |R|)$$

and the minimum values

$$p_{min} = \hat{p}_0(1 - |R|) \quad \text{and} \quad v_{min} = \frac{\hat{p}_0}{\rho_0 c}(1 - |R|)$$

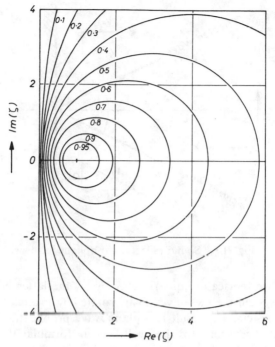

Fig. II.2. Circles of constant absorption coefficient in the complex wall impedance plane. The numbers denote the magnitude of the absorption coefficient.

but in such a way that each maximum of the pressure amplitude coincides with a minimum of the velocity amplitude and vice versa. The distance of one maximum to the next is $\pi/k = \lambda/2$. So, by measuring the pressure amplitude as a function of x, we can evaluate the wavelength. Furthermore, the absolute value and the phase angle of the reflection factor can also be evaluated. This leads to an important method of measuring the impedance and the absorption coefficient of wall materials (*see* Section VIII.7).

II.3 SOUND REFLECTION AT OBLIQUE INCIDENCE

In this section we consider the more general case of sound waves whose angles of incidence may be any value Θ. Without loss of generality, we can assume that the wall normal as well as the wave normal of the incident wave lie in the x–y plane of a rectangular coordinate system. The new situation is depicted in Fig. II.3.

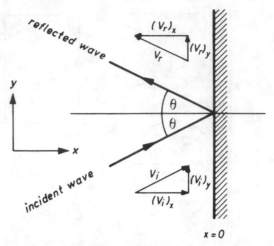

Fig. II.3. Sound reflection at oblique incidence.

Suppose we replace in eqn (II.4a) x by x', the latter belonging to a coordinate system, the axes of which are rotated by an angle Θ with respect to the x–y system. The result is a plane wave propagating in a positive x'-direction. According to the well-known formulae for coordinate transformation, x' and x are related by

$$x' = x \cos \Theta + y \sin \Theta$$

Inserting this into the previously mentioned expression for the incident plane wave we obtain for the latter

$$p_i = \hat{p}_0 \exp\left[-ik(x \cos \Theta + y \sin \Theta)\right] \qquad (\text{II.11}a)$$

(In this and the following expressions we omit, for the sake of simplicity, the factor $\exp(i\omega t)$, which is common to all pressures and particle velocities.) For the calculation of the wall impedance we require the velocity component normal to the wall, i.e. the x-component. It is obtained by applying the first version of eqn (I.12), which for the incident wave gives

$$(v_i)_x = \frac{\hat{p}_0}{\rho_0 c} \cos \Theta \exp\left[-ik(x \cos \Theta + y \sin \Theta)\right] \qquad (\text{II.11}b)$$

When the wave is reflected, as for normal incidence, the sign of x in the exponent is reversed, since the direction is altered with reference to this coordinate. Furthermore, the pressure and the velocity are multiplied by the reflection factor R and $-R$, respectively:

$$p_r = R\hat{p}_0 \exp\left[-ik(-x\cos\Theta + y\sin\Theta)\right] \qquad \text{(II.12a)}$$

$$(v_r)_x = -\frac{R\hat{p}_0}{\rho_0 c}\cos\Theta \exp\left[-ik(-x\cos\Theta + y\sin\Theta)\right] \qquad \text{(II.12b)}$$

The direction of propagation again includes an angle Θ with the wall normal, i.e. the reflection law well known in optics is also valid for the reflection of acoustical waves.

By setting $x=0$ in eqns (II.11a) to (II.12b) and by dividing $p_i + p_r$ by $(v_i)_x + (v_r)_x$ we obtain

$$Z = \frac{\rho_0 c}{\cos\Theta}\frac{1+R}{1-R} \qquad \text{(II.13)}$$

and from this

$$R = \frac{Z\cos\Theta - \rho_0 c}{Z\cos\Theta + \rho_0 c} = \frac{\zeta\cos\Theta - 1}{\zeta\cos\Theta + 1} \qquad \text{(II.14)}$$

The resulting sound pressure in front of the wall is given by

$$p(x, y) = \hat{p}_0[1 + |R|^2 + 2|R|\cos(2kx\cos\Theta + \chi)]^{1/2}\exp(-iky\sin\Theta) \qquad \text{(II.15)}$$

This pressure distribution again corresponds to a standing wave, the maxima of which are separated by a distance $\lambda/2\cos\Theta$ and which moves parallel to the wall with a velocity

$$c_y = \frac{\omega}{k_y} = \frac{\omega}{k\sin\Theta} = \frac{c}{\sin\Theta}$$

a result which is easily seen by multiplying eqn (II.15) by the time factor $\exp(i\omega t)$ and comparing the result with the expression for a plane wave, eqn (I.8).

As stated earlier, the wall impedance is independent of the angle of incidence if the wall surface is a locally reacting one. In this case, as shown by eqn (II.14), the reflection factor depends only on $\cos\Theta$. For $|\zeta| > 1$, its absolute value decreases at first until it reaches a minimum. If additionally the wall impedance is real, the reflection factor is real too. In this instance the sound reflection vanishes completely at a certain angle of incidence.

A locally reacting wall is encountered whenever the wall itself or the space behind it is unable to propagate waves or vibrations in a direction parallel to its surface. Obviously this is not true for a panel whose neighbouring elements are coupled together by bending stiffness.

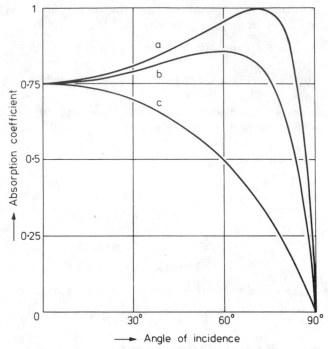

Fig. II.4. Absorption coefficient of walls with specific impedance: (a) $\zeta = 3$; (b) $\zeta = 1\cdot5 + 1\cdot323i$; (c) $\zeta = \frac{1}{3}$.

Moreover, this does not apply to a porous layer with an air space between it and a rigid rear wall. In the latter case, however, local reaction of the various surface elements of the arrangement can be brought about by rigid partitions which obstruct the air space in any lateral direction and prevent sound propagation parallel to the surface.

Using eqn (II.14) the absorption coefficient is given by

$$\alpha(\Theta) = \frac{4\,\mathrm{Re}\,(\zeta)\cos\Theta}{(|\zeta|\cos\Theta)^2 + 2\,\mathrm{Re}\,(\zeta)\cos\Theta + 1} \tag{II.16}$$

Its dependence on the angle of incidence is plotted in Fig. II.4 for various values of ζ.

II.4 A FEW EXAMPLES

In this section we consider as examples two types of surface which are of some practical importance as linings to room walls.

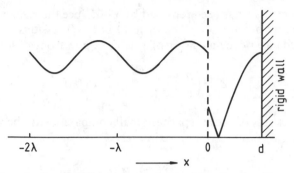

Fig. II.5. Sound reflection from a porous layer with a distance d from a rigid wall. The plotted curve is the pressure amplitude for $r_s = \rho_0 c$ and for $d/\lambda = \frac{5}{16}$.

The first arrangement consists of a porous layer of fabric or something similar which is stretched or hung in front of a rigid wall at a distance d from it and parallel to it. The x-axis is normal to the layer and the wall, the former having the coordinate $x = 0$. Hence, the wall is located at $x = d$ (*see* Fig. II.5). We assume that the porous layer is so heavy that it does not vibrate under the influence of an incident sound wave. Any pressure difference between the two sides of the layer forces an air stream through the pores with an air velocity v_s. The latter is related to the pressures p in front of and p' behind the layer by

$$r_s = \frac{p - p'}{v_s} \tag{II.17}$$

r_s being the flow resistance of the porous layer. We assume that this relation is valid for a steady flow of air as well as for alternating air flow.

In front of the rigid wall but behind the porous layer there is a standing wave which, for normal incidence of the original sound wave, is represented according to eqns (II.4a) to (II.5b) by

$$p'(x) = \hat{p}'\{\exp\left[-ik(x-d)\right] + \exp\left[ik(x-d)\right]\}$$
$$- 2\hat{p}' \cos\left[k(x-d)\right] \tag{II.18}$$

$$v'(x) = \frac{\hat{p}'}{\rho_0 c}\{\exp\left[-ik(x-d)\right] - \exp\left[ik(x-d)\right]\}$$

$$= -\frac{2i\hat{p}'}{\rho_0 c} \sin\left[k(x-d)\right] \tag{II.19}$$

(In the exponents x has been replaced by $x - d$ since the rigid wall is not at $x = 0$ as before but at $x = d$.) The ratio of both expressions at $x = 0$ is the 'wall' impedance of the air layer of thickness d in front of a rigid wall:

$$Z' = \left(\frac{p'}{v'}\right)_{x=0} = -i\rho_0 c \cot(kd) \tag{II.20}$$

If the thickness of the air space is small compared with the wavelength, i.e. if $kd \ll 1$, then we have approximately

$$Z' \approx \frac{\rho_0 c}{ikd} = \frac{\rho_0 c^2}{i\omega d} \tag{II.20a}$$

We shall make frequent use of these expressions in the following.

Because of the conservation of matter, the particle velocities in front of and behind the layer must be equal to each other, and to the flow velocity through the layer:

$$v(0) = v'(0) = v_s \tag{II.21}$$

Therefore the definition of the wall impedance of the whole arrangement (layer plus air space plus rigid wall) yields

$$p(0) = Z v_s \tag{II.22}$$

whereas eqn (II.20) now reads

$$p'(0) = -i\rho_0 c v_s \cot(kd) \tag{II.23}$$

Substitution of both these expressions into eqn (II.17) results in

$$Z = r_s - i\rho_0 c \cot(kd) \tag{II.24}$$

Hence the impedance of the air space behind the porous layer is simply added to the flow resistance to give the impedance of the complete arrangement.

In the complex plane of Fig. II.2, this wall impedance would be represented by a vertical line at a distance $r_s/\rho_0 c$ from the imaginary axis. Increasing the wave number or the frequency is equivalent to going repeatedly from $-i\infty$ to $+i\infty$ on that line. As can be seen from the circles of constant absorption coefficient, the latter has a maximum whenever Z is real, i.e. whenever the depth d of the air space is an odd multiple of $\lambda/4$. Introducing $\zeta = Z/\rho_0 c$ from eqn (II.24) into eqn (II.3) yields the following

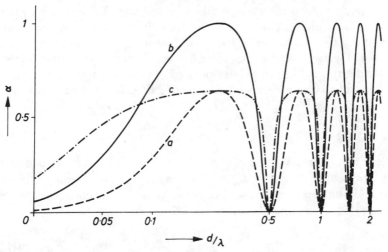

Fig. II.6. Absorption coefficient of porous layers with distance d from a rigid wall for normal incidence as a function of d/λ: (a) $r_s = 0.25\rho_0 c$; (b) $r_s = \rho_0 c$; (c) $r_s = 4\rho_0 c$.

formula for the absorption coefficient of a porous layer in front of a rigid wall:

$$\alpha(f) = \frac{4r_s}{(r_s' + 1)^2 + \cot^2(2\pi f d/c)} \tag{II.25}$$

with $r_s' = r_s/\rho_0 c$.

In Fig. II.6 the absorption coefficient of this arrangement is plotted as a function of the frequency for $r_s = \rho_0 c/4$, $r_s = \rho_0 c$ and $r_s = 4\rho_0 c$. Beginning from very low values, the absorption coefficient assumes alternate maximum and minimum values. Minimum absorption occurs for all such frequencies at which the distance d between the porous layer and the rigid rear wall is a multiple of half the wavelength. This can be easily understood since, at these distances, the standing wave behind the porous layer has a zero of particle velocity in the plane of the layer, but energy losses can take place only if the air is moving in the pores of the layer.

In practical cases it may be advisable to provide for a varying distance between the porous fabric and the rigid wall in order to smooth out the irregularities of the absorption coefficient. This can be done by hanging or stretching the fabric in deep folds. Since most materials are not heavy enough to guarantee the complete absence of vibrations of the porous layer, deviations from the absorption characteristics described above may occur, but the general features remain the same.

To this arrangement we now add a second layer or sheet which is not porous and which is placed immediately in front (as seen by the incident sound wave) of the porous layer, but in such a way that there is no contact between the two layers. Under the influence of a sound wave, it can vibrate in the direction of its normal. Its motion is merely controlled by its mass: if there is a pressure difference Δp between its faces this is related to v_s by

$$\Delta p = M \frac{dv_s}{dt} = i\omega M v_s$$

where M is the mass of the non-porous sheet per unit area. We denote the pressure behind the porous layer by p' and the pressure in front of the non-porous layer by p, i.e. at the surface of the whole construction, then, instead of eqn (II.17), we now obtain

$$\frac{p - p'}{v_s} = r_s + i\omega M \tag{II.26}$$

Hence the wall impedance which is determined in a manner similar to that used before is

$$Z = r_s + i\left(\omega M - \frac{\rho_0 c^2}{\omega d}\right) \tag{II.27}$$

where we have used instead of Z' the expression (II.20a), valid for small depths of the air space.

As in the preceding example, it is situated on a vertical line with distance r_s from the imaginary axis (*see* Fig. II.7a). If the frequency is increased from zero to infinity, the locus moves on this line from $-i\infty$ to $+i\infty$. When it crosses the real axis, the absolute value of the wall impedance reaches its minimum. Zince $Z = p/v_s$, a given sound pressure will then cause a particularly high velocity of the impervious sheet. According to eqn (II.27), this situation, which is usually referred to as 'resonance', occurs at an angular frequency:

$$\omega_0 = \left(\frac{\rho_0 c^2}{Md}\right)^{1/2} \tag{II.28}$$

where $f_0 = \omega_0/2\pi$ is the resonance frequency' of the system. As may also be seen from Fig. 11.7a and Fig. II.2, in resonance the absorption coefficient of the system assumes a maximum.

In Fig. II.7b the corresponding resonance curve is depicted, i.e. the

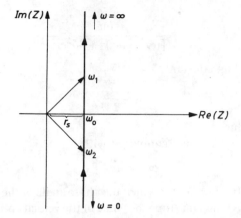

Fig. II.7a. Locus of the wall impedance in the complex impedance plane for a resonance system.

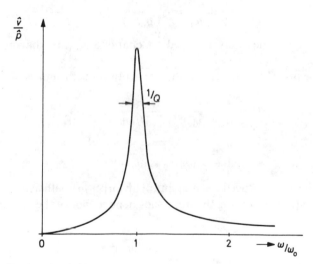

Fig. II.7b. Ratio of velocity to pressure amplitude as a function of the driving frequency for a resonance system.

velocity amplitude for a given pressure amplitude as a function of the sound frequency

$$|v_s| = \frac{\omega \hat{p}}{M[(\omega^2 - \omega_0^2)^2 + 4\delta^2\omega^2]^{1/2}} \tag{II.29}$$

where the damping constant

$$\delta = \frac{r_s}{2M} \tag{II.29a}$$

has been introduced.

Assuming that δ is small compared with ω_0,

$$\omega_{1,2} = \omega_0 \pm \delta \tag{II.29b}$$

are the angular frequencies for which the phase angle of the wall impedance becomes $\pm 45°$. At the same time the value of the velocity amplitude at these frequencies is lower than the maximum value $\hat{p}/2\delta M$ by a factor $(2)^{1/2}$. The difference $\Delta\omega = \omega_1 - \omega_2$ is the 'half-width' of the resonance system or, divided by the resonance angular frequency ω_0, the 'relative half-width', which is the reciprocal of the 'quality factor' or 'Q-factor' Q:

$$\frac{\Delta\omega}{\omega_0} = \frac{1}{Q} = \frac{2\delta}{\omega_0} = r_s\left(\frac{d}{\rho_0 c^2 M}\right)^{1/2} = \frac{r_s}{M\omega_0} \tag{II.29c}$$

All these quantities may be used to characterise the sharpness of the resonance.

Using eqns (II.8) and (II.27), the absorption coefficient is

$$\alpha = \frac{4r_s\rho_0 c}{(r_s + \rho_0 c)^2 + [(M/\omega)(\omega^2 - \omega_0^2)]^2}$$

$$= \frac{\alpha_{max}}{1 + Q_\alpha^2(\omega/\omega_0 - \omega_0/\omega)^2} \tag{II.30}$$

Here we have introduced the maximum absorption coefficient α_{max} and the 'quality factor' concerning the frequency dependence of the absorption, Q_α:

$$\alpha_{max} = \frac{4r_s\rho_0 c}{(r_s + \rho_0 c)^2} \tag{II.30a}$$

$$Q_\alpha = \frac{M\omega_0}{r_s + \rho_0 c} \tag{II.30b}$$

The physical meaning of Q_α is similar to that of Q: it is related to the frequencies at which the absorption coefficient has fallen to half its maximum value. It takes into account not only the losses caused by the porous sheet but also the loss of vibrational energy due to re-radiation (reflection) of sound from the surface of the whole arrangement.

Practical resonance absorbers will be discussed in Chapter VI.

As a last example we consider the 'open window', i.e. an imaginary, laterally bounded surface behind which free space extends. This concept played an important role as an absorption standard in the early days of modern room acoustics, since by definition its absorption coefficient is 1.

When a plane sound wave strikes an open window at an angle Θ to its normal, the component of the particle velocity normal to the 'wall' is $v \cos \Theta$, where v is the particle velocity in the direction of propagation. Hence the wall impedance is given by

$$Z = \frac{p}{v \cos \Theta} = \frac{\rho_0 c}{\cos \Theta} \qquad (II.31)$$

Thus the area does not react locally; its impedance depends on the angle of incidence. By inserting this into eqns (II.14) and (II.16) it is easily shown that $R = 0$ and $\alpha = 1$ for all angles of incidence.

We can introduce local reaction by filling the opening of the windows with a large number of parallel tubes with rigid walls and whose axes are perpendicular to the plane of the window. The entrances of these tubes are flush with the window opening; the tubes are either infinitely long or their opposite ends are sealed by a perfect absorber. In each of these tubes and hence on the front face of this 'wall' we can apply

$$\frac{p}{v_n} = \rho_0 c = Z$$

where v_n is the velocity component parallel to the tube axis. This expression leads to

$$R(\Theta) = \frac{\cos \Theta - 1}{\cos \Theta + 1} \qquad (II.32a)$$

$$\alpha(\Theta) = \frac{4 \cos \Theta}{(\cos \Theta + 1)^2} \qquad (II.32b)$$

The absorption is perfect only at normal incidence; at grazing incidence its value approaches zero. If the absorption coefficient is averaged over all directions of incidence (*see* Section II.5), a value of 0·912 is obtained, whereas if the lateral subdivision of the window opening is absent, the mean absorption coefficient is of course 1.

II.5 RANDOM SOUND INCIDENCE

In room acoustics we are interested not only in the reflection of one specified sound wave but very frequently in the simultaneous reflection of a large number of waves impinging from very different directions onto the wall under consideration and which have very different amplitudes and phases. Instead of investigating the reflection of each single wave and adding the energies of the reflected waves, we can average the effect of the reflecting wall over many directions. For this purpose we assume the amplitudes of the incident waves to be distributed uniformly over all possible directions of incidence in such a way that each element of solid angle carries the same intensity towards the wall. Furthermore, we can assume that the phases of the elementary waves are distributed at random so that interference effects can be neglected and we can simply add their energies. The latter are proportional to the squares of the pressure or the velocity amplitudes of the elementary plane waves.

In the literature on room acoustics this type of sound field is referred to as a 'diffuse sound field' and we shall frequently encounter it in this book.

Now let us concern ourselves with the geometry. We consider an element of area dS of the wall; the angle between its normal and the direction of incidence is denoted by Θ (*see* Fig. II.8). In addition, we characterise this direction by an azimuth angle Φ; thus the wall normal is the polar axis of a spherical polar coordinate system. Hence the element of the solid angle, viewed from the wall element, is d$\Omega = \sin \Theta\, \mathrm{d}\Theta\, \mathrm{d}\Phi$.

First we calculate the dependence of the energy density, which is

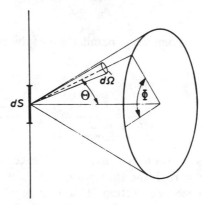

Fig. II.8.   Coordinates for sound incidence on to an area element dS at polar angle Θ and azimuth angle Φ.

essentially equal to the square of the sound pressure amplitude, on the distance from the wall which, for the moment, is assumed to be perfectly rigid $(R = 1)$. For this case, according to eqn (II.15), the square of the pressure amplitude with respect to a wave incident at angle Θ is

$$|p|^2 = 2\hat{p}_0^2[1 + \cos(2kx \cos \Theta)] \tag{II.33}$$

Multiplied by $d\Omega$ this represents the contribution to the total square pressure due to the solid angle element with polar angle Θ. By averaging eqn (II.33) over all directions on one side of the wall we obtain

$$\langle|p|^2\rangle = 2\hat{p}_0^2 \frac{1}{2\pi} \int_0^{2\pi} d\Phi \int_0^{\pi/2} [1 + \cos(2kx \cos \Theta)] \sin \Theta \, d\Theta$$

$$= 2\hat{p}_0^2 \left[1 + \frac{\sin(2kx)}{2kx} \right] \tag{II.34}$$

This quantity, divided by $|p_\infty|^2 = 2\hat{p}_0^2$, is plotted in Fig. II.9 as a function of the distance x from the wall. Immediately in front of the wall fluctuations of the square pressure occur, as they do in every standing wave. With increasing distance, however, they fade out and the square pressure approaches a constant limiting value which is half of that in front of the wall. A microphone which is sensitive to the sound pressure indicates a pressure level which is higher by 3 dB at the wall than at some distance from it. For the same reason, the sound absorption of an absorbent surface adjacent and perpendicular to a rigid wall is higher near the edge than at a distance of several wavelengths from the wall.

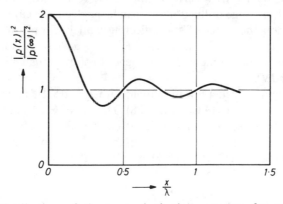

Fig. II.9. Distribution of the squared absolute pressure for random sound incidence in front of a perfectly reflecting wall.

Experimentally it may prove to be difficult to confirm eqn (II.34). The reason for this is not so much the difficulty of establishing a sufficiently diffuse sound field but rather the impossibility of realising the independence of phases among the various components, at least at one single frequency, as assumed in our derivation. When a room is acoustically excited by a sinusoidal signal, the resulting steady state sound field is made up of a number of 'characteristic vibrations' or normal modes (*see* Chapter III), the phases of which are inter-related in a well-defined way. These inter-relations may be destroyed to a certain extent by replacing the sinusoidal signal with random noise with a limited bandwidth. But then the pressure distribution must also be averaged with respect to frequency over the exciting frequency band.

The smoothing of the standing wave with increasing distance x as indicated by eqn (II.34) and Fig. II.9 is effected not only by averaging over various directions but also for normal incidence by averaging over a frequency band of finite bandwidth, since the argument of the cosine function in eqn (II.33) or (II.15) contains both the frequency $f = kc/2\pi$ and $\cos \Theta$. Thus it does not make a substantial difference which of the two variables is to be averaged. To demonstrate this, in Fig. II.10 the absolute square of the sound pressure has been plotted as a function of the distance from a wall having a reflection factor 0·7. The sound incidence in this plot is at $\Theta = 0$; the spectrum of the incident sound is assumed to be flat between a lower and an upper limiting frequency, the ratio of which is the parameter of these curves. For comparison, the standing wave for a sinusoidal sound signal is added. For signals of a non-vanishing bandwidth, the standing wave extends over only a certain range close to the wall. For very high frequencies, this range of fluctuations can be neglected because of its short extension; then the effect of the reflecting wall is simply to reduce the intensity of the wave by a factor $|R^2| = 1 - \alpha$. Use is made of this simplification in the geometrical treatment of room acoustical phenomena (*see* Chapter IV).

Now we again consider a wall element with area dS. Its projection in the direction Φ, Θ is $dS \cos \Theta$ (*see* Fig. II.8). Thus $I \cos \Theta \, dS \, d\Omega$ is the sound energy arriving per second on dS from an element $d\Omega$ of solid angle around the considered direction. By integrating this over all solid angle elements, assuming I independent of Φ and Θ, we obtain the total energy per second arriving at dS:

$$E_i = I \, dS \int_0^{2\pi} d\Phi \int_0^{\pi/2} \cos \Theta \sin \Theta \, d\Theta = \pi I \, dS \qquad (II.35)$$

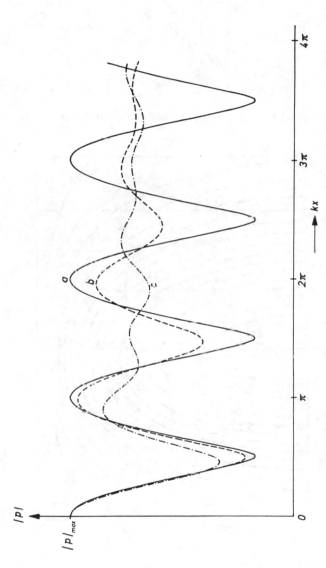

Fig. II.10. Standing waves in front of a plane wall with reflection factor $R = 0.7$ at normal incidence: (a) sine tone; (b) third octave band; (c) octave band. In the latter cases k refers to the centre frequency of the band.

From a sound wave incident at angle Θ on the wall, the fraction $\alpha(\Theta)$ is absorbed, thus the totally absorbed energy per second is

$$E_a = I\,dS \int_0^{2\pi} d\Phi \int_0^{\pi/2} \alpha(\Theta)\cos\Theta\sin\Theta\,d\Theta$$

$$= 2\pi I\,dS \int_0^{\pi/2} \alpha(\Theta)\cos\Theta\sin\Theta\,d\Theta \qquad (\text{II.36})$$

By dividing these two expressions we get the absorption coefficient for

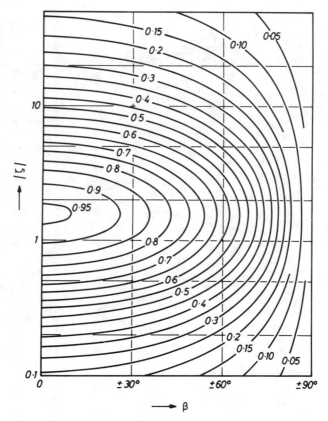

Fig. II.11. Curves of constant absorption coefficient in the impedance plane for random sound incidence: ordinate is the absolute value, abscissa the phase angle of the specific impedance.

random or uniformly distributed incidence:

$$\alpha_{uni} = \frac{E_a}{E_i} = 2 \int_0^{\pi/2} \alpha(\Theta) \cos\Theta \sin\Theta \, d\Theta = \int_0^{\pi/2} \alpha(\Theta) \sin(2\Theta) \, d\Theta \quad (\text{II.37})$$

This is occasionally referred to as the 'Paris' formula' in the literature.

For locally reacting surfaces we can express the angular dependence of the absorption coefficient by eqn (II.16). If this is done and the integration is performed, we obtain

$$\alpha_{uni} = \frac{8}{|\zeta|^2} \cos\beta \left[|\zeta| + \frac{\cos 2\beta}{\sin\beta} \arctan\left(\frac{|\zeta| \sin\beta}{1 + |\zeta| \cos\beta} \right) \right.$$

$$\left. - \cos\beta \ln(1 + 2|\zeta| \cos\beta + |\zeta|^2) \right] \quad (\text{II.38})$$

Here the wall impedance is characterised by the absolute value and the phase angle β of the specific impedance with

$$\beta = \arctan\left(\frac{\text{Im }\zeta}{\text{Re }\zeta} \right)$$

The content of this formula is represented in Fig. II.11 in the form of curves of constant absorption coefficient α_{uni} in a coordinate system, the abscissa and the ordinate of which are the phase angle and the absolute value of the specific impedance, respectively. The absorption coefficient has its absolute maximum 0·951 for the real impedance $\zeta = 1·567$. Thus, in a diffuse sound field, a locally reacting wall can never be totally absorbent.

It should be mentioned that recently the validity of the Paris' formula has been called into question by Makita and Hidaka.[1] These authors recommend replacing the factor $\cos\Theta$ in eqns (II.35) and (II.36) by a somewhat more complicated weighting function. This, of course, would also modify eqn (II.38).

REFERENCE

1. Makita, Y. & Hidaka, T., *Acustica*, **63** (1987) 163; *ibid.*, **67** (1988) 214.

III

The Sound Field in a Closed Space
(Wave Theory)

In the preceding chapter we saw the laws which a plane sound wave obeys upon reflection from a single plane wall and how this reflected wave is superimposed on the incident one. Now we shall try to obtain some insight into the complicated distribution of sound pressure or sound energy in a room which is enclosed on all sides by walls which are at least partially reflecting.

We could try to describe the resulting sound field by means of a detailed calculation of all the reflected sound components and by finally adding them together; that is to say, by a manifold application of the reflection laws which we dealt with in the previous chapter. Since each wave which has been reflected from a wall A will be reflected from walls B, C, D, etc., and will arrive eventually once more at wall A, this procedure leads only asymptotically to a final result, not to mention the calculations which grow like an avalanche. Nevertheless, this method is highly descriptive and therefore it is frequently applied in a much simplified form in geometrical room acoustics. We shall return to it in the next chapter.

In this chapter we shall choose a different way of tackling our problem which will lead to a solution in closed form—at least a formal one. This advantage is paid for by a higher degree of abstraction, however. Characteristic of this approach are certain boundary conditions which have to be set up along the room boundaries and which describe mathematically the acoustical properties of the walls, the ceiling and the other surfaces. Then solutions of the wave equations are sought which satisfy these boundary conditions. This method is the basis of what is frequently called 'the wave theory of room acoustics'.

It will turn out that this method in its exact form too can only be applied to highly idealised cases with reasonable effort. The rooms with which we are concerned in our daily life, however, are more or less irregular in shape, partly because of the furniture, which forms part of the room boundary. Rooms such as concert halls, theatres or churches deviate from their basic shape because of the presence of balconies, galleries, pillars, columns and other wall irregularities. The methods of wave theory cannot be applied to such enclosures because the boundary conditions cannot be formulated in a satisfactory way and so this theory can only yield approximate or qualitative results. For this reason the immediate application of wave theory to practical problems in room acoustics is very limited. Nevertheless, it is the most reliable and appropriate one from a physical point of view, and therefore it is essential for a more than superficial understanding of sound propagation in enclosures. For the same reason we should keep in mind the results of wave theory when we are applying more simplified methods, in order to keep our ideas in perspective.

III.1 FORMAL SOLUTION OF THE WAVE EQUATION FOR AN ENCLOSURE

The starting point for a wave theory representation of the sound field in a room is again the wave equation (I.5), which will be used here in a time-independent form. That is to say, we assume, as earlier, a harmonic time law for the pressure, the particle velocity, etc., with an angular frequency ω. Then eqn (I.5) reads

$$\Delta p + k^2 p = 0 \qquad k = \frac{\omega}{c} \qquad \text{(III.1)}$$

Furthermore, we assume that the room under consideration has locally reacting walls and ceiling, the acoustical properties of which are completely characterised by a wall impedance depending on the coordinates and the frequency but not on the angle of sound incidence.

According to eqn (I.2), the velocity component normal to any wall or boundary is

$$v_n = -\frac{1}{i\omega\rho_0}(\operatorname{grad} p)_n = \frac{i}{\omega\rho_0}\frac{\partial p}{\partial n} \qquad \text{(III.2)}$$

The symbol $\partial/\partial n$ denotes a differentiation in the direction of the outward normal to the wall. We replace v_n by p/Z (see eqn (II.2)) and obtain

$$Z\frac{\partial p}{\partial n} + i\omega\rho_0 p = 0 \qquad \text{(III.2a)}$$

or, using the specific impedance ζ,

$$\zeta \frac{\partial p}{\partial n} + ikp = 0 \tag{III.2b}$$

Now it can be shown that the wave equation yields non-zero solutions fulfilling the boundary condition (III.2a) or (III.2b) only for particular discrete values of k, called 'eigenvalues'.[1,2] In the following we shall frequently distinguish these quantities from each other by an index number n or m, though it is often more convenient to use a trio of subscripts because of the three-dimensional nature of the problem.

Each eigenvalue k_n is associated with a solution $p_n(\mathbf{r})$, which is known as an 'eigenfunction' or 'normal mode' of the room under consideration. Here $\mathbf{r}$ is used as an abbreviation for the three spatial coordinates.

At this point we need to comment on the quantity k in the boundary condition (III.2a) or (III.2b). Implicitly, it is also contained in ζ, since the specific wall impedance depends in general on the frequency $\omega = kc$. We can identify it with k_n, the eigenvalue to be evaluated, by solving our boundary problem. Then in general the boundary condition contains the parameters which we are looking for. Another possibility is to give k (and hence ω) in the boundary condition a fixed value, which may be given by the driving frequency of a sound source.

It is only the latter case for which one can prove that the eigenfunctions are mutually orthogonal, which means that

$$\int\int\int_V p_n(\mathbf{r})p_m(\mathbf{r})\,\mathrm{d}V = \begin{cases} K_n & \text{for } n = m \\ 0 & \text{for } n \neq m \end{cases} \tag{III.3}$$

where the integration has to be extended over the whole volume V enclosed by the walls. K_n is a constant.

If all the eigenvalues and eigenfunctions, which in general are functions of the frequency, are known, we can in principle evaluate any desired acoustical property of the room; for instance, its steady state response to arbitrary sound sources. Suppose the sound sources are distributed continuously over the room according to a density function $q(\mathbf{r})$, where $q(\mathbf{r})\,\mathrm{d}V$ is the volume velocity of a volume element $\mathrm{d}V$ at $\mathbf{r}$. $q(\mathbf{r})$ may be a complex function taking account of possible phase differences between the various infinitesimal sound sources. Furthermore, we assume a common driving frequency ω. By adding $\rho_0 q(\mathbf{r})$ to the right-hand side of eqn (I.3) it is easily seen that the wave equation (III.1) now has to be modified into

$$\Delta p + k^2 p = -i\omega\rho_0 q(\mathbf{r}) \tag{III.4}$$

with the same boundary condition as above. Since the eigenfunctions form a complete and orthogonal set of functions, we can expand the source function in a series of p_n:

$$q(\mathbf{r}) = \sum_n C_n p_n(\mathbf{r}) \quad \text{with } C_n = \frac{1}{K_n} \int\int\int_V p_n(\mathbf{r})q(\mathbf{r}) \, dV \quad \text{(III.5)}$$

where the summation is extended over all possible combinations of subscripts. In the same way the solution $p_\omega(\mathbf{r})$, which we are looking for, can be expanded in eigenfunctions:

$$p_\omega(\mathbf{r}) = \sum_n D_n p_n(\mathbf{r}) \quad \text{(III.6)}$$

Our problem is solved if the unknown coefficients D_n are expressed by the known coefficients C_n. For this purpose we insert both series into eqn (III.4):

$$\sum D_n(\Delta p_n + k^2 p_n) = i\omega\rho_0 \sum C_n p_n$$

Now $\Delta p_n = -k_n^2 p_n$. Using this relation and equating term by term in the equation above, we obtain:

$$D_n = i\omega\rho_0 \frac{C_n}{k^2 - k_n^2} \quad \text{(III.7)}$$

The final solution assumes a particularly simple form for the important case of a point source at the point $\mathbf{r}_0$ which has a volume velocity Q. The source function is represented mathematically by a delta function in this case:

$$q(\mathbf{r}) = Q\delta(\mathbf{r} - \mathbf{r}_0)$$

Because of eqn (I.36) the coefficients C_n in eqn (III.5) are then given by

$$C_n = \frac{1}{K_n} Q p_n(\mathbf{r}_0)$$

Using this relation and eqns (III.7) and (III.6), we finally find for the sound pressure in a room excited by a point source of angular frequency ω:

$$p_\omega(\mathbf{r}) = iQ\omega\rho_0 \sum \frac{p_n(\mathbf{r})p_n(\mathbf{r}_0)}{K_n(k^2 - k_n^2)} \quad \text{(III.8)}$$

This is called 'Green's function' of the room under consideration. It is interesting to note that it is symmetric in the coordinates of the sound source and of the point of observation. If we put the sound source at $\mathbf{r}$, we observe at point $\mathbf{r}_0$ the same sound pressure as we did before at $\mathbf{r}$, when the sound source was at $\mathbf{r}_0$. Thus eqn (III.8) is the mathematical expression of the famous reciprocity theorem which can be applied sometimes with advantage to measurements in room acoustics.

Since the boundary conditions are usually complex equations containing k_n, the latter are in general complex quantities. Putting

$$k_n = \frac{\omega_n}{c} + i\frac{\delta_n}{c}$$

and assuming that $\delta_n \ll \omega_n$, we obtain from eqn (III.8)

$$p_\omega(\mathbf{r}) = iQc^2\omega\rho_0 \sum_n \frac{p_n(\mathbf{r})p_n(\mathbf{r}_0)}{(\omega^2 - \omega_n^2 - 2i\delta_n\omega_n)K_n} \tag{III.9}$$

Considered as a function of the frequency, this expression is the transmission function of the room between the two points $\mathbf{r}$ and $\mathbf{r}_0$. At the angular frequencies $\omega = \omega_n$, the associated term of this series assumes a particularly high absolute value. The corresponding frequencies are called 'eigenfrequencies' of the room; sometimes they are referred to as 'resonance frequencies' because of some sort of resonance occurring in the vicinity of those frequencies. The δ_n will turn out later to be 'damping constants'.

If the sound source is not emitting a sinusoidal signal but instead a signal which is composed of several spectral components, then $Q = Q(\omega)$ can be considered as its spectral function and we can represent the source signal as a Fourier integral (see Section I.4):

$$s(t) = \int_{-\infty}^{+\infty} Q(\omega) \exp(i\omega t)\,d\omega$$

where we have used $\omega = 2\pi f$ as a variable of integration instead of f. Since the response to any spectral component with angular frequency ω is just given by eqns (III.8) or (III.9), the sound pressure at the point $\mathbf{r}$ as a function of time is

$$p(\mathbf{r}, t) = \int_{-\infty}^{+\infty} p_\omega(\mathbf{r}) \exp(i\omega t)\,d\omega \tag{III.10}$$

where Q in the formulae for p_ω has to be replaced by $Q(\omega)$.

III.2 NORMAL MODES OF VIBRATION IN RECTANGULAR ROOMS WITH RIGID BOUNDARIES

In order to put some life into the abstract formalism outlined in the preceding section, we consider a room with parallel pairs of walls, the pairs being perpendicular to each other. It will be referred to in the following as a 'rectangular room'. In practice rooms with exactly this shape do not exist. On the other hand, most concert halls or other halls, churches, lecture rooms and so on are much closer in shape to the rectangular room than to any other of simple geometry, and so the results obtained for strictly rectangular rooms can be applied at least qualitatively to many rooms encountered in practice. Therefore our example is not only intended for the elucidation of the theory discussed above but has some practical bearing as well.

Our room is assumed to extend from $x = 0$ to $x = L_x$ in the x-direction, and similarly from $y = 0$ to $y = L_y$ in the y-direction and from $z = 0$ to $z = L_z$ in the z-direction (*see* Fig. III.1). As far as the properties of the wall are concerned, we start with the simplest case, namely that of all walls being rigid. That is to say, that at the surface of the walls the normal components of the particle velocity must vanish.

In cartesian coordinates the wave equation may be written

$$\frac{\partial^2 p}{\partial x^2} + \frac{\partial^2 p}{\partial y^2} + \frac{\partial^2 p}{\partial z^2} + k^2 p = 0$$

The variables can be separated, which means that we can compose the solution of three factors:

$$p(x, y, z) = p_1(x)p_2(y)p_3(z)$$

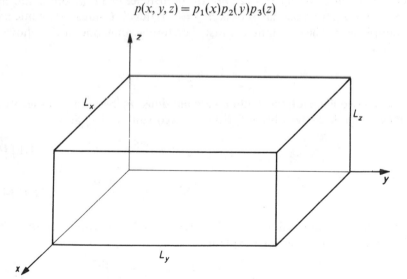

Fig. III.1. Dimensions of a rectangular room.

which depend on x only, on y only and on z only, respectively. If this product is inserted into the wave equation, the latter splits up into three ordinary differential equations. The same is true for the boundary conditions. p_1, for instance, must satisfy the equation

$$\frac{d^2 p_1}{dx^2} + k_x^2 p_1 = 0 \qquad (III.11)$$

together with the boundary condition

$$\frac{dp_1}{dx} = 0 \quad \text{for } x = 0 \text{ and } x = L_x \qquad (III.12)$$

Analogous equations hold for $p_2(y)$ and $p_3(z)$; the newly introduced constants are related by

$$k_x^2 + k_y^2 + k_z^2 = k^2 \qquad (III.13)$$

Equation (III.11) has the general solution

$$p_1(x) = A_1 \cos(k_x x) + B_1 \sin(k_x x)$$

The constants A_1 and B_1 are used for adapting this solution to the boundary conditions (III.12). So it is seen immediately that we must put $B_1 = 0$, since only the cosine function possesses at $x = 0$ the horizontal tangent required by eqn (III.12). For the occurrence of a horizontal tangent too at $x = L_x$, we must have $\cos(k_x L_x) = \pm 1$, thus $k_x L_x$ must be an integral multiple of π. The constant k_x must therefore assume one of the allowed values

$$k_x = \frac{n_x \pi}{L_x} \qquad (III.14a)$$

as a consequence of the boundary conditions, n_x being a non-negative integer. Similarly, we obtain for the allowed values of k_y and k_z

$$k_y = \frac{n_y \pi}{L_y} \qquad (III.14b)$$

$$k_z = \frac{n_z \pi}{L_z} \qquad (III.14c)$$

Inserting these values into eqn (III.13) results in the following equation for the eigenvalues of the wave equation:

$$k_{n_x n_y n_z} = \pi \left[\left(\frac{n_x}{L_x} \right)^2 + \left(\frac{n_y}{L_y} \right)^2 + \left(\frac{n_z}{L_z} \right)^2 \right]^{1/2} \qquad (III.15)$$

The eigenfunctions or normal modes associated with these eigenvalues are simply obtained by multiplication of the three cosines, each of which describes the dependence of the pressure on one coordinate:

$$p_{n_x n_y n_z}(x, y, z) = C \cos\left(\frac{n_x \pi x}{L_x}\right) \cos\left(\frac{n_y \pi y}{L_y}\right) \cos\left(\frac{n_z \pi z}{L_z}\right) \quad \text{(III.16)}$$

where C is an arbitrary constant. This formula represents a three-dimensional standing wave; of course, it is incomplete without the factor $\exp(i\omega t)$ describing the time dependence of the sound pressure. The sound pressure is zero for all times at those points, at which at least one of the cosines becomes zero. This occurs for all values of x which are odd integers of $L_x/2n_x$, and for the analogous values of y and z. So these points of vanishing sound pressure form three sets of equidistant planes, called 'nodal planes', which are mutually orthogonal. The numbers n_x, n_y and n_z indicate the numbers of nodal planes perpendicular to the x-axis, the y-axis and the z-axis, respectively. (For non-rectangular rooms the surfaces of vanishing sound pressure are generally no longer planes. They are referred to as 'nodal surfaces'.)

In Fig. III.2 the sound pressure distribution in the plane $z = 0$ is depicted for $n_x = 3$ and $n_y = 2$. The closed loops are curves of constant pressure amplitude, namely for $|p/p_{max}| = 0.25$, 0.5 and 0.75. The intersections of

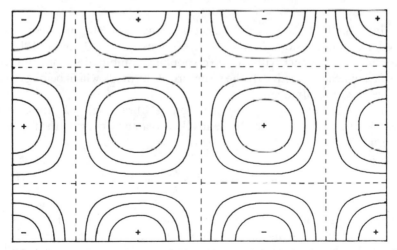

Fig. III.2.   Sound pressure distribution in the plane $z = 0$ of a rectangular room for $n_x = 3$ and $n_y = 2$.

Table III.1

Eigenfrequencies of a Rectangular Room with Dimensions $4\cdot7 \times 4\cdot1 \times 3\cdot1\,\text{m}^3$
(in Hertz)

f_n	n_x	n_y	n_z	f_n	n_x	n_y	n_z
36·17	1	0	0	90·47	1	2	0
41·46	0	1	0	90·78	2	0	1
54·84	0	0	1	99·42	0	2	1
55·02	1	1	0	99·80	2	1	1
65·69	1	0	1	105·79	1	2	1
68·55	0	1	1	108·51	3	0	0
72·34	2	0	0	109·68	0	0	2
77·68	1	1	1	110·05	2	2	0
82·93	0	2	0	115·49	1	0	2
83·38	2	1	0	116·16	3	1	0

vertical nodal planes with the plane $z = 0$ are indicated by dotted lines. On either side of such a line the sound pressures have opposite signs.

The eigenfrequencies corresponding to the eigenvalues of eqn (III.15), which are real because of the special boundary condition (III.12), are given by

$$f_{n_x n_y n_z} = \frac{C}{2\pi} k_{n_x n_y n_z} \qquad (\text{III.17})$$

In Table III.1 the lowest 20 eigenfrequencies (in Hz) of a rectangular room with dimensions $L_x = 4\cdot7\,\text{m}$, $L_y = 4\cdot1\,\text{m}$ and $L_z = 3\cdot1\,\text{m}$ are listed for $c = 340\,\text{m/s}$, together with the corresponding combinations of subscripts, which indicate immediately the structure of the mode which belongs to the respective engenfrequency.

By using the complex representation of vibrational quantities, i.e. by employing $\cos x = (e^{ix} + e^{-ix})/2$, eqn (III.16) can be written in the following form:

$$p_{n_x n_y n_z} = \frac{C}{8} \sum \exp\left[\pi i \left(\pm \frac{n_x}{L_x} x \pm \frac{n_y}{L_y} y \pm \frac{n_z}{L_z} z\right)\right] \qquad (\text{III.18})$$

wherein the summation has to be extended over the eight possible combinations of signs in the exponent. Each of these eight terms—multiplied by the usual time factor $\exp(i\omega t)$—represents a plane travelling wave, whose direction of propagation is defined by the angles β_x, β_y and β_z, which it makes with the coordinate axes, where

$$\cos \beta_x : \cos \beta_y : \cos \beta_z = \left(\pm \frac{n_x}{L_x} \right) : \left(\pm \frac{n_y}{L_y} \right) : \left(\pm \frac{n_z}{L_z} \right) \qquad \text{(III.19)}$$

If one of the three subscripts, for instance n_z, equals zero, then the corresponding angle (β_z in this example) is 90°; the propagation takes place perpendicularly to the respective axis, i.e. parallel to all planes which are perpendicular to that axis. The corresponding vibration pattern is frequently referred to as a 'tangential mode'. If there is only one non-zero subscript, the propagation is parallel to one of the coordinate axes, i.e. parallel to one of the room edges. Then we are speaking of an 'axial mode'. In Fig. III.3, for the analogous two-dimensional case, two combinations of plane waves are shown which correspond to certain eigenfunctions.

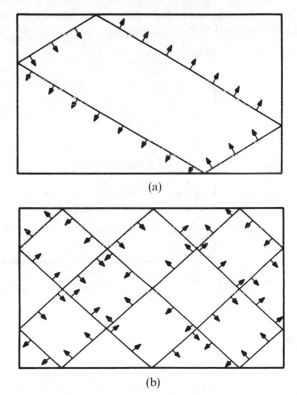

(a)

(b)

Fig. III.3. Plane wavefronts creating standing waves in a rectangular room: (a) $n_x : n_y = 1:1$; (b) $n_x : n_y = 3:2$.

We can get an illustrative survey on the arrangement, the types and the number of the eigenvalues by the following geometrical representation. We interpret k_x, k_y and k_z as cartesian coordinates in a k-space. Each of the allowed values of k_x, given by eqn (III.14a), corresponds to a plane perpendicular to the k_x-axis. The same statement holds for the values of k_y and k_z, given by eqns (III.14b) and (III.14c). These three equations therefore represent three sets of equidistant, mutually orthogonal planes in the k-space. Since for one eigenvalue these equations have to be satisfied simultaneously, each intersection of three mutually orthogonal planes corresponds to a certain eigenvalue in our representation. These intersections in their totality form a rectangular point lattice in the first octant of our k-space (*see* Fig. III.4). (Negative values obviously do not yield new eigenvalues, since eqn (III.15) is not sensitive to the signs of the subscripts!) The lattice points corresponding to tangential and to axial modes are situated on the coordinate planes and on the axes, respectively. The straight line connecting the origin of the coordinate system to a certain

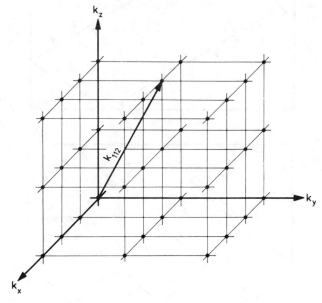

Fig. III.4. Eigenvalue lattice in the k-space for a rectangular room. The arrow pointing from the origin to an eigenvalue point indicates the direction of one of the eight plane waves which the corresponding mode consists of; its length is proportional to the eigenvalue.

lattice point has—according to eqn (III.19)—the same direction as one of the plane waves of which the associated mode is made up (*see* eqn (III.18)).

This representation allows a simple estimation of the number of eigenfrequencies which are located between the frequency 0 and some other given frequency. Considered geometrically, eqn (III.13) represents a spherical surface in the k-space with radius k, enclosing a 'volume' $4\pi k^3/3$. Of this volume, however, only the portion situated in the first octant is of interest, i.e. the volume $\pi k^3/6$. On the other hand, the distances between one certain lattice point and its nearest neighbours in the three coordinate directions are π/L_x, π/L_y and π/L_z. The k-'volume' per lattice point is therefore $\pi^3/L_xL_yL_z = \pi^3/V$, where V is the real geometrical volume of the room under consideration. Now we are ready to write down the number of lattice points inside the first octant up to radius k, which is equivalent to the number of eigenfrequencies from 0 to an upper limit $f = kc/2\pi$:

$$N_f = \frac{\pi k^3/6}{\pi^3/V} = \frac{Vk^3}{6\pi^2} = \frac{4\pi}{3}V\left(\frac{f}{c}\right)^3 \qquad \text{(III.20)}$$

The average density of eigenfrequencies on the frequency axis, i.e. the number of eigenfrequencies per Hz at the frequency f, is

$$\frac{\mathrm{d}N_f}{\mathrm{d}f} = 4\pi V\frac{f^2}{c^3} \qquad \text{(III.21)}$$

Strictly speaking, in the course of the derivation of the above formulae, we have made an error in as much as we have regarded the lattice points on the coordinate planes only as halves and those on the axes only as quarters, since we have restricted our consideration strictly to the first octant, although the points on the coordinate planes and the axes represent full eigenvalues. Correcting this yields, instead of eqn (III.20), the more exact formula

$$N_f = \frac{4\pi}{3}V\left(\frac{f}{c}\right)^3 + \frac{\pi}{4}S\left(\frac{f}{c}\right)^2 + \frac{L}{8}\frac{f}{c} \qquad \text{(III.20}a\text{)}$$

In this expression S is the area of all walls $2(L_xL_y + L_xL_z + L_yL_z)$ and $L = 4(L_x + L_y + L_z)$ the sum of all edge lengths occurring in the rectangular room.

It can be shown that in the limiting case $f \to \infty$ eqn (III.20) is valid not only for rectangular rooms but also for rooms of arbitrary shape. This is not too surprising since we can approximate the volume more or less by the total volume of a number of rectangular enclosures inside the room under consideration. At very high frequencies the dimensions of those rectangular enclosures or 'elementary rooms' are large compared with the wavelength. Thus to each of them we can apply eqn (III.20). Finally, since this equation is linear in V, we add all the calculated numbers of eigenfrequencies and obtain the total number of eigenfrequencies for the arbitrary room.

We bring this section to a close by applying our approximate formulae (III.20) and (III.21) to two simple examples. The volume of the rectangular room for which we have calculated the first eigenfrequencies in Table III.1 is $59.7 \, m^3$. For an upper frequency limit of $116 \, Hz$, eqn (III.20) indicates a total number of eigenfrequencies of 10 as compared with the 20 we have listed in the table. Using the more accurate formula (III.20a) we obtain exactly 20 eigenfrequencies. That means that we must not neglect the corrections due to tangential and axial modes when dealing with such small rooms at low frequencies. Now we consider a rectangular room with dimensions $50 \, m \times 24 \, m \times 14 \, m$ whose volume is $16\,800 \, m^3$. (This might be a large concert hall, for instance.) In the frequency range from 0 to $10\,000$ Hz there are, according to eqn (III.20), about 1.8×10^9 eigenvalues. At 1000 Hz the number of eigenfrequencies per Hertz is about 5400, thus the average distance of two eigenfrequencies on the frequency axis is less than $0.0002 \, Hz$. These figures underline the enormous volume of numerical calculation which would be required to evaluate accurately the sound field in a room of even the simplest geometry.

III.3 NON-RIGID WALLS

In this section we are still dealing with rectangular rooms. But now we assume that the walls are not completely rigid, but allow the normal components of particle velocity to have non-vanishing values. Therefore we have to replace the boundary condition (III.12) by the more general conditions of eqn (III.2b). For the walls perpendicular to the x-axis of our coordinate system we therefore require

$$\zeta_x \frac{dp_1}{dx} = ikp_1 \qquad \text{for } x = 0$$

$$\zeta_x \frac{dp_1}{dx} = -ikp_1 \qquad \text{for } x = L_x$$

(III.22)

The specific impedance ζ_x of the x-walls is assumed to be constant; the same holds for the analogous boundary conditions concerning the walls perpendicular to the y-axis and the z-axis, respectively. Thus each pair of walls has uniform acoustical properties. The frequency contained in k and in ζ is considered as constant, and so we expect the resulting eigenfunctions to be mutually orthogonal.

We have tacitly assumed that the solution of the wave equation—as in the preceding section— can be split into three factors p_1, p_2 and p_3, each of which depends on one spatial coordinate only.

For the present purpose it is more useful to write the general solution for p_1 in the complex form:

$$p_1(x) = C_1 \exp(-ik_x x) + D_1 \exp(ik_x x) \qquad \text{(III.23)}$$

which, however, is completely equivalent to the real expression for $p_1(x)$ on page 56. By inserting p_1 into the boundary conditions (III.22) we obtain two linear and homogeneous equations for the constants C_1 and D_1:

$$\begin{aligned}
C_1(k + k_x \zeta_x) + D_1(k - k_x \zeta_x) = 0 \\
C_1(k - k_x \zeta_x) \exp(-ik_x L_x) + D_1(k + k_x \zeta_x) \exp(ik_x L_x) = 0
\end{aligned} \qquad \text{(III.24)}$$

which have a non-vanishing solution only if the determinant of their coefficient is zero. This leads to the following equation, from which the allowed values of k_x can be determined:

$$\exp(ik_x L_x) = \pm \frac{k - k_x \zeta_x}{k + k_x \zeta_x} \qquad \text{(III.25)}$$

which is equivalent to

$$\tan u = i \frac{2u\zeta_x}{kL_x} \quad \text{and} \quad \tan u = i \frac{kL_x}{2u\zeta_x} \qquad \text{(III.25a)}$$

with

$$u = \tfrac{1}{2}k_x L_x$$

Since the specific wall impedance is usually complex, we must also expect complex values for the solution k_x:

$$\zeta_x = \xi_x + i\eta_x \qquad k_x = \beta_x + i\gamma_x$$

Once the allowed values of k_x have been determined, the ratio of the two constants C_1 and D_1 can be evaluated from eqns (III.24); for instance, from the first of them

$$\frac{C_1}{D_1} = -\frac{k - k_x \zeta_x}{k + k_x \zeta_x} = \mp \exp(ik_x L_x)$$

the latter equality resulting from eqn (III.25). Thus the x-dependent factor
of the eigenfunction reads

$$p(x) \sim \begin{cases} \cos\left[k_x(x - L_x/2)\right] & \text{(even)} \\ \sin\left[k_x(x - L_x/2)\right] & \text{(odd)} \end{cases} \tag{III.26}$$

The complete eigenfunction is made up of three such factors.

We do not pursue a thorough discussion of eqn (III.25) or (III.25a) and its
solutions here, which can be found elsewhere. (In fact, graphical solutions
to eqn (III.25a) obtained by conformal mapping are known as Morse's
charts in the literature.[3]) Here we restrict ourselves to two special cases
which make the contrast with a rigid wall sufficiently evident. In the
following we suppose $|\zeta| \gg 1$.

First let the wall impedance be purely imaginary, i.e. $\xi_x = 0$. At the walls,
therefore, no energy loss will occur, since the absolute value of the reflection
coefficient is one (*see* eqn (II.14)). The right-hand terms of eqns (III.25a) are
real in this case, and therefore the same is true for the allowed values of u
and k_x, as was the case for rigid walls. If $k_x \neq 0$, the assumption we are
making here, we can write instead of eqn (III.25), since $k_x|\zeta_x| \gg k$,

$$\exp\left(ik_xL_x\right) \approx \mp\left(1 + i\,\frac{2k}{k_x\eta_x}\right) \tag{III.25b}$$

If the wall possesses the impedance of a spring, i.e. if $\eta_x < 0$, the argument
of the exponential function decreases with increasing compliance. The
corresponding k_x is therefore lower than it was for rigid walls. If, on the
contrary, $\eta_x > 0$, i.e. if the impedance is that of a mass, all allowed values of
k_x become larger than with rigid walls. If the allowed values of k_x are
denoted by k_{xn_x}, so the eigenvalues of the original differential equation are
given as earlier by

$$k_{n_xn_yn_z} = (k_{xn_x}^2 + k_{yn_y}^2 + k_{zn_z}^2)^{1/2} \tag{III.27}$$

From this relation it can be concluded that for missing energy losses at
the wall, i.e. for purely imaginary wall impedances, all eigenvalues are only
shifted by a certain amount.

As a second case we consider walls with very large real impedances. From
eqns (III.25) we obtain

$$\exp\left(i\beta_xL_x\right)\exp\left(-\gamma_xL_x\right) = \pm\frac{k - k_x\xi_x}{k + k_x\xi_x} \approx \mp\left(1 - \frac{2k}{k_x\xi_x}\right) \tag{III.25c}$$

Since we have supposed $\xi_x \gg 1$, we conclude $\gamma_x \ll \beta_x$, and so we can safely replace k_x by β_x on the right-hand side. Then $\exp(i\beta_x L_x) \approx \mp 1$, the allowed values of β_x are nearly the same as those of k_x from eqn (III.14a). Furthermore, it follows from eqn (III.25c) that

$$\exp(-\gamma_x L_x) \approx 1 - \gamma_x L_x \approx 1 - \frac{2k}{\beta_x \xi_x}$$

hence

$$\gamma_x \approx \frac{2k}{\beta_x L_x \xi_x} \tag{III.28}$$

Analogous approximate formulae are obtained for the other coordinates. The quantities β are, by the way, called 'phase constants'.

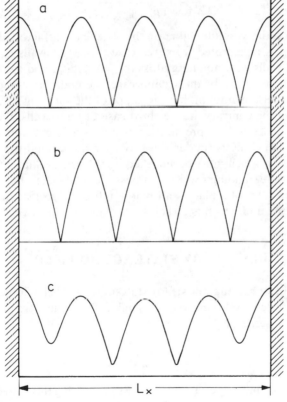

Fig. III.5. Standing waves in a one-dimensional room, $n_x = 4$: (a) $\zeta = \infty$; (b) $\zeta = i$; (c) $\zeta = 2$.

Now we put the calculated values of k_x, k_y and k_z into eqn (III.27) and obtain for the eigenvalues

$$k_{n_x n_y n_z} = [(\beta_{n_x} + i\gamma_{n_x})^2 + (\beta_{n_y} + i\gamma_{n_y})^2 + (\beta_{n_z} + i\gamma_{n_z})^2]^{1/2}$$

$$\approx \beta_{n_x n_y n_z} + i \frac{\gamma_{n_x}\beta_{n_x} + \gamma_{n_y}\beta_{n_y} + \gamma_{n_z}\beta_{n_z}}{\beta_{n_x n_y n_z}}$$

where

$$\beta_{n_x n_y n_z}^2 \approx \pi^2 \left[\left(\frac{n_x}{L_x}\right)^2 + \left(\frac{n_y}{L_y}\right)^2 + \left(\frac{n_z}{L_z}\right)^2 \right] \tag{III.15a}$$

If we finally insert the approximate values from eqn (III.28) into our expression for $k_{n_x n_y n_z}$, we get

$$k_{n_x n_y n_z} \approx \beta_{n_x n_y n_z} + i \frac{2\omega}{c\beta_{n_x n_y n_z}} \left(\frac{1}{L_x \xi_x} + \frac{1}{L_y \xi_y} + \frac{1}{L_z \xi_z} \right) \tag{III.29}$$

In Fig. III.5 the absolute value of the x-dependent factor of a certain eigenfunction is represented for three cases: for rigid walls ($\zeta_x = \infty$), for mass-loaded walls with no energy loss ($\xi_x = 0$, $\eta_x > 0$), and for walls with purely real impedances. In the second case, the nodes are simply shifted together by a certain amount, but the shape of the standing wave remains unaltered. On the contrary, in the third case of lossy walls, there are no longer exact nodes and the pressure amplitude is different from zero at all points. This can easily be understood by keeping in mind that the walls dissipate energy, which must be supplied by waves travelling towards the walls, thus a pure standing wave is not possible. The same situation occurs in principle in front of a plane wall whose reflection coefficient is slightly different from 1 and which is struck by a plane sound wave.

III.4 STEADY STATE SOUND FIELD

In Section III.1 we saw that the steady state acoustical behaviour of a room, when it is excited by a sinusoidal signal with angular frequency ω, is described by a series of the form

$$p_\omega = \sum_n \frac{A_n}{\omega^2 - \omega_n^2 - 2i\delta_n \omega_n} \tag{III.30}$$

where we are assuming $\delta_n \ll \omega_n$ as before. By comparing this with our earlier eqn (III.9) we learn that the coefficients A_n are functions of the source position, of the receiving position, and of the angular frequency ω. If both points are considered as fixed, eqn (III.30) is the transfer function of the room between both points. (If p_ω is to represent a true transfer function, certain relationships between the eigenvalues must be met, which we shall not discuss here.)

Since we have supposed that the constants δ_n are small compared with the corresponding ω_n, the absolute value of one series term changes so rapidly in the vicinity of $\omega = \omega_n$ if the frequency is altered that we can safely neglect any frequency dependence except that of the denominator. Since it is the term $\omega^2 - \omega_n^2$ which is responsible for the strong frequency dependence, ω_n can be replaced by ω in the last term of the denominator without any serious error. The absolute value of the nth series term then becomes

$$\frac{|A_n|}{[(\omega^2 - \omega_n^2)^2 + 4\omega^2\delta_n^2]^{1/2}}$$

and thus agrees with the amplitude–frequency characteristics of a resonance system, according to eqn (II.29). Therefore the stationary sound pressure in a room and at one single exciting frequency proves to be the combined effect of numerous resonance systems with resonance (angular) frequencies ω_n and damping constants δ_n. The half-widths of the various resonance curves are according to eqn (II.29c):

$$(\Delta f)_n = \frac{1}{2\pi}(\Delta\omega)_n = \frac{\delta_n}{\pi} \tag{III.31}$$

In the next section it will be seen that the damping constants in normal rooms lie mostly between 1 and $20\,s^{-1}$. Therefore our earlier assumption concerning the relative magnitude of the damping constants seems to be justified. Furthermore, we see from this that the corresponding half-widths, within which the various resonance terms assume their highest values, are of the order of magnitude of $1\,Hz$.

If one compares with this figure the average spacing of eigenfrequencies on the frequency axis which is the reciprocal of dN_f/df after eqn (III.21) and which is usually smaller by several orders of magnitude than the half-widths, it becomes evident that one single resonance peak always covers several, and frequently many, eigenfrequencies. With a sound source emitting a sinusoidal signal, it is thus impossible to excite a single resonance separately; instead, the resulting sound pressure is made up of many simultaneously excited vibrational modes. Exceptions may be observed only in small, relatively undamped rooms or chambers at low frequencies, since here the eigenfrequencies are well separated. Thus one can easily detect in a tiled bathroom, for example, one or several eigenfrequencies by singing or humming. In all other cases, however, there are always several or many terms of the series (III.30) which take part in the resulting steady state pressure, whose contributions are different in their strengths and exhibit mutual phase differences. Since the magnitudes of ω_n and δ_n are changing from one eigenfrequency to the neighbouring one in a very irregular way, the steady state sound pressure at one point of a room can be considered as the superposition of numerous components of the same frequency, but with randomly distributed amplitudes and phase angles.

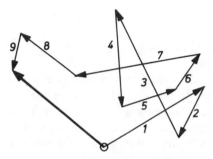

Fig. III.6. Vector diagram of the components of the steady state sound pressure in a room and their resultant for sinusoidal excitation (in most practical cases the number of components is much larger).

The situation is elucidated by Fig. III.6. The various arrows represent the contributions of the different terms of the series (III.30), the lengths being proportional to their absolute values and the angles between the arrows and a fixed direction corresponding to the phase angles. The resulting arrow is the vector sum of the various arrows. For a different frequency or at a different point in the room, this diagram has the same general character, but it looks quite different in detail, provided that the change in frequency or location is sufficiently great.

Since the different components (the different series terms) can be considered as mutually independent, we can apply to the real part as well as to the imaginary part of the resulting sound pressure p_ω the central limit theorem of probability theory, according to which both quantities are random variables obeying nearly a Gaussian distribution. This statement implies that the absolute value of p_ω is distributed according to a Rayleigh law. Let z denote the absolute value $|p_\omega|$ divided by its frequency (or space) average, then the probability of finding this quantity between z and $z + dz$ is given by

$$P(z)\,dz = \frac{\pi}{2}\exp\left(-\frac{\pi z^2}{4}\right)z\,dz \qquad\qquad (III.32)$$

This distribution is plotted in Fig. III.7. Its variance is

$$\langle z^2\rangle - 1 = \frac{4}{\pi} - 1$$

The relative mean standard deviation from the mean value is thus $[(4/\pi) - 1]^{1/2} = 0.523$. So the distribution of the sound pressure amplitude has proven to be completely independent of the type of room, of its volume, shape or acoustical qualities.

If, in any normal room or hall, we measure the absolute value of the sound pressure as a function of the frequency by feeding a loudspeaker with a sinusoidal signal of very slowly varying frequency and by recording the

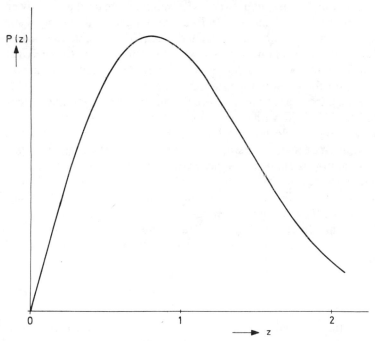

Fig. III.7. The probability density of the absolute sound pressure in a room excited by a sinusoidal signal.

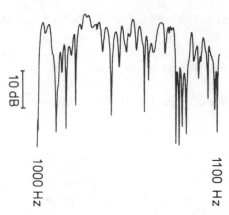

Fig. III.8. Logarithmic record of the sound pressure level at steady state conditions from 1000 to 1100 Hz (frequency curve), measured in a lecture room.

voltage amplitude of a microphone well separated from the loudspeaker, we obtain a highly irregular curve with minima, which may be lower by 40 dB or more than the maxima. In Fig. III.8 a logarithmic record of such a 'frequency curve' is shown, which has been obtained in the described manner. If the microphone is placed at a different point in the same room, or in a different room, the details of the new frequency curve are quite different, but the general appearance is similar.

According to the above discussion, the maxima of such frequency curves cannot be identified with single resonance peaks; the latter would be situated, if they could be detected experimentally, much closer. In fact, maxima of frequency curves appear when many simultaneously excited vibrational modes happen to superpose at in-phase conditions. Similarly, the minima are caused by mutual cancellation of modes, whose amplitudes and phases are distributed by chance in such a way as to make the resulting arrow in Fig. III.6 particularly small.

The average frequency spacing of adjacent maxima can be calculated under certain assumptions by applying a well-known formula of Rice.[4] The result is[5]

$$(\Delta f)_{max} = \frac{\bar{\delta}}{(3)^{1/2}} \tag{III.33}$$

where $\bar{\delta}$ is the mean value of many damping constants, which are associated with neighbouring eigenfrequencies. Hence the average separation of two adjacent frequency curve maxima is somewhat larger than the average half-width of the room resonances. This formula has also been confirmed experimentally; it turns out that the assumptions made for its derivation are justified for frequencies higher than

$$f_g \approx \frac{5000}{(V\bar{\delta})^{1/2}} \, \text{Hz} \approx 2000 \left(\frac{T}{V}\right)^{1/2} \quad \text{Hz} \tag{III.34}$$

where V is the room volume in m^3 and T denotes the reverberation time to be introduced in the following section. One can consider f_g as the lower limit of frequencies at which a statistical treatment of superimposed normal modes in a room is permissible.

Another quantity of interest especially concerning the performance of public address systems in rooms is the most probable value of the absolute maximum of a frequency curve in a prescribed frequency bandwidth B. In order to calculate this we assume, according to Schroeder,[6] that the frequency curve can be represented completely in that frequency band by N equidistant samples. Then the probability for exactly one sample assuming the absolute and normalised sound pressure z_0 (see pages 68–9), while all remaining samples are smaller than z_0 or equally large at best, is given by

$$N P(z_0) \left[\int_0^{z_0} P(z) \, dz \right]^{N-1}$$

Here $P(z)$ is the Rayleigh distribution of eqn (III.32). The expression above has its maximum for that z_0 at which its first derivative with respect to z_0 is zero. Into the equation resulting from this requirement we insert eqn (III.32) and obtain

$$\exp\left(-\frac{\pi}{4} z_0^2\right) = \frac{1 - (\pi/2) z_0^2}{1 - (\pi/2) N z_0^2} \approx \frac{1}{N}$$

the latter approximation being justified if $z_0 \gg 1$, which can safely be assumed. Solving for z_0 we get

$$z_0 \approx \left(\frac{4}{\pi} \ln N\right)^{1/2} \approx (\ln N)^{1/2}$$

or, for the corresponding level difference between the most probable maximum value and the mean value of the frequency curve,

$$\Delta L_{max} \approx 10 \log (\ln N) = 4 \cdot 3 \ln (\ln N) \quad \text{dB} \tag{III.35}$$

Because of the double logarithm it is not necessary to know the required number of samples accurately. If their distances are chosen as one-fourth of the mean spacing of frequency curve maxima, we obtain from eqn (III.33)

$$N = 4(3)^{1/2} \frac{B}{\bar{\delta}} \approx BT$$

where again we have introduced the 'reverberation time' $T = 6 \cdot 91/\bar{\delta}$ (*see* eqn (III.45)). The final result is

$$\Delta L_{max} \approx 4 \cdot 3 \ln(\ln BT) \quad dB \tag{III.36}$$

For a room with a reverberation time of 2 s, which is a typical value for a concert hall or other large hall, and for a bandwidth of 10 000 Hz, the absolute maximum of the frequency curve is most probably about 10 dB higher than its average value.

So far we have concentrated on the sound pressure amplitude in rooms as a function of the driving frequency. If we vary the driving frequency slowly at a fixed observation point, not only does the pressure amplitude change in an irregular manner but so does the phase. However, a monotonic increase (or decrease) in phase with respect to the driving frequency is superimposed on these quasi-statistical fluctuations. The average frequency dependence of the phase can be calculated as follows.

When the exciting signal is switched off at a certain moment $t = 0$, the excited modes start to decay exponentially, as we shall see in more detail in the next section. If the damping constants of the contributing modes are not too different from each other, the decay process of the envelope takes place according to a common exponential factor $\exp(-\bar{\delta}t)$. We transform the area enclosed by this curve and the t-axis for $t > 0$ into a rectangle of equal area which has the height 1 and a length $1/\bar{\delta}$. Therefore a signal originating from the sound source will be delayed on the average by a group delay time $1/(2\bar{\delta})$.

On the other hand, in the theory of linear systems, the group delay time is defined as the derivative of the frequency-dependent phase angle ψ with respect to the angular frequency. Hence we find immediately the average change per Hz in a room:

$$\left\langle \frac{d\psi}{df} \right\rangle = 2\pi \left\langle \frac{d\psi}{d\omega} \right\rangle = \frac{\pi}{\bar{\delta}} = \frac{T}{2 \cdot 2} \tag{III.37}$$

where we have again expressed the mean damping constant by the reverberation time. It is interesting to note that the formula above agrees exactly with the result of more sophisticated calculations.

We have seen so far that the general properties of the transfer function of a room, especially the distribution of its absolute values and thus the depth of its irregularities, the sequence of maxima and the phase change averaged over some frequency range, do not depend in a specific way on the room or on the point of observation. In particular, it is impossible to base a criterion of the acoustic quality on these quantities. This is in complete contrast to what has been expected in the past from an examination of frequency curves. From experience gained in the use of transmission lines, amplifiers and loudspeakers, etc., one had supposed originally that a room would be better acoustically if it had a smooth frequency curve. That this is not so is due to several reasons. First, speech and music exhibit such rapid variations in signal character that a large room does not reach steady state conditions when excited by them except perhaps during very slow musical passages. Furthermore, more recent investigations have shown that our hearing organ is unable to perceive fluctuations of the spectrum of a signal with respect to frequency if these irregularities are spaced closely enough on the frequency axis (*see* Section VII.3).

Finally, we come back once more to the spatial distribution of the sound pressure or the energy density for stationary, sinusoidal excitation. The distribution of the absolute sound pressure with respect to a variation of the location is the same as that with respect to a frequency variation, as given by eqn (III.32). An example of the pressure distribution along a straight line at fixed frequency is shown in Fig. III.9. The mean distance of pressure maxima along a certain measuring line can be estimated from the fact that each normal mode is a sort of standing wave which can be imagined as being composed of plane waves, at least for sufficiently high frequencies. The same is then true for the numerous modes interfering with each other which are simultaneously excited by a sinusoidal tone.

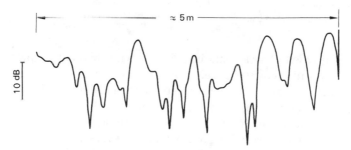

Fig. III.9. Logarithmic record of the steady state sound pressure level in a small lecture room at 1000 Hz; abscissa is the location of the measuring microphone on a certain line.

In a one-dimensional standing wave there are $(2/\lambda)|\cos \Theta|$ maxima per unit length in a straight line which makes an angle Θ with the wave normal. If one averages this expression over all possible directions, the resulting mean value is $1/\lambda$, i.e. the mean distance of adjacent pressure maxima is about one wavelength. A more accurate derivation along similar lines to that of eqn (III.33) yields the value

$$\langle \Delta x_{max} \rangle = 0.935\lambda \qquad \text{(III.38)}$$

This expression is again entirely independent of the sort of room; measurements of the steady state, spatial pressure distribution at a single frequency have no significance in describing the acoustical qualities of the room.

III.5 DECAYING MODES IN ROOMS, REVERBERATION

If a room is excited not by a stationary sinusoidal signal as in the preceding sections but instead by a very short sound pulse emitted at time $t = 0$, we obtain, in the limit of vanishing pulse duration, an impulse response $g(t)$ at some receiving point of the room. According to the discussion in Section I.5, this is the Fourier transform of the transfer function. Hence

$$g(t) = \int_{-\infty}^{+\infty} p_\omega \exp(i\omega t)\, d\omega$$

Generally the evaluation of this Fourier integral, applied to p_ω after eqn (III.9) or (III.30), is rather complicated since both ω_n and δ_n depend on the driving frequency ω. At any rate the solution has the form

$$g(t) = \begin{cases} 0 & \text{for } t < 0 \\ \sum_n A'_n \exp(-\delta'_n t) \cos(\omega'_n t + \psi'_n) & \text{for } t \geq 0 \end{cases} \qquad \text{(III.39)}$$

It is composed of sinusoidal oscillations with different frequencies, each dying out with its own particular damping constant. This is quite plausible since each term of eqn (III.30) corresponds to a resonator whose reaction to an excitation impulse is a damped oscillation. If the wall losses in the room are not too large, the frequencies ω'_n and damping constants δ'_n differ only slightly from those occurring in eqn (III.30). As is seen from the more exact representation (III.9), the coefficients A'_n contain implicitly the location of both the source and the receiving point.

If the room is excited not by an impulse but by a stationary signal $s(t)$

which is switched off at $t = 0$, the resulting room response $h(t)$ is, according to eqn (I.37),

$$h(t) = \int_{-\infty}^{0} s(\tau)g(t - \tau)\,d\tau$$

$$= \sum_{n} A'_n \exp(-\delta'_n t)[a_n \cos(\omega'_n t + \psi'_n) + b_n \sin(\omega'_n t + \psi'_n)] \quad \text{for } t \geq 0$$

where

$$\left.\begin{array}{c} a_n \\ b_n \end{array}\right\} = \int_{-\infty}^{0} s(x) \exp(\delta'_n x)\left\{\begin{array}{c} \cos \\ \sin \end{array}\right\}(\omega'_n x)\,dx$$

The above expression for $h(t)$ can be written more simply as

$$h(t) = \sum_{n} c_n \exp(-\delta'_n t)\cos(\omega'_n t - \phi_n) \quad \text{for } t > 0 \qquad \text{(III.40)}$$

with

$$c_n = A'_n\sqrt{a_n^2 + b_n^2}$$

It is evident that only such modes can contribute to the general decay process whose eigenfrequencies are not too remote from the frequencies which are contained in the spectrum of the driving signal. If the latter is a sinusoidal tone switched off at some time $t = 0$, then only such components contribute noticeably to $h(t)$, the frequencies ω'_n of which are separated from the driving frequency ω by not more than a half-width, i.e. by about δ'_n.

The decay process described by eqn (III.40) is called the 'reverberation' of the room. It is one of the most important acoustical phenomena of a room, familiar also to the layman. In this book we shall encounter it quite frequently.

An expression proportional to the energy density is obtained by squaring $h(t)$:

$$w(t) \sim [h(t)]^2 = \sum_{n}\sum_{m} c_n c_m \exp[-(\delta'_n + \delta'_m)t]\cos(\omega'_n t - \phi_n)\cos(\omega'_m t - \phi_m)$$
$$\text{(III.41)}$$

This expression can be considerably simplified by averaging it with respect to time. Since the damping constants are small compared with the eigenfrequencies, the exponential terms vary slowly and we are permitted to average the cosine products only. The products with $n \neq m$ will cancel on the average, whereas each term $n = m$ yields a value $\frac{1}{2}$. Thus we obtain

$$\overline{w(t)} = \sum_{n} c_n^2 \exp(-2\delta'_n t) \qquad \text{(III.41a)}$$

where all constants of no importance have been omitted.

Now we imagine that the sum is rearranged according to increasing damping constants δ'_n. Additionally, the sum is supposed to consist of many significant terms. Then we can replace it by an integral by introducing a damping density $H(\delta)$. This is done by denoting the sum of all c_n^2 with damping constants between δ and $\delta + d\delta$ by $H(\delta) \, d\delta$, and by normalising $H(\delta)$ so as to have

$$\int_0^\infty H(\delta) \, d\delta = 1$$

Then the integral envisaged becomes simply

$$\overline{w(t)} = \int_0^\infty H(\delta) \exp(-2\delta t) \, d\delta \tag{III.42}$$

Just as with the coefficient c_n, the damping distribution $H(\delta)$ depends on the sound signal, on the location of the sound source, and on the point of observation. From this representation we can derive some interesting general properties of reverberation.

Usually reverberation measurements are based on the sound pressure level of the decaying sound field:

$$L_r = 10 \log_{10}\left(\frac{\bar{w}}{w_0}\right) = 4\cdot34 \ln\left(\frac{\bar{w}}{w_0}\right) \quad \text{dB}$$

Its decay rate is

$$\frac{dL_r}{dt} = \frac{4\cdot34}{\bar{w}} \frac{d\bar{w}}{dt} \quad \text{dB/s}$$

If in this formula $\bar{w}$ and its time derivative are substituted from eqn (III.42), one obtains

$$-\frac{dL_r}{dt} = 8\cdot69 \frac{\int H(\delta) \exp(-2\delta t)\delta \, d\delta}{\int H(\delta) \exp(-2\delta t) \, d\delta} = 8\cdot69 \frac{\int H_t(\delta)\delta \, d\delta}{\int H_t(\delta) \, d\delta} \tag{III.43}$$

Here $H_t(\delta) = H(\delta) \exp(-2\delta t)$ has been introduced, the instantaneous damping distribution at time t. This formula indicates that the slope of the reverberation curve at a certain time t is given by the mean damping constant, weighted with the time-dependent distribution H_t. Since, at increasing time, the values for small δ in the function H_t become more and more pronounced, the slope of the curve decreases and the curve becomes flatter. That is to say, reverberation curves are generally curved convexly viewed from the time axis. As a limiting case they can be straight lines. The latter is the case if all damping constants which are involved in the decay process are equal, i.e. if the distribution function $H(\delta)$ is a delta function (or is at least very narrow).

For $t = 0$ the curve has its steepest part; its initial slope

$$\left(\frac{\mathrm{d}L_r}{\mathrm{d}t}\right)_{t=0} = -8{\cdot}69 \int H(\delta)\delta \, \mathrm{d}\delta = -8{\cdot}69\bar{\delta} \tag{III.44}$$

is determined by the mean value of the damping distribution.

In Fig. III.10 are shown some examples of distributions of damping constants together with the corresponding logarithmic reverberation curves. The distributions are normalised so that their mean values (and hence the initial slopes of the corresponding reverberation curves) agree

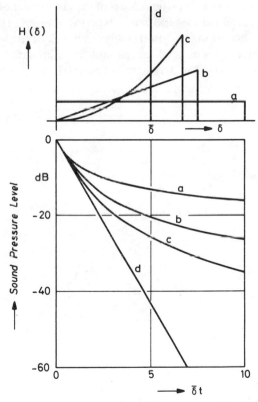

Fig. III.10. Various distributions of damping constants and corresponding reverberation curves.

with each other. Only when all the damping constants are equal (case d) straight curves are obtained.

The preceding considerations do not apply, however, for coupled rooms; that is to say, they are not valid for rooms which are composed of virtually separate rooms, connected by relatively small coupling apertures only or by partially transparent walls. That different conditions are to be expected can be understood in the following way.

Let us consider two partial rooms not too different from each other, which are coupled to each other and whose eigenfrequencies, if they were not coupled, would be $\omega_1, \omega_2, \ldots, \omega_n$ and $\omega_1', \omega_2', \ldots, \omega_n', \ldots$, respectively. For each eigenfrequency of the one room, we can find an eigenfrequency of the other room, having nearly the same value. By introducing the coupling element these pairs of eigenfrequencies—as with any coupled system—are pushed apart by a value $\Delta\omega$, where $\Delta\omega$ is of the same order of magnitude for all pairs of eigenfrequencies and depends on the amount of coupling. In the decay process, according to eqn (III.40), beats will occur with a relatively low beat frequency $\Delta\omega/2$ which cannot be eliminated by short-time averaging as applied in the derivation of eqn (III.41), and the shape of the

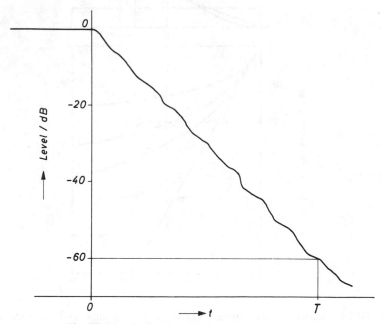

Fig. III.11. Definition of the reverberation time.

reverberation curve may exhibit more complicated features than described above. Only if the coupling is so strong that the frequency shifts, and hence the beat frequencies become comparable with the eigenfrequencies themselves, will a short-time averaging process remove everything except the exponential factors, and we can apply eqn (III.41). For that case, however, the coupling aperture has to be so large that we can speak of one single room and its splitting up into partial rooms would be artificial. In Chapter V we shall discuss the properties of coupled rooms from a statistical point of view. For the exact wave theoretical treatment of coupled rooms, the reader is referred to the literature.[7]

We come back once more to the case of nearly uniform damping constants, the weighted average of which is δ_0. As mentioned above, the reverberation level decreases linearly in this case. It is usual in room acoustics to characterise the duration of the reverberation not by the damping constant δ_0 but by the 'reverberation time' T, introduced by W. C. Sabine, the great pioneer of modern room acoustics. The reverberation time is the time interval in which the reverberation level drops down by 60 dB (see Fig. III.11). From

$$-60 = 10 \log_{10} [\exp(-2\delta_0 T)]$$

it follows that the reverberation time

$$T = \frac{6 \cdot 91}{\delta_0} \qquad (III.45)$$

a relation which we have made use of already in Section III.4.

For curved reverberation records, a reverberation time can also be evaluated, for instance by evaluating the moment at which the reverberation level has fallen by a certain value, or by determining an average slope in a certain section of the curve. In no case, however, is this procedure entirely free from some arbitrariness.

Fortunately the reverberation level falls in many practical cases in a fairly linear way, apart from minor random or quasi-random fluctuations, which are superimposed on the general shape and which are due to incomplete cancellation of terms with $n \neq m$ in the double series in eqn (III.41).

With suitable precautions it is possible to give the decay constants of a room fairly uniform values and thus to straighten the reverberation curves. This is important in certain measuring methods.

Typical values of reverberation times run from about 0·3 s (living rooms) up to 10 s (large churches, reverberation chambers). Most large rooms have reverberation times between 0·7 and 2 s. Thus the average damping constants encountered in practice are in the range 1 to $20 \, s^{-1}$.

REFERENCES

1. Morse, P. M. & Feshbach, H., *Methods of Theoretical Physics.* McGraw-Hill, New York, 1953, Chapter 11.
2. Morse, P. M. & Ingard, K. U., *Theoretical Acoustics.* McGraw-Hill, New York, 1968, Chapter 9.
3. Morse, P. M., *J. Acoust. Soc. America,* **11** (1939) 205.
4. Rice, S. O., Mathematical analysis of random noise. In *Selected Papers on Noise and Stochastic Processes,* ed. N. Wax. Dover Publ., New York, 1954, p. 209.
5. Schroeder, M. R. & Kuttruff, K. H., *J. Acoust. Soc. America,* **34** (1962) 76.
6. Schroeder, M. R., *Proceedings of the Third International Congress on Acoustics,* Stuttgart, 1959, ed. L. Cremer. Elsevier, Amsterdam, 1961, p. 771.
7. Morse, P. M. & Ingard, K. U., *Theoretical Acoustics.* McGraw-Hill, New York, 1968, Chapter 10.

IV

The Limiting Case of Very High Sound Frequencies: Geometrical Room Acoustics

The discussions of the preceding chapter have clearly shown that it is not very promising to apply the methods of wave theory in order to find answers to questions of practical interest, especially if the room under consideration is large and somewhat irregular in shape. In such cases even the calculation of one single eigenvalue and the associated normal mode is quite difficult. Moreover, in order to obtain a survey of the sound fields which are to be expected for different types of excitation it would be necessary to calculate not one but a very large number of modes. On the other hand, such a computation, supposing it were at all practicable, would yield far more detailed information than would be required and meaningful for the judgement of the acoustical properties of the room.

We arrive at a greatly simplified way of description—just as in geometrical optics—by employing the limiting case of vanishingly small wavelengths, i.e. the limiting case of very high frequencies. This assumption is permitted if the dimensions of the room and its walls are large compared with the wavelength of sound. This condition is frequently met in room acoustics; at a medium frequency of 1000 Hz, corresponding to a wavelength of 34 cm, the linear dimensions of the walls and the ceiling, and also the distances covered by the sound waves are usually larger than the wavelength by orders of magnitude. Even if the reflection of sound from a balcony face is to be discussed, for instance, a geometrical description is applicable, at least qualitatively.

In geometrical room acoustics, the concept of a wave is replaced by the concept of a sound ray. The latter is an idealisation just as much as the plane wave. As in geometrical optics, we mean by a sound ray a small portion of a spherical wave with vanishing aperture which originates from a certain point. It has a well-defined direction of propagation and is subject to the same laws of propagation as a light ray, apart from the different

81

propagation velocity. Thus, according to the above definition, the total energy conveyed by a ray remains constant provided the medium itself does not cause any energy losses. However, the intensity within a diverging bundle of rays falls as $1/r^2$, as in every spherical wave, where r denotes the distance from its origin. Another fact of particular importance for room acoustics is the law of reflection. In contrast, the transition to another medium and the refraction accompanying it does not occur in room acoustics, neither does the curvature of rays in an inhomogeneous medium. But the finite velocity of propagation must be considered in many cases, since it is responsible for many important effects such as reverberation, echoes and so on.

Diffraction phenomena are neglected in geometrical room acoustics, since propagation in straight lines is its main postulate. Likewise, interference is not considered, i.e. if several sound field components are superimposed their mutual phase relations are not taken into account; instead, simply their energy densities or their intensities are added. This simplified procedure is permissible if the different components are 'incoherent' with respect to each other, which is usually the case if the components have wide frequency spectra. Criteria for characterising the coherence of sound signals will be discussed in Chapters VII and VIII.

It is self-evident that geometrical room acoustics can reflect only a partial aspect of the acoustical phenomena occurring in a room. This aspect is, however, of great importance—especially of practical importance—and therefore we must deal with it in some detail.

IV.1 THE REFLECTION OF SOUND RAYS

If a sound ray strikes a plane surface it is usually reflected from it. This process takes place according to the reflection law well known in optics. It states that the ray during reflection remains in the plane, including the incident ray and the normal to the surface, and that the angle between the incident ray and reflected ray is halved by the normal to the wall.

Since the lateral extension of a sound ray is vanishingly small, the specular reflection law is valid for any part of a plane no matter how small. Therefore it can be applied equally well to the construction of the reflection of an extended ray bundle from a curved surface by imagining each ray in turn to be reflected from the tangential plane which it strikes. This is very important in room acoustics since the sound reflection from concave portions of walls or ceilings or balcony faces may give rise to non-uniform

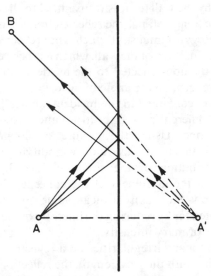

Fig. IV.1.   Construction of an image source.

distributions of sound energy and, as a consequence, to audible echoes and hence to deficiencies which can be detected immediately from ray diagrams.

The reflection of sound rays originating from a certain point can be illustrated by the construction of an image source, provided that the reflecting surface is plane (*see* Fig. IV.1). At some distance from the reflecting plane there is a sound source A. We are interested in the sound transmission to another point B. It takes place along the direct path AB on the one hand (direct sound) and on the other by reflection from the wall. To find the path of the reflected ray we make A′ the mirror image of A, connect A′ to B, and A to the point of intersection of A′B with the plane.

Once we have constructed the image source A′ associated with a given original source A, we can disregard the wall altogether, the effect of which is now replaced by that of the image source. Of course, we must assume that the image emits exactly the same sound signal as the original source and that its directional characteristics are symmetrical to those of A. If the extension of the reflecting wall is finite, then we must restrict the directions of emission of A′ accordingly. Or put in a different way: for certain positions of the observation point B the image source may become 'invisible'. This is the case if the line connecting B with the image source does not intersect the actual wall.

Usually not all the energy striking a wall is reflected from it; part of the energy is absorbed by the wall (or it is transmitted to the other side, which amounts to the same thing as far as the reflected fraction is concerned). The fraction of sound energy (or intensity) which is not reflected is characterised by the absorption coefficient α of the wall, which has been defined in Section II.2 as the ratio of the non-reflected to the incident intensity. It depends generally, as we have seen, on the angle of incidence and, of course, on the frequencies which are contained in the incident sound. Thus the reflected ray generally has a different power spectrum and a lower total intensity than the incident one. Using the picture of image sources, these circumstances can be taken into account by modifying the spectrum and the directional distribution of the sound emitted by A'. With such refinements, however, the usefulness of the concept of image sources is degraded considerably. So usually a mean value only of the absorption coefficient is accounted for by reducing the intensity of the reflected ray by a fraction $1 - \alpha$ of the primary intensity.

If there are a great many irregularities on a reflecting wall, the sizes of which are comparable with the wavelength, the reflection law is no longer valid in the form mentioned above. Instead, the incident sound energy is diffracted or scattered into an extended solid angle. In this case we speak of 'diffuse' or, more exactly, of 'partially diffuse' sound reflections. The reflection takes place in a totally diffuse manner if the directional distribution of the reflected or the scattered energy does not depend in any way on the direction of the incident sound. This case can be realised physically quite well in optics. In contrast, in acoustics and particularly in room acoustics, in most cases only partially diffuse reflections can be achieved. But nevertheless in many cases the assumption of totally diffuse reflections comes closer to the actual reflecting properties of real walls than that of specular reflection, particularly if we are concerned not only with one but instead with many successive ray reflections from different walls or portions of walls. This is the case with reverberation processes and in reverberant enclosures.

Totally diffuse reflections from a wall take place according to Lambert's cosine law: suppose an area element dS is 'illuminated' by a bundle of parallel or nearly parallel rays which make an angle ϑ_0 to the wall normal, whose intensity is I_0. Then the intensity of the sound which is scattered in a direction characterised by an angle ϑ, measured at a distance r from the surface (see Fig. IV.2), is given by

$$I(r) = I_0 \, dS \frac{\cos \vartheta \cos \vartheta_0}{\pi r^2} = B_0 \, dS \frac{\cos \vartheta}{\pi r^2} \qquad \text{(IV.1)}$$

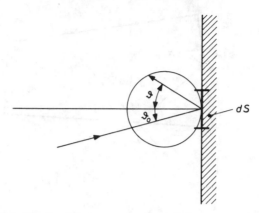

Fig. IV.2. Ideally diffuse sound reflection from a rough surface.

B_0 being the so-called 'irradiation strength', i.e. the energy incident on unit area of the wall per second. This formula holds provided that there is no absorption, i.e. the incident energy is re-emitted completely. If this is not the case, $I(r, \vartheta)$ has to be multiplied by an appropriate factor $1 - \alpha(\vartheta)$.

According to eqn (IV.1), each surface element has to be considered as a secondary sound source, which is expressed by the fact that the distance r, which determines the intensity reduction due to propagation, must be measured from the reflecting area element dS. This is not so with specular reflection: here the geometrical intensity decrease of a sound ray originating from a certain point is determined by the total length of the path between the sound source and the point of observation with no regard as to whether this path is bent or straight.

IV.2 SOUND REFLECTIONS IN A ROOM

Suppose we follow a sound ray originating from a sound source on its way through a closed room. Then we find that it is reflected not once but many times from the walls, the ceiling and perhaps also from the floor. This succession of reflections continues until the ray arrives at a perfectly absorbent surface. But even if there is no perfectly absorbent area in our enclosure the energy carried by the ray will become vanishingly small after some time, because with each reflection a certain part of it is lost by absorption.

If the room is bounded by plane surfaces, it may be advantageous to find

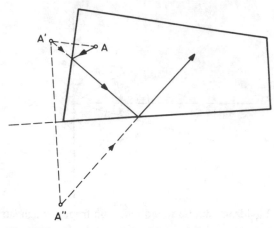

Fig. IV.3.   Image sources of first and second order.

the paths of the sound rays by constructing the image sources (*see* Fig. IV.3).
For this purpose consider the wall which is struck first and construct the
image A′ corresponding to that wall. This image source enables us to find
the next section of the ray path. Then a second image A″ is constructed from
A′ associated with the wall at which the ray will arrive next. We continue in
this way, obtaining more and more image sources as the total path length of
the ray increases.

For a given enclosure and sound source position, the image sources can
be constructed without referring to a particular sound path. Suppose the
enclosure is made up of N-plane walls. Each wall is associated with one
image of the original sound source. Now each of these image sources of first
order is mirrored by each wall, which leads to $N(N-1)$ new images which
are of second order. By repeating this procedure again and again a rapidly
growing number of images is generated with increasing distances from the
original source. The number of images of order i is $N(N-1)^{i-1}$ for $i \geq 1$; the
total number of images of order up to i_0 is obtained by adding all these
expressions:

$$N(i_0) = N \frac{(N-1)^{i_0} - 1}{N-2} \tag{IV.2}$$

It is obvious that in the general case the construction of the significant
image sources and the addition of the energies they contribute to the total
energy in some receiving point can be carried out, if at all, only by use of a
digital computer (*see* Section IX.6). Here we have to keep in mind that each

image source has its own directivity since it 'illuminates' only a limited solid angle, determined by the limited extension of the walls. This problem of the 'validity' of image sources has been carefully discussed by Borish.[1]

These complications are not encountered with enclosures of high regularity, which in turn produce regular patterns of image sources. As a simple example, which also may illustrate the usefulness of the image model, let us consider a very flat room, the height of which is small compared with its lateral dimensions. Since most points in this enclosure are far from the side walls, the effect of the latter may be totally neglected.

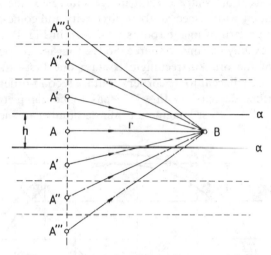

Fig. IV.4. System of image sources of an infinite flat room: A is the original sound source; A′, A″, etc., are image sources; B is the receiving point.

Then we arrive at a space which is bounded by two parallel, infinite planes. We assume a sound source A in the middle between both planes, radiating constant power P uniformly in all directions. The corresponding image sources (and image spaces) are depicted in Fig. IV.4. The source images form a simple pattern of equidistant points situated on a straight line, and each of them is a valid one, i.e. it is 'visible' from any observation point B. Its distance from an image of nth order is $(r^2 + n^2h^2)^{1/2}$, if r denotes the horizontal distance of B from the original source A and h is the 'height' of the room. If we furthermore assume, for the sake of simplicity, that both planes have the same absorption coefficient α independent of the angle of sound incidence, the total energy density in B is given by the following expression:

$$w = \frac{P}{4\pi c} \sum_{n=-\infty}^{\infty} \frac{(1-\alpha)^{|n|}}{r^2 + n^2 h^2} \tag{IV.3}$$

which can easily be evaluated with a programmable pocket calculator.

Another example is obtained by dropping the assumption of very large lateral dimensions. Then we have to take the side walls into account, which we assume to be perpendicular to the floor and the ceiling, and also to each other. The resulting enclosure is a rectangular room, as depicted in Fig. III.1. For this room shape certain image sources of the same order are complementary with respect to their directivity and coincide. The result is the regular pattern of image rooms as shown in Fig. IV.5, each of them containing exactly one image source. So the four image rooms adjacent to the sides of the original rectangle contain one first-order image each, whereas those adjacent to its corners contain second-order images and so on. The lattice depicted in Fig. IV.5 has to be completed in the third dimension, i.e. we must imagine an infinite number of such patterns one

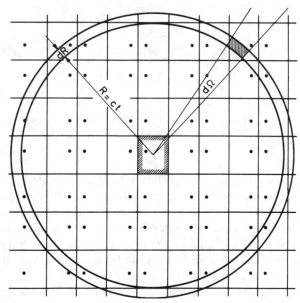

Fig. IV.5. Image sound sources for a rectangular room. The pattern continues in an analogous manner in the direction perpendicular to the drawing plane.

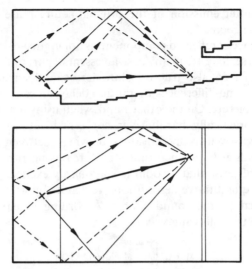

Fig. IV.6. Direct sound and a few reflected components in a room. The dashed lines denote the paths of double reflections.

upon the other at equal distances, one of them containing the original room.

Leaving apart the image concept for the remainder of this section, let us examine how a room of arbitrary shape with given locations of the sound source and the receiving point modifies a sound signal.

We assume the sound source to emit at a certain time a very short sound pulse with equal intensity in all directions. This pulse will reach the observation point (*see* Fig. IV.6) not only by the direct path but also via numerous partly single, partly multiple reflections, of which only a few are indicated in Fig. IV.6. The total sound field is thus composed of the 'direct sound' and of many 'reflections'. (In the following we use the term 'reflection' with a two-fold meaning: first to indicate the process of reflecting sound from a wall and secondly as the name for a sound component which has been reflected.) These reflections reach the observer from various directions, moreover their strengths may be quite different and finally they are delayed with respect to the direct sound by different times, corresponding to the total path lengths they have covered until they reach the observation point. Thus each reflection must be characterised by three quantities: its direction, its relative strength, and its relative time of arrival, i.e. its delay time. The sum total of the reflections arriving at a certain point after emission of the original sound pulse is the acoustic response of the room.

The occurrence of reflected components is not limited to impulsive sound signals, of course; they are in any case an essential part of the sound field in an enclosure. This is also true for stationary sound signals. In this case, however, their time differences or mutual delay times themselves do not come into the picture. On the other hand, when using a room in a normal way, we are practically hardly ever concerned with stationary sound signals; music as well as speech are somewhere between stationary and impulsive signals as far as their time structure is concerned. It is only with certain types of noise that a room is stationarily excited.

For a more quantitative description, we denote by $s(t)$ the sound signal being produced by the sound source. According to eqn (I.36) we can represent it in the following way:

$$s(t) = \int_{-\infty}^{+\infty} s(x)\delta(t-x)\,\mathrm{d}x$$

Thus $s(t)$ is considered as a close succession of Dirac pulses. As described before, each of them gives rise to numerous reflections in the observation point. Generally the shapes of these reflected impulses will differ from the original Dirac pulse since the wall reflectivities and also the air absorption are frequency dependent. If we neglect this effect, the response of the room to a single pulse is just

$$g(t) = \sum_n A_n \delta(t-t_n)$$

where A_n are the strengths and t_n the times of arrival of the reflections (t_0 denotes the arrival time of the direct sound). According to eqn (I.37), the whole signal arriving at the observation point is given by

$$s'(t) = \int_{-\infty}^{+\infty} s(x)g(t-x)\,\mathrm{d}x = \sum_n A_n s(t-t_n) \qquad \text{(IV.4)}$$

Hence it is composed of numerous repetitions of the original signal, which gradually become weaker and weaker, since the A_n generally decrease with increasing n. It is evident that $s'(t)$ may sound quite different from $s(t)$ and that therefore the temporal structure of a reflection pattern is a quite important if not even the most important characteristic feature of the acoustics of any room. We should add that the directional distribution of the received reflections also influences to a great extent what we hear in a room.

Since an enumeration of the great number of reflections, of their strengths, their directions and their delay times would not be very illustrative and would yield much more information on the sound field than is meaningful because of our limited hearing abilities, we shall again prefer statistical methods in what follows.

IV.3 THE TEMPORAL DISTRIBUTION OF REFLECTIONS

If we mark the arrival times of the various reflections by perpendicular dashes over a horizontal time axis and choose the heights of the dashes proportional to the relative strengths of reflections, i.e. to the coefficients A_n, we obtain what is frequently called a 'reflection diagram' or 'echogram'. It contains all significant information on the temporal structure of the sound field at a certain room point. In Fig. IV.7 a schematical reflection diagram is plotted. After the direct sound, arriving at $t = 0$, the first strong reflections occur at first sporadically, later their temporal density increases rapidly, however; at the same time the reflections carry less and less energy. As we shall see later in more detail, the role of the first isolated reflections with respect to our subjective hearing impression is quite different from that of the very numerous weak reflections arriving at later times, which merge into what we perceive subjectively as reverberation. Thus we can consider the reverberation of a room not only as the common effect of free decaying vibrational modes, as we did in Chapter III, but also as the sum total of all reflections—except the very first ones.

A survey on the temporal structure of reflections and hence of the law of

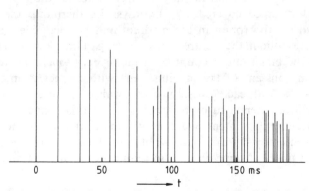

Fig. IV.7. Schematical reflection diagram. Abscissa is the delay time of a reflection, ordinate its level, both with respect to the direct sound arriving at $t = 0$.

reverberation in a rectangular room can easily be obtained by using the system of image rooms and image sound sources (*see* Fig. IV.5). We suppose for this purpose that at some time $t = 0$ all mirror sources generate impulses of equal strengths. In the time interval from t to $t + dt$, all those reflections will arrive in the centre of the original room which originate from image sources whose distances to the centre are between ct and $c(t + dt)$. These sources are located in a spherical shell with radius ct. The thickness of this shell (which is supposed to be very small as compared with ct) is $c\,dt$ and its volume is $4\pi c^3 t^2\,dt$. In this shell volume, the volume V of an image room is contained $4\pi c^3 t^2\,dt/V$ times; this figure is also the number of mirror sources contained in the shell volume. Therefore the temporal density of the reflections arriving at time t is

$$\frac{dN_r}{dt} = 4\pi \frac{c^3 t^2}{V} \tag{IV.5}$$

The mean density of sound reflections increases according to a quadratic law with respect to time, a result which is meaningful only if the reflection density is already high enough to make a statistical approach applicable.

It is interesting to note, by the way, that the above approach is the same as we applied to estimate the mean density of eigenfrequencies in a rectangular room (eqn (III.21)) with about the same result. In fact, the pattern of mirror sources and the eigenfrequency lattice are closely related to each other. Moreover, it can be shown[2] that eqn (IV.5) does not only apply to rectangular rooms but to rooms with arbitrary shape as well.

Each reflection—considered physically—corresponds to a bundle of rays originating from the respective image source in which the sound intensity decreases proportionally as $(ct)^{-2}$, i.e. as the square of the reciprocal distance covered by the rays. Furthermore, the rays are attenuated by absorption in the medium and by incomplete reflections which correspond in the picture to the crossing of image walls. The former effect can be taken into account by a factor $\exp(-mct)$, where m is the absorption constant of the medium (air) with respect to intensity (*see* Section VI.1). With each crossing of any wall of an image room the ray bundle will be attenuated by a factor $1 - \alpha$; if this happens n-times per second, the energy or intensity of the ray bundle after some time t will have become smaller by $(1 - \alpha)^{nt} = \exp[nt \ln(1 - \alpha)]$. On average the reflections arriving at time t at some observation point in the original room have an intensity

$$\frac{A}{(ct^2)} \exp\{[-mc + n \ln(1 - \alpha)]t\}$$

A being a constant factor. Therefore the whole energy of all reflections at the point of observation (the exact location of which is of minor importance) as a function of time is

$$E(t) = E_0 \exp\{[-mc + n\ln(1-\alpha)]t\} \qquad \text{(IV.6)}$$

Now we must calculate the average number of wall reflections or wall crossings per second. For this purpose, as in Section III.2, the dimensions of the rectangular room are denoted by L_x, L_y, L_z. A sound ray whose angle with respect to the x-axis is β_x undergoes n_x crossings of mirror walls per second perpendicular to the x-axis where

$$n_x(\beta_x) = \left|\frac{c}{L_x}\cos\beta_x\right| \qquad \text{(IV.7)}$$

Averaging of $|\cos\beta_x|$ over all possible directions (where for the moment we choose the x-axis as a polar axis) yields

$$\frac{1}{4\pi} \times 2\pi \times 2 \int_0^{\pi/2} \cos\beta_x \sin\beta_x \, d\beta_x = \tfrac{1}{2}$$

The average of n_x over all directions is thus $c/2L_x$. Similar expressions are obtained for the average number of crossings of walls which are perpendicular to the y-axis and z-axis. The average total number of wall reflections per second is therefore

$$\bar{n} = \frac{c}{2}\left(\frac{1}{L_x} + \frac{1}{L_y} + \frac{1}{L_z}\right) = \frac{cS}{4V} \qquad \text{(IV.8)}$$

Here S is the total area of all walls of the original rectangular room. We want to put some emphasis on the statement that this expression is the number of crossings or of wall reflections per second, averaged over a large number of rays or ray bundles which are assumed to be distributed uniformly over all possible directions of propagation. It is not the average number of crossings of one single ray, since each of these has its particular and well defined direction in our picture. The latter number is instead $n_x + n_y + n_z$ and depends, according to eqn (IV.7) and the similar equations, on the specific ray direction. If we want the calculated figure $\bar{n}$ to represent the mean number of crossings or wall reflections for each ray separately, we must arrange in some way for each ray to change its direction many times during the reverberation process so that the difference between the time average and the directional average will disappear. This can be achieved either by walls which reflect the impinging sound rays not specularly but diffusely or by obstacles in the room which are struck by each ray with some probability and which cause quasi-random deviations from the original directions of propagation. Or, put in still another way, the sound field in the room must be made diffuse.

If this condition is met, we can insert $\bar{n}$ from eqn (IV.8) into our 'reverberation law' (IV.6) and obtain

$$E(t) = E_0 \exp\left[-ct\,\frac{4mV - S\ln(1-\alpha)}{4V}\right] \qquad \text{(IV.9)}$$

The reverberation time, that is the time in which the total energy falls to one millionth of its initial value, is thus

$$T = \frac{1}{c}\,\frac{24V\ln 10}{4mV - S\ln(1-\alpha)} \qquad \text{(IV.10)}$$

or, if we use the value of the sound velocity in air and express the volume V in m³ and the wall area S in m²,

$$T = 0\cdot163\,\frac{V}{4mV - S\ln(1-\alpha)} \qquad \text{(IV.11)}$$

In the preceding, we have derived by rather simple geometric considerations the most important formula of room acoustics which relates the reverberation time, that is the most characteristic figure with respect to the acoustics of a room, to its geometrical data and to the absorption coefficient of its walls. We have assumed tacitly that the latter is the same for all wall portions and that it does not depend on the angle at which a wall is struck by the sound rays. In the next chapter we shall try to look more closely into the laws of reverberation by applying somewhat more refined methods, but the result will be essentially the same.

The exponential law of eqn (IV.9) represents an approximate description of the temporal change of the energy carried by the reflections, neglecting many details which may be of great importance for the acoustics of a room. In practical cases the actual decrease of reflected energy succeeding an impulsive sound signal always exhibits greater or lesser pronounced deviations from this ideal law. Sometimes such deviations may be heard subjectively in a very unpleasant way and spoil the acoustical quality of a room. So it may happen, for instance, that a reflection arriving at a relatively large time delay carries far more energy than its contemporaries and stands out of the general reverberation. This can occur when the sound rays of which it is made up have undergone a reflection from a remote concave portion of wall. Such a reflected component is perceived as a distinct echo and is particularly disturbing if the portion of wall which is responsible is irradiated by a loudspeaker. Another unfavourable condition is that of many reflections clustered together in a narrow time interval. Since our hearing has a limited time resolution and therefore performs some sort of short-time integration, this lack of uniformity may be audible and may exhibit undesirable effects which are similar to a single reflection of exceptional strength.

Particularly disturbing are reflections which form a periodic or a nearly periodic succession. This is true even if this periodicity is hidden in a great number of reflections distributed irregularly over the time axis, since our hearing is very sensitive to periodic repetitions of certain sound signals. For short periods, i.e. for repetition times of a few milliseconds, such periodic components are perceived as a 'colouration' of the reverberation; then a certain pitch and timbre can be associated with the sound decay itself. Hence speech or music in such a room will have their spectra changed. If the periods are longer, if they amount to 30, 50 or even 100 ms, the regular temporal structure itself becomes audible. This case, which is frequently referred to as 'flutter echo', occurs if sound is reflected repeatedly to and fro between parallel walls. Flutter echoes can be observed quite distinctly in corridors or other longish rooms where the end walls are rigid but the ceiling, floor and side walls are absorbent. They can also occur in rooms the shapes of which are less extreme, but then their audibility is mostly restricted to particular locations of source and observer.

IV.4 THE DIRECTIONAL DISTRIBUTION OF REFLECTIONS, DIFFUSION

We shall now take into consideration the third property which characterises a reflection, namely the direction from which it reaches an observer. As before, we shall not attribute to each single reflection its proper direction, but we shall apply a summarising method, which commends itself not only because of the great number of reflections making up the resulting sound field in a room but also because we are usually not able to locate subjectively the directions from which reflected and hence delayed components reach our ears. Nevertheless, whether the reflected components arrive uniformly from all directions or whether they all come from one single direction has considerable bearing on the acoustical properties of a room. The directional distribution of sound is also important for certain measuring techniques.

Consider a short time interval dt (in the vicinity of time t) on the time axis of a reflection diagram or echogram. As before, let the origin of the time axis be the moment at which the direct sound arrives. Furthermore, define some polar angle ϑ and azimuth angle φ as the quantities which characterise certain directions. Around a certain direction, imagine a 'directional cone' with a small aperture, i.e. solid angle $d\Omega$. The total energy contributed by reflections arriving in dt from the solid angle element $d\Omega$ is denoted by

$$d^3E = E_t(\varphi, \vartheta)\,dt\,d\Omega \tag{IV.12}$$

$E_t(\varphi, \vartheta)$ is the time-dependent directional distribution of the reflection energy or reverberation energy.

If we integrate eqn (IV.12) over all directions, we obtain the time distribution of the reflected sound energy discussed in the preceding section:

$$E(t) = \int\int E_t(\varphi, \vartheta)\,d\Omega \tag{IV.13}$$

If we integrate, however, eqn (IV.12) over all times from zero to infinity, we obtain the steady state directional distribution:

$$I(\varphi, \vartheta) = \int_0^\infty E_t(\varphi, \vartheta)\,dt \tag{IV.14}$$

This can be determined experimentally by exciting the room with a stationary sound signal and by measuring the sound components arriving from the various directions by the use of a directional microphone. The result, however, is always modified to some extent by the limited directional resolution of the microphone.

The difference between the time-dependent and the steady state directional distribution can be illustrated by invoking the system of image sound sources shown in Fig. IV.5. For the energy arriving at time t from the solid angle element $d\Omega$ those image sources are responsible which are located in the area common to the cone $d\Omega$ and to the circular belt (in the cross-section shown) of width $c\,dt$ and radius ct; the stationary energy incident from the same solid angle element is due to all image sources in the whole cone.

If the directional distribution does not depend in any way on the angles φ and ϑ, the stationary sound field is called 'diffuse'. If in addition to this condition $E_t(\varphi, \vartheta)$ is independent of the angles φ and ϑ for all t, the decaying sound field is also diffuse for all t.

In a certain sense the diffuse sound field is the counterpart of a plane wave. Just as certain properties can be attributed to plane waves, so relationships describing the properties of diffuse sound can be enumerated. A number of more important relationships have already been encountered in Chapter II. These are of particular interest to the whole of room acoustics, since, although the sound field in a concert hall or theatre is not completely diffuse, its directional structure resembles much more that of a diffuse field than that of a plane wave. Or, put in another way: the sound field in an actual room, which always contains some irregularities in shape, can be approximated fairly well by a sound field with uniform directional distribution on account of its great complexity. In contrast to this, a single plane wave is hardly ever encountered in a real situation.

The directional distribution in a rectangular room can be discussed again—at least qualitatively—by the use of Fig. IV.5. The cross-hatched region, which of course must be imagined as continued into the third dimension, has the volume $c^3 t^2 \, dt \, d\Omega$. If V again denotes the volume of the original room, the region referred to contains on the average $c^3 t^2 \, dt \, d\Omega / V$ image sources, their number thus being independent of the direction. Because of the absence of any absorption by the walls, the sound components reaching the centre of the original room are not subject to any directionally dependent attenuation; the time-dependent as well as the stationary directional distribution is therefore uniform.

Matters are not the same if the walls have an absorption coefficient different from zero. In this case there are directions from which the strength of arriving reflections is particularly reduced, since the mirror sources in these directions are predominantly of higher order. It is only in the directions of the axes that the image sources of first order are received, i.e. components which have undergone one reflection only from a wall. The resulting sound field is therefore by no means diffuse. This means that the averaging which we have performed between eqns (IV.7) and (IV.8) is not, strictly speaking, permissible in this form and ought to be replaced by some weighted average which would yield a result different from eqn (IV.9).

A somewhat extreme example of a room with non-diffuse conditions is presented by a strictly rectangular room, whose walls are perfectly rigid except for one which absorbs the incident sound energy completely. Its behaviour with respect to the formation and distribution of reflections is elucidated by the image room system depicted in Fig. IV.8, consisting of only two 'stores' since the absorbing wall generates no images of the room

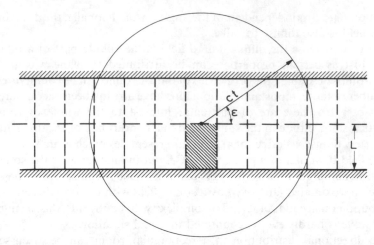

Fig. IV.8. System of image rooms for a rectangular room, one side of which is perfectly sound absorbing. The original room is cross-hatched.

and the sound source. In the lateral directions, however (and perpendicular to the plane of the figure), the system is extended infinitely.

We denote the distance between the absorbing wall and the wall opposite to it by L and the elevation angle by ε, measured from the point of observation which may be located in the centre of the reflecting floor for the sake of simplicity. The time-dependent directional distribution is then given by

$$E_t(\varphi, \varepsilon) = \begin{cases} \text{const} & \text{for } |\varepsilon| \leq \varepsilon_0 \\ 0 & \text{for } |\varepsilon| > \varepsilon_0 \end{cases} \qquad \text{(IV.15)}$$

where

$$\varepsilon_0(t) = \arcsin\left(\frac{L}{ct}\right) \quad \text{for } t \geq \frac{L}{c}$$

The range of elevation angle subtended by the image sources contracts more and more with increasing time. With the presently used meaning of the angle ε, the element of solid angle becomes $\cos \varepsilon \, \mathrm{d}\varepsilon \, \mathrm{d}\varphi$; hence the integration indicated by eqn (IV.13) yields the following expression for the sound decay:

$$E(t) = 2 \int_0^{2\pi} \mathrm{d}\varphi \int_0^{\varepsilon_0} E_t(\varphi, \varepsilon) \cos \varepsilon \, \mathrm{d}\varepsilon = \text{const} \frac{4\pi L}{ct} \quad \text{for } t \geq \frac{L}{c} \qquad \text{(IV.16)}$$

By reasoning similar to that on page 97 we find for the steady state directional distribution:

$$I(\varepsilon) - \frac{\text{const}}{|\sin \varepsilon|} \tag{IV.17}$$

$I(\varepsilon)$ is far from being uniform and hence the time decay of the reverberant sound energy is not described by an exponential law as in eqn (IV.9), but instead is inversely proportional to the time.

REFERENCES

1. Borish, S., *J. Acoust. Soc. America*, **75** (1985) 1827.
2. Vorländer, M., Untersuchungen zur Leistungsfähigkeit des raumakustischen Schallteilchenmodells. Dissertation, Technische Hochschule Aachen, 1988.

V

Reverberation and Steady State Energy Density in Diffuse Sound Fields

Reverberation is a phenomenon which plays a major role in every aspect of room acoustics and which as yet yields the least controversial criterion for the judgement of the acoustical qualities of every kind of room. It is this fact which justifies devoting the major part of a chapter to reverberation and to the laws which govern it. Another important subject to be dealt with in this chapter is the diffuse sound field. Both reverberation and diffusion are closely related to each other: the laws of reverberation can be formulated in a simple way only for sound fields where all directions of sound propagation contribute equal sound intensities, not only in steady state conditions but at each moment in decaying sound fields, at least in the average over time intervals which are short compared with the duration of the whole decaying process. Likewise, simple relationships for the steady state energy density in a room as will be derived in Section V.5 are also based on the assumption of a diffuse field. It is clear that in practical situations these stringent conditions are met only approximately. A completely diffuse sound field can be realised fairly well in certain types of measuring rooms, such as reverberation chambers. But in other rooms, too, the approximation of the actual sound fields by diffuse ones is not too crude an approach. In most instances in this chapter we shall therefore assume complete uniformity of sound field with respect to directional distribution; deviations from this condition will be dealt with only briefly.

In Chapter III we regarded reverberation as the common decaying of free vibrational modes. In Chapter IV, however, reverberation was understood to be the sum total of all sound reflections arriving at a certain point in the room after the room was excited by an impulsive sound signal. In this chapter we shall adopt a slightly different point of view. As in the preceding chapter, we shall consider the case of relatively high frequencies, i.e. we shall neglect interference and diffraction effects which are typical wave phenomena and which only appear in the immediate vicinity of reflecting walls or when obstacle dimensions are comparable with the wavelength. We therefore suppose that the applied sound signals are of such a kind that the direct sound and all reflections from the walls are mutually incoherent, i.e. that they cannot interfere with each other. Consequently, their energies or intensities can simply be added together regardless of mutual phase relations. Under these assumptions sound behaves in much the same way as white light. We shall, however, not so much consider sound rays but instead we shall stress the notion of 'sound particles' carrying a certain amount of energy. Sound particles are propagated with a constant velocity c along straight lines—except for wall reflections—and are supposed to be present in very large numbers. If they strike a wall with absorption coefficient α, only the fraction $1 - \alpha$ is reflected from the wall. Thus the absorption coefficient will be interpreted as an 'absorption probability'.

In order to bestow more physical reality upon the concept of sound particles—which appears a bit artificial at first glance—we can consider the sound particles to be short sound pulses with a broad spectral distribution propagating along sound ray paths. Their shape is not important; in principle they are not even required to have uniform shapes, but they must all have the same power spectrum. The most important condition is their mutual incoherence.

V.1 BASIC PROPERTIES AND REALISATION OF DIFFUSE SOUND FIELDS

As mentioned before, the uniform distribution of sound energy in a room is the crucial condition for the validity of most common expressions describing either the decay of sound fields or the steady state energy contained in them. Therefore it is appropriate to deal first with some properties of diffuse sound fields and, furthermore, to discuss the circumstances under which we can expect them in enclosures.

Suppose we select from all sound rays crossing an arbitrary point P in a room a bundle within a vanishingly small solid angle $d\Omega$. Since the rays of the bundle are nearly parallel, an intensity $I(\varphi, \vartheta)\,d\Omega$ can be attributed to them with φ and ϑ characterising their direction (see Fig. V.1). Furthermore, we can apply eqn (I.15) to these rays, according to which the energy density

$$dw = \frac{I(\varphi, \vartheta)}{c}\,d\Omega \tag{V.1}$$

is associated with them.

Fig. V.1. Bundle of nearly parallel
            sound rays.

Now the condition of a diffuse sound field requires that the quantity I does not depend on the angles φ and ϑ, hence integrating over all directions is achieved by multiplication of 4π, and the total energy density is

$$w = \frac{4\pi I}{c} \qquad (V.2)$$

Since we did not specify the location of P, the independence of I of the direction of propagation implies that I is constant throughout the considered enclosure, and the same holds for the energy density w.

Another important property of a diffuse sound field has already been derived in Section II.5. According to eqn (II.35), the energy incident on a wall element dS per second is $\pi I\, dS$ if I does not depend on the angle of incidence or, if we introduce the 'irradiation strength' B obtained by dividing that energy by dS (*see* Section IV.1):

$$B = \pi I \qquad (V.3)$$

With the same argument as above we can conclude that the irradiation strength B is also constant over the whole wall if the sound field is diffuse. Combining eqns (V.2) and (V.3) leads to the important relation

$$B = \frac{c}{4} w \qquad (V.4)$$

which is to be compared with the corresponding eqn (I.15) for a plane wave. As we shall see it is this relation which enables us to derive simple formulae for the sound decay and the energy density under steady state conditions.

It is obvious that a diffuse sound field cannot exist in enclosures whose walls have the tendency to concentrate the reflected sound energy in certain regions or directions. Likewise, a very non-uniform distribution of wall absorption will continuously extinguish potential ray paths and hence impede the formation of a diffuse sound field. In contrast, highly irregular room shapes help to establish a diffuse sound field by continuously redistributing the energy in all possible directions. Particularly efficient in this respect are rooms with acoustically rough walls, the irregularities of which scatter the incident sound energy in a wide range of directions, as has been already described in Section IV.1. Such walls are referred to as 'diffusely reflecting', either partially or completely. The latter case is characterised by Lambert's law as expressed in eqn (IV.1). Although this ideal behaviour is frequently assumed as a model of diffuse reflection, it will hardly ever be encountered in practical situations. Any wall or ceiling will, although it may be structured by numerous columns, niches, cofferings and other 'irregular' decorations, diffuse only a certain fraction of the incident sound whereas the remaining part of it is reflected into specular directions.

This may be demonstrated by Fig. V.2, which shows the directional distribution of sound reflected from the ceiling of a particular concert hall.[1] This ceiling is covered with many irregular shapes made of gypsum. The average depth of these irregularities is about 30 cm. (This measurement has been carried out in a model scale at normal sound incidence; the frequency corresponds to 1000 Hz. The plotted quantity is the sound pressure

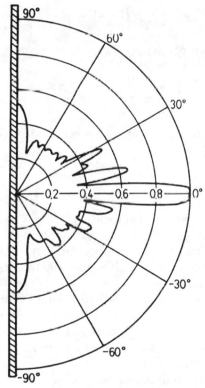

Fig. V.2. Directional distribution of sound, scattered from a highly irregular ceiling. (Polar representation of the pressure amplitude.)

amplitude.) Despite the irregular ceiling shape, there is still a pronounced maximum at 0° due to specular reflection.

Although only a part of the incident sound energy is usually scattered into non-specular directions, this part makes the resulting stationary sound field fairly diffuse, since this field is made up of sound portions having undergone not only one but several or many reflections. During each reflection, specular sound energy is partially transformed into non-specular energy; the reverse process, however, will never occur.

In order to calculate the fraction of diffuse sound in a steady state sound field, we split up the reflected energy fraction $(1 - \alpha)$ into two parts, namely into the portion $g(1 - \alpha)$, which is reflected specularly, and the portion $(1 - g)(1 - \alpha)$, which is scattered in non-specular directions. Under steady state conditions the regularly reflected components add up to

$$w_g \sim \sum_{n=1}^{\infty} g^n(1 - \alpha)^n = \frac{g(1 - \alpha)}{1 - g(1 - \alpha)}$$

whereas the total energy density except for the contribution due to direct sound is given by

$$w \propto \sum_{n=1}^{\infty} (1 - \alpha)^n = \frac{1 - \alpha}{\alpha}$$

Hence the fraction of non-specularly reflected energy in the stationary sound field is

$$\frac{w - w_g}{w} = 1 - \frac{\alpha g}{1 - g(1 - \alpha)} \qquad (V.5)$$

This relation is represented graphically in Fig. V.3. The contribution of diffuse sound components to the total energy density is actually higher than indicated by these curves, since the specularly reflected components travel across the room in quite different directions and thus themselves contribute to the increase in diffusion.

Diffuse or partially diffuse reflections do not occur only at walls with geometrical irregularities but also at walls which are smooth and have non-uniform impedance instead. To understand this we have for the moment to leave the world of rays and particles and to return to our original sound wave concept. According to eqn (II.7) or (II.14), the reflection factor is closely related to the wall impedance and is—like the latter—a complex quantity $R = |R| \exp(i\chi)$. This means that not only the amplitude but also the phase of a sound wave is changed when it is reflected. Generally a wall with

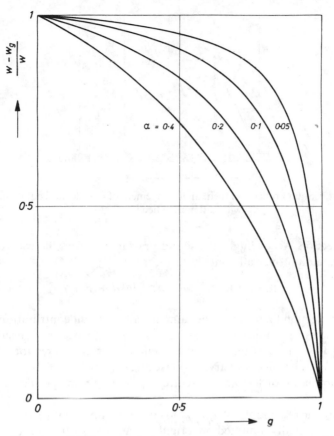

Fig. V.3.   Fraction of diffuse sound components in a steady state sound field for partially diffuse wall reflections.

locally varying wall impedances will re-emit elementary waves or 'wavelets' with different phase angles which interfere with each other to form a complicated wave field. This may be illustrated by Fig. V.4, which shows a plane wall subdivided into strips with constant width d and with different complex reflection factors. To avoid unnecessary complication we assume a plane wave arriving at the wall at normal incidence. It will excite each strip with equal amplitude and phase. We consider those wave portions which are re-emitted (i.e. reflected) from corresponding points of the strips under some angle ϑ. Their phases contain contributions due to the path differences $d \sin \vartheta$ between wavelets from adjacent strips and the phase jumps caused

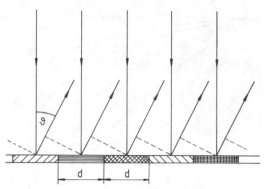

Fig. V.4. Sound reflection from an arrangement of parallel and equidistant strips
with different reflection factors.

by reflection. Accordingly, the sound pressure far from the wall, obtained
by summation over all contributions, is

$$p \sim \exp\left(i\omega t\right) \sum_{n} |R_n| \exp\left[i(nkd \sin \vartheta + \chi_n)\right] \tag{V.6}$$

If the reflection factor were the same for all strips, all contributions would
have the same amplitudes and phases for $\vartheta = 0$, hence the reflected wave
would have a particularly high amplitude for this direction (specular
reflection). The effect of varying phase angles χ_n is to destroy this specular
reflection more or less and to scatter sound into non-specular directions
instead.

A practical example of this kind are walls lined with wooden panels
which are usually mounted on a rigid framework. At the points where the
lining is fixed to the supporting construction, the lining is virtually rigid
whereas at the other points it has a different impedance and can perform
vibrations enforced by the pressure fluctuations of the sound field.
Scattering into non-specular directions occurs mainly in the low-frequency
range, where the non-supported portions may assume relatively large
vibrational amplitudes (compare Section VI.4). Still more efficient are
variations of the depth of air space behind the panels, which tune them to
different resonance frequencies.

For the following we assume that the width d of the strips in Fig. V.4 is
small compared with the acoustical wavelength. If the scattering wall is to
be free of absorption, the magnitude $|R|$ of the reflection factor must be 1
everywhere. Then the arrangement shown in Fig. V.4 acts as a kind of phase
grating. Its diffusing effect is best if the phases of the re-emitted wavelets are

randomly distributed. Complete randomness, however, requires a very large number of elements. Therefore the best that can be achieved practically is a pseudo-random pattern of the phase jumps χ_n.

Pseudo-random sequences play an important role in many branches of signal theory and measuring techniques, and we shall encounter them again in Section VIII.2. Of particular interest are periodic sequences which repeat after a certain number of elements. Their application to the present problem is due to Schroeder,[2,3] and consequently reflective phase gratings employing pseudo-random phase shifts are known as Schroeder diffusors. They can be based upon various number-theoretical schemes such as quadratic residues, Galois fields, primitive roots, etc.[4] We shall describe here in some more detail diffusors employing primitive roots.

Let m be a prime number and g some other integer $< m$. Then we choose the phase jumps effected by the elements according to

$$\chi_n = 2\pi g^n / m$$

with n denoting natural numbers. Since the phase of a harmonic oscillation or wave remains unchanged if multiples of 2π are added to or subtracted from it, it is sufficient to replace g^n with the remainder s_n obtained by repeatedly subtracting m from g^n until the result is one of the numbers $1, 2, \ldots, m-1$, or, in the language of number theory,

$$s_n = g^n (\mathrm{mod}\ m)$$

For instance, for $m = 7$ and $g = 2$ the sequence s_n is

$$2, 4, 1, 2, 4, 1, 2, \ldots$$

and its period obviously comprises three elements. For a given m, one period will contain all integers from 1 to $m-1$ in a pseudo-random order if g is a so-called primitive root of m. Thus, for $m = 7$ and $g = 3$ (which is a primitive root of 7), the sequences s_n would read

$$3, 2, 6, 4, 5, 1, 3, 2, \ldots$$

Particularly important are the spectral properties[4] of the sequence $\exp(2\pi i s_n / m)$, with the s_n derived from a primitive root of m. Its discrete Fourier transform can be written as

$$S = \sum_{n=0}^{m-2} \exp\left[i(nkd \sin \vartheta + 2\pi s_n / m)\right]$$

Because of the periodicity of s_n the transform S has non-zero values only if the Fourier variable $kd \sin \vartheta$ is an integer multiple of $2\pi / (m-1)$.

Fig. V.5. Pseudo-random phase
grating for $m = 7$ and $g = 3$.

Furthermore, these discrete values of S have equal magnitudes except those
for $(m-1)kd\sin\vartheta/2\pi = 0, m, 2m, \ldots$, which are smaller than the others by a
factor $\sqrt{m-1}$. Since S is contained several or many times in the sum of eqn
(V.6) (with $R_n = 1$), we can conclude that most of the impinging sound
energy is scattered into discrete angles $\neq 0$ while only a small fraction of it
will go into the specular direction $\vartheta = 0$.

A diffusing phase grating can be realised as a rigid surface with 'wells' in it
whose depths h_n are proportional to χ_n (Fig. V.5). A wave entering one of
these wells is reflected from its bottom; when it appears again in the
opening, it has undergone a phase shift $-2kh_n$. Accordingly, the depths of
the wells must be

$$h_n = \pi s_n/mk \qquad (V.7)$$

Figure V.6 shows the diffraction pattern experimentally obtained for a
primitive root phase grating with $m = 7$ and $g = 3$. It is clearly seen that the
specular component is almost completely extinguished and that the energy
is scattered into discrete angles.

At first glance it seems that the condition for optimum scattering can be
fulfilled for one single frequency $\omega = ck$ only. However, it is easy to check
that if the elements of the sequence s_n obtained for a primitive root are
multiplied by any integer (except multiples of m), and the products are
taken modulo m, the sequence is restored, apart from some cyclic
permutation. This means that optimum performance of a primitive root
diffusor is obtained not only for the design frequency ck but also for (nearly)
all multiples of it. It may be added that not only one-dimensional Schroeder

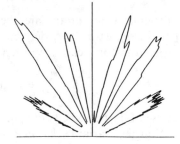

Fig. V.6. Angular distribution of the
sound energy scattered by the phase
grating shown in Fig. V.5.

diffusors can be designed but also two-dimensional ones consisting of troughs in a rigid surface, the depths of which are chosen according to some two-dimensional pseudo-random pattern. For more information the reader is referred to the cited literature.

Quite a different method of achieving a diffuse sound field is to provide not for rough or corrugated walls, and thus to destroy specular reflections, but instead to disturb the free propagation of sound in the space. This is effected by suitable objects—rigid bodies or shells—which are suspended freely in the room at random positions and orientations, and which scatter the arriving sound waves or sound particles in all directions. This method is quite efficient even when applied only to parts of the room, or in enclosures with partially absorbing walls. Of course, no architect would agree to fill the free space of a concert hall or a theatre completely with such 'volume diffusors', therefore a uniform distribution of them can only be installed in certain measuring rooms, so-called reverberation chambers (see Section VIII.7), for which achieving a diffuse sound field is of particular importance.

To estimate the efficiency of volume scatterers we assume N of them to be randomly distributed in a room with volume V, but with constant mean density $\langle n \rangle = N/V$. The scattering efficiency of a single obstacle or diffusor is characterised by its 'scattering cross-section' Q_0, which is defined as the sound energy it scatters per second divided by the intensity of an incident plane sound wave. If we again stress the notion of sound particles, the probability that a particle will travel a distance r or more without being scattered by a diffusor is $\exp(-\langle n \rangle Q_s r)$ or $\exp(-r/\bar{r})$, where we have introduced the mean free path $\bar{r}$ with respect to collisions of sound particles with diffusors. In Section V.2 we shall introduce the mean free path of sound particles between successive wall reflection $\bar{l} - 4V/S$, with S denoting the wall surface of a room. Obviously the efficiency of volume diffusors depends on the ratio $\bar{r}/\bar{l}$. The probability that a sound particle will undergo no collision between two successive wall reflections and hence the fraction of unscattered sound energy is

$$g = \exp(-\bar{l}/\bar{r}) \approx 1 - \bar{l}/\bar{r}$$

The latter approximation is permitted since in most cases $\bar{r} \gg \bar{l}$.

This expression is inserted into eqn (V.5) assuming small wall absorption ($\alpha \ll 1$). Then the fraction of diffused sound energy in a stationary sound field is obtained as

$$\frac{w - w_g}{w} \approx \frac{1}{1 + \alpha \bar{r}/\bar{l}} \qquad (V.5a)$$

If the diffusors are not small compared with the acoustical wavelength, the scattering cross-section Q_s of a diffusor is roughly half its specular cross-section; the other half corresponds to the energy scattered in the forward direction which causes the 'shadow' behind the obstacle by interfering with the incident sound wave. For non-spherical diffusors, the cross-section has to be averaged over all directions of incidence.

We conclude this section by emphasising that sound field diffusion must strictly be distinguished from diffuse wall reflections or scattering by volume scatterers. The diffuse sound field in a room is an ideal condition which can only be approximated by wall or volume diffusors. Even if the latter diffuse the incident sound perfectly, the result—namely the diffusion of the sound field—may be much less than ideal.

V.2 MEAN FREE PATH AND AVERAGE NUMBER OF REFLECTIONS PER SECOND

In the following we shall make use of the concept of 'sound particles', already introduced at the beginning of this chapter. We imagine that the sound field is composed of a very great number of sound particles. Our goal is the evaluation of the laws according to which the sound energy decreases with time in a decaying sound field. For this purpose we have firstly to follow the 'fate' of one sound particle and subsequently to average over many of these fates.

In this connection the notion of the 'mean free path' of a sound particle is frequently encountered in literature on room acoustics. The notion itself appears at first glance to be quite clear, but its use is sometimes misleading, partly because it is not always evident whether it refers to the time average or the particle (ensemble) average.

We shall start here from the simplest concept: a sound particle is observed during a very long time interval t; the total path length ct covered by it during this time is divided by N, the number of wall reflections which have occurred in the time t:

$$\bar{l} = \frac{ct}{N} = \frac{c}{\bar{n}} \tag{V.8}$$

where $\bar{n} = N/t$ is the average reflection frequency, i.e. the average number of wall reflections per second.

$\bar{l}$ and $\bar{n}$ are clearly defined as time averages for a single sound particle; they may differ from one particle to another. In order to obtain averages which are representative of all sound particles, we should average $\bar{l}$ and $\bar{n}$ once more, namely over all possible particle fates. In general, the result of such a procedure would depend on the shape of the room as well as on the chosen directional distribution of sound paths.

Fortunately we can avoid such cumbersome methods and arrive at simple and general relations between room geometry and the required averages by assuming the sound field to be diffuse. Then no additional specification of the directional distribution is required. Furthermore, no other averaging is necessary. This is so because—according to our earlier discussions—a diffuse sound field is established by non-predictable changes in the particle directions either by diffuse wall reflections or by particles being scattered by obstacles during their free propagation. In any case the sound particles change their roles and their direction again and again, and during this process they completely lose their individuality. Thus the distinction between time averages and particle or ensemble averages is no longer meaningful; it does not matter whether the mean free path and all other averages are evaluated by averaging over many free paths traversed by one particle or by averaging for one instant over a great number of different particles. Or in short:

$$\text{time average} = \text{ensemble average}$$

Now we shall calculate the mean free path of sound particles in rooms of arbitrary shape with walls which reflect the incident sound in an ideally diffuse fashion, i.e. according to Lambert's cosine law of eqn (IV.1). For the present purpose we shall formulate that law in a slightly different way: the probability of a sound particle being reflected or re-emitted into a solid angle element $d\Omega$, which includes an angle ϑ with the wall element under consideration, is

$$P(\vartheta)\,d\Omega = \frac{1}{\pi}\cos\vartheta\,d\Omega \qquad (\text{V.9})$$

It is thus entirely independent of the particle's previous history.

We consider all possible free paths, i.e. all possible chords in the enclosure (*see also* Fig. V.10) and intend to carry out an averaging of their lengths R over all wall elements dS as well as over its directions.

These paths are, however, not traversed with equal probabilities. When averaging over all directions we have to concede a greater chance to the small angles ϑ according to eqn (V.9) by using a proper weighting function.

Therefore we obtain

$$\bar{l} = \frac{1}{S} \iint_S \mathrm{d}S \frac{1}{\pi} \iint_{2\pi} R_{\mathrm{d}S}(\vartheta) \cos\vartheta \, \mathrm{d}\Omega' \qquad (V.10)$$

$R_{\mathrm{d}S}(\vartheta)$ is the length of the chord originating from $\mathrm{d}S$ under an angle ϑ with respect to the wall normal and S is the total wall area of the room. Now we interchange the order of integrations, keeping in mind, however, that ϑ is not measured against a fixed direction but against the wall normal, which changes its direction from one wall point to another. Thus we obtain

$$\bar{l} = \frac{1}{\pi S} \iint_{2\pi} \mathrm{d}\Omega' \iint_S R_{\mathrm{d}S}(\vartheta) \cos\vartheta \, \mathrm{d}S \qquad (V.11)$$

The second integrant is the volume of an infinitesimal cylinder with axis $R_{\mathrm{d}S}$ and basis $\mathrm{d}S$; the second integral is thus the double volume $2V$ of the room. The remaining integral simply yields 2π and therefore our final result is

$$\bar{l} = \frac{4V}{S} \qquad (V.12)$$

We should remember that this formula, which has been derived by Kosten[5] in a somewhat similar way, is valid only for rooms with diffusely reflecting walls.

The direct calculation of the mean reflection frequency $\bar{n}$ is even simpler. Let us suppose that a single sound particle carries the energy e_0. Its contribution to the energy density of the room is

$$w = \frac{e_0}{V} \qquad (V.13)$$

On the other hand, if the sound particle strikes the wall $\bar{n}$ times per second, it transports on average the energy per second and unit area

$$B = \bar{n}\frac{e_0}{S} \qquad (V.14)$$

to the wall. According to eqn (V.4), w and B are simply related to each other; invoking this relation yields

$$\bar{n} = \frac{cS}{4V} \qquad (V.15)$$

This expression, which is the time average as well as the particle average, has already been derived in Section IV.3 for rectangular rooms with specularly reflecting walls. But there it was the result only of directional averaging over many particles and not of time averaging. Together with the mean free path according to eqn (V.12), this expression fulfils eqn (V.8).

The mean free path is the mean value of the probability density governing the occurrence of a free path l between two subsequent wall reflections. The probability density itself depends on the shape of the room, and the same is true for other characteristic values such as the variance. As an illustration Fig. V.7 shows the distributions of free path lengths for three different shapes of rectangular rooms with diffusely reflecting walls; abscissa is the path length divided by its mean value $\bar{l}$. These distributions

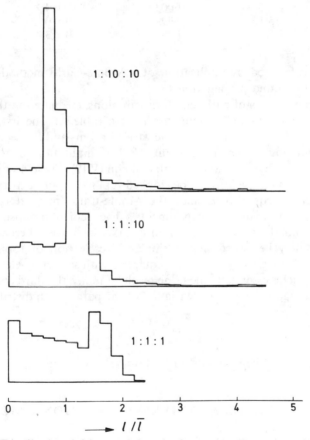

Fig. V.7. Distributions of free path lengths for rectangular rooms with diffusely reflecting walls.

Table V.1

Some Monte-Carlo Results of Mean Free Paths and of γ^2 for Rectangular Rooms with Diffusely Reflecting Walls

Relative dimensions	$\bar{l}_{MC}/\bar{l}$	γ^2
1:1:1	1·009 0	0·342
1:1:2	1·005 0	0·356
1:1:5	1·006 6	0·412
1:1:10	1·004 2	0·415
1:2:2	1·002 0	0·363
1:2:5	1·008 5	0·403
1:2:10	0·992 8	0·465
1:5:5	1·003 5	0·464
1:5:10	0·999 3	0·510
1:10:10	1·002 4	0·613

have been calculated by application of a Monte-Carlo method, i.e. by simulating the sound propagation.[6]

Typical parameters of path length distributions, evaluated in the same way for different rectangular rooms, are listed in Table V.1. The first column contains the relative dimensions of the various rooms and the second lists the corresponding results of the Monte-Carlo computation for the mean free path divided by the 'classical' value of eqn (V.12). These numbers are very close to unity and can be looked upon as an 'experimental' confirmation of eqn (V.12), since the Monte-Carlo method could be characterised as 'computer experiments'. The remaining insignificant deviations from 1 are due to random errors which are inherent in the method. It may be added that a similar investigation of rooms with specularly reflecting walls, which are equipped with scattering elements in the interior, yields essentially the same result.[6] Finally, the third column of Table V.1 contains the 'relative variance' of the path length distributions:

$$\gamma^2 = \frac{\overline{l^2} - \bar{l}^2}{\bar{l}^2} \tag{V.16}$$

Its significance will be discussed in Section V.4.

V.3 SOUND DECAY AND REVERBERATION TIME

As far back as Chapter IV, formulae have been derived for the time dependence of decaying sound energy in rooms and for the reverberation time of rectangular rooms (eqns (IV.9) to (IV.11)). In the preceding section it has been shown that the value $cS/4V$ of the mean reflection frequency, which we have used in Chapter IV, is valid not only for rectangular rooms but for rooms of arbitrary shape provided that the sound field in their interior is diffuse. Thus the general validity of those reverberation formulae has been proven.

If the sound absorption coefficient of the walls depends on the direction of sound incidence, which will usually be the case, we must use the average value α_{uni} of eqn (II.37) instead of α.

Further consideration is necessary if the absorption coefficient is not constant along the walls but depends on the location of a certain wall element. For the sake of simplicity we assume that there are only two different absorption coefficients in the room under consideration. The subsequent generalisation of the results for more than two different types of wall will be obvious.

We therefore attribute an absorption coefficient α_1 to the wall portion with area S_1 and α_2 to the portion with area S_2, where $S_1 + S_2 = S$. We follow the life of a particular sound particle over N wall reflections, among which there are N_1 reflections from S_1 and $N_2 = N - N_1$ reflections from S_2. These numbers can be assumed to be distributed in some way about their mean values

$$\bar{N}_1 = N\frac{S_1}{S} \quad \text{and} \quad \bar{N}_2 = N\frac{S_2}{S} \tag{V.17}$$

S_1/S and S_2/S are the *a priori* probabilities for the arrival of a sound particle at wall portion S_1 and S_2, respectively.

In a sound field which has been made diffuse by one means or another, subsequent wall reflections are stochastically independent from each other, i.e. the probability of hitting one or other portion of the wall does not depend on the past history of the particle. In this case the probability of N_1 collisions with wall portion S_1 among a total number of reflections N is given by the binomial distribution

$$P_N(N_1) = \binom{N_1}{N} \cdot \left(\frac{S_1}{S}\right)^{N_1} \left(\frac{S_2}{S}\right)^{N-N_1} \tag{V.18}$$

After N_1 collisions with S_1 and $N_2 = N - N_1$ collisions with S_2, a sound particle has the remaining energy

$$E_N(N_1) = E_0(1 - \alpha_1)^{N_1}(1 - \alpha_2)^{N-N_1} \tag{V.19}$$

The expectation value of this expression with respect to the distribution (V.18) is

$$\langle E_N \rangle = \sum_{N_1=0}^{N} E_N(N_1) P_N(N_1) = E_0 \left[\frac{S_1}{S}(1-\alpha_1) + \frac{S_2}{S}(1-\alpha_2) \right]^N$$

where we have applied the binomial theorem. Since $S_1 + S_2 = S$, this can be written as

$$\langle E_N \rangle = E_0(1-\bar{\alpha})^N = E_0 \exp[N \ln(1-\bar{\alpha})] \tag{V.20}$$

with

$$\bar{\alpha} = \frac{1}{S}(S_1\alpha_1 + S_2\alpha_2) \tag{V.20a}$$

This latter formula is the most important result of the foregoing derivation. It indicates that the absorption coefficients of the various portions of wall have to be averaged arithmetically using the respective areas as weighting factors. Finally, we replace the total number N of wall reflections in time t by its expectation value or mean value $\bar{n}t$ with $\bar{n} = cS/4V$ and obtain for the energy of the 'average' sound particle and hence for the total energy in the room

$$E(t) = E_0 \exp\left[\frac{cS}{4V} t \ln(1-\bar{\alpha}) \right] \tag{V.21}$$

From this we can evaluate the reverberation time, i.e. the time interval T, in which the reverberating sound energy reaches one millionth of its initial value

$$T = -\frac{24V \ln 10}{cS \ln(1-\bar{\alpha})} \tag{V.22}$$

We can complete this formula by taking into account, as in eqns (IV.6) to (IV.11), the attenuation constant m of air which is responsible for the attenuation of sound during its free propagation and by inserting the numerical value of the sound velocity of air

$$T = -0 \cdot 163 \frac{V}{S \ln(1-\bar{\alpha}) - 4mV} \tag{V.23}$$

with

$$\bar{\alpha} = \frac{1}{S} \sum S_i \alpha_i \tag{V.23a}$$

where we have already generalised eqn (V.20a) for any number of different portions of the wall. In this formula, which is probably the most important relation of room acoustics, all lengths have to be expressed in metres; T is measured in seconds.

Equations (V.22) or (V.23) together with (V.23a) are known as Eyring's reverberation formula, although they have been derived independently by Norris as well as by Schuster and Waetzmann.

For many practical purposes it is safe to assume that the average absorption coefficient $\bar{\alpha}$ is small compared with unity. Then the logarithm in eqn (V.23) can be expanded into a series and all terms of higher than the first order in $\bar{\alpha}$ may be neglected. This results in a reverberation formula originally derived by Sabine:

$$T = 0 \cdot 163 \frac{V}{S\bar{\alpha} + 4mV} \tag{V.24}$$

For small rooms the term $4mV$ related to air absorption can be neglected.

If, in our derivation of eqn (V.20), we had considered the quantities NS_1/S and NS_2/S not as mean values of a probability distribution but instead as exact numbers of collisions with the wall portions S_1 and S_2, then eqn (V.19) would be the final expression for the reverberant energy after a total of N reflections. It can equally well be written in the following way:

$$E(t) = E_0 \exp(-N\bar{a}') = E_0 \exp\left(-\frac{cS}{4V}\bar{a}'t\right) \tag{V.25}$$

with the average 'absorption exponent'

$$\bar{a}' = -\frac{1}{S}\sum_i S_i \ln(1 - \alpha_i) \tag{V.25a}$$

The resulting equation

$$T = 0 \cdot 163 \frac{V}{S\bar{a}'} \tag{V.26}$$

which could again be completed by taking into account the air attenuation by adding a term $4mV$ to the denominator, is known as Millington–Sette's formula. It differs from eqn (V.23) only in the manner in which the absorption coefficients of the various portions of wall are averaged; here the average absorption coefficient is replaced by the average absorption exponent.

The application of eqns (V.26) and (V.25a) has a strange consequence: let us suppose that a room has a portion of wall, however small, with the absorption coefficient $\alpha_i = 1$. It would make the average (V.25a) infinitely large and hence the reverberation time evaluated by eqn (V.26) would be zero. This is obviously an unreasonable result.

V.4 THE INFLUENCE OF UNEQUAL PATH LENGTHS

The incorrect averaging rule of eqn (V.25a) was the result of replacing a probability distribution by its mean value. However, in the derivation of eqn (V.21) we have practised a similar simplification in that we have replaced the actual number of reflections in the time t by its average $\bar{n}t$. For a more correct treatment we ought to introduce the probability $P_t(N)$ of exactly N wall reflections occurring in a time t and to calculate $E(t)$ as the expectation value of eqn (V.20) with respect to this probability distribution:

$$E(t) = E_0 \sum_{N=0}^{\infty} P_t(N) \exp\left[N \ln(1 - \bar{\alpha})\right] \qquad (\text{V.27})$$

To derive a correction term from eqns (V.21) and (V.22) which can account for varying collision numbers N it is sufficient to restrict the discussion to enclosures with uniform absorption coefficient α and to introduce, in a similar way as in eqn (V.25), the 'absorption exponent'

$$a = -\ln(1 - \alpha) \qquad (\text{V.28})$$

If, for the moment, N is considered as a continuous variable, the function $\exp(-Na)$ in eqn (V.27) can be expanded in a Taylor series around $\bar{n}t$. Truncating this series after its third term yields

$$\exp(-Na) \approx \exp(-\bar{n}ta)\left[1 - \frac{N - \bar{n}t}{1!}a + \frac{(N - \bar{n}t)^2}{2!}a^2\right]$$

Before inserting this expression into eqn (V.27) it should be kept in mind that

$$\sum P_t(N) = 1 \quad \text{and} \quad \sum (N - \bar{n}t)P_t(N) = 0$$

whereas

$$\sum (N - \bar{n}t)^2 P_t(N) = \sigma_N^2$$

is the variance of the distribution $P_t(N)$. Hence

$$E(t) \approx E_0 \exp(-\bar{n}ta)(1 + \tfrac{1}{2}\sigma_N^2 a^2) \approx E_0 \exp(-\bar{n}ta + \tfrac{1}{2}\sigma_N^2 a^2) \qquad (\text{V.29})$$

The latter approximation is permissible if the second term in the bracket is small compared with unity. On the other hand, σ_N^2 is closely related to the relative variance γ^2 of the path length distribution as defined in eqn (V.16). In fact, since the successive free paths $l_1, l_2, \ldots, l_N$ of one particle are statistically independent in a diffuse sound field, their sum has the mean value $N\bar{l}$ and the variance $N\bar{l}^2\gamma^2$ according to basic laws of probability. Furthermore, any increment ΔN in the total number of reflections is associated with an increment $\bar{l}\Delta N$ in the aforementioned sum, and the same argument applies to the standard deviations of these quantities:

$$\sqrt{N\bar{l}^2\gamma^2} = \bar{l}\sigma_N$$

or, if we finally replace N by its mean value $\bar{n}t$,

$$\sigma_N^2 \approx \bar{n}t\gamma^2 \tag{V.30}$$

This expression, inserted into eqn (V.29), yields the final result

$$E(t) \approx E_0 \exp\left(-\frac{cS}{4V}a't\right) \tag{V.31}$$

from which the reverberation time is derived as

$$T = 0.163\frac{V}{Sa'} \tag{V.32}$$

with the modified absorption exponent

$$a'' = -\ln(1-\alpha)\left[1 + \frac{\gamma^2}{2}\ln(1-\alpha)\right] \tag{V.33}$$

In Fig. V.8 the 'effective absorption exponent' a'' is compared with the absorption coefficient α as is used in Sabine's formula (eqn (V.24) with $m = 0$ and uniform absorption). It plots the relative difference between both quantities for various parameters γ^2. The curve $\gamma^2 = 0$ corresponds to Eyring's formula (V.22 and V.23). Accordingly, the latter is strictly valid for one-dimensional enclosures only where all paths have exactly the same length. For $\gamma^2 \neq 0$, a'' is smaller than $-\ln(1-\alpha)$. Hence the reverberation time is longer than that evaluated by the Eyring formula.

With eqn (V.32) we have for the first time arrived at a reverberation formula in which the shape of the room is accounted for by the quantity γ^2. Unfortunately the latter can be calculated directly only for a limited number of room shapes with high symmetry. For a sphere, for instance, it turns out to be 1/8. For other shapes γ^2 can be determined by computer

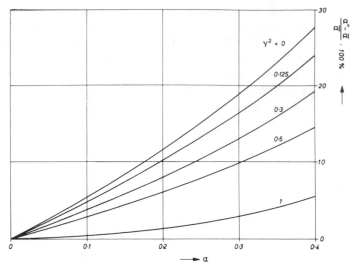

Fig. V.8. Relative difference between a'' and α in per cent after eqn (V.32).

simulation. Results obtained in this way for rectangular rooms have already been presented in Table V.1. It is seen that for most shapes γ^2 is close to 0·4 and it is likely that this value can also be applied to other enclosures provided that their shapes do not deviate too much from that of a rectangular room.

For rooms with suspended 'volume diffusors' (*see* Section V.1), the distribution of free path lengths is greatly modified by the scattering obstacles. The same applies to γ^2 but not to the mean free path.[6]

V.5 STEADY STATE ENERGY DENSITY IN A REVERBERANT SPACE WITH DIFFUSE SOUND FIELD

Equation (V.21) describes the temporal decay of the sound energy at times during which no sound source is in operation. It can also be considered as the energetic response of the room to a short impulse which releases the energy E_0 into the room, i.e. to a sound source which supplies the acoustical power $P(t) = E_0 \delta(t)$.

If acoustical power is continuously supplied to a room, we can make use of the relations of Section I.4, according to which the power $P(t)$ can be regarded as a close succession of short energy impulses (*see* eqn (I.36)), while the energetic response of the room after eqn (I.37) is given by

$$E(t) = \int_{-\infty}^{t} P(\tau) \exp\left[\frac{cS}{4V}(t-\tau)\ln(1-\bar{\alpha})\right] d\tau$$

$$= \int_{0}^{\infty} P(t-\tau) \exp\left[\frac{cS}{4V}\tau \ln(1-\bar{\alpha})\right] d\tau \qquad (V.34)$$

the latter expression being the result of a change in the integration variable.

For a constant source power P, we can carry out the integration and obtain the stationary sound energy in the room:

$$E = -\frac{4PV}{cS\ln(1-\bar{\alpha})} \qquad (V.35)$$

or the energy density

$$w = -\frac{4P}{cS\ln(1-\alpha)} \qquad (V.36)$$

If we want to exclude the contribution of the direct sound in order to obtain the energy density of the reverberant sound field only, we can replace the lower limit of the second integral in eqn (V.34) by $\bar{l}/c = 1/\bar{n}$, the average time for a sound particle to reach the observation point via one wall reflection. This yields

$$w_r = -\frac{4P}{cS}\frac{1-\bar{\alpha}}{\ln(1-\bar{\alpha})} \qquad (V.36a)$$

An alternative derivation starts from eqn (V.20) which represents the expected energy of a sound particle after N wall reflections. By summation of this expression for N running from 1 to infinity we obtain the energy of all particles:

$$E = E_0 \frac{1-\bar{\alpha}}{\bar{\alpha}}$$

Steady state conditions are met if one sound particle with energy E_0 per time interval $1/\bar{n}$ is emitted by the sound source since this is the time pattern imposed by the sequence of wall reflections. Therefore the source power is $P = \bar{n}E_0 = cSE_0/4V$. Substituting E_0 from this' relation into the above formula yields

$$w_r = \frac{4P}{cS}\frac{1-\bar{\alpha}}{\bar{\alpha}} \qquad (V.36b)$$

This expression is similar to eqn (V.36a); the difference is due to the fact that we have performed an integration of a continuous function in one case but a summation over a stepwise changing function in the other.

It is not very meaningful to investigate which of these two formulae is more correct. At any rate they merge for low values of the average absorption coefficient and yield

$$w_r = \frac{4P}{cS\bar{\alpha}} \qquad (V.37)$$

The application of the statistical reverberation theory for the calculation of the steady state energy density becomes questionable for absorption coefficients of such a magnitude where there is a significant difference between $\bar{\alpha}$ and $-\ln(1-\bar{\alpha})$. This is because the contribution of the very first reflections, which are not randomly distributed, to the total energy density is relatively high then. Therefore the range of validity of the above formulae with respect to $\bar{\alpha}$ is substantially smaller than that of the reverberation formulae developed in the preceding sections.

This is one of the reasons why the absorption of a room and its reverberation time is determined by decay measurements and not usually by steady state measurements and by the application of one of the eqns (V.36) to (V.37) (which would be possible in principle).

On the other hand, however, steady state measurements are quite useful for the evaluation of the total power N of a sound source using eqn (V.37) if $\bar{\alpha}$ is known or determined by a reverberation measurement. This procedure is free from objection as long as the room utilised for this purpose is a 'reverberation chamber' with a long reverberation time and hence with low absorption. We should bear in mind that in the measurement of acoustic power an error of 10% (corresponding to 0·4 dB) can usually be tolerated, but not so in the determination of absorption or reverberation time.

The above formulae for the stationary energy density are only valid with some degree of accuracy as long as the point of observation is not too close to the sound source, otherwise direct sound would prevail. Assuming omnidirectional sound radiation, the direct sound energy density is given by (compare eqns (I.15) and (I.19))

$$w_d = \frac{P}{4\pi c r^2}$$

In Fig. V.9 w_r and w_d are presented schematically as a function of distance r from the sound source. For a certain distance $r = r_h$ both energy densities

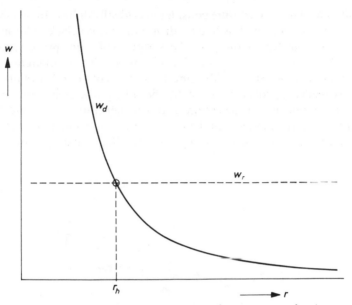

Fig. V.9.   Space dependence of direct and reverberant energy density w_d and w_r.

are equal. This quantity r_h is called the 'reverberation distance' and is given by

$$r_h = \frac{1}{4}\left(\frac{S\bar{\alpha}}{\pi}\right)^{1/2} = 0 \cdot 1\left(\frac{V}{\pi T}\right)^{1/2} \tag{V.38}$$

In the latter expression we have introduced the reverberation time T from Sabine's formula (with $m \approx 0$); V is to be measured in m^3.

If, however, the sound source has a certain directionality, its gain G has to be considered, defined in eqn (I.26). In this case $w_d = GP/4\pi cr^2$ and we obtain

$$r_h = \frac{1}{4}\left(\frac{GS\bar{\alpha}}{\pi}\right)^{1/2} = 0 \cdot 1\left(\frac{GV}{\pi T}\right)^{1/2} \tag{V.38a}$$

for the maximum 'reverberation distance'.

V.6 PARTIALLY DIFFUSE SOUND FIELD

All the previous equations for the sound decay, the reverberation time and the steady state energy density have been derived on the assumption that the sound field in the enclosure considered is ideally diffuse. In this section, however, we are leaving this line by dropping this crucial condition. This will lead to a somewhat more general description of sound propagation in a room. As before, we restrict the discussion to incoherent sound propagation, i.e. we still use the simple concept of sound rays or sound particles, neglecting all effects brought about by phase differences between different components of the sound field. Furthermore, we assume diffuse sound reflection from each wall element. As we know from the discussion of Section V.1, this condition is less stringent than that of a diffuse sound field.

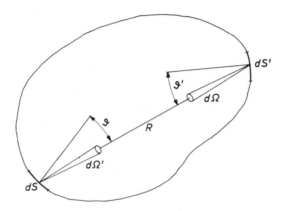

Fig. V.10.   Illustration of coordinates for the derivation of eqn (V.41).

We start by considering two wall elements, dS and dS', of a room of arbitrary shape (*see* Fig. V.10). Their locations are characterised by the vectors **r** and **r'**, respectively, each of them standing for a trio of suitable coordinates. The straight line connecting them has the length R, and the angles between this line and the wall normals in dS and dS' are denoted by ϑ and ϑ'.

Suppose the element dS' is irradiated by the energy $B(\mathbf{r'})\,\mathrm{d}S'$ per second, where B is the 'irradiation strength' introduced in Section V.1. The fraction ρ of it will be re-radiated from dS' into the space, where the 'reflection coefficient'

$$\rho = 1 - \alpha \tag{V.39}$$

was introduced. To avoid unnecessary complication we assume that the absorption coefficient α and hence ρ is independent of the angles ϑ and ϑ'.

According to Lambert's law of diffuse reflection as formulated in eqn (IV.1), the intensity of the energy re-radiated by dS' and received at dS is

$$dI = B(\mathbf{r}')\rho(\mathbf{r}') \frac{\cos \vartheta'}{\pi R^2}\, dS' \qquad (V.40)$$

The total energy per second and unit area received at $\mathbf{r}$ from the whole boundary is obtained by multiplying this equation with $\cos \vartheta$ and integrating it over all wall elements dS'. If the direct contribution B_d from some sound source is added, the following relation is obtained:[7,8]

$$B(\mathbf{r}, t) = \frac{1}{\pi} \int\!\!\int_S \rho(\mathbf{r}')B\!\left(\mathbf{r}', t - \frac{R}{c}\right) \frac{\cos \vartheta \cos \vartheta'}{R'}\, dS' + B_d(\mathbf{r}, t) \qquad (V.41)$$

It takes regard of the finite travelling time of sound energy from the transmitting wall element dS' to the receiving one dS by replacing the argument t with $t - R/c$.

Equation (V.41) is an inhomogeneous integral equation for the irradiation strength B of the wall. It is fairly general in that it contains both the steady state case (for B_d and B independent of time t) and that of a decaying sound field (for $B_d = 0$). Once it were solved, the energy density at any point $\mathbf{r}$ inside the room could be obtained from

$$w(\mathbf{r}, t) = \frac{1}{\pi c} \int\!\!\int_S \rho(\mathbf{r}')B\!\left(\mathbf{r}', t - \frac{R}{c}\right) \frac{\cos \vartheta'}{R^2}\, dS' + w_d(\mathbf{r}, t) \qquad (V.42)$$

For the stationary case there is a general solution of eqn (V.41),[9] which, however, is of little practical use. The same holds for solutions for geometrically simple shapes such as spherical rooms. One exception is the flat room consisting of two parallel unbounded planes with distance h as already discussed in Section IV.2 for the case of specular reflection. For diffusely reflecting walls with constant reflectivity ρ the solution can be expressed as an integral and, what is even more useful, approximated by[10]

$$w(r) \approx \frac{P}{\pi c}\left\{ \frac{4}{r^2} + \frac{\mu}{h^2}\left[\left(1 + \frac{r^2}{h^2}\right)^{-3/2} + \frac{\rho b}{1 - \rho}\left(b^2 + \frac{r^2}{h^2}\right)^{-3/2}\right]\right\} \qquad (V.43)$$

In this expression P denotes the acoustic power of a non-directional sound source, r is its distance from the observation point, and b is a number which is in most cases between 2 and 3, depending on ρ.

For more complicated room shapes solutions must be worked out by numerical methods.

To some extent the same holds for the evaluation of the decaying sound field. However, if we focus our attention on the overall reverberation time, neglecting details of the decay process, we may assume an exponential law for the time dependence of B in eqn (V.41):

$$B(\mathbf{r}, t) = B(\mathbf{r}) \exp(-\bar{n}a^* t) \qquad (V.44)$$

where a^* denotes the absorption exponent (see eqn (V.28)), which is valid under our present assumptions and which is to be determined. In fact, numerical calculations carried out by Miles[11] indicate that after the very first phases of the decay process the sound energy will decrease exponentially, at least in rectangular enclosures.

Equation (V.44) is the basis of an iteration scheme developed by Gilbert,[12] who supplemented eqn (V.41) by another integral equation for the total energy. We shall not discuss it here; instead we shall draw a few general conclusions from eqn (V.41) and derive a correction to Eyring's formula (V.22 and V.23). For this purpose it is sufficient to apply eqn (V.44) and to replace the distance R in the argument of B in eqn (V.41) by the mean free path $\bar{l}$. Then the above integral equation reads (with $B_d = 0$)

$$B(\mathbf{r}) = \frac{\exp a^*}{\pi} \int \int \rho(\mathbf{r}')B(\mathbf{r}') \frac{\cos \vartheta \cos \vartheta'}{R^2} \, dS' \qquad (V.45)$$

After integrating this equation over the whole wall area S and interchanging the order of integrations on the right-hand side, one obtains the result

$$a^* = \ln\left(\frac{\iint B \, dS}{\iint \rho B \, dS}\right) \qquad (V.46)$$

It tells us that the absorption exponent would assume its Eyring value, $a_{ey} = -\ln \bar{\rho} = -\ln(1 - \bar{\alpha})$ (apart from the deviations we have discussed in Section V.4), if the irradiation strength were constant. This may happen for certain distributions of the absorption, but it is certainly the case if ρ and hence the absorption coefficient α has everywhere the same value. In general, however, the effective absorption exponent will be smaller or larger than $-\ln \bar{\rho}$, depending on the room shape and on the distribution of the wall absorption. To illustrate this Fig. V.11 presents the results of some computer simulations carried out for rectangular rooms of various shapes. In these examples one of the six walls is assumed to be totally absorbent ($\alpha = 1$) while the remaining ones are supposed to be free of absorption ($\alpha = 0$). Each room is characterised by its relative dimensions; the first two numbers refer to the absorbing wall. The plotted quantity is the effective

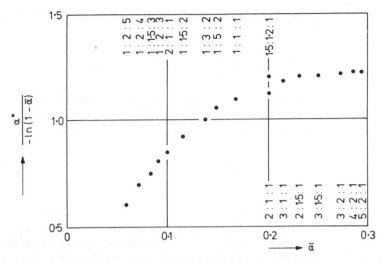

Fig. V.11. Effective absorption exponents α^*, divided by $-\ln(1-\bar{\alpha})$, as obtained from Monte-Carlo computations for rectangular rooms with $\alpha = 1$ for one wall and $\alpha = 0$ for the others. Numbers in the figure indicate the relative room dimensions; the first two numbers refer to the absorbing wall.

absorption exponent divided by its Eyring value $-\ln\bar{\rho}$; the abscissa is the mean absorption coefficient $\bar{\alpha}$. It is seen that the results deviate from the ordinate 1 in both directions; in particular, for relatively flat rooms with a highly absorbing floor (see right side of the figure) the absorption exponent is higher, hence the reverberation time is shorter than predicted by the Eyring formulae. This is of practical interest since virtually all auditoria are of this general type because of the high audience absorption.

To obtain the mentioned correction formula we restrict ourselves to enclosures of polyhedral shape, i.e. to rooms bounded by N plane walls with areas S_n. Furthermore, we assume the reflection coefficient and the irradiation strength to be constant over each wall. Then the double integrals in eqn (V.46) become sums over the wall index. Now we replace the missing knowledge of the exact irradiation strengths by a reasonable guess. Obviously the irradiation strength of one particular wall with index n consists of the contributions from the $N-1$ remaining walls, and each of them is proportional to the reflection coefficient and to the area of the wall which produces it:

$$B_n \sim \sum_{m=1}^{N} \rho_m S_m - \rho_n S_n = \bar{\rho} S - \rho_n S_n \tag{V.47}$$

Inserting the latter expression into the modified eqn (V.46) yields, after some easy manipulation,

$$a^* \approx \ln\left(\frac{1}{\bar{\rho}}\right) + \ln\left(1 + \frac{\sum \rho_n(\rho_n - \bar{\rho})S_n^2}{\bar{\rho}^2 S^2 - \sum \rho_n^2 S_n^2}\right)$$

In most cases the second term in the denominator is much smaller than the first and hence can be neglected. Finally, we can expand the second logarithm into a power series and neglect all terms of higher than first order:

$$a^* \approx a_{ey} + \frac{\sum \rho_n(\rho_n - \bar{\rho})S_n^2}{(\bar{\rho}S)^2} \qquad (V.48)$$

The second term of this expression is always positive—a consequence of our somewhat crude approach. Therefore this correction formula applies only to situations in which the effective absorption exponent is expected to exceed the Eyring value (right side of Fig. V.11). According to the previous discussion, however, these are the practically important cases, and it is easily verified that eqn (V.48) accounts quite well for the deviations.

V.7 COUPLED ROOMS

Sometimes a room is shaped in such a way that it can barely be considered as a single enclosure but rather as a collection composed of partial rooms separated by virtually non-transparent walls. The only communication is by relatively small apertures in these walls. The same situation is encountered if the partition walls are totally closed but are not completely rigid, and have some slight sound transparency. A particular aspect of such 'coupled rooms' has been discussed in Chapter III. Now their acoustical properties will be dealt with from a geometrical and statistical point of view.

Let us suppose that the sound field in every partial room is a diffuse one and that reverberation would follow an exponential law if there were no interaction between them. Then for the ith partial room we have

$$\frac{dw_i}{dt} = -2\delta_i w_i$$

δ_i being the damping constant of that room without coupling.

The coupling elements permit an energy exchange between the partial rooms. If there are wall apertures with areas S_{ij} between rooms i and j, the energy loss in room i per second due to coupling is $\sum_j' B_i S_{ij} = cS_i' w_i/4$ with

$S_i' = \sum_j' S_{ij}$. On the other hand, the energy increase contributed by room j per second is $cS_{ij}w_j/4$. Hence the energy balance yields for the ith room

$$\frac{dw_i}{dt} + \left(2\delta_i + \frac{cS_i'}{4V_i}\right)w_i = \sum_j' \frac{cS_{ij}}{4V_i} w_j \qquad \text{(V.49)}$$

The apostrophe indicates that the summation index must be extended over all integers from 1 to m except i, where m is the total number of partial rooms. This system of linear differential equations can be further simplified to read

$$\frac{dw_i}{dt} = \sum_{j=1}^{m} k_{ij}w_j \qquad (i = 1, 2, \ldots, m) \qquad \text{(V.50)}$$

where

$$k_{ii} = -\left(2\delta_i + \frac{cS_i'}{4V_i}\right) \qquad k_{ij} = \frac{cS_{ij}}{4V_i} \qquad \text{for } i \neq j$$

First we look for the conditions under which the decay process obeys an exponential law with only one damping constant δ', which is the same for all partial rooms. In this case we would obtain $dw_i/dt = -2\delta'w_i$. Inserting this into eqns (V.50) yields m homogeneous linear equations

$$k_{i1}w_1 + k_{i2}w_2 + \cdots + (k_{ii} + 2\delta')w_i + \cdots + k_{im}w_m = 0$$
$$(i = 1, 2, \ldots, m) \quad \text{(V.51)}$$

which have non-vanishing solutions only if their coefficient determinant is zero. This condition is an equation of degree m (secular equation) for δ' with m roots $\delta_1', \delta_2', \ldots, \delta_m'$. If they are inserted one after the other into eqns (V.51), the energy densities associated with a certain root can be determined except for a common factor

$$w_1^{(r)}, w_2^{(r)}, \ldots, w_m^{(r)}$$

For a certain root δ_r' the mutual ratios of the $w_i^{(r)}$ remain constant during the whole decay process. Hence they also represent the ratios of the initial values. This result can be summarised as follows. There are at most (since in principle several roots δ' can happen to coincide) m possibilities for the reverberation to follow the same exponential law throughout the whole room system. A particular set of initial energy densities is required for each of these possibilities.

The general solution is obtained as a linear superposition of the special solutions evaluated above:

$$w_i(t) = c_1 w_{i0}^{(1)} \exp(-2\delta_1't) + c_2 w_{i0}^{(2)} \exp(-2\delta_2't) + \cdots + c_m w_{i0}^{(m)} \exp(-2\delta_m't)$$
$$(i = 1, 2, \ldots, m) \quad \text{(V.52)}$$

If the energy densities $w_i(0)$ of all partial rooms at the beginning of the decay process are given, the constants c_r can be determined unambiguously from eqn (V.52) by setting $t = 0$. The decay of sound energy in the ith partial room is then represented by

$$w_i(t) = \sum_{j=1}^{m} a_{ij} \exp\left(-2\delta'_j t\right) \qquad\qquad (\text{V.52}a)$$

which is similar to eqn (III.41a). In contrast to the coefficients c_n^2 of the latter, however, the a_{ij} are not necessarily all positive and so we cannot draw the conclusion (as we did in Section III.5) that the logarithmic decay curves are either straight lines or curved upwards.

The stationary energy densities in the various partial rooms can be determined from eqns (V.50) if the derivatives dw_i/dt are replaced by the ratios $-P_i/V_i$. Here $-P_i$ is the power output of the sound source which is in action in the room i and which, of course, can also be zero (provided that there is at least one active sound source in some other partial room). In the latter case, the decay curve in the ith room starts with a horizontal tangent because up to the moment of switching off the sound source ($t = 0$)

$$\frac{P_i}{V_i} = \sum_j k_{ij} w_j = 0$$

and hence, immediately after switching off all sound sources,

$$\left(\frac{dw_i}{dt}\right)_{t=0} = 0$$

according to eqn (V.50). We can proceed along this line by differentiating eqn (V.50):

$$\left(\frac{d^2 w_i}{dt^2}\right)_{t=0} = \sum_j k_{ij} \left(\frac{dw_j}{dt}\right)_{t=0}$$

This formula is to be interpreted as follows. If neither the ith partial room nor one of its nearest neighbours is driven directly by a sound source, the decay curve in the ith room starts not only with zero slope but also with zero curvature.

These findings may be illustrated by an example depicted in Fig. V.12. It refers to three coupled rooms of equal volumes in a line, but only one of them is driven directly by a sound source. Accordingly the steady state level from which the decay process starts is highest in room 1, and only in this room the decay curve begins with a negative slope. The decay rate in this room becomes gradually less steep since the adjacent rooms feed some of

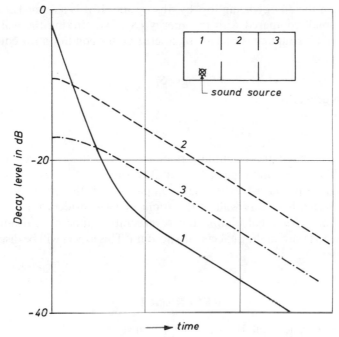

Fig. V.12.   Example for sound decay in three coupled rooms: $\delta_2 = k_{12} = \delta_1/10$, $\delta_3 = \delta_1/2$, $k_{13} = 0$, $k_{23} = \delta_1/5$.

the energy stored in them back to room 1. The decay curves in the rooms 2 and 3 have horizontal tangents at $t = 0$; moreover, the initial curvature of decay curve 3 is zero.

On the whole we can see that in coupled rooms the variety of possible decay curves is considerably greater than it is in a single uncoupled room.

The occurrence of typical coupling effects as outlined above is not restricted to room systems of a special geometrical structure. They can also be observed in apparently normal rooms if the exciting conditions are such that they excite one or several normal modes whose eigenfrequencies are close to those of other modes but whose energy exchange is only slight. Convexly curved decay curves (viewed from the positive ordinate direction) are a safe indication of the presence of several energy stores which are only weakly coupled to each other.

The transition from coupled systems to normal rooms is, of course, a gradual one. The simple theory of coupled rooms applies to all cases where the energy per second being exchanged by coupling is not substantially larger than the energy being lost by absorption. If it is assumed that the latter is small compared with the energy $cS_iw_i/4V_i$ striking the walls per second, and if coupling is effected by apertures, the condition for coupling reads simply

$$S_i' \ll S_i$$

or, more generally,

$$|k_{ii}| \ll \frac{cS_i}{4V_i} \tag{V.53}$$

This means that typical coupling phenomena are to be expected if the probability of a sound particle being absorbed or of escaping to a neighbouring partial room is small compared with the probability of it being reflected from any wall of the room under consideration.

Sometimes, when calculating the reverberation time of a room, it is advisable to take coupling effects into account. This aspect will be discussed in Chapter IX.

REFERENCES

1. Meyer, E. & Kuttruff, H., *Acustica*, **9** (1959) 465.
2. Schroeder, M. R., *J. Acoust. Soc. America*, **65** (1979) 958.
3. Schroeder, M. R., Proc. Vancouver Symposium (1986), p. 104 (12th Int. Congr. on Acoustics, Toronto, 1986).
4. Schroeder, M. R., *Number Theory in Science and Communication*, 2nd edn. Springer-Verlag, Berlin, 1986.
5. Kosten, C. W., *Acustica*, **10** (1960) 245.
6. Kuttruff, H., *Acustica*, **23** (1970) 238; *ibid.*, **24** (1971) 356.
7. Kuttruff, H., *Acustica*, **25** (1971) 333; *ibid.*, **35** (1976) 141.
8. Joyce, W. B., *J. Acoust. Soc. America*, **64** (1978) 1429; *ibid.*, **65** (1979) 51(A).
9. Carrol, M. M. & Miles, R. N., *J. Acoust. Soc. America*, **64** (1978) 1424.
10. Kuttruff, H., *Acustica*, **57** (1985) 62.
11. Miles, R. N., *J. Sound Vibr.*, **92**(2) (1984) 203.
12. Gilbert, E. N., *J. Acoust. Soc. America*, **69** (1981) 178.

VI

Sound Absorption and Sound Absorbers

Of considerable importance to the acoustics of a room are the loss mechanisms which reduce the energy of sound waves when they are reflected from walls as well as during their free propagation in the air. They influence the strengths of the direct sound and of all reflected components and therefore all acoustical properties of the room.

The attenuation of sound waves in the free medium becomes significant only in large rooms and at relatively high frequencies; for scale model experiments, however, it causes serious limitations. We have to consider it inevitable and something which cannot be influenced by the efforts of the acoustician. Nevertheless, in reverberation calculations it has to be taken into account. Therefore it is sufficient in this context to give a brief description of the causes of air attenuation and to present the important numerical values.

The situation is different in the case of the absorption to which sound waves are subjected when they are reflected. The magnitude of wall absorption and its frequency dependence varies considerably from one material to another. With the proper choice of materials used in construction and finish or by applying special arrangements, the absorption and hence the sound transmission in a room can be substantially influenced in a desired way; furthermore, a particular frequency dependence can be given to it. There is also an unavoidable contribution to the wall absorption which depends on certain physical properties of the medium, but it is so small that in most cases it is not evident.

Since it is one of the most common tasks of an acoustic consultant to achieve a desired reverberation time in a room with a prescribed frequency dependence and since this is done by selecting the proper wall materials and absorbers, this chapter will discuss in some detail the principles and mechanisms of the most important types of sound absorbers. For a comprehensive account the reader is referred to F. Mechel's book on sound absorption.[1]

VI.1 THE ATTENUATION OF SOUND IN AIR

In the derivation of the wave equation (I.5) it was tacitly assumed that the changes in the state of the air, caused by the sound waves, occurred without loss. This is not quite true, however. We shall refrain here from a proper amendment of the basic equations and from a quantitative treatment of the attenuation. Instead the most prominent loss mechanisms are briefly described in the following.

(a) Equation (I.4) is based on the assumption that the changes in the state of a volume of gas take place adiabatically, i.e. there is no heat exchange between neighbouring volume elements. The equation states that a compressed volume element has a slightly higher temperature than an element which is rarefied by the action of the sound wave. Although the temperature differences occurring at normal sound intensities amount to small fractions of a degree centigrade only, they cause a heat flow because of the finite thermal conductivity of the air. This flow is directed from the warmer to the cooler volume elements. The changes of state are therefore not taking place entirely adiabatically. According to basic principles of physics, the energy transported by these thermal currents cannot be reconverted completely into mechanical, i.e. into acoustical energy; they are partially lost to the sound wave. The corresponding portion of the attenuation constant m increases with the square of the frequency.

(b) In a plane sound wave each volume element becomes periodically longer or shorter in the direction of sound propagation. This distortion of the original element can be considered as a superposition of an omnidirectional compression or rarefaction and of a shear deformation, i.e. of a pure change of shape. The medium offers an elastic reaction to the omnidirectional compression proportional to the amount of compression, whereas the shear is controlled by viscous forces which are proportional to the shear velocity. Hence—as with every frictional process—mechanical energy is irreversibly converted into heat. This 'viscous portion' of the attenuation constant m also increases proportionally with the square of the frequency.

(c) Under normal conditions the above-mentioned causes of attenuation in air are negligibly small compared with the attenuation caused by what is called 'thermal relaxation'. It can be described briefly as follows. Under equilibrium conditions the total thermal energy contained in a certain quantity of a uniform polyatomic gas is distributed among several energy stores (degrees of freedom) of the gas molecules, namely as translational, vibrational and rotational energy of the molecules. If the gas is suddenly compressed, i.e. if its energy is suddenly increased, the whole additional energy will be stored at first in the form of translational energy. Afterwards a gradual redistribution among the other stores will take place. Or in other words: the establishment of a new equilibrium requires a finite time. If compressions and rarefactions change periodically as in a sound wave, a thermal equilibrium can be maintained—if at all—only at very low frequencies; with increasing frequency the actual energy content of certain molecular stores will lag behind the external changes and will accept or deliver energy at the wrong moments.

This is a sort of 'internal heat conduction' which weakens the sound wave just like the normal heat conduction with which we are more familiar. The relative amount of energy being dissipated along one wavelength has a maximum when the duration of one sound period is comparable with a specific time interval, the so-called 'relaxation time' being characteristic of the time lag in internal energy distribution.

In Fig. VI.1 the attenuation constant m multiplied by the wavelength for a single relaxation process is plotted in arbitrary units as a function of the product of frequency and relaxation time. The very broad frequency range in which it appears is characteristic of a relaxation process. (For

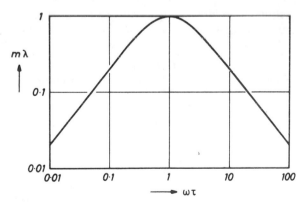

Fig. VI.1. Intensity attenuation constant (per wavelength) for a relaxation process. Abscissa is the product of angular frequency and relaxation time τ.

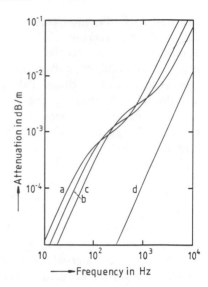

Fig. VI.2. Sound attenuation of air at normal conditions. Relative humidity: (a) 20%; (b) 40%; (c) 80%. (d) Classical attenuation (after Bass *et al.*[2]).

comparison we refer to the resonance curve in Fig. II.7b.) Moreover, the relaxation of a medium causes not only a substantial increase in absorption but also a slight change in sound velocity which, however, is not of importance in this connection.

For mixtures of polyatomic gases such as air, which consists mainly of nitrogen and oxygen, matters are much more complicated because there are many more possibilities of internal energy exchange which we shall not discuss here. Figure VI.2 shows the attenuation of sound in air at 20°C as a function of frequency and for various relative humidities. Each bump of an otherwise straight curve is due to a relaxation process of the kind described

Table VI.1

Attenuation Constant m of Air at 20°C and Normal Atmospheric Pressure, in 10^{-3} m^{-1} (after Ref. 2)

Relative humidity (%)	Frequency (kHz)						
	0·5	1	2	3	4	6	8
40	0·43	0·75	1·94	3·88	6·58	14·11	24·23
50	0·47	0·74	1·64	3·12	5·18	10·98	18·94
60	0·50	0·76	1·49	2·68	4·34	9·04	15·53
70	0·53	0·79	1·42	2·42	3·81	7·75	13·22

above. For comparison the attenuation due solely to the 'classical' effects is also plotted (curve d).

Because of their importance in room acoustics and, in particular for the calculation of reverberation time, a few numerical values of the intensity-related absorption constant m are listed in Table VI.1. This quantity is defined by the exponential decrease of intensity in a plane wave:

$$I(x) = I_0 \exp(-mx)$$

VI.2 UNAVOIDABLE WALL ABSORPTION

Even if the walls, the ceiling and the floor of a room are completely rigid and free from pores, they cause a sound absorption which is small but different from zero. It only becomes noticeable, however, when there are no other absorbents or absorbent portions of wall in the room, no people, no porous or vibrating walls. This is the case for measuring rooms which have been specially built to obtain a high reverberation time (reverberation chambers; *see* Section VIII.7). Physically this kind of absorption is again caused by the finite heat conductivity and viscosity of the air.

According to eqn (I.4), the periodic temperature changes caused by a sound wave are in phase with the corresponding pressure changes—apart from the slight deviations discussed in the preceding section. Therefore the maximum sound pressure amplitude which is observed immediately in front of a rigid wall should be associated with a maximum of 'temperature amplitude', which in turn is possible only if the wall temperature can completely follow the temperature fluctuations produced by the sound field. In reality the contrary is true: because of its high thermal capacity the wall surface remains virtually at a constant temperature. Therefore, in some boundary layer adjacent to the wall, strong temperature gradients will develop and hence a periodically alternating heat flow will be directed to and from the wall. This energy transport occurs at the expense of the sound energy, since the heat which was produced by the wave in a compression phase can only be partly reconverted into mechanical energy during the rarefaction phase.

As we saw earlier, the component of the particle velocity which is normal to the wall vanishes in front of a perfectly rigid wall. The parallel component, i.e. the y-component of the particle velocity, can be calculated from eqn (II.15) by applying

$$v_y = -\frac{1}{i\omega\rho_0}\frac{\partial p}{\partial y} \qquad (\text{VI.1})$$

which is analogous to eqn (I.12). The result (for $x = 0$ and $R = 1$) is

$$v_y = \frac{2\hat{p}_0}{\rho_0 c} \sin \theta \exp(-\mathrm{i}ky \sin \theta) \tag{VI.2}$$

It indicates that the parallel component does not vanish for oblique sound incidence ($\theta \neq 0$). This, however, cannot be true, since in a real medium the molecular layer immediately on the wall is fixed to the latter, which means $v_y = 0$ for $x = 0$. For this reason our assumption of a perfectly reflecting wall is not correct, in spite of its rigidity. In reality a boundary layer is again formed between the region of unhindered parallel motion in the air and the wall; at oblique incidence particularly high viscous forces and hence a substantial conversion of mechanical energy into heat takes place in the boundary layer.

Although the energy dissipation occurs due to both loss processes in a certain layer of air, its effect is commonly described by an absorption coefficient ascribed to the wall. It can be shown that the thicknesses of the boundary layers are inversely proportional to the square root of the frequency. Since, on the other hand, the gradients of the temperature and of the parallel velocity component increase proportionally with frequency, both contributions to the absorption coefficient are proportional to the square root of the frequency. Their dependence on the angle of incidence, however, is different. The viscous portion is zero for normal sound incidence, as can easily be seen from eqn (VI.1), whereas the heat flow to and from the wall does not vanish at normal incidence.

Both effects are very small even at the highest frequencies relevant in room acoustics. For practical design purposes they can be safely neglected.

VI.3 SOUND ABSORPTION BY VIBRATING OR PERFORATED WALLS

For the acoustics of a room it does not make any difference whether the apparent absorption of a wall is physically brought about by dissipative processes, i.e. by conversion of sound energy into heat, or by parts of the energy penetrating through the wall into the outer space. In this respect an open window is a very effective absorber, since it acts as a sink for all the arriving sound energy.

A less trivial case is that of a wall or some part of a wall forced by a sound field into vibration with a substantial amplitude. (Strictly speaking, this happens more or less with any wall, since completely rigid walls cannot be constructed.) Then a part of the wall's vibrational energy is re-radiated into the outer space. This part is withdrawn from the incident sound energy, viewed from the interior of the room. Thus the effect is the same as if it were really absorbed. It can therefore also be described by an absorption coefficient. In practice this sort of 'absorption' occurs with doors, windows, light partition walls, suspended ceilings, circus tents and similar 'walls'.

This process, which may be quite involved especially for oblique sound incidence, is very important in all problems of sound insulation. From the viewpoint of room acoustics, it is sufficient, however, to restrict discussions to the simplest case of a plane sound wave impinging perpendicularly onto the wall whose dynamic properties are completely characterised by its mass inertia. Then we need not consider the propagation of bending waves on the wall.

Let us denote the sound pressures of the incident and of the reflected waves on the surface of a wall (*see* Fig. VI.3(a)) by p_1 and p_2, and the sound pressure of the transmitted wave by p_3. The total pressure acting on the wall is then $p_1 + p_2 - p_3$. It is balanced by the inertial force $i\omega M v$, where M denotes the mass per unit area of the wall and v the velocity of the wall vibrations. This velocity is equal to the particle velocity of the wave radiated from the rear side, for which $p_3 = \rho_0 c v$ holds. Therefore we have $p_1 + p_2 - \rho_0 c v = i\omega M v$, from which we obtain

$$Z = i\omega M + \rho_0 c \qquad (VI.3)$$

for the wall impedance. Inserting this into eqn (II.8) yields

$$\alpha = \left[1 + \left(\frac{\omega M}{2\rho_0 c}\right)^2\right]^{-1} \approx \left(\frac{2\rho_0 c}{\omega M}\right)^2 \qquad (VI.4)$$

This simplification is permissible for the case frequently encountered in practice in which the characteristic impedance of air is small compared with the mass reactance of the wall. Thus the 'absorption' becomes noticeable only at low frequencies.

At a frequency of 100 Hz the absorption coefficient of a glass pane with 4 mm thickness is—according to eqn (VI.4)—as low as 0·02 approximately. For oblique or random incidence this value is a bit higher due to the better matching between the air and the glass pane, but it is still very low. Nevertheless, the increase in absorption with decreasing frequency has the effect that rooms with many windows sometimes sound 'crisp' since the reverberation at low frequency is not as long as it would be in the same room without windows.

The absorption caused by vibrations of normal and single walls and

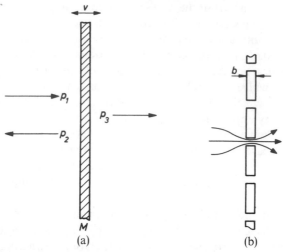

Fig. VI.3.   (a) Pressures acting on a layer with mass M per unit area. (b) Perforated panel.

ceilings is thus very low. Matters are different for double or multiple walls, provided that the partition on the side of the room under consideration is mounted in such a way that vibrations are not hindered and provided that it is not too heavy. Because of the interaction between the leaves and the enclosed volume of air such a system behaves as a resonance system. This will be discussed in the next section.

It is a fact of great practical interest that a rigid perforated plate or panel has essentially the same properties as a mass-loaded wall or foil. Let us look at Fig. VI.3(b). Each hole in a plate may be considered as a short tube or channel with length b; the mass of air contained in it, divided by the cross-section, is $\rho_0 b$. Because of the contraction of the air stream passing through the hole, the air vibrates with a greater velocity than that in the sound wave remote from the wall, and hence the inertial forces of the air included in the hole are increased. The increase is given by the ratio S_2/S_1, where S_1 is the area of the hole and S_2 is the plate area per hole. Hence the equivalent mass of the perforated panel per unit area is

$$M = \frac{\rho_0 b'}{\sigma} \tag{VI.5}$$

with

$$\sigma = \frac{S_1}{S_2} \tag{VI.6}$$

The latter quantity is the perforation ratio of the plate; sometimes it is also called 'porosity' (generally in a different context).

In eqn (VI.5) the geometrical tube length (or plate thickness) b has been replaced by an 'effective length' b', which is somewhat larger than b:

$$b' = b + 2\delta b \qquad (VI.7)$$

The correction term $2\delta b$, known as the 'end correction', accounts for the fact that the streamlines cannot contract or diverge abruptly but only gradually when entering or leaving a hole (see Fig. VI.3(b)). For circular apertures with radius a and with relatively large mutual distances it is given by

$$\delta b = 0\cdot 8a \qquad (VI.8)$$

Finally, the absorption coefficient of a perforated panel is obtained from eqn (VI.4) by substituting M from eqn (VI.5).

The absorption coefficient given by eqn (VI.4) is also the fraction of sound energy which is transmitted by a wall or a perforated panel (in the latter case it is necessary to use the first form of eqn (VI.4)). It thus characterises the sound transparency of the wall. Let us illustrate this by an example: to yield a transparency of 90%, $\omega M/2\rho_0 c$ must have the value $\frac{1}{3}$. At 1000 Hz this is the case with a foil or perforated panel with an (equivalent) mass per unit area of about 45 g/m^2, which can be realised for instance by a 1-mm thick sheet with 7·5% perforation with holes having diameters of 2 mm.

VI.4 EXTENDED RESONANCE ABSORBERS

In this section we take up again the earlier discussion of extended resonance absorbers (see Section II.4). As shown in Fig. VI.4, such an absorber consists basically of a layer with mass M per unit area, for instance a panel of wood or chipboard, which is mounted in front of a rigid wall at a certain distance d. Under the influence of an impinging sound wave it will perform vibrations, the amplitude of which depends strongly on the sound frequency. The wall impedance of this system is given by eqn (II.27). Its real part r_s represents all vibrational losses of this system which may have several physical reasons. One of them has to do with the fact that any kind of panel must be fixed at certain points or along certain lines to a supporting construction which forces the panel to be bent when it vibrates. Now all elastic deformations of a solid, including those by bending, are associated with internal losses depending on the material and other circumstances. In metals, for instance, the intrinsic losses of the material are relatively small, but they may be substantial for plates made of wood or of plastic. If necessary the losses may be increased by certain paints or surface layers.

According to the discussion of the preceding section, the mass layer in Fig. VI.4 can also be realised as a perforated plate. In this case the losses are caused by the viscosity of the air, the effect of which is enhanced by the constriction of the air flow through the holes (*see* Fig. VI.3(b)). If desired they can be augmented by covering the holes by a porous fabric. Another method of adapting the magnitude of r_s for either kind of resonance absorbers to a desired value is to fill the air space behind the panel partially or completely with porous material.

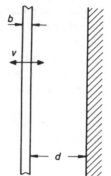

Fig. VI.4.   Resonance absorber consisting of a layer with mass M per unit area in front of a rigid wall.

In the following discussion we assume the real part r_s of the wall impedance to be constant. Then all the eqns (II.27)–(II.30b) can be applied to these structures. The absorption coefficient in particular reaches a maximum caused by resonance at the angular frequency ω_0 given by eqn (II.28). In Fig. VI.5 calculated absorption coefficients of panel resonators are plotted as a function of the ratio ω/ω_0 under the additional assumption $M\omega_0 = 10\rho_0 c$. The parameter of the curves is the quantity $r_s/\rho_0 c$. A maximum absorption coefficient of 1 is reached only for exact matching, i.e. for $r_s = \rho_0 c$. For $r_s > \rho_0 c$ the maximum absorption is less than unity and the curves are broadening. This is qualitatively the same behaviour as that of a porous layer which is arranged at some distance and in front of a rigid wall (compare Fig. II.6). The resonance frequency of a panel absorber can be

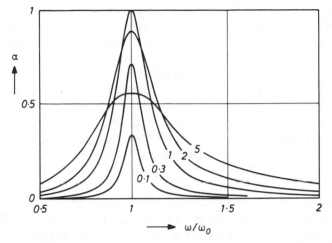

Fig. VI.5. Absorption coefficient α (calculated) of resonance absorbers, similar to Fig. VI.4, as a function of frequency for normal sound incidence and for $M\omega_0 = 10\rho_0 c$. Parameter is the ratio $r_s/\rho_0 c$.

expressed equally well in the following form as this is more useful for its practical application:

$$f_0 = \frac{600}{(Md)^{1/2}} \tag{VI.9}$$

where M is in kg/m^2 and d in cm.

There is no doubt as to the practical validity of this formula for absorbers with perforated panels. As far as unperforated panels are concerned, one may wonder whether the elastic bending stiffness will not influence the resonance frequency and modify the above formula which contains merely the stiffness of the air space behind the plate. In many practical cases, however, the air stiffness is much larger than the bending stiffness and thus the latter can safely be neglected. This is true at least for wall linings with wooden panels and for similar constructions which are the main applications being considered at present. Equation (VI.9) may be regarded as sufficiently correct for the usual plate thicknesses of up to 20 mm, as long as the distance of the points or lines at which the plates are fixed are not closer than about 80 cm. We should bear in mind that this equation applies only to normal sound incidence and should therefore anyway only be considered as a clue to the actual frequency of maximum absorption. Since the losses and hence the Q-factor of the resonator are determined by numerous factors which do not lend themselves to mathematical expression, it will be necessary to measure the actual absorption coefficient in any case except where the values are known from experience with sufficient accuracy.

The practical importance of resonance absorbers stems from the possibility of choosing their significant data (dimensions, materials) from a wide range so as to give them the desired absorption characteristics. By a suitable combination of several types of resonance absorbers the acoustic consultant is able to achieve a prescribed frequency dependence of the reverberation time. The most common application of vibrating panels is to effect a low frequency balance for the strong absorption of the audience at medium and high frequencies, and thus to equalise the reverberation time. This is the reason for the generally favourable acoustical conditions which are frequently met in halls whose walls are lined with wooden panels or are equipped with similar components, i.e. walls or suspended decoration ceilings made of thin plaster. Thus it is not, as is sometimes believed by laymen, a sort of 'amplification' caused by 'resonance' which is responsible for the reasonable acoustics of many concert halls lined with wooden panels. Likewise, audible decay processes of the wall linings, which are sometimes also believed to be responsible for good acoustics, do not occur in practical situations although they might be possible in principle. If a resonance system with the relative half-width (reciprocal of the Q-factor) $\Delta\omega/\omega_0$ is excited by an impulsive signal, its amplitude will decay with a damping constant $\delta = \Delta\omega/2$ according to eqn (II.29c); thus the reverberation time of the resonator is

$$T' = \frac{13 \cdot 8}{\Delta\omega} = \frac{2 \cdot 2}{\Delta f}$$

To be comparable with the reverberation time of a room which is of the order of magnitude of 1 s, the frequency half-width Δf should be about 2 Hz. Such resonators can indeed be constructed. However, wall linings with vibrating or perforated panels in front of rigid walls usually have half-widths larger by several orders of magnitude.

Since neighbouring area elements of unperforated panels are strongly coupled one to the other by bending forces, they cannot be considered as 'locally reacting wall surfaces'. Therefore the simple angle dependence of the reflection factor or of the absorption coefficient expressed by eqns (II.14) and (II.16) is not valid for them. On the contrary, at oblique incidence a forced bending wave is excited in the panel. The propagation of this wave is strongly affected by the sort of mounting, the arrangement of timber battening which carries the panels, also by the elastic properties of the plate material and by interaction with the air volume behind the panels. It is the structure of these bending waves which strongly affects the absorption coefficient of the whole arrangement at oblique incidence. Since general statements in this respect cannot be made, we shall not discuss this point in any further detail.

For resonators with perforated panels, the coupling of neighbouring holes is effected by the air space behind the panels. The coupling can be destroyed by hindering the lateral sound propagation in that air space. This is done by lateral partitions made of rigid material, or by filling the air space with porous and hence sound absorbent materials like glass or mineral wool. Neighbouring elements of the plate can then be regarded as independent; the wall impedance and similarly the resonance frequency is independent of the direction of sound incidence. To achieve this it is

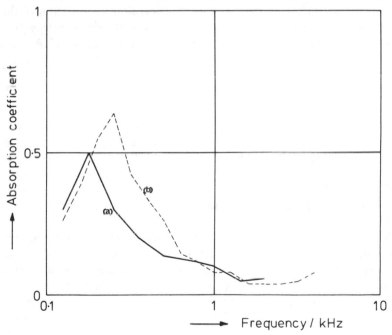

Fig. VI.6. Measured absorption coefficient of resonance absorbers at random sound incidence. (a) Wooden panels, 8 mm thick, 5 kg/m² in 30 mm distance from rigid wall, with 20 mm thick rock wool plate behind (33·2 Rayl/cm). (b) Panels, 9·5 mm thick, perforated at 1·6% (diameter of holes 6 mm), with 5 cm distance from wall; air space filled with glass wool.

sufficient to reduce the range of lateral coupling to about half a wavelength, since smaller regions at oblique incidence are excited at equal phases.

In Fig. VI.6 the absorption coefficients of a wooden wall lining and of a resonance absorber with perforated panels are plotted as functions of the frequency, measured at omnidirectional sound incidence.

VI.5 SINGLE RESONATORS

Sometimes sound absorbent elements are not distributed so as to cover the wall or the ceiling of a room but instead they are single or separate objects or things arranged either on a wall or in free space. Examples of this are chairs, small wall openings or lamps; musical instruments too can absorb sound. To sound absorbers of this sort we cannot attribute an absorption coefficient, since the latter always refers to a uniform surface. Instead their absorbing power is characterised by their 'absorption cross-section' or their absorption area, which is defined as the ratio of sound energy being absorbed per second by them and the intensity which the incident sound wave would have at the place of the absorbent object if it were not present:

$$A = \frac{P_{abs}}{I_0} \qquad (VI.10)$$

When calculating the reverberation time of a room, absorption of this type of absorber is taken into account by adding their absorption areas A_i to the sum $\sum \alpha_i S_i$ (*see* eqn (V.23a)). The analogue holds for all other formulae and calculations in which the total absorption or the mean absorption coefficient $\bar{\alpha}$ of a room appears, as for instance in the calculation of the steady state energy density in a sound field according to eqns (V.36) to (V.37).

In this section we are discussing single sound absorbers with pronounced resonant behaviour. Their characteristic feature is an air volume which is enclosed by rigid boundaries and which is coupled to the surrounding space by an aperture. The latter may equally well be a channel or a 'neck'. The whole structure is assumed to be small compared with the wavelength of sound and thus it has one single resonance only in the corresponding frequency range. It is brought about by interaction of the air contained in the neck or in the aperture which is moved to and fro by the sound and acts essentially as a mass load while the air cushion in the enclosure is periodically compressed and rarefied, and opposes these changes of state with the stiffness of a spring. Arrangements of this type are called

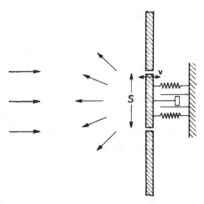

Fig. VI.7. Principle of mechanical resonator in a sound field. Part of the incident sound energy is re-radiated uniformly.

'Helmholtz resonators'; examples of these are all kinds of bottles, vases and similar vessels. In ancient times, as 'Vitruv's sound vessels', they played an unknown, possibly only a surmised, acoustical role.

In order to calculate the absorption of a single absorber, we shall represent it (*see* Fig. VI.7) by a piston, with area S, inserted so that it is flush with the surface of a rigid wall of infinite extension. The dimension of the piston should be small compared with the wavelength. If the piston is moved, its mass inertia, the elastic stiffness of a spring and certain frictional resistances have to be overcome; furthermore, the piston radiates sound in all directions of the adjacent half space which exerts a corresponding reaction on it. The latter may be characterised by the 'radiation impedance' of the piston whose real part we denote by R_r.

Next we assume that the resonator is working at its resonance frequency. In this case all the imaginary parts of the mechanical load will mutually cancel each other, including that of the radiation impedance. The remainder of the impedance, the ratio of the force F acting on the piston and its velocity v is

$$\frac{F}{v} = R_0 + R_r \qquad (VI.11)$$

where R_0 is the frictional resistance in which we include all mechanical losses except those caused by radiation. Furthermore, we assume that the resonator is matched to the surrounding medium, i.e. that its frictional resistance equals the radiation resistance

$$R_0 = R_r$$

The energy converted to heat per second by the internal friction is

$$P_{abs} = R_0 \overline{v^2} = R_0 \frac{\overline{F^2}}{(2R_r)^2} = \frac{\overline{F^2}}{4R_r} \tag{VI.12}$$

where we have used eqn (VI.11) to express the velocity v in terms of the force F (the bars indicate time averaging). The force exerted externally on the piston arises from the sound field. If p denotes the sound pressure, the force is $F = 2pS$. The factor 2 takes into account the reflection from the rigid wall surrounding the piston. By application of eqn (I.14) we can express the sound pressure and hence the force in terms of the intensity I of the incident sound wave:

$$\overline{F^2} = 4S^2 \overline{p^2} = 4\rho_0 c S^2 I \tag{VI.13}$$

Finally, we need an expression for the radiation resistance R_r, which is generally defined by

$$P_r = R_r \overline{v^2} \tag{VI.14}$$

P_r is the acoustic power of a sound source whose surface vibrates with a velocity v. Since the piston to which this relation is applied is small compared with the wavelength, P_r can be substituted from eqn (I.24) using $\hat{Q}^2 = (S\hat{v})^2 = 2S^2 \overline{v^2}$, but we must bear in mind that the re-radiation of sound from the piston is restricted to the half space and hence is a factor of 2 higher than in eqn (I.24). Thus eqn (VI.14) yields

$$R_r = \frac{\rho_0 \omega^2 S^2}{2\pi c} = 2\pi \rho_0 c \left(\frac{S}{\lambda}\right)^2 \tag{VI.15}$$

Now we are ready to evaluate eqn (VI.12) by substituting from eqns (VI.13) and (VI.15), and we obtain as a final result

$$P_{abs} = \frac{\lambda_0^2}{2\pi} I \quad \text{and} \quad A_{max} = \frac{\lambda_0^2}{2\pi} \tag{VI.16}$$

where λ_0 is the wavelength corresponding to the resonance frequency.

For the frequency dependence of the absorption area, we can essentially adopt eqn (II.30):

$$A(\omega) = \frac{A_{max}}{1 + Q_A^2[(\omega/\omega_0) - (\omega_0/\omega)]^2} \tag{VI.17}$$

with

$$Q_A = \frac{M\omega_0}{2R_r} \tag{VI.17a}$$

As for any resonance system, the angular resonance frequency is given by

$$\omega_0^2 = \frac{s}{M}$$

In the present case M is the mass of the air in the resonator neck, whose geometrical length has to be completed by a correction term, as was the case in eqn (VI.7), and whose cross-sectional area is equal to the piston area S in Fig. VI.7. s is the elastic stiffness of the air enclosed in the resonator volume. To calculate it we suppose an imaginary piston in the neck displaced by δx; the corresponding change in air pressure is p_i. According to the usual definition of the stiffness,

$$s = -\frac{p_i S}{\delta x}$$

On the other hand, the pressure change is associated with a change $\delta \rho$ in air density, which in turn is due to the volume change $S\delta x$. These quantities are related to each other by (see eqns (I.4) and (I.5a))

$$p_i = c^2 \delta \rho = -\rho_0 c^2 \frac{S\delta x}{V_0}$$

V_0 denoting the resonator volume. Thus we obtain

$$s = \frac{\rho_0 c^2 S^2}{V_0}$$

Next we insert this value for s into the equation for ω_0^2, eliminate the mass M from the resulting relation and from eqn (VI.17a), and apply eqn (VI.15) for the radiation resistance. This procedure will finally result in

$$Q_A = \frac{\pi}{V_0}\left(\frac{c}{\omega_0}\right)^3 = \frac{\pi}{V_0}\left(\frac{\lambda_0}{2\pi}\right)^3 \qquad \text{(VI.18)}$$

where V_0 is the volume of the resonator.

We observe that the maximum absorption area of a resonator matched to the sound field is fairly large, according to eqn (VI.16). On the other hand, the Q-factor given by eqn (VI.18) is very large too, which means that the relative frequency half-width which is the reciprocal of the Q-factor is very small, i.e. large absorption will occur only in a very narrow frequency range. This is clearly illustrated by the following numerical example: suppose a resonator is tuned to a frequency of 100 Hz corresponding to an angular frequency of $628\,s^{-1}$. This can be achieved conveniently by a resonator volume of 1 litre. If it is matched, the resonator has a maximum absorption area which is as large as $1{\cdot}87\,\text{m}^2$. Its Q-factor is—according to eqn (VI.18)—about 500, the relative half-width is thus $0{\cdot}002$. At frequencies of $99{\cdot}9$ and $100{\cdot}1\,\text{Hz}$ the absorption area has already fallen to one half of its maximum of $100\,\text{Hz}$. Therefore the very high absorption in the resonance is paid for by the exceedingly narrow frequency bandwidth. This is why the application of such weakly damped resonators does not seem too promising. It is more promising to increase the losses and hence the useful bandwidth at the expense of maximum absorption.

Finally, we investigate the problem of audible decay processes, which we have already touched on in the preceding section. The reverberation time of the resonator can again be calculated by the relation

$$T' = \frac{13{\cdot}8}{\Delta\omega} = 13{\cdot}8\,\frac{Q_A}{\omega_0} \tag{VI.19}$$

In many cases this time cannot be ignored when considering the reverberation time of a room. What about the perceptibility of the decay process?

It is evident from the derivation of the absorption area, eqn (VI.16), that the same amount of energy per second which is converted to heat in the interior of the resonator is being re-emitted by it, since we have assumed $R_0 = R_r$. Its maximum radiation power is thus $I(\lambda_0^2/2\pi)$, I being the intensity of the incident sound waves. Thus the intensity of the re-radiated sound at distance r is

$$I_s = \left(\frac{\lambda_0}{2\pi r}\right)^2 I = \left(\frac{c}{r\omega_0}\right)^2 I$$

Both intensities are equal at a distance

$$r = \frac{c}{\omega_0} = \frac{54}{f_0}\quad\text{m} \tag{VI.20}$$

The decay process of the resonator is therefore only audible in its immediate vicinity. In the example mentioned above this critical distance would be $0{\cdot}54\,\text{m}$; at substantially larger distances the decay cannot be heard.

VI.6 SOUND ABSORPTION BY POROUS MATERIALS

We refer now to the contents of Section VI.2, in which we discussed the reflection losses caused by a viscous boundary layer adjacent to smooth surfaces. The extension of this boundary layer will be larger if the surface of the wall is contoured, i.e. if the wall has a rough surface. Correspondingly, the absorption coefficient of a rough wall will become larger since it refers to the 'visual area' of the wall.

The increase of the absorption coefficient becomes even more pronounced when the sound waves strike a material which is traversed by a great number of channels which the sound can enter. The viscous boundary layer (and likewise the thermal boundary layer) extends over the whole internal surface of the structure, i.e. over all channel walls. These walls contribute to the absorption of the surface of the material to the same degree as their accessibility to the incident sound.

This mechanism of sound absorption concerns all porous materials with pores accessible from the outside. They usually consist of granular or fibrous substances which have been made reasonably compact by pressing or weaving them and very frequently by adding suitable adhesives. Commercial absorbent materials of this kind are often manufactured from glass or mineral fibres pressed into plates or felts.

Of course it is not possible to describe exactly and in every detail the acoustical properties of such complicated structures; one usually has to resort to simplifying assumptions. In this presentation we do not attempt to give a description which pretends to be quantitative; instead we shall restrict our discussions to a highly idealised model of a porous material, the so-called Rayleigh model, which qualitatively exhibits the essential features. In any case it is absolutely essential to test a new and unknown material experimentally before applying it in practice.

The Rayleigh model consists of a great number of similar equally spaced parallel channels which traverse a skeleton material considered to be completely rigid (*see* Fig. VI.8). It is assumed that the surface of that system, being located at $x = 0$, is perpendicular to the axes of the channels; in the positive x-direction it is assumed that the model is unbounded.

First we consider the sound propagation in a single channel. We suppose that it is so narrow that the profile of the air stream is determined almost completely by the viscosity of the air and not by any inertial forces. This is always the case at sufficiently low frequencies (compare also eqn (VI.25)). Then the same lateral distribution of flow velocities prevails in the inerior of the channel as for constant (i.e. for non-alternating) flows; and likewise the flow resistance of the channel per unit length, which is defined by

$$\Xi' = -\frac{1}{\bar{v}}\frac{\partial p}{\partial x} \qquad (VI.21)$$

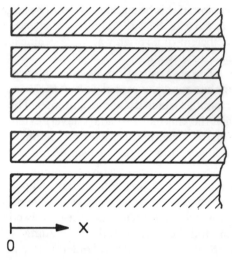

Fig. VI.8. Rayleigh model, schematic representation.

has virtually the same value as for constant flow velocity. (In this formula $\bar{v}$ is the flow velocity averaged over the cross-section of the channel.) It is known from flow dynamics that for shallow channels between parallel planes at distance b, Ξ' is given by

$$\Xi' = \frac{12\eta}{b^2} \tag{VI.22}$$

whereas for channels with circular cross-section (radius a)

$$\Xi' = \frac{8\eta}{a^2} \tag{VI.23}$$

In these formulae η denotes the viscosity of the streaming medium. For air under normal conditions $\eta = 1{\cdot}8 \times 10^{-5}\,\mathrm{kg\,cm^{-1}\,s^{-1}}$. In some texts on acoustics specific flow resistances are measured in units of 'Rayl/cm'. The conversion into the mks system is effected by the formula

$$1\,\mathrm{Rayl/cm} = 1000\,\mathrm{kg\,m^{-3}\,s^{-1}}$$

In order to establish the balance of forces, we now consider a length element $\mathrm{d}x$ in the channel (*see* Fig. VI.9). The net force acting on it in positive x-direction is $-(\partial p/\partial x)\,\mathrm{d}x\,\mathrm{d}S$, with $\mathrm{d}S$ denoting the cross-sectional area of the channel. It is kept at equilibrium by an inertial force

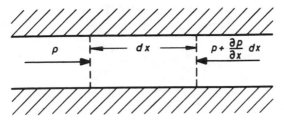

Fig. VI.9. Forces acting on a length element in a rigid channel.

$\rho_0(\partial\bar{v}/\partial t)\,dx\,dS$ and a frictional force $\Xi'\bar{v}\,dx\,dS$, according to eqn (VI.21). Thus the force equation which is analogous to eqn (I.2) reads

$$-\frac{\partial p}{\partial x} = \rho_0\frac{\partial\bar{v}}{\partial t} + \Xi'\bar{v} \tag{VI.24}$$

This relation assumes that the flow velocity (or the particle velocity) is constant over the whole cross-section and equal to $\bar{v}$. This is of course not true. In reality a certain velocity distribution develops across and in the channel. However, a more thorough investigation shows that the representation (VI.24) can be applied with sufficient accuracy so long as

$$\frac{\rho_0\omega}{\Xi'} \lesssim 4 \tag{VI.25}$$

The equation of continuity (I.3) is not affected by the viscosity, thus

$$\rho_0\frac{\partial\bar{v}}{\partial x} = -\frac{\partial\rho}{\partial t} = -\frac{1}{c^2}\frac{\partial p}{\partial t} \tag{VI.26}$$

Into eqns (VI.24) and (VI.26) we insert the following plane wave relations:

$$p = \hat{p}\exp\left[i(\omega t - k'x)\right] \qquad \bar{v} = \hat{\bar{v}}\exp\left[i(\omega t - k'x)\right]$$

and obtain two homogeneous equations for p and $\bar{v}$:

$$k'p - (\omega\rho_0 - i\Xi')\bar{v} = 0 \qquad \omega p - \rho_0 c^2 k'\bar{v} = 0 \tag{VI.27}$$

Setting the determinant, formed of the coefficients of p and $\bar{v}$, equal to zero yields the complex propagation constant

$$k' = \beta' - i\gamma' = \frac{\omega}{c}\left(1 - \frac{i\Xi'}{\rho_0\omega}\right)^{1/2} \tag{VI.28}$$

If we insert this result into one of eqns (VI.27), we obtain the ratio of sound pressure to velocity, i.e. the characteristic impedance in the channel:

$$Z'_0 = \frac{p}{\bar{v}} = \rho_0 c \left(1 - \frac{i\Xi'}{\rho_0 \omega} \right)^{1/2} \tag{VI.29}$$

For very high frequencies—or for very wide channels—these expressions approach the values ω/c and $\rho_0 c$, valid for free sound propagation, because then the viscous boundary layer occupies only a very small fraction of the cross-section. In contrast to this, at very low frequencies eqn (VI.28) yields

$$\beta' = \gamma' \approx \left(\frac{\omega\Xi'}{2\rho_0 c^2} \right)^{1/2} \tag{VI.30}$$

The attenuation in this range is thus considerable: a wave is reduced in its amplitude by 54·6 dB per wavelength.

From the characteristic impedance Z'_0 inside the channels we pass to the 'average characteristic impedance' Z_0 of a porous material by use of the porosity σ as already introduced in eqn (VI.6), which is the ratio of the cross-sectional area of one channel and the surface area per channel:

$$Z_0 = \frac{Z'_0}{\sigma} \tag{VI.31}$$

Likewise, the 'outer flow resistance' Ξ, which can be measured directly by forcing air through a test sample of the material, is related to Ξ' by

$$\Xi = \frac{\Xi'}{\sigma} \tag{VI.32}$$

For highly porous materials such as rock wool or mineral wool the porosity is close to unity.

Now we apply the above relations to a typical arrangement consisting of a homogeneous layer of porous material in front of a rigid wall. The thickness of the layer is d (see Fig. VI.10). A sound wave arriving at the surface of the layer will be partially reflected from it; the remaining part of the sound energy will penetrate into the material and reach again the surface after its reflection from the rigid rear wall. Then it will again split up into one portion penetrating the surface and another one returning to the rear wall, and so on. This qualitative consideration shows that the reflected sound wave can be thought of as being made up of an infinite number of successive contributions, each of them weaker than the preceding one because of the considerable attenuation of the interior wave. Furthermore,

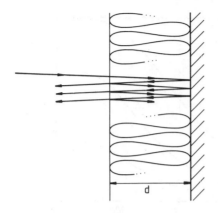

Fig. VI.10. Porous layer in front of a rigid wall.

it shows that the reflection factor and hence the absorption coefficient may show maxima and minima, depending on whether the various components interfere constructively or destructively at a given frequency.

For a quantitative treatment which will be restricted, however, to normal sound incidence we refer to eqn (II.20), according to which the 'wall impedance' of an air layer of thickness d in front of a rigid wall is $-i\rho_0 c \cot(kd)$. By replacing $\rho_0 c$ with Z_0 and k with k' we obtain for the wall impedance of the porous layer

$$Z = -iZ_0 \cot(k'd) \tag{VI.33}$$

From this expression the reflection factor and the absorption coefficient can be calculated using eqns (II.7) and (II.8).

For the following discussion it is useful to separate the real and the imaginary part of the cotangent:

$$\cot(k'd) = \frac{\sin(2\beta'd) + i \sinh(2\gamma'd)}{\cosh(2\gamma'd) - \cos(2\beta'd)} \tag{VI.34}$$

Then one can draw the following qualitative conclusions:

(a) For a layer which is thin compared with the sound wavelength, i.e. for $kd \ll 1$, $\cot(k'd)$ can be replaced with $1/k'd$. Hence the porous layer has a very large impedance and accordingly low absorption. In other words: substantial sound absorption cannot be achieved by just applying some kind of paint to a wall.

(b) If the sound waves inside the porous material undergo strong attenuation during one round trip, i.e. for $\gamma'd \gg 1$, the cotangent

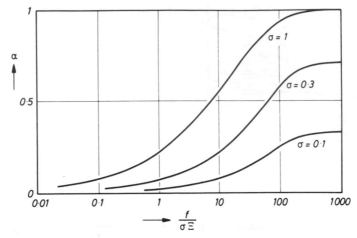

Fig. VI.11. Normal incidence absorption coefficient of a porous layer (Rayleigh model) for $\gamma'd \gg 1$ (frequency f in Hz, Ξ in $1000\,\mathrm{kg\,m^{-3}\,s^{-1}}$).

becomes i, according to eqn (VI.34), and the wall impedance is

$$Z = \frac{Z_0'}{\sigma} = \frac{\rho_0 c}{\sigma}\left(1 - \frac{i\sigma\Xi}{\rho_0\omega}\right)^{1/2} \tag{VI.35}$$

Figure VI.11 shows the absorption coefficient of the layer calculated from eqn (VI.35). For high frequencies it approaches asymptotically the value

$$\alpha_\infty = \frac{4\sigma}{(1+\sigma)^2} \tag{VI.36}$$

(c) If, on the contrary, $\gamma'd \ll 1$, i.e. for small attenuation inside the material, the periodicity of the trigonometric functions in eqn (VI.34) will dominate in the frequency dependence of the cotangent, and the same holds for that of the absorption coefficient. The latter has a maximum whenever $\beta'd$ equals $\pi/2$ or an odd multiple of it, i.e. at all frequencies for which the thickness d of the layer is an odd integer of $\lambda'/4$, with $\lambda' = 2\pi/\beta'$ denoting the wavelength inside the porous material.

If we want a high absorption coefficient at low frequencies, we do not necessarily need a thick porous layer. The only essential thing is that there is a porous sheet with a sufficiently high flow resistance at a distance in front of a rigid wall which, at the interesting frequencies, amounts to about a quarter wavelength; between the porous layer and the wall there may simply be air. If we only have thin sheets of absorbent material at our disposal, it is better to mount them at a certain distance from the wall than directly onto the wall. This saving in material is offset by an absorption coefficient which decreases at higher frequencies. In the limiting case of vanishingly thin absorbent sheets we ultimately arrive at the stretched fabric which we have already dealt with in Section II.4.

In the ideal Rayleigh model with rigid channel walls, which we have been discussing, there is no lateral coupling. A surface perpendicular to the channel axes therefore has a wall impedance which is independent of the angle of sound incidence. Its absorption coefficient at oblique incidence can be calculated from the impedance by eqn (II.16). Real absorbent materials behave differently in this respect, at least in principle, since their internal channels run in all directions and are interconnected by a great many side branches, thus effecting lateral coupling at oblique incidence. Lateral coupling can be neglected, however, at low frequencies, since this has a substantial effect only if its range of influence is comparable with the wavelength. In the low frequency range, however, the limiting equation (VI.30) is applicable, indicating very high attenuation per wavelength in the material. On the other hand, at higher frequencies the attenuation per wavelength γ/β decreases and therefore the absorption coefficient depends in a different way on the angle of incidence.

We want to emphasise here that the Rayleigh model, even at normal sound incidence, is only useful for a qualitative understanding of the effects in a porous material but not for a quantitative calculation of the acoustical properties of real absorbent materials. The assumed rigidity of its skeleton is a simplification which is not entirely justified in practice. Furthermore, these materials do not contain well separated and distinguishable channels but rather irregularly shaped cavities which are mutually connected. The pores or channels are so narrow that there must surely be a heat exchange between the air contained in the channels and the walls, and therefore heat conduction can be expected to play a substantial role; or, in other words, the changes of state of the air occur neither adiabatically nor according to an isothermal law but somehow in between these limiting cases and this causes an additional complication. In the past attempts have been made to take these effects, which are not covered by our simple Rayleigh model, into account by introducing a 'structure factor' which can, however, only be evaluated experimentally. From a practical point of view it therefore seems more advantageous to omit such a sophisticated treatment and to obtain the absorption coefficient by measurement. This procedure is recommended all the more because the performance of porous absorbers depends only partially on the properties of the material and to a greater extent on its arrangement, on the covering and on other constructional details, which vary substantially from one situation to another.

When porous absorbent materials are used for reducing the reverberation time of a room, it will usually be necessary to cover these materials in some way on the side exposed to the room. Many of these materials will in the course of time shed small particles which must be prevented from polluting the air in the room. If the absorbent portions of wall are within the reach of people, a suitable covering is desirable too as a protection against unintentional thoughtless damage of the materials which are not usually very hard wearing. And, finally, the architect usually wishes to hide the rock wool layer which is not aesthetically pleasing behind a surface which he can treat as he wishes.

To prevent purling (or to keep water away from the pores, as for instance in swimming baths) it is sufficient to bag the absorbent materials in very thin plastic foils. Furthermore, purling can be avoided by a somewhat denser porous front layer on the bulk of the material. Very heavily perforated or slotted panels of wood, metal, plaster (with additives) or plastic materials are used for making more hard-wearing coverings.

According to Section VI.3, foils, as well as perforated or slotted panels, have a certain sound transmissibility which may be close to unity at low frequencies and which is identical to the absorption coefficient in eqn (VI.4). It would be wrong, however, to calculate the absorption of the combination of porous material plus covering by multiplying the absorption coefficient of the uncovered layer by the transmissibility of the covering. Instead one has to add the wall impedance $i\omega M$ of the perforated panel or of the foil to the impedance of the porous layer. The resulting impedance can be better matched in certain frequency ranges to the characteristic impedance of the air, in which case the absorption is increased by the covering. This will occur if the wall impedance of the uncovered arrangement has a negative imaginary part, i.e. if the distance between the surface of the porous layer and the rigid wall behind it is less than a quarter wavelength. The added mass reduces this imaginary part and this results in a higher absorption coefficient according to Fig. II.2. The resonance absorbers discussed in Section VI.4 are obtained once again with lightly perforated plates or with heavy non-perforated panels.

Perforated or slotted panels may have such small apertures that these are only visible at short distances. The surfaces of these panels can be painted and can be cleaned from time to time; however, care must be taken that the holes are not obstructed. Hence this kind of covering is widely used. Likewise, parallel rods may be used for this purpose so that they do not impair the absorption too severely.[3,4]

We close this section by illustrating a few more typical measured results. In Fig. VI.12 the absorption coefficient of two porous layers, which are 50 mm thick, is shown as a function of the frequency which has been obtained by measurement in the reverberation chamber, i.e. for random sound incidence (*see* Section VIII.8). Both materials differ in their densities as well as in their flow resistances. Obviously the denser material exhibits an absorption coefficient close to 1 even at lower frequencies. (Absorption

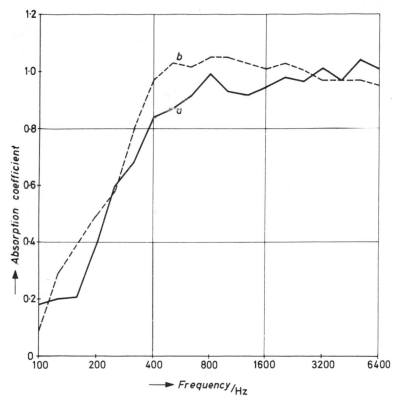

Fig. VI.12. Absorption coefficient of rock wool layers of 50 mm thickness, mounted immediately on concrete (random incidence). (a) Density 40 kg/m³, 12·7 Rayl/cm; (b) density 100 kg/m³, 22 Rayl/cm.

coefficients higher than unity occurring in the diagrams are due to peculiarities of the measuring method.)

Figure VI.13 shows the absorption coefficient of a porous sheet with 30 mm thickness and a density of 46·5 kg/m³ which is mounted directly in front of a rigid wall in the first case; in the other case there is an air space of 50 mm between the sheet and the wall. The latter is partitioned off by wooden lattices with a pattern of 50 cm × 50 cm. The second method of mounting leads to an absorption coefficient of 0·9 at 300 Hz, whereas when there is no air space double the frequency at least is required for the same value. Thus an air space behind the absorbent material considerably improves its effectiveness.

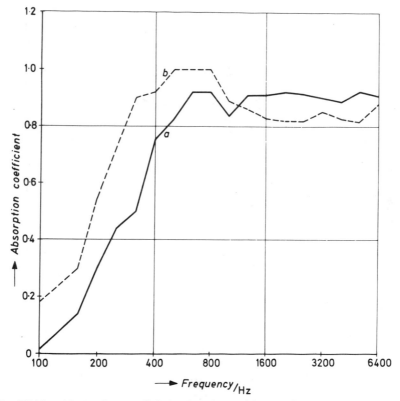

Fig. VI.13. Absorption coefficient of rock wool layer of 30 mm thickness and density 46·5 kg/m³ (12 Rayl/cm), random incidence. (a) Mounted immediately on concrete; (b) mounted in 50 mm distance from concrete rear wall; air space laterally partitioned.

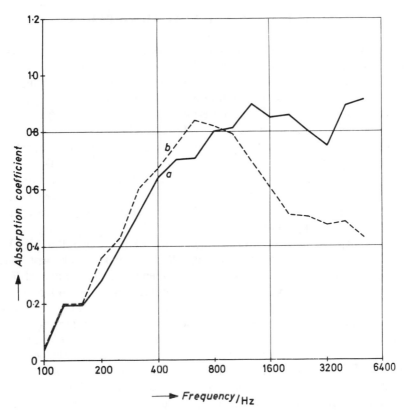

Fig. VI.14. Absorption coefficient of 50-mm glass wool, mounted immediately on concrete (random incidence). (a) Uncovered; (b) covered by a panel of 5 mm thickness, perforated at 14%.

The influence of a covering is demonstrated in Fig. VI.14. In both cases the porous layer has a thickness of 50 mm and is mounted directly onto the wall. The fraction of hole areas, i.e. the perforation, is 14%. The mass load corresponding to it is responsible for an absorption maximum at 800 Hz which is not present for the bare material. This shift of the absorption to lower frequencies can sometimes be very desirable. It must be paid for, however, by a loss of absorption at higher frequencies. At a higher degree of perforation this influence is much less pronounced, and with a perforation of 25% or more the effect of the covering plate can virtually be neglected.

VI.7 AUDIENCE AND SEAT ABSORPTION

The purpose of most medium to large size halls is to accommodate a large number of spectators or listeners and thus enable them to watch events or functions of common interest. This is true for concert halls and lecture rooms, for theatres and opera houses, for churches and sports halls, cinemas, council chambers and entertainment halls of every kind. The important acoustical properties are therefore those which are present when the rooms are occupied or at least partially occupied. These properties, however, are largely determined by the audience itself, especially by the sound absorption effected by the people or, strictly speaking, by their clothing. The only exceptions are broadcasting and television studios, which are not intended to be used with an audience present, and certain acoustical measuring rooms.

The absorption effected by an audience is due mainly to people's clothing and its porosity. Since clothing is not usually very thick, the absorption is considerable only at medium and high frequencies; in the range of low frequencies it is relatively small. Since people's clothing differs from individual to individual, only average values of the audience absorption are available and it is quite possible that these values are changing with the passage of time according to changing fashion. Furthermore, audience absorption depends on the arrangement of the row of seats, on the portions which are exposed to the incident sound, on the density of seats, and on the interruption of occupied 'blocks' by aisles, stairs, etc. It is quite evident that a person seated at the rear of a box with a small opening, as was typical in 18th- to 19th-century theatres, absorbs much less sound energy than a person sitting among steeply raked rows of seats and who is thus well exposed to the sound. Therefore it is not surprising that there are considerable differences in the data on audience absorption which have been given by different authors who have carried out their measurements in a reverberation chamber or who have based their calculations on the reverberation time of existing halls.

The absorption of persons standing singly or seated is characterised most appropriately by their absorption cross-section or absorption area A, already defined in eqn (VI.10) in Section VI.5. The absorption area of each person is added to the sum of eqn (V.23a), which in this case reads

$$\bar{\alpha} = \frac{1}{S}\left(\sum_i S_i\alpha_i + N_pA\right)$$

N_p being the number of persons.

Table VI.2
Absorption Areas of Single Persons in m²

Type of persons	Frequency (Hz)					
	125	250	500	1000	2000	4000
Male standing in heavy coat	0·17	0·41	0·91	1·30	1·43	1·47
Male standing without coat	0·12	0·24	0·59	0·98	1·13	1·12
Musician sitting with instrument (after Kuhl)	0·60	0·95	1·06	1·08	1·08	1·08

Table VI.2 lists some absorption areas as a function of the frequency measured by Kath and Kuhl[5] in the diffuse sound field.

When people are seated close together (which is usual in occupied rooms) it seems to be more correct[6] to use an absorption coefficient instead of absorbent areas, i.e. not to indicate the absorption per person but per square metre instead. In Table VI.3 measured absorption coefficients are presented for several conditions of a closely seated audience.[6,7] For the reasons mentioned, however, these values cannot be considered as being

Table VI.3
Absorption Coefficients of Audience and Chairs

Type of seats	Frequency (Hz)						
	125	250	500	1000	2000	4000	6000
Audience seated on wooden chairs, two persons per m²	0·24	0·40	0·78	0·98	0·96	0·87	0·80
Audience seated on wooden chairs, one person per m²	0·16	0·24	0·56	0·69	0·81	0·78	0·75
Audience on moderately upholstered chairs, 0·85 m × 0·63 m	0·72	0·82	0·91	0·93	0·94	0·87	0·77
Audience on moderately upholstered chairs, 0·90 m × 0·55 m	0·55	0·86	0·83	0·87	0·90	0·87	0·80
Moderately upholstered chairs, unoccupied, 0·90 m × 0·55 m	0·44	0·56	0·67	0·74	0·83	0·87	0·80
Occupied audience, orchestra and chorus area[a,b]	0·60	0·74	0·88	0·96	0·93	0·85	0·80
Unoccupied 'average' cloth-covered, well-upholstered areas (seats with perforated bottoms)[b]	0·49	0·66	0·80	0·88	0·82	0·70	0·64

[a] The occupied areas include aisle widths up to but not exceeding 1 m.
[b] Values evaluated by application of Sabine's formula.[6]

applicable to all cases. Furthermore, the absorption of empty chairs is indicated and this is important to the judging of the difference in reverberation times for the occupied and the unoccupied hall.

Although the sound absorption of audience and chairs may in actual cases be different from those of Table VI.3, the latter at least demonstrates the general features of audience absorption: at increasing frequencies the absorption coefficients increase at first. For frequencies higher than 2000 Hz, however, they decrease. This decrease is presumably due to mutual shadowing of absorbent surface areas; this shadowing becomes more prominent at high frequencies because at higher frequencies it is not overcome by diffraction around the heads, arms and other parts of the listeners' bodies.

The effect of upholstered chairs essentially consists of an increase in absorption at low frequencies, whereas at frequencies of about 1000 Hz and above there is no significant difference between the absorption of audiences seated on upholstered or on unupholstered chairs.

If the audience absorption is calculated from observed reverberation times of completed halls by application of the reverberation formulae, results are obtained as shown in Fig. VI.15. Hence the absorption area may vary per person at 1000 Hz between 0·63 and 0·2 m^2. These differences must be attributed to the different arrangement of the seats and the different structure of sound fields in the various rooms. Of course we must bear in mind that these values are subject to considerable errors due to the lack of knowledge of the absorption coefficients of the other surfaces and materials; nevertheless, they demonstrate clearly that even nowadays the absorption of an audience is a major source of uncertainty for the prediction of reverberation times.

If there are many listeners in a room or a hall with almost completely rigid walls, the reverberation time is expected to be particularly high at low frequencies; in any case it will be higher than at medium and high frequencies. This long low frequency sound decay is detrimental especially for speech intelligibility but it is also undesirable for many forms of music. It can be avoided or reduced by utilising resonant absorbers tuned to low frequencies. In Section 4 of this chapter we have already discussed the possibility of balancing the reverberation time.

It has been known for a long time that an audience does not only absorb the impinging sound waves, thus reducing the reverberation time of the room, but it also attenuates the sound waves propagating parallel to the audience. This effect is actually observed along each absorbent surface and is due to some sort of diffraction which partially directs the sound waves

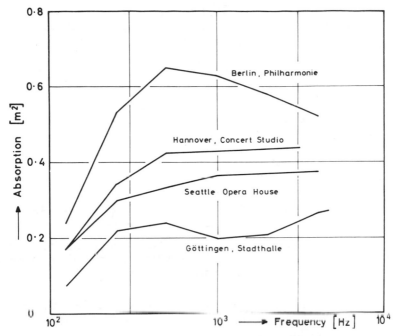

Fig. VI.15. Apparent audience absorption in several halls in square metres per seat, estimated from observed reverberation times.

into the absorbent material. In an auditorium the attenuation of the directly received sound in excess of eqn (I.19) depends strongly on the way in which the audience is seated. Free field measurements of sound propagation parallel to an audience have shown that a pronounced drop in the pressure level occurs over the very first rows of listeners at frequencies of 1000 Hz and more, if the listeners are seated one behind the other.[8]

Quite different results were obtained by more realistic measurements in concert halls performed with tone bursts on a model scale as well as in real halls.[9,10] They indicated that there is strong selective attenuation with a maximum in the range from about 100 to 200 Hz. A typical result is presented in Fig. VI.16, which plots the transmission characteristics of the direct sound as a function of frequency. In other halls somewhat different curves have been obtained. However, they all have in common the fact that the attenuation has a pronounced maximum in the low frequency range, which seems to be caused by a vertical resonance in the gaps between the seating rows. Accordingly, the amount of attenuation is not greatly

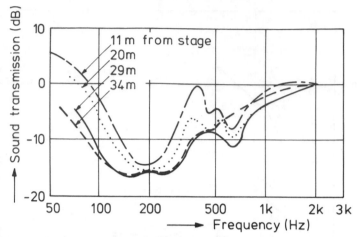

Fig. VI.16. Transmission characteristics of the direct sound, measured at various seats of the main floor in the Boston Symphony Hall.[9] The numbers in the figure indicate the distance from the stage.

influenced by the presence or absence of an audience. Furthermore, it is not only the direct sound but sound reflected from side walls as well which is subject to excess attenuation.

The selective attenuation of low frequency components cannot be considered as an acoustical fault since it takes place in good concert halls as well as in poorer ones (except, of course, in the very first seating rows of main floors and balconies). Obviously it is not the spectral composition of the direct sound and of the very first reflections which is responsible for the tonal balance but rather that of all contributions to the intensity at the listeners' ears.

Listening conditions will be impaired, however, if the sight lines from the listeners to the sound source are obscured by the heads of other listeners sitting in front of them or by other obstacles. Therefore it is important that the seats are arranged in such a way that the listeners are freely exposed to the direct sound and to the reflections arriving from the side walls (*see* also Section IX.1 and IX.2).

VI.8 ANECHOIC ROOMS

In the acoustical design of rooms, sound absorbers mounted on walls and ceilings are usually employed to meet one of the following objectives:

—to adapt the reverberation of the room, for instance of a concert hall, to the type of performances which are to be staged in it;

—to suppress sound reflections from remote walls which might be heard as echoes;

—to reduce the acoustical energy density and hence the sound pressure level in noisy rooms such as factories, for instance.

All these goals can be reached by sound absorbers of the kind described so far, although the elimination of echoes may require particular care, especially when the echo-producing wall shows a concave curvature. Matters are different for spaces which are intended for certain acoustical free field measurements such as the calibration of microphones or the determination of directional patterns of sound sources, etc. The same holds for psychoacoustic experiments. In all these cases the accuracy and the reliability of results would be impaired by the interference of the direct sound with sound components reflected from the boundaries.

One way to avoid reflections—except that from the ground—would be to perform such measurements or experiments in the open air. It has the disadvantage, however, that the experimenter depends on favourable weather conditions, which implies not only the absence of rain but of wind too. Furthermore, the measurements can be affected by ambient noise.

A more convenient way is to use a so-called anechoic room or chamber, all boundaries of which are treated in such a way that virtually no sound reflections are produced by them, at least in the frequency range of interest. How stringent the conditions are which have to be met by the acoustical treatment may be illustrated by a simple example. If all boundaries of an enclosure have an absorption coefficient of 0·90, everybody would agree that the acoustics of this room is extremely 'dry' on account of its very low reverberation time. Nevertheless, the sound pressure level of a wave reflected from a wall would be only 10 dB lower than that of the incident wave! Therefore the usual requirement for the walls of an anechoic room is that the absorption coefficient is at least 0·99 for all angles of incidence. This requirement cannot be fulfilled with plane homogeneous layers of absorbent material; it can only be satisfied with a wall covering which achieves a stepwise or continuous transition · of the characteristic impedance from that of the air to that of a highly lossy material.

In principle, this transition can be accomplished by a porous wall coating whose flow resistance increases in a well-defined way from the surface to the wall. It must be expected, however, that, at grazing sound incidence, the absorption of such a plane layer would be zero on account of total reflection. Therefore it is more usual to achieve the desired transition by choosing a proper geometrical structure of the acoustical treatment than by varying the properties of the material. This can be achieved by pyramids of absorbent material which are mounted onto the walls. An incident sound wave then runs into channels with absorbent walls whose cross-sections steadily decrease in size, i.e. into reversed horns. The apertures at the front of these channels are very well matched to the characteristic impedance of the air and thus no significant reflection will occur.

This is only true, however, as long as the length of the channels, i.e. the thickness of the lining, is at least about one-third of the acoustical wavelength. This condition can easily be fulfilled at high frequencies, but only with great expense at frequencies of 100 Hz or below. For this reason every anechoic room has a certain lower limiting frequency, usually defined as the frequency at which the absorption coefficient of its walls becomes less than 0·99.

As to the production of such a lining, it is easier to utilise wedges instead of pyramids. The wedges must be made of a material with suitable flow resistance and sufficient mechanical solidity, and the front edges of neighbouring wedges or packets of wedges must be arranged at right angles to each other.

Since the floor, as well as the other walls, must be treated in the way just described, a net of steel cables or plastic wires must be installed in order to give access above the floor of the room. The reflections from this net can be safely neglected at audio frequencies.

The lower limiting frequency of an anechoic room can be further reduced by combining the pyramids or wedges with cavity resonators which are located between the latter and the rigid wall.[11] By choosing the apertures and the depths of the resonators carefully, the reflection can be suppressed at frequencies at which substantial reflection would occur without resonators.

In this way, for a particular anechoic room,[12] a lower limiting frequency of 80 Hz could be achieved by lining to a total depth of 1 m. The absorber material has a density of 150 kg/m³ and a flow resistance of about 10^5 kg/m³ s. It is fabricated in wedges of 13 cm × 40 cm base area and 80 cm length, which terminate in rectangular blocks of the same base area and 10 cm length. Between these blocks there are narrow gaps of 1 cm width which run into an air cushion of 10 cm depth between the absorber material and the concrete wall (*see* Fig. VI.17). The latter acts as a resonator volume, the necks of which are the gaps between the wedges. Three wedges with parallel edges are joined together in a packet; neighbouring packets are

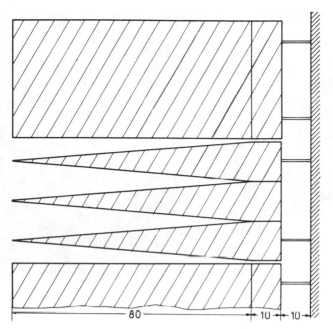

Fig. VI.17. Absorbing wall lining of an anechoic room (dimensions in cm).

rotated by 90° with respect to each other. A view of the interior of this anechoic room is presented in Fig. VI.18.

Another way of achieving a continuous transition towards the wall is to string dense rock wool cubes of increasing size onto wires—like strings of pearls. These wires are stretched in parallel planes in front of the wall.[13] Next to the wall, the cubes merge to form closed layers of rock wool. At the ceiling the absorbent cubes are strung onto wires suspended from the ceiling and, similarly, at floor level they are pushed onto steel rods in a specific way and at prefixed distances. This arrangement seems to be advantageous especially for sound at grazing incidence, since the fraction which is not absorbed is scattered uniformly rather than reflected in certain directions.

Anechoic rooms are usually checked by observing the way in which the sound amplitude decreases when the distance from a sound source is increased. This decrease should take place according to a $1/r$ law to simulate perfect outdoor conditions. In practice, with increasing distance, deviations from this simple law become more and more apparent in the form of random fluctuations. Since these fluctuations are caused by wall reflections,

Fig. VI.18. Anechoic room fitted with 65 loudspeakers for synthesising complex sound fields.

they can be used to evaluate the average absorption coefficient of the walls. Several methods have been worked out to perform these measurements and to determine the wall absorption from their results.[14,15]

REFERENCES

1. Mechel, F. P., *Schallabsorber*. S. Hirzel Verlag, Stuttgart, 1989.
2. Bass, H. E., Bauer, H.-J. & Evans, L. B., *J. Acoust. Soc. America*, **52** (1972) 821.
3. Meyer, E., Kuttruff, H. & Matthaei, H., *Acustica*, **15** (1965) 285.
4. Budach, P., *Zeitschr. Hochfrequenztechn. u. Elektroakust.*, **77** (1968) 5, 134, 164.
5. Kath, U. & Kuhl, W., *Acustica*, **15** (1965) 127.
6. Beranek, L. L., *J. Acoust. Soc. America*, **32** (1960) 661.
7. Meyer, E., Kunstmann, D. & Kuttruff, H., *Acustica*, **14** (1964) 119.
8. Meyer, E., Kuttruff, H. & Schulte, F., *Acustica*, **15** (1964) 175.
9. Schultz, T. J. & Watters, B. G., *J. Acoust. Soc. America*, **36** (1964) 885.
10. Sessler, G. M. & West, J. E., *J. Acoust. Soc. America*, **36** (1964) 1725.
11. Kurtze, G., *Acustica*, **2** (Akust. Beihefte) (1951/2) 104.
12. Meyer, E., Kurtze, G., Severin, H. & Tamm, K., *Acustica*, **3** (1953) 409.
13. Rother, P. & Nutsch, J., Proceedings of the Fourth International Congress on Acoustics, Copenhagen, 1962, paper M44.
14. Diestel, H. G., *Acustica*, **12** (1962) 113.
15. Delany, M. E. & Bazley, E. N., Proceedings of the Seventh International Congress on Acoustics, Budapest, 1971, paper 24A6.

VII

The Subjective Effects of Combined Sound Fields

The preceding chapters were devoted exclusively to the physical side of room acoustics, i.e. the objectively measurable properties of sound fields in a room and to the circumstances which are responsible for their origin. We could be satisfied with this aspect if the only problems at stake were those of noise abatement by reverberation reduction and hence by reduction of the energy density, or if we only had to deal with problems of measuring techniques, which will be discussed in more detail in Chapter VIII.

In most cases, however, the 'final consumer' of acoustics is the listener who listens to a concert, for example, or who attends a lecture or a theatre performance. This listener does not by any means require the reverberation time, at the various frequencies, to have certain values; neither does he insist that the sound energy at his seat should exhibit a certain directional distribution. Instead he expects the room with its 'acoustics' to support the music being performed or to render speech easily intelligible (as far as this depends on acoustic properties). This is true not only in the case of listeners who are personally present in the room under consideration but also when the sounds are transferred to another room, as for instance in broadcasting. Similarly, it does not matter whether the perceived sounds originate from the lips of an orator or from the membrane of a loudspeaker as long as the latter does not attract the listener's attention because of poor tonal quality or other undesirable effects.

Hence we must now focus our attention on the question as to which properties of the sound field are related to certain hearing impressions: whether and how a particular reflection will be perceived, which values of reverberation times at various frequencies are preferable for a particular kind of performance, or which other physical parameters may influence the listener's impression of the acoustics of a room in one way or another. With

171

these considerations we leave the region of purely physical fact and enter
the realm of psychoacoustics.

The previously mentioned questions and similar problems have in the
past been the subject of numerous investigations—experimental investigations—since answers to these problems, which are not affected by the
stigma of pure speculation, can only be obtained by experiments.
Unfortunately their results do not form an unequivocal picture, in contrast
to what we are accustomed to in the purely physical branch of acoustics.
This is ascribed to the very involved physiological properties of our hearing
organ but perhaps even more to the manner in which hearing sensations are
processed by our brain; it can also be attributed to our hearing habits and,
last but not least, to the personal aesthetic sensitivity of the listener—at
least as far as musical productions are concerned. Another reason for our
incomplete knowledge in this field is the great number of sound field
components, which all may influence the subjective hearing impression.
The experimental results which are available to date must therefore be
considered in spite of the fact that many are unrelated or sometimes even
inconsistent, and that every day new and highly surprising insights into
psychoacoustic effects and their significance in room acoustics can be
found.

There are basically two methods which are employed for investigating
the subjective effects of complex sound fields, namely to synthesise sound
fields with well-defined properties in an anechoic room or to judge directly
the acoustical qualities of completed halls, the objective properties of which
are known from previous measurement. Each of these methods has its own
merits and limitations, and each of them has contributed to understanding.
The synthesis or laboratory simulation of sound fields permits easy and
rapid variations of sound field parameters and the immediate comparison
of different field configurations. It is not free, however, from a somewhat
artificial character in that it is impossible to simulate sound fields of real
halls in their full complexity. Instead certain simplifications have to be
made which restrict the application of this method to the investigation of
particular aspects.

The direct judgement of real halls leads to relatively reliable results if
speech intelligibility is the only property in question since the latter can be
determined by counting the number of correctly understood syllables in a
given text. The subjective assessment of the acoustics of concert halls or
opera theatres, however, is affected by great uncertainties, one of which is
the limited memory which impedes the direct comparison of different halls.
Furthermore, two halls differ invariably in more than one respect which

makes it difficult to correlate subjective opinions with acoustical properties such as, for instance, reverberation time. Nevertheless, many important facts have become known in the course of time just by interviewing many concert or opera goers.

Moreover, this has been greatly improved by progress in sound reproduction technique. It allows music samples played in different concert halls to be recorded and then reproduced with high fidelity, either by earphones or by loudspeakers in an anechoic room. Therefore the presented sound signals are realistic in that they contain the full complexity of sound fields in a room and, on the other hand, music motifs transplanted from different halls or from different places of one hall can be compared immediately by the listener. Of course, all electroacoustic components such as microphones, recorders and earphones or loudspeakers must be of excellent quality; moreover, the transmission chain must effect a correct reproduction of the directional structure of the original sound field as far as this is significant for our hearing. The usual stereophonic techniques are not sufficient for this purpose since they are unable to create the illusion of sound arriving from above, from the rear, or from lateral directions. For recording the sounds a carefully designed artificial head with two built-in microphones has to be utilised. If the recorded sound signals are to be re-created by loudspeakers, a special filtering procedure is required which eliminates the signal travelling from the left loudspeaker to the right ear and vice versa. Such a reproduction system as developed by Damaske and Mellert[1] yields a surprisingly realistic impression since the listener perceives sound from exactly the same directions as he would in the original room and thus has also the same acoustical sensation.

Recently another procedure seems very promising, which in one way can be considered as a combination of both aforementioned methods. It is based upon the simulation of sound propagation in rooms with given geometrical and acoustical data (absorption coefficients, for instance) by means of digital computers. Once the binaural impulse response for a particular listening position has been evaluated in this way, it can be converted into a digital filter to which music or speech samples are applied. Then a test person, the ear transfer functions of whom (see Section I.5) must be known beforehand, can listen to music or speech presented in a room which does not exist physically but is in effect stored in the memory of the computer.[2,3] This method is not only very useful for psychoacoustic experiments related to room acoustics but may be as well a powerful tool in the acoustical design of rooms. More will be said on computer simulation of rooms in Section XI.

VII.1 SOME GENERAL REMARKS ON REFLECTIONS AND ECHOES

In the following discussion we shall regard the sound transmission between two points of a room as formally represented by the impulse response of the transmission path. According to eqn (IV.4), this impulse response is composed of numerous repetitions of the original sound signal as it is generated by the sound source. Since our hearing is sensitive to the direction of sound incidence, this description has to be completed by indicating the direction from which each repetition will arrive at the receiving point. As already mentioned in Section VI.2, the various components of the impulse response are not exact replicas of the original sound signal, strictly speaking, because of the frequency dependence of the wall reflectivities. In the following two sections this fact will be disregarded, as has been done in eqn (IV.4).

There are two experiences of the subjective effect of reflected portions of sound which are familiar to everyone: under certain conditions such a reflection can become a distinct 'echo'. In that case it is heard consciously as a repetition of the original signal. This can frequently be observed outdoors with sound reflections from the walls of houses or from the edge of forests. In closed rooms such experiences are less familiar, since the echoes in them are fortunately usually masked by the general reverberation of the room. Whether a reflection will become an echo or not depends on its delay with respect to the direct sound, on its relative strength, on the nature of the sound signal, and on the presence of other reflections which eventually mask the reflection under consideration.

The second common experience concerns our ability to localise sound sources in closed rooms. Although in a room which is not too heavily damped the sum of all reflected sound energies is mostly a multiple of the directly received energy, our hearing can usually localise the direction of the sound source without any difficulty. Obviously it is the sound signal to reach the listener first which subjectively determines the direction from which the sound comes. This fact is called—according to L. Cremer—the 'law of the first wave front'. In Section VII.3 we shall discuss the conditions under which it is valid.

In the following sections the subjective effects of sound fields with increasing complexity will be discussed. It is quite natural that the criteria of judgement become less and less detailed: in a sound field consisting of 1000 reflections we cannot investigate the effect of each reflection separately.

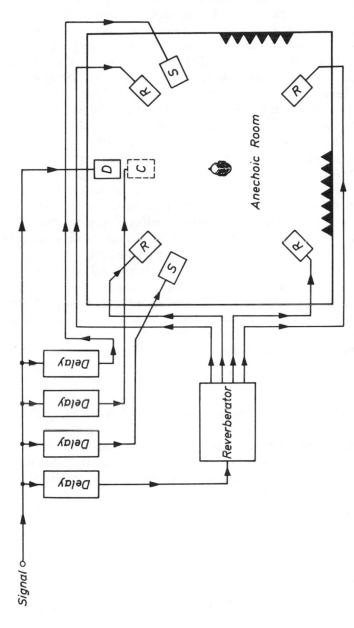

Fig. VII.1.   Schematic representation of simulation of sound fields in an anechoic room. The loudspeakers are denoted by D = direct sound, S = side wall reflections, C = ceiling reflections (elevated), R = reverberation.

Many of the experimental results to be reported on have been obtained with the use of synthetic sound fields, as mentioned earlier: in an anechoic chamber the reflections, as well as the direct sound, are 'simulated' by loudspeakers which have certain positions *vis-à-vis* the test subject; these positions correspond to the desired directional distribution. The differences in the strengths of the various reflections are achieved by attenuators in the electrical lines feeding the loudspeakers, whereas their mutual delay differences are produced by electrical delay units. In the past small signal delays have been achieved by means of certain electrical allpass networks, whereas for longer delay times tape recorders with endless tape loops have been employed on which the signal is recorded and subsequently replayed by suitably arranged reproducing heads. Nowadays such analogue devices are widely replaced with digital delay units which allow a wide variety of delay times without any noticeable signal deterioration. When necessary or desired, the reverberation with prescribed properties can be added to the signals. For this purpose signals are passed through a so-called reverberator, which is also most conveniently realised with digital methods nowadays. (Other methods of reverberating signals will be mentioned in Section X.5.) A typical setup for psychoacoustic experiments related to room acoustics is sketched in Fig. VII.1; it allows simulation of the direct sound, two side wall reflections and one ceiling reflection. The reverberated signal is reproduced by four additional loudspeakers. A more complete and flexible loudspeaker arrangement for similar purposes was shown in Fig. VI.18.

VII.2 THE PERCEPTIBILITY OF SINGLE REFLECTIONS

In this and the next section we consider impulse responses with a very simple structure: they consist of the direct sound component and only one repetition of it, i.e. only one reflection. There are two questions which can be raised in this case, namely:

(1)   Under what condition is a reflection perceivable at all, without regard to the way in which its presence is manifested, and under what condition is it masked by the direct sound?

(2)   Under what condition does the presence of a reflection rate as a disturbance of the listening impression?

In the present section we deal with the first question, postponing the discussion of the second one to the next section. We start with the hypothesis that there is a threshold level separating the levels at which a reflection is audible from those at which it is completely masked. This 'threshold of absolute perceptibility' is a function not only of the time delay with respect to the direct sound but also of the direction of its incidence (and probably of other parameters). Through all the further discussions we assume the listener looking into the direction of direct sound incidence.

To find this threshold two alternate sound field configurations which differ in the presence or absence of a specified reflection are presented to test persons who have to decide whether they notice a difference or not. (One has to make sure, of course, that the test subjects do not know beforehand to which configuration they are listening at a given moment.) The answers of the subjects are evaluated statistically; the level at which 50% of the answers are positive is regarded as the threshold of absolute perceptibility.

For speech with a level of 70 dB, and for frontal incidence of the direct sound as well as of the reflected component, this threshold is given by

$$\Delta L \approx -0.6 t_0 - 8 \quad \text{decibels} \tag{VII.1}$$

where ΔL is the pressure level of the reflected sound signal relative to the sound pressure of the direct sound and t_0 is the time delay in milliseconds. For an example take a reflection delayed by 60 ms with respect to the direct sound. According to eqn (VII.1) it is audible even when its level is lower by 40 dB than that of the direct signal.

Figure VII.2 plots for three different signals (continuous speech, a short syllable and a white noise pulse with a duration of 50 ms) the thresholds of absolute perceptibility of a reflection delayed by 50 ms as a function of the angle under which the reflection arrives. (The investigated directions have been restricted to a horizontal plane.) It is evident to which extent the thresholds depend on the type of sound signal. In any case, however, the masking effect of the direct sound is most pronounced at equal directions or, in other words, our hearing is more sensitive to reflections arriving from lateral directions than to those arriving from the front or the rear. It should be added that reflections arriving from above are also masked more effectively by the direct sound than are lateral reflections.

If the sound signal is not speech but music, our hearing is generally much less sensitive to reflections. This is the general result of investigations carried out by Schubert,[5] who measured the threshold with various music motifs. One of his typical results is presented in Fig. VII.3, which plots the average threshold taken over six different music samples. With increasing delay time it falls much less rapidly than according to eqn (VII.1); its maximum slope is about -0.13 dB/ms. As with speech, the threshold is

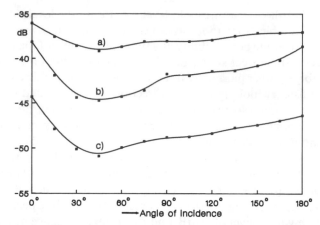

Fig. VII.2. Threshold of absolute perceptibility of a reflection with 50 ms delay, obtained with (a) continuous speech, (b) a short syllable, (c) noise pulses of 50 ms duration. Abscissa is the horizontal angle at which the reflection arrives. The direct signal arrives from the front at a level of 75 dB (after Burgtorf and Oehlschlägel[4]).

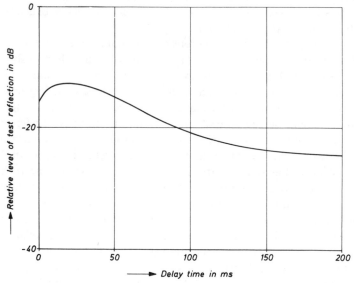

Fig. VII.3. Threshold of absolute perceptibility of a delayed reflection as a function of delay time. The threshold is an average taken over six different music samples (frontal incidence of reflection).

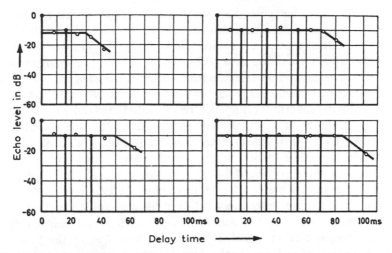

Fig. VII.4. Threshold of absolute perceptibility of a delayed signal (reflection) being added to a sound field consisting of direct sound plus one, two, three of four reflections at fixed delay times and relative levels, which are denoted by vertical lines. The original sound signal is speech. All sound components arriving from the front.

noticeably lower for reflections arriving from lateral directions than with frontal incidence. Furthermore, added reverberation renders the detection of a reflection more difficult. Obviously reverberated sound components cause additional masking, at least with continuous sound signals.

For more than one reflection the number of parameters to be varied increases rapidly. Fortunately each additional reflection does not create a completely new situation for our hearing. This is demonstrated in Fig. VII.4, which shows the absolute threshold for a variable reflection which is added to a primary sound field consisting of one, two, three or four reflections at fixed delay times.[6] In this case all the reflections arrive from the same direction as the direct sound. The fixed reflections are indicated as vertical lines over the delay times belonging to them; their heights are a measure of the strength of the reflections. If all the reflections—the fixed ones as well as the variable one—and the direct sound arrive from different directions, the thresholds are different from those of Fig. VII.4 in that they immediately begin to fall and then jump back to the initial value at the delay time of one of the fixed reflections.

Apart from the thresholds of perceptibility, the differential thresholds for reflections are also of great interest. They have been measured by Reichardt

and Schmidt[7] utilising synthetic sound fields which simulated the direct
sound, two lateral 'wall reflections' (delay time 35 ms), a 'ceiling reflection'
(delay time 60 ms) and reverberation (delay of the beginning by about
100 ms) with a reverberation time of 2 s (*see* Fig. VII.1). The loudspeakers
for the direct sound and the lateral reflections appeared between $\pm 20°$ and
$\pm 60°$, respectively; the ceiling reflection arrived at an elevation angle of 60°.
The four loudspeakers emitting the reverberated signal had elevation
angles of 20° and lateral angles of $\pm 45°$ and $\pm 135°$; the signal was
reverberated by a reverberation plate (compare Section X.5). A short piece
of music, lasting only a few seconds, was used as a test signal. The absolute
differential threshold (i.e. not taking into account the way in which the
difference became audible) was found to be about ± 1.5 dB; it was larger for
very low or very high reflection levels and likewise for reflections with
reduced frequency bandwidth. Similarly the threshold was slightly larger
for the ceiling reflection, which is along the same line as the findings
previously reported. Changes in the delay time had also been investigated
but these could only be detected with considerable uncertainty.

VII.3 ECHOES AND COLOURATION

A reflection which is perceived at all does not necessarily reach the
consciousness of a listener. At low levels it manifests itself only by an
increase of loudness of the total sound signal, by a change in timbre, or by
an increase of the apparent size of the sound source. But at higher levels a
reflection can be heard as a separate event, i.e. as a repetition of the original
sound signal. This effect is commonly known as 'echo', as already
mentioned in Section VII.1. But what outdoors usually appears as an
interesting experience may be rather unpleasant in a concert hall or in a
lecture room in that it distracts the listeners' attention. In severe cases an
echo may severely reduce our enjoyment of music or impair the
intelligibility of speech, since subsequent speech sounds or syllables are
mixed up and the text is confused.

In the following the term 'echo' will be used for any sound reflection
which is subjectively noticeable as a temporal or spatially separated
repetition of the original sound signal, and we are discussing the conditions
under which a reflection will be an echo. Thus we are taking up again the
second question raised at the outset of the foregoing section.

From his outdoor experience the reader may know that the echo
produced by sound reflection from a house front, etc., disappears when he

approaches the reflecting wall and when his distance from it becomes less than about 10 m, although the wall still reflects the sound. Obviously it is the reduction of the delay time between the primary sound and its repetition which makes the echo vanish. This shows that our hearing has only a restricted ability to resolve succeeding acoustical events, a fact which is sometimes attributed to some kind of 'inertia' of hearing. Like the absolute threshold of perceptibility, however, the echo disturbance depends not only on the delay of the repetition but also on its relative strength, its direction, on the type of sound signal, on the presence of additional components in the impulse response and other circumstances.

Systematic experiments to find the critical echo level of reflections are performed in much the same way as those for investigating the threshold of absolute perceptibility, but with a different instruction given to the test subjects. It is clear that there is more ambiguity in fixing the critical echo levels than in establishing the absolute perception threshold since an event which is considered as disturbing by one person may be found quite tolerable by others.

Classical experiments of this kind were carried out as early as 1950 by Haas[8] using continuous speech as a primary sound signal. This signal was presented by two loudspeakers: the input signal of one of them could be attenuated (or amplified) and delayed with respect to the other.

Figure VII.5 shows one of Haas' typical results. It plots the percentage of

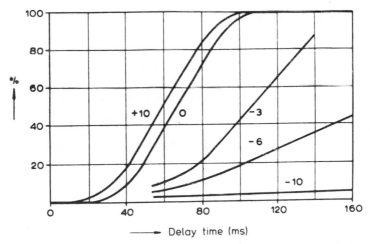

Fig. VII.5.   Percentage of listeners disturbed by a delayed speech signal. Speaking rate is 5·3 syllables per second. The relative echo levels (in dB) are indicated by numbers next to the curves.

subjects who felt disturbed by an echo of given relative level as a function of the time delay between the undelayed signal (or primary sound) and the delayed one (reflection). The numbers next to the curves indicate the level of the artificial reflection in dB relative to that of the primary sound. The rate of speech was 5·3 syllables per second; the listening room had a reverberation time of 0·8 s. At a delay time of 80 ms, for instance, only about 20% of the observers felt irritated by the presence of a reflection with a relative level of −3 dB, but the percentage was more than 80% when the level was +10 dB.

Table VII.1
Critical Echo Delays at Equal Levels of Direct Sound and Reflection

Reverberation time of listening room (s)	Speaking rate (syllables/s)	Critical delay time (ms)
0	5·3	43
0·8	5·3	68
1·6	5·3	78
0·8	3·5	93
0·8	5·3	68
0·8	7·4	41

Analogue results have been obtained for different speaking rates or reverberation times of the listening room. They are summarised in Table VII.1. The numbers in the last column denote the median values of the delay time distributions, i.e. the delay times in milliseconds at which the curves analogue to those of Fig. VII.5 cross the 50% line.

Muncey et al.[9] have performed similar experiments for speech as well as for various kinds of music. As could be expected, these investigations clearly showed that our hearing is less sensitive to echoes in music than in speech. The reason for this is obviously the fact that music does not have to be 'understood' in the same sense as speech. The annoyance of echoes in very slow music, as for example organ music, is particularly low. In Fig. VII.6 the critical echo level (50% level) for fast string music and organ music is plotted as a function of time delay.

The most striking result of all these experiments can be seen most clearly from Fig. VII.5: if the relative echo level is raised from 0 to +10 dB, there is only a small change in the percentage of observers feeling disturbed by the reflected sound signal. Hence no disturbance is expected to occur for a

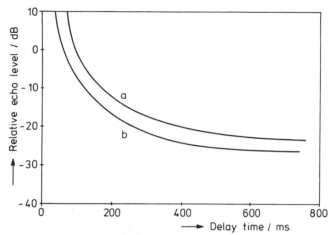

Fig. VII.6.   Critical echo level (re-direct sound pressure) as a function of delay time for (a) organ music and (b) string music.

reflection with time delay of, say, 20 ms even if its energy is ten times the energy of the direct sound. This finding is frequently referred to as 'Haas effect' and has important applications in the design of public address systems.

Careful investigations into the above-mentioned Haas effect and of related phenomena have been performed by Meyer and Schodder.[10] In order to restrict the range of possible judgements, the test subjects were not asked to indicate the level at which they were disturbed by an echo; instead they had to indicate the level at which they heard both the delayed signal and the undelayed one equally loudly. Since in these tests the undelayed signal reached the test subject from the front, the delayed one from a lateral angle of 90°, the test subjects could also be asked to indicate the echo level at which the sound seemed to arrive from halfway between both directions. Both criteria of judgement led to the same results. One of them is shown in Fig. VII.7, where the critical level difference between primary sound and reflection is plotted as a function of the delay time. It virtually agrees with the test results obtained by Haas and renders them somewhat more precise. For our hearing sensation the primary sound determines the impression of direction even when the reflection—provided it has a suitable delay time— is stronger by up to 10·5 dB. If the reflection is split up into several small reflections of equal strengths and with successive mutual delay times of 2·5 ms, leaving constant the total reflection energy, the curve shown in Fig. VII.7 is shifted upwards by another 2·5 dB at maximum.

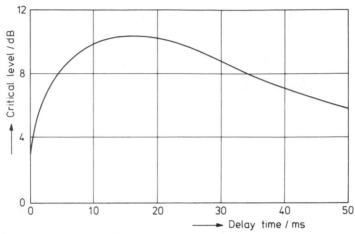

Fig. VII.7. Critical level difference between echo and undelayed signal, resulting in apparently equal loudness of both signals (speech). Abscissa is the delay time.

This result shows that many small reflections separated by short time intervals of the order of milliseconds cause about the same disturbance as one single reflection provided the total reflected energy and the (centre) delay time are the same for both configurations.

These results can be summarised in the following statement: in room acoustics the law of the first wave front can be considered to be valid in general. Exceptions, i.e. erroneous localisations and reflections which are audible as echoes, will occur only in special situations, as for example when most of the room boundaries, except for a few remote portions of wall, are lined with an absorbent material or when certain portions of wall are concavely curved and hence produce reflections of more than average intensity by focusing the sound.

The superposition of a strong isolated reflection onto the direct sound can cause another undesirable effect, especially with music, namely a 'colouration', i.e. a characteristic change of timbre. The same is true for a regular, i.e. equidistant, succession of reflections.

If the impulse response $g_1(t)$ of a room were to consist only of the direct sound and one reflection which is weaker by a factor of q,

$$g_1(t) = \delta(t) + q\delta(t - t_0) \tag{VII.2}$$

the corresponding squared absolute value of its Fourier transform is given according to eqn (I.39) by

$$|G_1(f)|^2 = |1 + q \exp(2\pi i f t_0)|^2 = 1 + q^2 + 2q \cos(2\pi f t_0) \tag{VII.3}$$

This is the squared transfer function of a comb filter with a ratio of maximum to minimum of $(1+q)^2/(1-q)^2$; the separation of adjacent maxima is $1/t_0$. An infinite and regular succession of reflections would be given by

$$g_2(t) = \sum_{n=0}^{\infty} q^n \delta(t - nt_0) \qquad \text{(VII.4)}$$

and its squared absolute spectrum

$$|G_2(f)|^2 = [1 + q^2 - 2q \cos(2\pi f t_0)]^{-1} \qquad \text{(VII.5)}$$

with the same distance of the maxima and the same relative 'roughness' as before. However, the peaks are much sharper here than with a single reflection, except for $q \ll 1$ (*see* Fig. VII.8).

Whether such a comb filter—and likewise a room with similar impulse response—will produce audible colourations or not depends on the delay time t_0 and on the relative heights of the maxima.[11] The absolute threshold for audible colourations rises as the delay time or distance t_0 increases, i.e. when the distance $1/t_0$ between subsequent maxima on the frequency axis is smaller (see Fig. VII.9). This finding makes understandable why the very high but closely spaced irregularities of room frequency curves do not cause audible colourations.

If t_0 exceeds a certain value, say 25 ms or so, the regularity of impulse responses does not appear subjectively as colouration, i.e. of changes of the

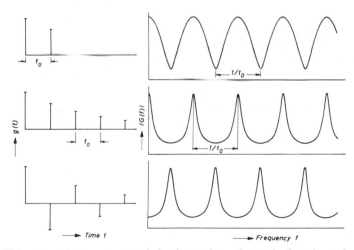

Fig. VII.8. Impulse responses and absolute values of transfer functions of various comb filters ($q = 0.7$).

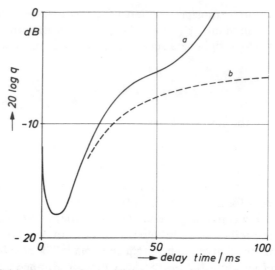

Fig. VII.9. Critical values of q resulting in just audible colouration of white noise passed through (a) comb filter according to eqn (VII.3) and (b) comb filter according to eqn (VII.5).

timbre of sound, but rather the sounds have a rough character, which means that we become aware of the regular repetitions of the signal as a phenomenon occurring in the time domain (echo or flutter echo). This is because our ear is not just a sort of frequency analyser but is also sensitive to the temporal structure of the sound signals. Or more correctly expressed: our hearing performs a short-time spectral analysis.

In Section VIII.4 we shall discuss a criterion for the perceptibility of sound colouration or of a flutter echo which is applicable to the measuring techniques and which is based on thresholds of the kind shown in Fig. VII.9.

So far this discussion has been restricted to the somewhat artificial case that the sound field consists of the primary or direct sound followed by just one single repetition of the sound signal. As we know from Chapter IV, however, impulse responses of most real rooms have a much more complicated structure, and it is clear that the presence of numerous reflections must influence the way we perceive one of them in particular. On the other hand, from a practical point of view it would be desirable to have a criterion to indicate whether a certain peak in a measured impulse response or 'reflectogram' (*see*, for instance, Fig. VIII.7 or VIII.8) hints at an audible echo and should be removed by suitable constructive measures.

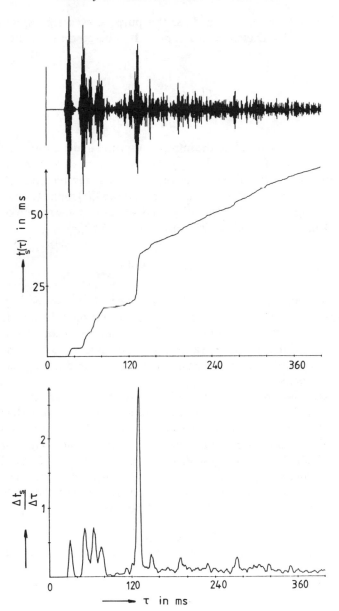

Fig. VII.10.   First 400 ms of an impulse, response build-up function of the first moment of $|g(t)|^n$ (with $n = 2$) and running difference quotient $\Delta t_s(\tau)/\Delta\tau$ (with $\Delta\tau = 5$ ms). *EC* is 2·75 in this example.

Out of several criteria intended for this purpose we are going to describe
that proposed by Dietsch and Kraak.[12] It is based on the ratio

$$t_s(\tau) = \frac{\int_0^\tau |g(t)|^n t \, dt}{\int_0^\tau |g(t)|^n \, dt} \qquad\qquad (VII.6)$$

with $g(t)$ denoting as before the impulse response under consideration. $t_s(\tau)$
is a monotonous function of τ approaching a certain limiting value $t_s =$
$t_s(\infty)$ for $\tau \to \infty$. This value is some kind of 'centre of gravity time';[13] indeed,
t_s is the first moment of $[g(t)]^n$, and the function $t_s(\tau)$ indicates its temporal
build-up (Fig. VII.10). The quantity used for rating the strength of an echo
is based upon the running difference quotient of $t_s(\tau)$:

$$EC = \text{maximum of } \frac{\Delta t_s(\tau)}{\Delta \tau} \qquad\qquad (VII.7)$$

where $\Delta \tau$ can be adapted to the character of the sound signal. The
dependence of the echo criterion EC on the directional distribution of the
various reflections is accounted for by recording two impulse responses
with an artificial head (i.e. with a dummy head made of plastic or wood with
microphones in the place of the human ear drums) and adding the energies
of both responses.

By numerous subjective tests, both with synthetic sound fields and in real
halls, the authors referred to determined not only suitable values for the
exponent n and for $\Delta \tau$ but also the critical values EC_{crit}, which must not be
exceeded to ensure that not more than 50% of the listeners will hear an echo
(Table VII.2). (The 10% thresholds are slightly lower.) It should be noted
that particularly high frequency spectral components may cause echo
disturbances. For practical purposes, however, it seems sufficient to employ
test signals with a bandwidth of 1 or 2 octaves.

Table VII.2
Characteristic Data for the Echo Criterion of Dietsch and Kraak[12]

Sound signal	n	τ (ms)	EC_{crit}	Bandwidth of test signal (Hz)
Speech	2/3	9	1·0	700–1 400
Music	1	14	1·8	700–2 800

VII.4 EARLY ENERGY AND ITS RELATION TO SPEECH INTELLIGIBILITY AND TO CLARITY

The occurrence of echoes is not the only factor which can impair speech intelligibility; another one is too long a sound decay which is brought about by the great number of sound reflections with relatively long delay times following each other in closer and closer succession. Of course, it would be hopeless to consider each of them separately in order to assess its effect on the listening conditions. Instead several authors have proposed somewhat coarser criteria which compare different parts of the impulse response with each other in order to arrive at objective measures for the intelligibility of speech, for the 'clarity' or 'transparency' of the perceived sounds and similar categories. Such a procedure is not just an expedient dictated by the limitations of time and facilities but is justified by the limited ability of our hearing to distinguish all the countless repeated sound signals.

In the preceding sections it was shown that a reflection is not perceived subjectively as something separate from the direct sound as long as its delay does not exceed a certain limit. Its only effect is to make the sound source appear somewhat more extended and to increase the apparent loudness of the direct sound. Since such reflections give support to the sound source they are considered useful.

Reflections which arrive at the listener with longer delays are noticed as echoes in unfavourable cases; in favourable cases they contribute to the reverberation of the room. Since any reverberation impairs the intelligibility of speech because it causes speech sounds and syllables to merge, more delayed reflections are considered to be detrimental from the viewpoint of speech transmission. From our everyday experience with outdoor echoes, but even more precisely from Haas' results (see Fig. VII.5) and similar findings, it can be concluded that the critical delay time separating useful from detrimental reflections is somewhere in the range from 50 to 100 ms.

Most of the following criteria compare the energy conveyed in useful reflections, including that of the direct sound with the energy contained in the remaining ones. To validate them it is necessary to determine the speech intelligibility directly. This can be done in the following way. A sequence of meaningless syllables (so-called 'logatoms') is read aloud in the environment under test. To obtain representative results it is advisable to use phonetically balanced material (from so-called PB lists) for this purpose, i.e. sets of syllables in which initial consonants, vowels and final consonants are properly distributed. Listeners placed at various positions are asked to write down what they have heard. The percentage of syllables which have been correctly understood is considered to be a relatively reliable measure of speech intelligibility, called 'syllable intelligibility'.

One of the earliest attempts to define an objective criterion of what may be called the distinctness of sound, derived from the impulse response, is due to Thiele,[14] who named it 'definition' (originally 'Deutlichkeit'):

$$D = \frac{\displaystyle\int_0^{50\,\mathrm{ms}} [g(t)]^2\,\mathrm{d}t}{\displaystyle\int_0^{\infty} [g(t)]^2\,\mathrm{d}t}\ 100\% \qquad\qquad (\mathrm{VII.8})$$

The lower limit of integration $t = 0$ coincides with the arrival of the direct sound at the point of observation.

The relation between D and the syllable intelligibility has been established by Boré,[15] who performed subjective tests in different rooms, both with and without a public address system in operation. As test signals for the impulse response he used tone impulses with a duration of 20 ms; the final value of the 'definition' was obtained by a somewhat involved averaging process over the frequency range 340–3500 Hz. The results are shown in Fig. VII.11;

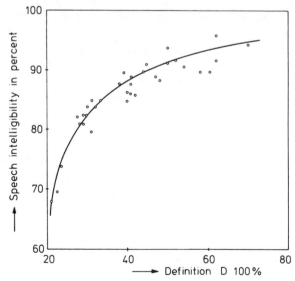

Fig. VII.11. Relation between syllable intelligibility and 'definition'.

they indicate that there is indeed a good correlation between the intelligibility and the 'definition' D.

A quantity which is formally similar to 'definition' but intended to characterise the transparency of music in a concert hall is the 'clarity index' C as introduced by Reichardt et al.[16] It is defined by

$$C = 10 \log_{10} \left\{ \frac{\displaystyle\int_0^{80\,\mathrm{ms}} [g(t)]^2 \, dt}{\displaystyle\int_{80\,\mathrm{ms}}^{\infty} [g(t)]^2 \, dt} \right\} \quad \mathrm{dB} \tag{VII.9}$$

The higher limit of delay time (80 ms compared with 50 ms) makes allowance for the fact that with music a reflection is less detectable than it is with speech signals. By subjective tests with synthetic sound fields these authors have determined the values of C preferred for the presentation of various styles of orchestral music. They found that $C = 0\,\mathrm{dB}$ indicates that the subjective clarity is sufficient even for fast musical passages, whereas a value of $C = -3\,\mathrm{dB}$ seems to be still tolerable.

The assumption of a sharp delay limit separating useful from non-useful reflections is certainly a crude approximation to the way in which repetitions of sound signals are processed by our hearing. From a practical point of view it has the unfavourable effect that in critical cases a small change of the arrival time of a strong reflection may result in a significant change of D or C. Therefore several authors have proposed a gradual transition from useful to detrimental reflections by calculating the useful energy with a continuous weighting function $a(t)$:

$$E_E = \int_0^{\infty} a(t)[g(t)]^2 \, dt \tag{VII.10}$$

For a linear transition $a(t)$ is given by

$$a(t) = \begin{cases} 1 & \text{for } 0 \le t < t_1 \\ \dfrac{t_2 - t}{t_2 - t_1} & \text{for } t_1 \le t \le t_2 \\ 0 & \text{for } t > t_2 \end{cases} \tag{VII.10a}$$

Based on the results of very detailed experimental studies, Niese[17] recommends use of $t_1 = 17$ ms and $t_2 = 33$ ms in eqn (VII.10a). He places the 'useful sound' calculated (or measured) according to this prescription in

contrast with the 'detrimental sound' E_{NE} obtained by integrating the
reflection energies which are in excess of a certain idealised decay curve and
which are delayed by more than 33 ms. This decay curve is given by

$$h(t) = \begin{cases} 0 & \text{for } 0 < t < 30\,\text{ms} \\ \left(\dfrac{2E_E}{30\,\text{ms}}\right)^{1/2} \exp\left[\dfrac{-6\cdot9(t - 30\,\text{ms})}{T}\right] & \text{for } t > 30\,\text{ms} \end{cases}$$

(VII.11)

T being the actual reverberation time in seconds of the room under
consideration. This definition is based on the consideration that
reverberation itself is not an acoustical fault in a room. (This is probably a
controversial point, at least as far as speech intelligibility is concerned.)
Using the quantities defined in the described way, the 'echo degree' is
calculated by

$$\varepsilon = \frac{E_{NE}}{E_E + E_{NE}}$$

(VII.12)

Niese compared the 'definition' D and the 'echo degree' ε with the
subjective syllable intelligibility determined by the method described above
for numerous seats in several halls. He found that the 'echo degree' is
somewhat better correlated to syllable intelligibility than Thiele's
'definition'. This advantage has to be paid for, on the other hand, by more
complicated evaluation.

Lochner and Burger[18] also used eqns (VII.10) and (VII.10a) to calculate
the useful energy portion of the impulse response, but with $t_1 = 35$ ms and
$t_2 = 95$ ms. In contrast to Niese, however, they considered all reflections
with delay times exceeding 95 ms as detrimental, i.e. as contributing to the
noise level

$$E_{NE} = \int_{95\,\text{ms}}^{\infty} [g(t)]^2 \, dt$$

(VII.13)

The level difference of both energy portions is regarded as some sort of
'signal-to-noise ratio':

$$\Delta L_{LB} = 10 \log (E_E / E_{NE}) \quad \text{dB}$$

(VII.14)

To test the significance of their criterion Lochner and Burger have
measured the syllable intelligibility as a function of the speech level and the
noise level, in the first instance without specifying the origin of the noise but
under the presupposition that both noise and speech have the same

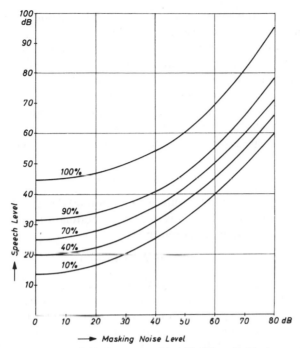

Fig. VII.12. Speech intelligibility (rate of intelligible syllables) as a function of speech level and noise level.

spectrum. Their result is presented in Fig. VII.12 in the form of curves of constant intelligibility. If the noise energy is identified with the energy of late reflections given by eqn (VII.13), the speech intelligibility can be directly determined from the absolute speech level and from ΔL_{LB} using Fig. VII.12. Let ΔL_{LB} as obtained from $g(t)$ have the value of -5 dB, for instance. The useful speech level at the same place is 60 dB (ordinate of Fig. VII.12), accordingly the 'noise' level is 65 dB (abscissa), and from Fig. VII.12 the syllable intelligibility can be seen to be about 90%. It is clear that Lochner and Burger's 'signal-to-noise ratio' is only one component of speech intelligibility, the other one is speech level at the listener's ears. The same holds probably as well for the 'definition' and for the 'echo degree'.

Still another criterion for the intelligibility of speech and the transparency of music to be derived from the impulse response was proposed by Kürer:[13] the 'centre of gravity time' t_s already introduced in the preceding section. It is obtained from eqn (VII.6) by setting $\tau = \infty$ and

$n = 2$. Obviously a reflection with given strength contributes the more to t_s the longer it is delayed with respect to the direct sound. High transparency or intelligibility is expected to be associated with low values of t_s, which has been proven by comparing measured values of t_s with intelligibility scores.

Quite a different approach to rate the speech intelligibility from objective sound field data is due to Houtgast and Steeneken.[19] Its basis is not the impulse response of a particular transmission path but the so-called 'modulation transfer function' (MTF). Suppose a sound source produces some stationary sound signal, the power of which is modulated sinusoidally according to

$$P(t) = P_0(1 + \cos \Omega t) \qquad \text{(VII.15)}$$

then the intensity in any observation point is modulated with the same angular frequency Ω but the relative depth of modulation is reduced by a factor $m < 1$, called the modulation index:

$$I(t) = I_0\{1 + m \cos [\Omega(t - t_0)]\} \qquad \text{(VII.16)}$$

with t_0 denoting some delay (*see* Fig. VII.13). One reason for the reduction of the modulation index is the smearing effect of reverberation. Let, for instance, the sound decay of the room be given by a simple exponential law, i.e. insert eqn (VII.15) into eqn (V.34), then the modulation index or, as we may call it now, the modulation transfer function turns out to be

$$m(\Omega) = \left[1 + \left(\frac{\Omega T}{13 \cdot 8}\right)^2\right]^{-1/2} \qquad \text{(VII.17)}$$

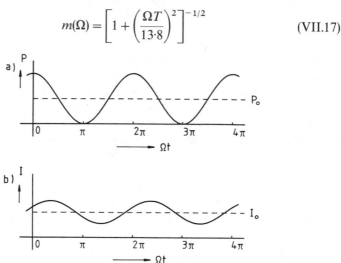

Fig. VII.13. Flattening effect of transmission in a room on the modulation of sound signals: (a) power of original sound signal; (b) received intensity.

with T denoting the reverberation time. Another reason may be ambient noise interfering with the test signal.

In general, the MTF will be much more complicated than according to eqn (VII.17); furthermore, it is not only a function of the modulation frequency Ω but depends also on the type of stationary signal the sound source emits, for instance on the sound frequency ω if the source generates a sine wave. Since the complete MTF describes in a fairly general way the flattening of power fluctuations by reverberation and noise, it can be applied to the inherent level fluctuations of speech and to the way they are affected by transmission in a particular room. Houtgast and Steeneken have developed a procedure to convert MTF data measured in seven octave bands and at several modulation frequencies into one single figure of merit, which they called the 'speech transmission index' (STI). This conversion involves averaging over a certain range of modulation frequencies; furthermore, it makes allowance for the different contributions of the various frequency bands to speech quality and also for the mutual masking between adjacent frequency bands occurring in our hearing organ. Finally, they have shown in numerous experiments that the STI is very closely related to the speech intelligibility determined with various types of speech signals (Fig. VII.14).

We conclude this section with a few observations which apply more or less to all the above criteria. Firstly, it is evident that they are highly

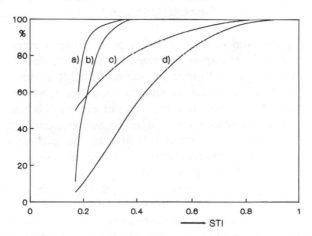

Fig. VII.14. Relation between STI and the scores of intelligibility, obtained with: (a) numbers and spell alphabet; (b) short sentences; (c) diagnostic rhyme test; (d) logatoms (after Houtgast and Steeneken[19]).

correlated among each other. If, for example, a particular impulse response is associated with a short 'centre of gravity time' t_s, its evaluation according to eqn (VII.8) will yield a high value of 'definition' D and vice versa. Therefore there is no point in measuring many or all of them in order to collect as much information as possible.

Secondly, if the sound decay in the room under consideration would strictly obey an exponential law according to eqn (IV.9) or (V.21), all the parameters defined above could be directly expressed by the reverberation time, as has already been done in eqn (VII.17). Hence they would not yield any information beyond the reverberation time. In real situations, however, the exponential law is a useful but nevertheless crude approximation to a much more complicated process. Especially in its early portions an impulse response is far from being a smooth function of time; furthermore, the pattern of reflections (*see*, for example, Fig. IV.7) usually varies from one observation point to the other, accordingly these parameters too may vary over a wide range within one hall and are quite sensitive to geometrical and acoustical details of a room. Therefore they are well suited to describe differences of listening conditions at different seats in a hall whereas the reverberation time does not significantly depend on the place where it has been measured.

VII.5 EARLY LATERAL ENERGY AND ITS RELATION TO 'SPACIOUSNESS'

The preceding discussions of this chapter predominantly referred to the temporal structure of the impulse response of a room and to the subjective consequences associated with them. A subjective effect not mentioned so far, which is nevertheless of utmost importance, is the acoustical 'sensation of space' which a listener usually experiences in a room. It is caused by the fact that the sound in a closed room reaches the listener from quite different directions and that our hearing is not able to locate these directions separately but has to process them into an overall impression, namely the mentioned sensation of feeling of space.

It is quite evident that this sensation is not achieved just by reverberation itself; if music with reverberation is replayed through a single loudspeaker in a relatively 'dry' environment, it never suggests acoustically the illusion of being in a room of some size, no matter if the reverberation time is long or short. Likewise, if the music is replayed through several loudspeakers which are placed at equal distance but in different directions seen from the listener, and which are fed by identical signals, the situation is not improved to any great extent: a so-called 'phantom sound source' is formed, which means that all the sound seems to arrive from a single imaginary sound source which can easily be located and which seems, at best, somewhat more extended than a single loudspeaker. The same effect occurs if a great number of loudspeakers in an anechoic room are arranged in a hemisphere (*see* Fig. VI.18) and are connected to the same signal source. A listener in the centre of the hemisphere does not perceive a 'spacious' or 'subjectively diffuse' sound field but instead he perceives a phantom sound source immediately overhead. Even the usual two-channel stereophony employing two similar loudspeaker signals, which differ in a certain way from each other, cannot provide a full acoustical impression of space since the apparent directions of sound incidence remain restricted to the region between both loudspeakers.

The 'sensation of space' has attracted the interest of acoustic researchers for many years, but only since the late 1960s has real progress been made in finding the cause of this subjective property of sound fields. The different authors used expressions like 'spatial responsiveness', 'spatial impression', 'ambience', 'apparent source width', 'subjective diffusion', 'Räumlichkeit', 'spaciousness' and others to circumscribe this sensation. Assuming that all these verbal descriptions are to signify the same thing, we shall prefer the term 'spaciousness' in the following.

For a long time it was common belief among acousticians that spaciousness was a direct function of the uniformity of the directional distribution (*see* Section IV.4) in a sound field: the higher the diffusion, the higher the degree of spaciousness. This belief originated from the fact that many old and highly renowned concert halls are decorated with statuettes, pillars, coffered ceilings and other projections which supposedly reflect the sound rather in a diffuse manner than specularly.

It was the introduction of synthetic sound fields as a research tool which led to the insight that the uniformity of the stationary directional distribution is not the primary cause of spaciousness. Indeed a spatial listening impression can be brought about by a few reflections only, provided they satisfy the following conditions:

(a)   the reflected sound signals have to be mutually incoherent;
(b)   their intensities must surpass a certain threshold (*see* Section VII.2);
(c)   their delay times with respect to the direct sound must not exceed 100 ms, i.e. they have to be 'early reflections';
(d)   they must arrive from lateral directions.

Regarding the condition (a), a few remarks on coherence may be in order. Two signals are called coherent if they can interfere with each other, i.e. if they can intensify or cancel each other depending on their mutual phase relations. For instance, noise signals taken from different noise sources are incoherent, but two sine signals of the same frequency are coherent.

Mathematically, the degree of coherence can be expressed by the correlation coefficient or correlation factor ψ: let $p_1(t)$ and $p_2(t)$ denote the sound pressures of two acoustic signals, then

$$\Psi = \frac{\overline{p_1 p_2}}{(\overline{p_1^2} \cdot \overline{p_2^2})^{1/2}} \qquad \text{(VII.18)}$$

(The horizontal dash indicates averaging withh respect to time.) For complete coherence this quantity assumes the value $+1$ or -1 (the second value occurs when both signals are equal but of opposite sign). $\Psi = 0$ is the condition for complete incoherence. (Strictly speaking, $\Psi = 0$ is only a necessary but not a sufficient condition for incoherence. If pure tones are excluded, however, the magnitude of Ψ can be taken as a good measure for the degree of coherence.)

Partially coherent signals can be derived experimentally from an original signal by replaying this signal through a loudspeaker in a fairly reverberant enclosure in which a diffuse sound field is established. The sound signal is picked up again by two microphones being set up at different points in the enclosure. The output signals of the microphones are only partially coherent, the degree of coherence depending on the distance between them (*see* Section VIII.6).

A different and even simpler method for generating partially coherent signals is to delay two identical signals with respect to each other. For if we insert $p_2(t) = p_1(t - \tau)$ into eqn (VII.18), we obtain essentially for Ψ the autocorrelation function of the original signal p_1, defined by eqn (I.33). The value which this function assumes for a given delay time τ depends on the type of signal. If the delay time exceeds a certain value τ_e characteristic for that particular kind of signal (*see* Table I.1), both final signals are virtually incoherent.

The relation between the directional distribution and the mutual coherence in synthetic sound fields on the one hand and the associated subjective impression of spaciousness on the other hand has been investigated by Damaske.[20] He established a reverberant sound field in an anechoic room by utilising four loudspeakers at equal distances from a certain point arranged at an elevation angle of $9°$ (with respect to that point) and lateral angles of $\pm 54°$ and $\pm 126°$, the reference direction being the viewing direction of a test subject seated at the point mentioned. The loudspeakers were fed with partially coherent signals which were obtained in the following way: a primary signal was replayed by loudspeakers in a separate room with a volume of $120\,m^3$ and with a reverberation time of 2 s, and the same signal was picked up again by four microphones arranged in the corners of an (imagined) tetrahedron. The distances between the microphones and hence the mutual coherence of their output signals could be varied over a wide range.

Damaske used a stationary random noise band limited at 250 and 2000 Hz as a test signal; the listeners were asked to indicate the solid angle from which the sound apparently arrived. This solid angle, divided by 2π, can be considered to be a measure of the spatial impression and is plotted in Fig. VII.15 as a function of the correlation coefficient Ψ. With almost incoherent signals the sound source seems to be distributed over more than 70% of the upper hemisphere, and with completely coherent signals the sound seems to arrive from a single direction, as mentioned above. This is only one result out of many similar ones which on the whole justify the condition (a) on page 197.

In practical concert hall situations the incoherence of lateral reflections

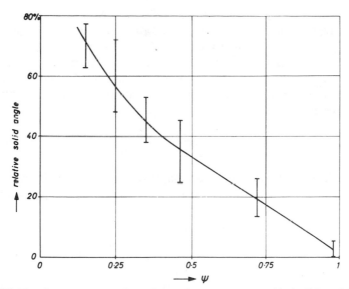

Fig. VII.15. Apparent extension of sound source, measured in (solid angle)/2π, as a function of correlation coefficient Ψ of the various sound field components.

with respect to each other and especially to the direct sound can be assumed to be achieved by their mutual time delays in connection with the broad frequency spectrum of music.

That only the lateral reflections (i.e. not reflections from the front, from overhead or from the rear) contribute to spaciousness has been emphasised especially by Marshall,[21] although it had been observed already by earlier authors.[22] Virtually all the later publications have confirmed this statement. The most extensive investigation at present on early reflections is due to Barron.[23] He found the contribution of a reflection to spaciousness to be independent of the style of music, of the presence or absence of reverberation, and to be almost independent of its time delay in the range 5–80 ms and of the presence of additional reflections. This contribution is proportional to the energy of the reflection and to $\cos \theta$, θ being the angle between the lateral axis through the listener's ears and the direction of sound incidence. Accordingly, an objective measure for the spaciousness of a sound field is the 'early lateral energy fraction', defined by

$$S = \frac{\sum_i' E_i \cos \theta_i}{\sum_i'' E_i (1 - \cos \theta_i)} \qquad (VII.19)$$

The sum in the numerator contains all reflections with delays between 5 and 80 ms; the sum in the denominator embraces the reflections with delays between 0 and 80 ms, thus including the direct sound.

Furthermore, Barron established a relation between S and a subjective scale of spaciousness developed by Reichardt and Schmidt[7] from their measurements on the difference limen for early reflections. This relation can be expressed by

$$\text{subjective spaciousness} = \frac{14 \cdot 5 S}{1 + S} - 0 \cdot 7 \quad \text{units} \qquad (VII.20)$$

It is important to note, however, that this formula is valid only for a total music level of about 70 dB, since Reichardt and Schmidt's experiments have been carried out at about this level. Indeed Keet[24] has found a strong dependence of spaciousness (or 'apparent source width') on the listening level. Accordingly, the presence and the relative strengths of early lateral reflections are only one component of spaciousness, the other being the total level at which music is heard by listeners.

The quantity S defined in eqn (VII.19) cannot be measured directly without difficulties. On the other hand, only sound impinging from the vertical symmetry plane of a listener's head will produce equal sound pressures at both ears, whereas sound from lateral directions will produce different ear signals. Therefore a practical measure can be based upon the similarity or dissimilarity of the sound pressures at the ears of a listener's (or of an artificial) head. Such a comparison is most readily accomplished by a correlation analysis and leads to a quantity similar to the correlation coefficient defined in eqn (VII.18). The restriction to early energy only can be effected by specifying p_1 and p_2 of eqn (VII.18) as the impulse responses $g_r(t)$ and $g_l(t)$ at both ears, and by imposing an upper limit on the time interval during which averaging is performed.

As a further refinement, a time shift τ can be included of one impulse response with respect to the other, taking into account that the listener's head may not be exactly directed toward the sound source. Then we arrive at a normalised short-time cross-correlation function of both impulse responses:

$$\varphi_{rl}(\tau) = \frac{\displaystyle\int_0^{t_0} g_r(t)g_l(t+\tau)\,dt}{\left\{\displaystyle\int_0^{t_0}[g_r(t)]^2\,dt\int_0^{t_0}[g_l(t)]^2\,dt\right\}^{1/2}} \qquad \text{(VII.21)}$$

(compare to eqn (I.33a)). A useful quantity, named 'interaural cross-correlation' (IACC), can be derived from this function with $t_0 = 100$ ms by defining[25,26]

$$\text{IACC} = \text{maximum of } \varphi_{rl}(\tau) \quad \text{within } |\tau| < 1 \text{ ms} \qquad \text{(VII.22)}$$

It is approximately related to the ratio of lateral to non-lateral early energy by

$$\text{IACC} \approx \frac{1}{1+S} \qquad \text{(VII.23)}$$

We shall come back to this quantity in Section VII.8.

VII.6 THE SUBJECTIVE EFFECT OF REVERBERATION: OPTIMUM REVERBERATION TIMES AND EARLY DECAY TIME

If we disregard all details of the impulse response of a room, we finally arrive at the general decay the sound energy undergoes after an impulse excitation or after a sound source has been stopped. As discussed in earlier chapters of this book, the duration of this decay is characterised by the reverberation time or decay time, at least if the energy decay obeys an exponential law in its gross appearance.

Historically, the reverberation time was the first quantity which could be measured objectively and could be expected to reflect the acoustical merits of a room. It was introduced into room acoustics by W. C. Sabine[27] during the last years of the 19th century. Sabine has also developed numerous methods to measure reverberation times with ever increasing accuracy, and he was the first to formulate the laws of reverberation. Furthermore, he investigated the sound absorbing power of numerous materials. So he was not just an outstanding pioneer but rather the inventor and founder of the science of room acoustics. The measuring techniques and many other things have changed since then, but Sabine's ideas continue to be the basis of modern room acoustics.

In particular, the reverberation time (or decay time) is still considered as the most important objective quantity in room acoustics, although it has been evident for some time that it characterises only one special aspect of sound propagation in rooms and needs to be supplemented by additional parameters if a full description of the prevailing listening conditions is to be obtained. This predominance of reverberation time has at least three reasons. Firstly, it can be measured and predicted with reasonable accuracy and moderate expenditure. Secondly, the reverberation time of a room does not usually depend significantly on the observer's position in a room, a fact which is also underlined by the simple structure of the formulae by which it can be calculated from room data (see Sections V.3 and V.4). Hence it is well suited to characterise the overall acoustic properties of a hall, neglecting details which may vary from one place to another. And, finally, abundant data on reverberation times of existing halls are available nowadays, including their frequency dependence. They can be used as a yardstick, so to speak, namely to get an idea of how the result of a particular reverberation measurement or calculation is to be judged.

Before discussing the important question which reverberation times are desirable or optimal for the various types of rooms and halls a remark on the just audible differences in reverberation time, i.e. on the difference threshold of reverberation time, may be in order. By presenting exponentially decaying noise impulses with variable decay times, bandwidths and centre frequencies to a large number of test subjects, Seraphim[28] was able to show that the relative difference threshold of the decay time is about 4% of its actual value, at least in the most important range of decay times. Although these results were obtained under somewhat unrealistic conditions, they show at least that there is no point in stating reverberation times with a greater accuracy than about 0·05 or 0·1 s.

In principle, preferred ranges of the reverberation time can be obtained by subjective tests, for instance by intelligibility scores of speech, or by judging music samples of various types. To lead to meaningful results such tests should be performed, strictly speaking, in environments (real enclosures or synthetic sound fields) which allow suitable variations of the reverberation time under otherwise unchanged conditions. This cannot be achieved just by comparing sound recordings from different halls unless the answers of test persons are subject to a more involved procedure of evaluation (see next section).

A more empirical approach consists in collecting the reverberation times of halls which are generally considered as acoustically satisfactory or even excellent for the purpose they have to serve (lectures, drama theatre, operatic performances, orchestra or chamber music, etc.). Sometimes the acoustical acceptance of a hall or of several of them is assessed by systematic enquiries (for instance on 11 British concert halls carried out by Barron[29]). In any case it should be noted that the collection of subjective opinions on acoustical qualities and hence the conclusions drawn from them are afflicted with several factors of uncertainty. This holds especially for music. One of them is the question of who is able to utter meaningful acoustical criticism. Certainly musicians have the best opportunity of comparison, since many of them perform in different concert halls. On the other hand, musicians have a very special standpoint (meant literally as well as metaphorically) which does not necessarily agree with that of a listener. The same is true for acousticians and sound recording engineers, who have a professional attitude towards acoustical matters and may frequently concentrate their attention on special properties which are insignificant to the average concert listeners. The latter, however, as for example the concert subscribers, often lack the opportunity or the desire to compare several concert halls or else they are not very critically minded in acoustical matters, or their opinion is influenced from the point of view of local patriotism. Furthermore, there are—and again this applies particularly to musical events and their appropriate surroundings—individual differences in taste which cannot be discussed in scientific terms. And, finally, it is quite possible that there are certain trends of 'fashion' towards longer or shorter reverberation times. All these uncertainties make it understandable that it is impossible to specify one single optimum value of reverberation time for each room type or type of presentation, instead only ranges of favourable values can be set up.

We start with rooms used only for speech, such as lecture rooms, congress halls, parliament, theatres for dramatic performances and so on. In principle, no reverberation whatsoever is required for such rooms, since any noticeable sound decay has the tendency to blur the syllables and thus to reduce speech intelligibility. On the other hand, a highly absorbing treatment of all walls and of the ceiling of a room would certainly remove virtually all the reverberation, but at the same time it would prevent the formation of useful reflections which increase the loudness of the perceived sounds and which are responsible for the relative ease at which communication is possible in enclosures as compared to outdoors communication. Furthermore, the lack of any audible reverberation in a closed space creates an unnatural and uncomfortable feeling, as can be observed when entering an anechoic room, for instance. Obviously one subconsciously expects to encounter some reverberation which bears a certain relation to the size of the room. Therefore the reverberation time in rooms of this kind should not fall short of 0·5 s approximately (except for very small rooms such as living rooms), and values of about 1·2 s are still tolerable especially for larger rooms.

In contrast to this purely empirical way of fixing optimum reverberation times, Lochner and Burger[18] have attempted to derive objectively the proper decay time from impulse responses calculated for particular room shapes and wall absorption. By evaluating the signal-to-noise ratio ΔL_{LB} according to eqn (VII.14) they obtained a relation between reverberation time and speech intelligibility, and from this derived an optimum reverberation time of about 1 s in accordance with the range of values given above.

As is well known, low frequencies contribute very little to speech intelligibility. Therefore it is an advantage to apply suitably designed sound absorbers to the walls of rooms used for speech in order to reduce the reverberation time and hence the stationary sound level at low frequencies.

Now we shall turn to the reverberation times which can be considered to be optimum for concert halls. In order to discover these values, we are completely dependent on subjective opinions concerning existing halls, at least so long as there are no results available of systematic investigations with synthetic or simulated sound fields. As has been pointed out before, there is always some divergence of opinion about a certain concert hall; furthermore, they are not always constant in time. Old concert halls particularly are often commented on enthusiastically, probably more than is justified by their real acoustical merits. (This is true especially for some halls which were destroyed by war or other catastrophes.)

In spite of all these reservations, it is a matter of fact that certain concert halls enjoy a high reputation for acoustical reasons. This means, among other things, that at least their reverberation time does not give cause for complaint. On the whole it seems that the optimum values for occupied concert halls is in the range from about 1·6 to 2·1 s at mid frequencies. Table VII.3 lists the reverberation times of several old and new concert halls, both for low frequencies (125 Hz) and for the medium frequency range (500–1000 Hz).

At first glance it may seem curious that that which is good for speech, namely a relatively short reverberation time, should be bad for music. This discrepancy can be resolved by bearing in mind that, when listening to speech, we are interested in perceiving each element of the sound signal, since this increases the ease with which we can understand what the speaker is saying. When listening to music, it would be rather disturbing to hear every detail including the bowing noise of the string instruments or the air flow noise of flutes, or minor shortcomings of the synchronism among the instruments of an orchestra. These and similar imperfections are hidden or masked by reverberation. What is even more important, reverberation of sufficient strength effects the blending of musical sounds and increases their loudness and richness as well as the continuity of musical line. The importance of all these effects for musical enjoyment becomes obvious if one listens to music in an environment virtually free of reverberation, as for example to a military band or a light orchestra playing outdoors: the sounds are brittle and harsh, and it is obvious that it is of no advantage to be able to hear every detail. Furthermore, the loudness of music heard outdoors is reduced rapidly as the distance increases from the sound source.

But perhaps the most important reason why relatively long reverberation times are adequate for music is simply the fact that listeners are accustomed to hearing music in environments which happen to have reverberation times of the order of magnitude mentioned. This applies equally well to composers who unconsciously take into account the blending of sounds which is produced in concert halls of normal size.

As regards the frequency dependence of the reverberation time, it is generally considered tolerable, if not as favourable, to have an increase of the reverberation time towards lower frequencies, beginning at about 500 Hz (*see* Table VII.3). On the other hand, there are quite a number of concert halls with reverberation times which do not increase towards the low frequencies or which even have a slightly decreasing reverberation time and which are nevertheless considered to be excellent acoustically.

The optimum range of reverberation time as indicated above refers to the

Table VII.3
Reverberation Time of Occupied Concert Halls

Hall	Volume (m^3)	Number of seats	Year of completion (reconstruction)	T_{125}	$T_{500-1000}$	Source
Großer Musikvereinssaal, Wien	14 600	2 000	1870	2·3	2·05	Beranek[34]
St Andrew's Hall, Glasgow	16 100	2 130	1877	2·1	2·2	Parkin et al.
Chiang Kai Shek Memorial, Taipei	16 700	2 077	1987	1·95	2·0	Kuttruff
Symphony Hall, Boston	18 800	2 630	1900	2·2	1·8	Beranek[34]
Concertgebouw, Amsterdam	19 000	2 200	1887	2·3	2·2	Geluk
Neues Gewandhaus, Leipzig	21 000	1 900	1884 (1981)	2·0	2·0	Fasold
Neue Philharmonie, Berlin	24 500	2 230	1963	2·4	1·95	Cremer
Concert Hall 'De Doelen', Rotterdam	27 000	2 220	1979	2·3	2·2	De Lange

Table VII.4
Reverberation Time of Occupied Opera Theatres

Opera house	Volume (m^3)	Number of seats	Year of completion (reconstruction)	T_{125}	$T_{500-1000}$	Source
La Scala, Milano	10 000	2 290/400	1778 (1946)	1·2	0·95	Furrer
Covent Garden, London	10 100	2 180/60	1858	1·2	1·1	Parkin et al.
Festspielhaus, Bayreuth	11 000	1 800	1876	1·7	1·5	Reichardt
National Theatre, Taipei	11 200	1 522	1987	1·6	1·4	Kuttruff
Staatsoper, Wien	11 600	1 658/560	1869 (1955)	1·5	1·3	Reichardt
Staatsoper, Dresden	12 500	1 290	1878 (1985)	2·3	1·7	Kraak
Neues Festspielhaus, Salzburg	14 000	2 158	1960	1·7	1·5	Schwaiger
Metropolitan Opera House, New York	30 500	3 800	1966	2·25[a]	1·8[a]	Jordan

[a] With 80% occupancy only.

performance of orchestral and choral music. For smaller ensembles, starting with soloists and including all kinds of chamber music, a reverberation time of 1·4 to 1·6 s is certainly more adequate.

Apart from this dependence of the reverberation time on the ensemble size, there is another one on the style of music to be performed. It has been investigated by Kuhl[30] in a remarkable round robin experiment. In this experiment three different pieces of music were recorded in many concert halls and broadcasting studios with widely varying reverberation times. These recordings were later replayed to a great number of listeners— musicians as well as acousticians, music historians, recording engineers and other engineers, i.e. individuals who were competent in that field in one way or another. They were asked to indicate whether the reverberation times in the different recordings, whose origin they did not know, appeared too short or too long. The pieces of music played back were the first movement of Mozart's Jupiter Symphony (KV551), the fourth movement of Brahms' 4th Symphony (E minor) and the 'Danse Sacrale' of Stravinsky's 'Le Sacre du Printemps'.

The final result was that a reverberation time of 1·5 s was considered to be most appropriate for the Mozart symphony as well as for the Stravinsky piece, whereas 2·1 s was felt to be most suitable for the Brahms symphony. In the first two pieces there was almost complete agreement in the listeners' opinions; in the Brahms symphony, however, there was considerable divergence of opinion.

These results should certainly not be overvalued since the conditions under which they have been obtained were far from ideal in that they were based on monophonic recordings, replayed in rooms with some reverberation. But they show clearly that no hall can offer optimum conditions for all types of music and explain the large range of 'optimum' reverberation times for concert halls.

In opera houses the listener should be able to enjoy the full sound of music as well as to understand the text, at least partially. Therefore one would expect that these somewhat contradictory requirements can be reconciled by a compromise as far as the reverberation time is concerned, and that consequently the optimum of the latter would be somewhere about 1·5 s. As a matter of fact, however, the reverberation times of well-renowned opera theatres scatter over a wide range (see Table VII.4). Traditional theatres have reverberation times close to 1 s only, whereas more modern ones show a definite trend towards longer values. One is tempted to explain these differences by a changed attitude of the listeners, who nowadays seem to give more preference to a full and smooth sound of music than to the intelligibility of the text, whereas earlier opera goers presumably just wanted to be entertained by the plot. The truth, however, is probably much simpler. Old theatres were designed in such a way as to seat as many spectators as possible, while the architects of more modern ones (including the Festsspielhaus in Bayreuth, which was specially designed to stage Wagner's operas) tried to follow more or less elaborate acoustical concepts.

The question of optimum reverberation times is even more difficult to answer if we turn to churches and other places of worship which cannot be considered merely under the heading of acoustics. It depends on the character of the service whether more emphasis is given to organ music and liturgical chants or to the sermon. In the first case longer reverberation times are to be preferred, but in the latter case the reverberation time should certainly not exceed 2 s. Frequently, however, churches with still shorter reverberation times are not well accepted by the congregation for reasons which have nothing to do with acoustics. This shows that the churchgoers' acoustical expectations are not only influenced by rational arguments such as that of speech intelligibility but also by hearing habits.

As mentioned above, the reverberation time is a meaningful measure for the duration of the decay process only if the latter is exponential, i.e. if the decay level decreases linearly with time. If, on the contrary, a logarithmic decay curve is bent and consequently each section of it has its own decay rate, the question arises which of these sections is most significant for the subjectively perceived 'reverberance' of a room.

To answer this question Atal et al.[31] added non-exponential artificial reverberation produced by a number of computer-simulated comb filters (see Section X.4) to speech and music samples. The signals modified in this way were presented over earphones to test subjects, who were asked to compare them with exponentially reverberated signals in order to find the effective decay rate of the non-exponential decays. The results are plotted in Fig. VII.16. The abscissa represents the reverberation time corresponding to the initial slope (first 160 ms) of the non-exponential decay; the ordinate is the reverberation time of an exponential decay giving the same impression of reverberance, i.e. the subjective or effective reverberation time. Similar results were obtained with sound signals reverberated in concert halls.

These findings can be explained by the fact that the smoothing effect of reverberation on the irregular level fluctuations of continuous speech or music is mainly achieved by the initial portion of the decay process, while its later portions add up to a general 'background' which is not felt subjectively as a typical effect of reverberation but rather as some sort of noise. Only final or other isolated chords present the listener with the opportunity of hearing the complete decay process; but these chords occur too rarely for them to influence to any great degree the overall impression which a listener gains of the hall's reverberance.

Nowadays there seems to be some agreement to characterise the rate of sound decay in its initial portion by the 'early decay time' (EDT) following a

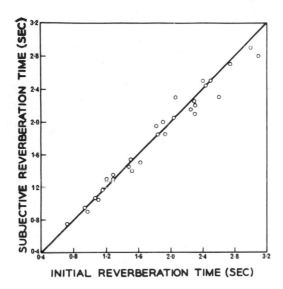

Fig. VII.16.   Subjective reverberation time as a function of the initial reverberation time T_{160}.

proposal of V. Jordan.[32] This is the time in which the first 10 dB fall of a decay process occurs, multiplied by a factor 6.

The overall reverberation time does not show substantial variations with room shape. This is so because the decay process as a whole is made up of numerous reflections with different delays, strengths and wall portions where they originated. On the contrary, the 'early decay time' is determined by quite a few strong and isolated reflections, and therefore depends noticeably on the measuring position; furthermore, it is sensitive to details of the room geometry. In this respect it resembles to some extent the parameters discussed in the preceding sections.

VII.7 STEADY STATE SOUND PRESSURE LEVEL AND ACOUSTICAL QUALITY

Usually the stationary sound pressure level or energy density a sound source produces in a hall is not considered as an acoustical quality criterion of a hall since, according to eqn (V.36), it depends mainly on the power output of the source and the reverberation time of the hall. On the other hand, high definition or clarity is of little use if the sound is too weak to be heard at proper loudness. Moreover, eqn (V.36) is valid for diffuse sound fields only, and the sound field in a real hall deviates more or less from this ideal condition.

The dependence of the sound pressure level (*SPL*) on the sound power the source generates is easily removed by subtracting its power level *PL* (*see* eqn (I.41)) from the measured (or calculated) pressure level:

$$L = SPL - PL \qquad\qquad (VII.24)$$

A similar normalisation is achieved by the following quantity, which is derived from the impulse response $g(t)$:

$$G = 10 \log_{10} \left\{ \frac{\int_0^\infty [g(t)]^2 \, dt}{\int_0^{\Delta t} [g_0(t)]^2 \, dt} \right\} \quad dB \qquad\qquad (VII.25)$$

In this expression g_0 denotes the impulse response at a specified distance (5 or 10 m, for example) from the sound source and Δt is the duration of the excitation impulse.

Employing eqn (VII.25), Gade and Rindel[33] measured the normalised levels in 21 Danish concert halls. They found that the stationary levels show a typical dependence on the distance from the sound source corresponding to 1·2–3·3 dB per distance doubling, and that their average in each hall falls short of the value predicted by eqn (V.36) by 2–3 dB. Furthermore, the steady state level does not depend in a simple way on the reverberation time or on geometrical data of the halls. From these results it may be concluded that—at least in concert halls—the steady state level does not lend itself to indicating acoustical faults or merits.

VII.8 ASSESSMENT OF CONCERT HALL ACOUSTICS

Although nowadays quite a number of parameters are at the acousticians' disposal to quantify the listening conditions in a concert hall (or particular aspects of them), the situation is still unsatisfactory in that important questions remain unanswered. Do these parameters yield a complete description of the acoustics of a hall? Are they independent from each other? Which relative weight is to be given to each of them? Is it possible, for instance, to compensate insufficient reverberation by a large amount of early lateral energy?

Conventional attempts to correlate the acoustical quality of a concert hall with an objective measure or a set of them have not been very satisfactory because they concentrated on one particular aspect only or, as for instance Beranek's elaborate rating system,[34] relied on plausible but unproven assumptions. Since about 1970, however, researchers have tried to get a complete picture of the factors which contribute to good acoustics, including their relative significance, by employing modern psychometric methods.

The basic idea of this new approach is first to detect the number and significance of independent scales of subjective acoustical experience and then, as a second step, to find out the physical parameters which show the highest correlation to these scales.

The first step is performed by presenting music samples recorded in different concert halls or at different places of one hall to test subjects. They are asked either to assess in some way the differences between subsequent listening impressions[35,36] or to give scores to the presented signals using a number of bipolar rating scales with verbally labelled extremes such as 'dull—brilliant', 'cold—warm', etc.,[37,38] or simply to say which of two presentations they prefer.[39,40] Such data are collected from many listeners and then are subjected to a mathematical procedure called factor analysis, which somewhat resembles the determination of the major axes of a multidimensional ellipsoid with the difference that the number r of dimensions is not known *a priori*. The result of such an analysis is the number r of independent perceptual scales, called 'factors', and the relative significance of each of these factors.

The meaning of these factors or scales is principally unknown, but sometimes they can be circumscribed vaguely by verbal labels such as 'resonance' or 'proximity'.

These factors can be thought of as coordinate axes of an r-dimensional 'perceptual space' in which each concert hall or sound field is represented by a point. Suppose $r = 2$; accordingly, the perceptual space is a plane with rectangular coordinates F_1 and F_2. If the preceding factor analysis was based on preference tests, the individual preference scale of one subject can be represented by a vector in this plane (*see* Fig. VII.17). According to the

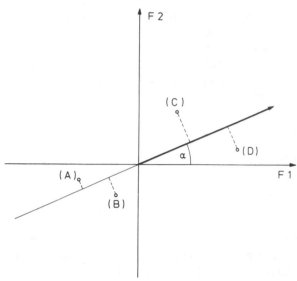

Fig. VII.17. Two-dimensional perceptual space with factors F_1 and F_2. The vector represents the preference scale of one subject; the points A, B, C, etc., denote concert halls.

angle α which it includes with the axis F_1, this particular listener gives in his preference judgement a weight of $\cos \alpha$ to the factor F_1 and of $\sin \alpha$ to the factor F_2. The projections of the 'concert hall points' A, B, C, etc., on this vector indicate this listener's personal preference rating of these halls. Similarly, if bipolar rating scales have been used, these scales can be presented as directions in such a diagram.

The successful application of factor analysis to the problems of concert hall acoustics requires refined methods of sound field reproduction which permit alternate presentations of different recordings without relying on the subject's memory. We have mentioned two possible methods already at the end of the introduction to this chapter. Common to them is the use of a very good artificial head for recording the sounds.

Wilkens and Plenge[38,41] collected their test samples by following an orchestra on its tour playing the same programme (Mozart, Bartok, Brahms) in six different halls. They used headphones for the reproduction and found three factors to be relevant, which they labelled as follows:

F_1: strength factor (47%)
F_2: distinctness factor (28%)
F_3: timbre factor (14%)

The numbers in the brackets denote the relative significance of the three factors. They add up to 89% only, which means that there are further, however insignificant, factors. It is interesting to note that there seem to be two groups of listeners: one group which prefers loud sounds (high values of F_1) and one giving more preference to distinct sounds (high values of F_2). (A similar division of the subjects into two groups with different preferences has been found by Barron.[29])

In the course of this research project, physical sound field parameters have been measured at the same positions in which the sound recordings have been made. Lehmann[42] has analysed them in order to select those which show highest correlation with the factors F_1 to F_3. He found that F_1 is highly correlated with the quantity G from eqn (VII.25), whereas F_2 shows high (negative) correlation with Kürer's 'centre of gravity time' t_s (see Section VII.4). Finally, the factor F_3 seems to be related to the frequency dependence of the 'early decay time'.

In contrast to the aforementioned authors, Siebrasse[40] collected his test samples by replaying 'dry', i.e. reverberation-free music, namely a motif of Mozart's Jupiter Symphony, stereophonically from the stages of 25 European concert halls and by re-recording them with an artificial head. The samples prepared in this way were presented to the test subjects in the free field at constant level employing the compensation system mentioned in the introduction to this chapter.[1] The subjects were asked to judge preference between pairs of sound fields. Application of factor analysis indicated four factors F_1 to F_4 with relative significances of 45%, 16%, 12% and 7%. In Fig. VII.18, which is analogous to Fig. VII.17, part of his results are plotted in the plane of factors F_1 and F_2. The vectors representing the individual preference scales have different lengths since they have non-vanishing components also in F_3- and F_4-directions. The fact that all these vectors are directed towards the right side leads to the conclusion that F_1 is a 'consensus factor', whereas the components in F_2-direction reflect differences in the listeners' personal taste. This holds as well with regard to the factors F_3 and F_4. Therefore further investigations can be concentrated on F_1 because one is interested mainly in criteria of general validity.

Gottlob[26] has analysed impulse responses recorded in the same halls with the aim of detecting the sound field parameters with the highest correlation to the consensus factor F_1. The reverberation time proved to be important only when it deviated substantially from an optimum range centred on 2 s. If halls with unfavourable reverberation times are excluded, F_1 shows high correlation with several parameters, of which the interaural cross-correlation (IACC) (see eqns (VII.21) and (VII.22)) seems to be of

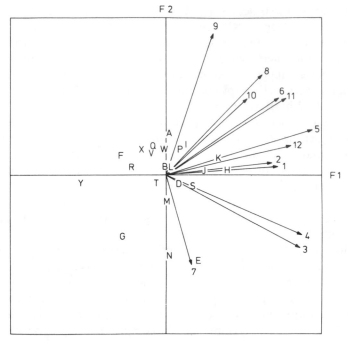

Fig. VII.18. Individual preference scales of 12 test subjects and 22 concert hall points (A, B,..., Y) represented in the F_1–F_2 plane of a four-dimensional perceptual space.

particular interest, since it is virtually independent of the reverberation time. Another highly correlated quantity is the width of a concert hall. Both the IACC and the width of a hall are negatively correlated to F_1, i.e. narrow concert halls are generally preferred. This again proves the importance of early lateral reflections which are stronger in narrow halls and, on the other hand, lead to a low value of the IACC. In a more recent publication[43] an even higher correlation to F_1 has been reported for the sum of the early lateral energy and the reverberant energy, where the latter is obtained by integrating the squared impulse response from 80 ms to infinity.

The fact that both investigations reported above show such poor agreement may have several explanations: the differences in the way the test samples were collected and presented to the subjects, different choice of halls, and different judging schemes. It is not surprising, however, that in the second study the strength or loudness of the sound signal does not show up since here all test samples were presented to the subjects at equal loudness.

A somewhat different approach to arrive at a consistent rating system for concert halls is due to Ando,[44] who simulated sound fields with various combinations of four objective parameters by means of a digital computer. These sound fields consisted of the direct sound, two distinct reflections, and subsequent reverberation generated by a set of comb filters (*see* Section X.4). The parameters which reportedly contribute almost independently to subjective preference judgement are: the level of listening, the delay time of the first reflection with respect to the direct sound Δt_1 (initial time delay gap), the subsequent reverberation time T, and the magnitude of the interaural cross-correlation (IACC). Based on subjective preference tests carried out with these sound fields, Ando finally proposed the following figure of merit, called 'total subjective preference':

$$S_a = - \sum_{i=1}^{4} \alpha_i |X_i|^{3/2} \qquad (VII.26)$$

with

$$X_1 = 20 \log_{10}\left(\frac{p}{p_p}\right) \qquad \alpha_1 = \begin{cases} 0\cdot07 \text{ for } X_1 \geq 0 \\ 0\cdot04 \text{ for } X_1 < 0 \end{cases}$$

(p = rms sound pressure in arbitrary units)

$$X_2 = \log_{10}\left[\frac{\Delta t_1}{(\Delta t_1)_p}\right] \qquad \alpha_2 = \begin{cases} 1\cdot42 \text{ for } X_2 \geq 0 \\ 1\cdot11 \text{ for } X_2 < 0 \end{cases}$$

$$X_3 = \log_{10}\left(\frac{T}{T_p}\right) \qquad \alpha_3 = \begin{cases} 0\cdot45 + 0\cdot74A \text{ for } X_3 \geq 0 \\ 2\cdot36 - 0\cdot42A \text{ for } X_3 < 0 \end{cases}$$

$$X_4 = \text{IACC} \qquad \alpha_4 = 1\cdot45$$

The quantity A in α_3 is the square root of the total energy contained in all reflections, divided by the amplitude of the direct sound; the symbols with the index p denote 'the most preferred value' of the respective quantity. These latter values depend on the type of music. In particular, $(\Delta t_1)_p$ is $(\log_{10} A - 1)\tau_e$ and T_p is $23\tau_e$, with τ_e denoting the effective duration of the autocorrelation function of the sound signal (*see* Section I.7).

According to this rating system there exists one sound field configuration ($X_1 = X_2 = X_3 = 0$, X_4 as high as possible) which is expected to yield an absolute optimum of listening conditions—which is hard to believe when one takes note of the considerable differences in the music lovers' tastes. Furthermore, if all designers of concert halls consequently decided to follow the guidelines of this system, the result would be halls not only equally good but of equal acoustics. We doubt whether this is a desirable goal of room acoustical effort, since variations in acoustical impressions are just as enjoyable as different architectural solutions.

Meanwhile, we are still far from this state of the art: the insights which have been reported do not combine to form a well-rounded picture of concert hall acoustics; they are not free of inconsistencies and even contradictions, and hence are to be considered as preliminary only. Nevertheless, it is obvious that major progress has been made during the past few decades; there is at least some agreement on likely important issues for concert hall design.

REFERENCES

1. Damaske, P. & Mellert, V., *Acustica*, **22** (1969/70) 153; *ibid.*, **24** (1971) 222.
2. Martin, J. & Vian, S. P., Proceedings of the 13th International Congress on Acoustics, Belgrade, 1989, p. 253.
3. Kuttruff, H., Vorländer, M. & Classen, T., *Acustica*, **70** (1990) 230.
4. Burgtorf, W. & Oehlschlägel, H. K., *Acustica*, **14** (1964) 254.
5. Schubert, P., *Zeitschr. Hochfrequenztechn. u. Elektroakust.*, **78** (1969) 230.
6. Seraphim, H. P., *Acustica*, **11** (1961) 80.
7. Reichardt, W. & Schmidt, W., *Acustica*, **18** (1967) 274.
8. Haas, H., *Acustica*, **1** (1951) 49.
9. Muncey, R. W., Nickson, A. F. B. & Dubout, P., *Acustica*, **3** (1953) 168.
10. Meyer, E. & Schodder, G. R., *Nachr. Akad. Wissensch. Göttingen, Math.-Phys. Kl.*, No. 6 (1952) 31.
11. Atal, B. S., Schroeder, M. R. & Kuttruff, H., Proceedings of the Fourth International Congress on Acoustics, Copenhagen, 1962, paper H31.
12. Dietsch, L. & Kraak, W., *Acustica*, **60** (1986) 205.
13. Kürer, R., *Acustica*, **21** (1969) 370.
14. Thiele, R., *Acustica*, **3** (1953) 291.
15. Boré, G., Kurzton-Meßverfahren zur punktweisen Ermittlung der Sprachverständlichkeit in lautsprecherbeschallten Räumen. Dissertation, Technische Hochschule Aachen, 1956.
16. Reichardt, W., Abdel Alim, O. & Schmidt, W., *Appl. Acoustics*, **7** (1974) 243.
17. Niese, H., *Zeitschr. Hochfrequenztechn. u. Elektroakust.*, **65** (1956) 4; *ibid.*, **66** (1957) 70; *Acustica*, **11** (1961) 199.
18. Lochner, J. P. A. & Burger, J. F., *Acustica*, **11** (1961) 195.
19. Houtgast, T. & Steeneken, H. J. M., *Acustica*, **28** (1973) 66. Steeneken, H. J. M. & Houtgast, T., *J. Acoust. Soc. America*, **67** (1980) 318. Houtgast, T., Proceedings of the 12th International Congress on Acoustics, Toronto, 1986, paper E4-13.
20. Damaske, P., *Acustica*, **19** (1967/68) 199.
21. Marshall, A. H., Proceedings of the Sixth International Congress on Acoustics, Tokyo, 1968, paper E-2-3.
22. Meyer, E. & Kuhl, W., *Acustica*, **2** (1952) 77.
23. Barron, M., *J. Sound Vibr.*, **15** (1971) 475. The effects of early reflections on

subjective acoustical quality in concert halls. PhD thesis, University of Southampton, 1974.

24. Keet, W. de Villiers, Proceedings of the Sixth International Congress on Acoustics, Tokyo, 1968, paper E-2-4.

25. Damaske, P. & Ando, Y., *Acustica*, **27** (1972) 232.

26. Gottlob, D., Vergleich objektiver akustischer Parameter mit Ergebnissen subjektiver Untersuchungen an Konzertsälen. Dissertation, University of Göttingen, 1973.

27. Sabine, W. C., *Collected Papers on Acoustics*. Dover Publ., 1964 (first published 1922).

28. Seraphim, H.-P., *Acustica*, **8** (1958) 280.

29. Barron, M., *Acustica*, **66** (1988) 1.

30. Kuhl, W., *Acustica*, **4** (1954) 618.

31. Atal, B. S., Schroeder, M. R. & Sessler, G. M., Proceedings of the Fifth International Congress on Acoustics, Liège, 1965, paper G32.

32. Jordan, V. L., *J. Acoust. Soc. America*, **47** (1970) 408.

33. Gade, A. C. & Rindel, J. H., in *Fortschr. d. Akustik—DAGA '85*. Bad Honnef, DPG-GmbH, 1985.

34. Beranek, L. L., *Music, Acoustics and Architecture*. John Wiley, New York/London, 1962.

35. Yamaguchi, K., *J. Acoust. Soc. America*, **52** (1972) 1271.

36. Edwards, R. M., *Acustica*, **30** (1974) 183.

37. Hawkes, R. J. & Douglas, H., *Acustica*, **24** (1971) 235.

38. Wilkens, H. & Plenge, G., The correlation between subjective and objective data of concert halls. In *Auditorium Acoustics*, ed. R. Mackenzie. Applied Science Publishers, London, 1974.

39. Schroeder, M. R., Gottlob, D. & Siebrasse, F., *J. Acoust. Soc. America*, **56** (1974) 1195.

40. Siebrasse, K. F., Vergleichende subjektive Untersuchungen zur Akustik von Konzertsälen. Dissertation, University of Göttingen, 1973.

41. Wilkens, H., *Acustica*, **38** (1977) 10.

42. Lehmann, P., Über die Ermittlung raumakustischer Kriterien und deren Zusammenhang mit subjektiven Beurteilungen der Hörsamkeit. Dissertation, Technical University of Berlin, 1976.

43. Gottlob, D., Siebrasse, F. & Schroeder, M. R., in *Fortschr. d. Akustik—DAGA '75*. Physik-Verlag GmbH, Weinheim, 1975.

44. Ando, Y., *J. Acoust. Soc. America*, **74** (1983) 873.

VIII

Measuring Techniques in Room Acoustics

The starting point of modern room acoustics is marked by attempts to find and to define objective parameters which have a mediatory function, in that they are related in a known way with geometrical and other room data on the one hand and with certain listening impressions on the other. As we have seen in the preceding chapter, quite a number of such parameters have been introduced in room acoustics since then with varied justification and significance, and it is the object of the present chapter to describe how such quantities can be measured and which kind of equipment is required for this purpose.

Measurements in room acoustics are not only necessary to increase our knowledge of the factors which govern the subjectively perceivable acoustical qualities of a room but they are also a valuable diagnostic tool and can give useful supporting information in the design of large halls. If, for instance, an existing hall is to be used for other purposes than was originally intended, or if there are certain acoustical deficiencies to be eliminated by constructive modifications, measurements of at least the reverberation time are indispensable. When a new hall is being designed, it may be very advantageous to perform measurements on a model of this hall in order to predict its acoustical behaviour and to detect possible acoustical faults and their causes as early as possible. Furthermore, it is advisable to carry out measurements during the various phases of the construction of a hall in order to check the acoustical concepts upon which the designs are based and, if necessary, to propose modifications in the inner finish, for instance in the choice of wall materials, seat upholstery and so on, at a time when this can be realised without much additional costs.

Other acoustical measurements which are not directly related to subjective impressions concern the investigation of the acoustic properties of materials, especially of the absorption of materials for walls and ceiling, of seats, etc. Knowledge of such data is absolutely essential for any planning in room acoustics.

During the past decade, the conventional measuring equipment which consisted of electronic 'hardware' has been widely replaced with digital components (digital computers in connection with analogue-to-digital converters, transient recorders, printers and plotters, etc.) which are generally more powerful, precise and flexible—and generally less expensive. Nevertheless, some of the traditional measuring procedures still keep their place nowadays. Since the sound waves are basically 'analogue', i.e. not digital, at least the transducers (sound sources, microphones) continue to be of the analogue type. In the following we are going to describe both kinds of measuring procedures and equipment.

VIII.1 GENERAL REMARKS ON INSTRUMENTATION AND PROCEDURES FOR ACOUSTICAL MEASUREMENTS

In order to carry out any acoustical measurement in a room, it is necessary first of all to excite the room by a suitable sound source. Sinusoidal steady state signals are hardly ever used for this purpose, with the exception of basic investigations or the exploration of special problems. On the contrary, one usually prefers to avoid standing wave systems which are inherent in steady state excitation with sinusoidal signals. The measuring signals most commonly used usually have a finite frequency bandwidth.

If impulsive signals are to be applied, simple non-electric devices are frequently used, such as pistols, sometimes even wooden clappers or air balloons, which are blown up and burst. Pulses, which can be reproduced and triggered off more easily, can be produced by spark gaps. In all these cases frequency discrimination, which may be desirable for several reasons, must be achieved on the receiving side of the whole system. If analogue filters are used for this purpose, such as octave or third octave filters, unwanted spectral components cannot be suppressed completely.

A better frequency discrimination and hence a better signal-to-noise ratio is obtained by restricting the bandwidth of the excitation signal on the transmitting side as well. This is achieved by using loudspeakers which are fed by proper electrical signals (frequency modulated sinusoidal signals, filtered random noise or tone impulses with defined and reproducible envelopes).

If the sound source has a certain directionality, which is usually the case if no special measures are taken to avoid it, the result of the measurement will depend not only on the position but also on the orientation of the source. These influences can usually be neglected in reverberation measurements, since the various sound components will anyway be mixed up during the decay process. They are very pronounced, however, if the impulse response or the directional distribution of the sound energy is to be observed. Therefore such measurements should be carried out with non-directional sound sources. One way to obtain uniform sound radiation is to employ 12 or 20 equal loudspeaker systems mounted on the faces of a regular polyhedron (dodecaeder or icosaeder). It should be noted that even this kind of source is not free of any directionality, especially at higher frequencies. A different approach is to employ a powerful electrodynamic driver as used in horn loudspeakers and to replace the horn by a tube, the open end of which radiates the sound uniformly provided its diameter is small compared with the wavelength. The resonance of the tube is avoided by proper choice of its length or by inserting some absorbent material into the tube. Spark gaps for the generation of wide-band impulses can also be designed in such a way that the sound is radiated almost uniformly in all directions.[1]

Pressure-sensitive microphones with omnidirectional characteristics are usually employed as sound receivers, whereas microphones which are sensitive to the sound pressure gradient or to the particle velocity are only useful for special purposes. Microphones with a pronounced directionality, which are required for the determination of the directional distribution of sound energy in a room, usually consist of a standard microphone which is fitted with an additional device such as a concave mirror or a slotted tube, which make it selective to the direction of sound incidence. If frequency selective filters are employed during the measurement, which is usually the case, no special requirements concerning the flatness of the frequency response have to be met by the microphone.

If measurements outside the laboratory (field measurements) are to be carried out, the amount of time and wealth of equipment can be reduced by recording the measuring signals picked up in the room with a tape recorder; these signals can then be evaluated in the laboratory, provided that the precision and signal-to-noise ratio of the recorder is high enough.

Interim or final results such as decay curves, impulse responses, etc., can be made visible either by analogue devices such as level recorders or conventional oscilloscopes. If the measured signals are subject to digital processing, it is more convenient to use the monitor of the computer for this purpose or a plotter connected to it.

VIII.2 MEASUREMENT OF THE IMPULSE RESPONSE

According to system theory all properties of a linear transmission system are contained in its impulse response or, alternatively, in its transfer function, which is the Fourier transform of the impulse response. Since a room can be considered as an acoustical transmission system, the impulse response yields a complete description of the changes a sound signal undergoes when it travels from one point in a room to another, and almost all of the parameters we discussed in the preceding chapter can be derived from it, at least in principle. Parameters related to spatial or directional effects can be based upon the 'binaural impulse response' determined for both ears of a listener (or of an artificial head). From these remarks it is clear that the experimental determination of impulse responses is one of the most fundamental tasks in room acoustics. It requires high quality standards for all measuring components, which must be free not only of linear amplitude distortions but also of phase shifts. If the output of the microphone is to be stored, digital memories or digital tape recorders are preferable.

By its very definition the impulse response of a system is the signal obtained at the system's output after its excitation by a vanishingly short impulse (yet with non-vanishing energy), i.e. by a Dirac or delta impulse (see Section I.4). In practice, this signal can be approximated by a rectangular impulse, the duration of which is short compared with the period of the highest spectral component. However, this may prove difficult in practical situations, not only because most loudspeakers are unable to reproduce impulsive signals correctly but also for a more serious reason: in order to obtain a sufficiently high signal-to-noise ratio, the energy of the excitation signal must not fall short of a certain limit. But since all the energy is concentrated into a short time interval, the necessary amplitude of the signal may be so high that the loudspeaker is no longer operated in its linear range or will even be destroyed by the signal.

One way to improve the signal-to-noise ratio is to restrict the frequency range of the measurement by some kind of bandpass filtering, which may often be desirable for other reasons as well, namely to achieve some frequency discrimination. This can be done by inserting an octave or third octave filter, for example, into the electrical signal path. As an alternative the room can be excited with a test signal which has the desired spectrum. The simplest way to produce such test signals is to cut out tone bursts from a sinusoidal electrical signal by an electronic gate. More advantageous is the use of analogue or digital function generators which produce sinusoids with particular envelopes, for instance with pseudo-Gaussian or Hamming envelope:

$$s(t) = a(t) \cos(\omega t) \qquad\qquad \text{(VIII.1)}$$

with

$$a(t) = \begin{cases} 0{\cdot}54 + 0{\cdot}46 \cos\left(2\pi \dfrac{t}{T_0}\right) & \text{(Hamming)} \\[2mm] \exp(-bt^2) & \text{(pseudo-Gaussian)} \end{cases} \qquad \text{(VIII.1}a)$$

both for $|t| \le T_0/2$, while $a(t) = 0$ outside this interval. These envelopes (*see* Fig. VIII.1) have more favourable spectral properties than the tone bursts mentioned above.

As can be seen from Fig. VIII.1, limiting the frequency band is tantamount to spreading the excitatory signal in time. Now there are more sophisticated methods of obtaining the latter effect without limiting the frequency range of the measurement. To see which condition has to be fulfilled by a suitable test signal, let $s(t)$ be a stationary sound signal which is applied to the room through a loudspeaker (*see* Fig. VIII.2). Then the signal received by a microphone is, according to eqn (I.37),

$$s'(t) = \int_{-\infty}^{+\infty} s(t')g(t-t')\,dt' = \int_{-\infty}^{+\infty} g(t')s(t-t')\,dt' \qquad \text{(VIII.2)}$$

with $g(t)$ denoting the impulse response of the transmission path we want to measure. Now we form the cross-correlation function of the excitation

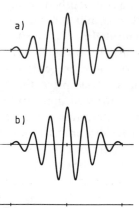

Fig. VIII.1. Test signals: (a) with Hamming and (b) with pseudo-Gaussian envelope ($\omega T_0 = 40$).

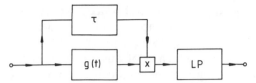

Fig. VIII.2. Measurement of the impulse response by cross-correlation (LP = lowpass filter).

signal s and the received signal s' by inserting the second version of eqn (VIII.2) into eqn (I.33a):

$$\phi_{ss'}(\tau) = \lim_{T_0 \to \infty} \frac{1}{T_0} \int_{-T_0/2}^{+T_0/2} s(t)\,dt \int_{-\infty}^{+\infty} g(t')s(t + \tau - t')\,dt'$$

or, after interchanging the order of integrations,

$$\phi_{ss'}(\tau) = \int_{-\infty}^{+\infty} g(t') \left[\lim_{T_0 \to \infty} \frac{1}{T_0} \int_{-T_0/2}^{+T_0/2} s(t)s(t + \tau - t')\,dt \right] dt'$$

$$= \int g(t')\phi_{ss}(\tau - t')\,dt' \tag{VIII.3}$$

according to eqn (I.33). Comparing the latter expression with eqn (I.36) leads to the conclusion that a measuring procedure corresponding to the above formalism (*see* Fig. VIII.2) results in $\phi_{ss'}(\tau) = g(\tau)$, i.e. will yield the impulse response g if the autocorrelation function of the exciting sound signal is the delta function or at least approximates it. This statement applies as well to transient excitation signals; in that case, however, the integrals defining the correlation functions are extended from $-\infty$ to $+\infty$ and need not be divided by some time interval T_0 (*see* Section VIII.3).

One 'signal' with an autocorrelation function concentrated at $\tau = 0$, which therefore could be used for this measurement, is random noise. To obtain a reasonable signal-to-noise ratio, however, the averaging time T_0 for each choice of the delay τ must not be too short (typically of the order 0·1 s). On the other hand, quite a number of delays are needed to resolve all details of an impulse response of some length. Therefore the measurement of impulse responses using white noise is a relatively time-consuming procedure.

More useful than random noise are 'pseudo-random' test signals, which have similar properties to random noise in a way although they are deterministic. Among these signals, binary impulse sequences are especially well suited for digital generation and processing. These are sequences of delta impulses or rectangular impulses with equal amplitudes, but with polarities changing according to a particular pattern.

An example of transient signals of this type are Barker coded impulse sequences. Since the length of these sequences do not exceed 13 elements, the achieved improvement of the signal-to-noise ratio is limited.[2] Another extremely powerful measuring scheme is based on 'maximum length sequences', which are stationary and have a period comprising

$$l = 2^n - 1 \tag{VIII.4}$$

elements s_k, where n is a positive integer. They can be generated by a digital n-step shift register with the outputs of certain stages fed back to the input.[3] Their main advantage, however, is that the required correlation process can be performed in a very efficient way by employing fast Hadamard transform. This method, which was introduced into room acoustics by Schroeder and Alrutz,[4] will be described in more detail in the following.

Let s_k (with $k = 0, 1, \ldots, l$) be a maximum length sequence with the length l, for instance for $n = 3$:

$$-1, +1, +1, -1, +1, -1, -1$$

Because of its periodicity we have $s_{k+l} = s_k$, and it has the general property

$$\sum_{k=0}^{l-1} s_k = -1$$

Since s_k is a discrete function, its autocorrelation function is defined by analogy with eqn (I.33) by

$$(\phi_{ss})_m = \sum_{k=0}^{l-1} s_k s_{k+m} \tag{VIII.5}$$

and has the values l for $m = 0, l, 2l, \ldots$ and -1 for all other values of m (Fig. VIII.3).

Now we excite the room under consideration with delta impulses following each other in time intervals Δt and which have equal strengths but signs corresponding to the sequence s_k. As indicated by eqn (I.37), the received signal is the 'convolution' of the room's impulse response $g(t)$ with the excitatory signal. If it is sampled at moments which are multiples of Δt, it reads

$$s'_k = \sum_{j=0}^{l-1} s_j g_{k-j} \tag{VIII.6}$$

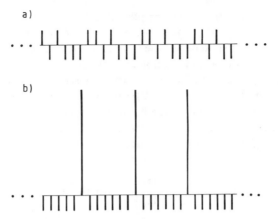

Fig. VIII.3. Maximum length sequence with $n = 3$ and its autocorrelation function.

This equation can equally well be formulated by means of a matrix **S** which consists of a cyclic arrangement of the elements s_k and one additional row and column of ones:

$$
\begin{bmatrix} s \\ s'_0 \\ s'_1 \\ s'_2 \\ \vdots \\ s'_{l-1} \end{bmatrix} = \begin{bmatrix} 1 & 1 & 1 & 1 & \cdots & 1 \\ 1 & s_0 & s_1 & s_2 & \cdots & s_{l-1} \\ 1 & s_1 & s_2 & s_3 & \cdots & s_0 \\ 1 & s_2 & s_3 & s_4 & \cdots & s_1 \\ \vdots & \vdots & \vdots & \vdots & \vdots & \vdots \\ 1 & s_{l-1} & s_0 & s_1 & \cdots & s_{l-2} \end{bmatrix} \begin{bmatrix} 0 \\ g_l \\ g_{l-1} \\ g_{l-2} \\ \vdots \\ g_1 \end{bmatrix} \qquad \text{(VIII.6}a\text{)}
$$

or in short-hand notation:

$$
\mathbf{s}' = \mathbf{S} \cdot \mathbf{g} \qquad \text{(VIII.6}b\text{)}
$$

In eqn (VIII.6a) we introduced $\bar{s}$ as the negative sum of all values of s'_k:

$$
\bar{s} \equiv -\sum_{k=0}^{l-1} s'_k = \sum_{k=0}^{l-1} g_k
$$

Now it is not difficult to verify that

$$
\mathbf{g} = \frac{1}{l+1} \mathbf{S} \cdot \mathbf{s}' \qquad \text{(VIII.7)}
$$

which corresponds to eqn (VIII.3) and is the formal solution of our problem, namely to recover the impulse response $g(t)$ (or the g_k) from the measured function $s'(t)$ or the samples s'_k taken from it, provided the duration of $g(t)$ is shorter than the period l of the maximum length sequence. It should be noted that the operation $\mathbf{S}.\mathbf{s}'$ requires considerable computing time if the period l is not very short.

At first glance the introduction of the matrix $\mathbf{S}$ may appear as an unnecessary complication of eqn (VIII.6). The great advantage of this formalism, however, is that by interchanging rows and columns according to a certain scheme this matrix can be transformed into a Hadamard matrix which contains $(l+1)(l+1) = 2^{2n}$ elements $+1$ or -1 in a highly regular pattern and which can be obtained by a simple recursion:

$$\mathbf{H}_{n+1} = \begin{bmatrix} \mathbf{H}_n & \mathbf{H}_n \\ \mathbf{H}_n & -\mathbf{H}_n \end{bmatrix} \quad \text{with } \mathbf{H}_0 = (1) \qquad \text{(VIII.8)}$$

For our previous example with $n = 3$ the matrix $\mathbf{S}$ reads

$$\begin{bmatrix}
1 & 1 & 1 & 1 & 1 & 1 & 1 & 1 \\
1 & -1 & 1 & 1 & -1 & 1 & -1 & -1 \\
1 & 1 & 1 & -1 & 1 & -1 & -1 & -1 \\
1 & 1 & -1 & 1 & -1 & -1 & -1 & 1 \\
1 & -1 & 1 & -1 & -1 & -1 & 1 & 1 \\
1 & 1 & -1 & -1 & -1 & 1 & 1 & -1 \\
1 & -1 & -1 & -1 & 1 & 1 & -1 & 1 \\
1 & -1 & -1 & 1 & 1 & -1 & 1 & -1
\end{bmatrix}$$

After interchanging its rows as well as its columns according to the following scheme:

old number: 1 2 3 4 5 6 7 8
new number: 1 8 7 4 2 6 3 5

the re-ordered matrix is

$$\begin{bmatrix}
1 & 1 & 1 & 1 & 1 & 1 & 1 & 1 \\
1 & -1 & 1 & -1 & 1 & -1 & 1 & -1 \\
1 & 1 & -1 & -1 & 1 & 1 & -1 & -1 \\
1 & -1 & -1 & 1 & 1 & -1 & -1 & 1 \\
1 & 1 & 1 & 1 & -1 & -1 & -1 & -1 \\
1 & -1 & 1 & -1 & -1 & 1 & -1 & 1 \\
1 & 1 & -1 & -1 & -1 & -1 & 1 & 1 \\
1 & -1 & -1 & 1 & -1 & 1 & 1 & -1
\end{bmatrix}$$

which is the Hadamard matrix $\mathbf{H}_3$.

To obtain the same result as with the matrix $\mathbf{S}$, the Hadamard matrix must not be applied to the sequence or one-column matrix $\mathbf{s}'$ but to a modified version $\mathbf{s}''$ of it, which is obtained by interchanging its elements according to the above scheme, and after execution of the matrix multiplication $\mathbf{H}_n \cdot \mathbf{s}''$ the elements of the resulting one-column matrix have to be rearranged into the original order to yield $\mathbf{g}$.

The important point is that, on account of the regular structure of $\mathbf{H}_n$, the multiplication $\mathbf{H}_n \cdot \mathbf{s}'$ can be carried out with a very time-efficient algorithm, a so-called 'butterfly' algorithm.

The necessary length l of the maximum length sequence s_k depends, of course, on the desired length of the impulse response. If the latter is to contain all sound frequencies up to f_m, it has to be sampled with a rate of at least $2f_m$ samples per second, and if it has significant components in the time interval from 0 to t_m, the inequality

$$l \geq 2f_m t_m \qquad \qquad (\text{VIII.9})$$

has to be fulfilled. It is of crucial importance, of course, that the sampling rate of the received signal $s'(t)$ agrees exactly with the rate at which the excitatory impulses $s(t)$ are generated and emitted.

It is beyond the scope of this representation to describe the algorithm of fast Hadamard transform, i.e. for the multiplication $\mathbf{H}_n \cdot \mathbf{s}'$; the same holds for the general rule according to which the elements of $\mathbf{s}'$ have to be permutated. For these details the reader is referred to the literature.[4,5]

VIII.3 CORRELATION MEASUREMENTS

Besides the impulse responses, various types of correlation functions have several important applications in room acoustics. One of them was mentioned in the preceding section, where the cross-correlation of two signals was used to determine the impulse response of a linear system, in particular of a room. In this section a few procedures to measure correlation functions will be described.

Generally correlation functions can be used to detect or to characterise the causal relationship between two different time functions or other continuous functions (cross-correlation function), or the degree of randomness of one function (autocorrelation function). They are especially useful in such cases where the functions to be compared are stochastic functions or have at least such a complicated structure that a mutual relationship cannot be recognised by simple inspection. It is just this aspect which frequently applies to room acoustics, as for instance in the impulse response of the transmission path between two points of a room.

Let $s_1(t)$ and $s_2(t)$ be two stationary time functions. Their cross-correlation function $\phi_{12}(\tau)$ is formed according to eqn (I.33a). Its evaluation or experimental determination is meaningful only in such cases where no analytical representation of both functions is possible or available. A special case of it with $s_1 = s_2$ is the autocorrelation function ϕ_{11}, already defined in eqn (I.33). It compares different sections of the same function and thus is a measure of how far functional relationship extends. Obviously ϕ_{11} is an even function in τ.

The function to be investigated most frequently in room acoustics is the impulse response $g(t)$ for the transmission between two points. In contrast to s_1 and s_2 it is, however, not a stationary function of time; instead it begins at a certain time and for $t \to \infty$ decays exponentially (*see* eqn (III.39)). If the

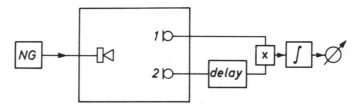

Fig. VIII.4. Measurement of cross-correlation functions in a room employing steady state excitation.

room under investigation (*see* Fig. VIII.4) is excited by white noise $r(t)$, the response to this sound signal at two different points in the room is given according to eqn (I.37) by

$$s_{1,2}(t) = \int_{-\infty}^{t} r(x) g_{1,2}(t-x)\,dx = \int_{0}^{\infty} g_{1,2}(x) r(t-x)\,dx \quad (VIII.10)$$

These functions are stationary and can be inserted into eqn (I.33a), which, after interchanging the order of integration, yields

$$\Phi_{12}(\tau) = \int_{0}^{\infty} g_1(x)\,dx \int_{0}^{\infty} g_2(y)\,dy \left[\lim \frac{1}{T_0} \int_{0}^{T_0} r(t-x) r(t-y+\tau)\,dt \right]$$

The expression in the brackets is the autocorrelation function of the random noise signal $r(t)$, taken at the argument $\tau + x - y$, which has virtually the character of a delta function because of the flat frequency spectrum of $r(t)$. Thus we obtain

$$\Phi_{12}(\tau) = \int_{-\infty}^{\infty} g_1(x)g_2(x+\tau)\,dx \qquad\qquad \text{(VIII.11)}$$

Thus there are two alternatives for measuring the cross-correlation function of g_1 and g_2. Either, as shown in Fig. VIII.4, by exciting the room with random noise or by replacing the noise generator (NG) with an impulse generator and correlating directly g_1 and g_2 according to eqn (VIII.11). The same holds for the measurement of the autocorrelation function of one impulse response, say of g_1; in this case the input of the delaying device is connected to microphone 1 too, with the result

$$\Phi_{11}(\tau) = \int_{-\infty}^{\infty} g_1(x)g_1(x+\tau)\,dx \qquad\qquad \text{(VIII.12)}$$

Another quite useful method for performing correlation measurement is the play-back method depicted schematically in Fig. VIII.5.[6] Again the room is excited by a short impulse at switch position I; the output of microphone 1 yields the impulse response $g_1(t)$, which is stored at first on a magnetic tape or a digital transient recorder. Then the signal is replayed with the recorder operated in reverse; the reversed impulse response $g_1(-t)$ thus obtained is applied once more to the room as an exciting signal (switch position II). As a result the output voltage of the microphone will be proportional to the function

$$\int_{-\infty}^{+\infty} g_1(-x)g_2(t-x)\,dx = \int_{-\infty}^{+\infty} g_1(x)g_2(x+t)\,dx$$

which agrees with eqn (VIII.11) and is thus the cross-correlation function

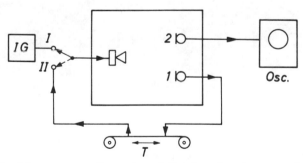

Fig. VIII.5.   Measurement of cross-correlation functions in a room by play-back.

$\Phi_{12}(t)$ which is obtained as a function of real time and can hence be observed directly on the screen of an oscilloscope. During the same phase of the measurement, the microphone 1 yields the autocorrelation function of the impulse response g_1 according to eqn (VIII.12).

As with the measurement of impulse responses, it may sometimes be

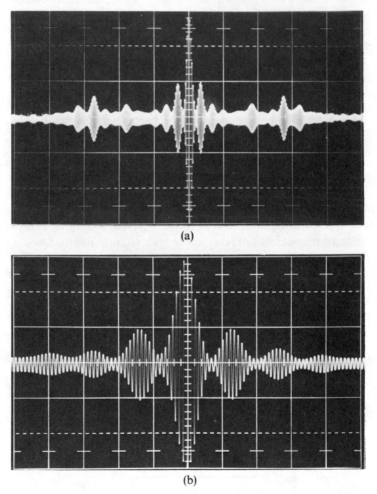

(a)

(b)

Fig. VIII.6. Autocorrelogram taken in a reverberation chamber by the play-back method. The room was excited with a Gaussian impulse with about 1 ms duration and a centre frequency of 2000 Hz. (a) Abscissa unit corresponding to 20 ms; (b) same as (a) but abscissa unit 5 ms.

desirable or necessary to restrict the frequency range of a correlation measurement. Again this can be achieved by inserting a proper bandpass filter into the electrical signal path or—if the measurement is carried out with impulse excitation—to employ test signals with the desired frequency spectrum, for instance sine bursts with Hamming or pseudo-Gaussian envelope (*see* eqns (VIII.1) and (VIII.1*a*)). As an example Fig. VIII.6 shows an autocorrelogram obtained with the play-back method in a reverberation chamber which was excited by a Gaussian impulse with about 1 ms duration and a centre frequency of 2000 Hz.

If correlation functions are determined by means of a digital computer, the most convenient way is to carry out the necessary operations in the frequency domain. Thus, to compute the autocorrelation function of some function $s(t)$, its Fourier transform is calculated by applying the FFT algorithm to $s(t)$ and its power spectrum is formed according to eqn (I.31). Finally, the autocorrelation function is obtained by applying the Wiener–Khintchine relation (I.32), i.e. by transforming the result back into the time domain. The cross-correlation function of two functions s_1 and s_2 with Fourier transforms $S_1(f)$ and $S_2(f)$ follows the same scheme: the product $S_1 S_2^*$ is known as the cross-power spectrum of both signals, and its (inverse) Fourier transform is the desired cross-correlation function.

VIII.4 EXAMINATION OF THE TIME STRUCTURE OF THE IMPULSE RESPONSE

After this digression into correlation analysis we return now to the impulse response of a room or, more precisely, to the impulse response of a particular transmission path within a room. Some of the information it contains on the acoustics of the room can be found directly by inspection of a 'reflectogram', by which term we mean the graphical representation of the impulse response or another time function which is closely related to it. Other properties require the extraction of certain parameters which have been discussed in the preceding chapter. (The measurement of reverberation time will be postponed to a separate section below.) In any case, however, some further processing of the measured impulse response is useful or necessary.

From the visual inspection of a reflectogram the experienced acoustician may learn quite a bit about the acoustical merits and faults of the place for which it has been measured. One important question is, for instance, to what extent the direct sound will be supported by shortly delayed reflections, and how these are distributed in time. Furthermore, the occurrence of strong and isolated peaks with long delays hints at the danger of audible echoes and may suggest the application of quantitative echo criteria, as for instance that of Dietsch and Kraak (*see* Ref. 12 of Chapter VII).

The direct examination of a reflectogram is greatly facilitated—especially that of a band-limited reflectogram—if insignificant details of it are removed beforehand. In principle, this can be effected by rectifying and smoothing the impulse response. This process, however, introduces some arbitrariness into the obtained reflectogram with regard to the applied time constant: if it is too short, the smoothing effect may be insufficient; if it is too long, important details of the reflectogram will be suppressed. One way to avoid this uncertainty is to apply a mathematically well-defined procedure to the impulse response, namely to form its 'envelope'. Let $s(t)$ denote any signal, then its envelope is defined as

$$e(t) = \sqrt{[s(t)]^2 + [\breve{s}(t)]^2} \qquad \text{(VIII.13)}$$

Here $\breve{s}(t)$ denotes the Hilbert transform of $s(t)$:

$$\breve{s}(t) = \frac{1}{\pi} \int_{-\infty}^{+\infty} \frac{s(t-t')}{t'} \, dt' \equiv \mathscr{H}[s(t)] \qquad \text{(VIII.14)}$$

which has quite a number of interesting properties and applications (see Ref. 1 of Chapter I, for instance). Of course the operation prescribed by eqn (VIII.14) can readily be carried out with a digital computer. Apart from this there are several ways to perform the Hilbert transform with analogue circuits. Since

$$\mathscr{H}[\cos(\omega t)] = \sin(\omega t) \quad \text{and} \quad \mathscr{H}[\sin(\omega t)] = -\cos(\omega t)$$

the Hilbert transform can be equally well described as a 90° phase shift of all spectral components of $s(t)$. Thus what is necessary to obtain the Hilbert transform of the impulse response $g(t)$ in order to form its envelope is just to apply it to a wide-band phase shifter. In a subsequent step $g(t)$ and $\breve{g}(t)$ must be squared and added. The final operation of drawing the square root from the sum can be omitted; then the result is the squared envelope of the impulse response.

Figure VIII.7 illustrates how an experimental reflectogram is modified by forming its squared envelope $[e(t)]^2$. It is obvious that the latter exhibits the significant components much more clearly.

But the simpler process of rectifying and smoothing the impulse response

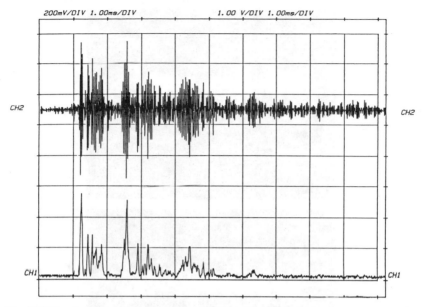

Fig. VIII.7. Impulse response (upper part) and its squared envelope, obtained by means of an analogue Hilbert transformer. Total range of abscissa is 400 ms.

may also have its merits, provided the time constant of smoothing is chosen in such a way as to reflect the inertia of our hearing organ (*see* Sections VII.2 and VII.3). A reflectogram processed in this way will account for the fact that an audible echo is not necessarily brought about by a single strong reflection but may be caused by several or many reflections of moderate strength concentrated in a narrow time interval and which are accumulated by the inertia of our hearing subjectively into one single event—namely an echo. This can be achieved by a simple electrical network consisting of a capacitor and a resistor, to which the rectified impulse response is applied. Each reflection provides a charge increase to the capacitor, which on the other hand disappears gradually through the resistor. Closely spaced reflections show up as a 'mountain' with several steps in the capacitor voltage, whereas details which are insignificant to our ear are virtually suppressed since they contribute to the slowly varying 'background' voltage only. According to Niese the time constant of the RC combination should be about 25 ms (*see* Ref. 17 of Chapter VII).

In Fig. VIII.8 a few experimental 'reflectograms' are shown as an example, obtained at several places in a lecture room which was excited by

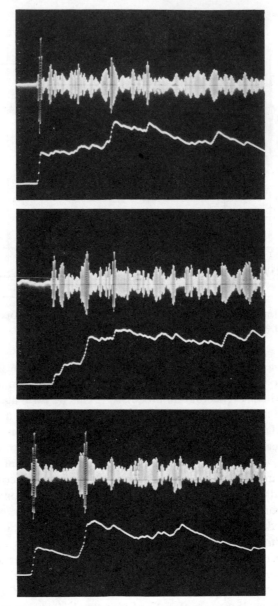

Fig. VIII.8.   Reflectograms of a lecture room at different places (centre frequency 3000 Hz, impulse duration about 1 ms). Upper traces without and lower traces with weighting RC network.

Gaussian impulses at a frequency of 3000 Hz and a pulse duration of about 1 ms, which had roughly a frequency bandwidth of 500 Hz. The lower trace of each registration shows the result of the weighting described above. The total length of an oscillogram corresponds to a time interval of 190 ms. The uppermost reflectogram was taken at a place close to the sound source, consequently the direct sound is relatively strong. The most outstanding feature in the lowest oscillogram is the strong reflection delayed by about 40 ms with regard to the direct sound. It is not heard as an echo, since it still lies within the integration time of our ear (*see* Section VII.4).

Of course the impulse response can be smoothed as well or even more conveniently by simulating the effect of an RC network with a digital computer. The same holds for the evaluation of the single number parameters discussed in Section VII.4 (definition D, clarity C, echo degree ε, etc.).

As we mentioned earlier, periodic successions in the impulse response of a room can appear subjectively in a very undesirable way. This is true even when the periodic components are obscured by other non-periodically distributed reflections and therefore cannot be detected simply by visual examination of a reflectogram. Usually the periodic components are caused by repeated reflections of sound rays between parallel walls, or generally in rooms with a very regular shape, as for instance in rooms which are circular or regularly polygonal in cross-section. At relatively short repetition times they are perceived as colouration, at least under certain conditions (*see* Section VII.3). But even a single dominating reflection may cause audible colouration, especially of music, since the corresponding transmission function has a regular structure or substructure.

The most adequate techniques for the investigation of the randomness or pseudo-randomness of an impulse response is the autocorrelation analysis. In this procedure all the irregularly distributed components are swept together into a single central peak (*see* Fig. VIII.6), whereas the remaining reflections will form side components and satellite maxima in the autocorrelogram. In order to decide the question of whether or not a certain side maximum might indicate audible colouration, we at first form, from the experimental autocorrelation function ϕ_{gg}, a 'weighted auto-correlation function':[7]

$$\phi'_{gg}(\tau) = b(\tau)\phi_{gg}(\tau) \qquad (VIII.15)$$

The weighting function $b(\tau)$ can be calculated from the thresholds represented in Fig. VII.9 and is shown in Fig. VIII.9.

Let us denote by τ_0 the value of the argument at which the side maximum

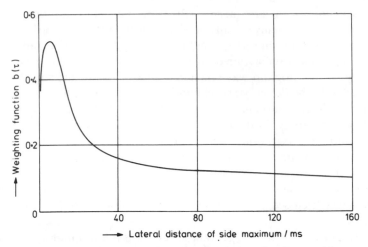

Fig. VIII.9. Weighting function for autocorrelation functions with respect to colouration.[7]

second to the central maximum (at $t = 0$) appears. Then we have to expect audible colouration if

$$\phi'_{gg}(\tau_0) > 0{\cdot}06\phi'_{gg}(0) \qquad\qquad\text{(VIII.16)}$$

no matter if this side maximum is caused by a single strong reflection or by a periodic succession of reflections.[8]

The temporal structure of a room's impulse response determines not only the shape of the autocorrelation function obtained in this room but also its modulation transfer function (MTF), which was introduced in Section VII.4. Indeed, as was shown by M. R. Schroeder,[9] the complex MTF for white noise as a primary sound signal (in the notation of eqn (VII.16))

$$\underline{m}(\Omega) = m \exp\left(-\mathrm{i}\Omega t_0\right) \qquad\qquad\text{(VIII.17)}$$

is related to the impulse response by

$$\underline{m}\,(\Omega) = \frac{\displaystyle\int_0^{\infty} [g(t)]^2 \exp\left(\mathrm{i}\Omega t\right)\mathrm{d}t}{\displaystyle\int_0^{\infty} [g(t)]^2\,\mathrm{d}t} \qquad\qquad\text{(VIII.18)}$$

As described in Section VII.4, a reliable criterion for the intelligibility of speech in auditoria, the 'speech transmission index' (STI), can be deduced from the magnitude of the complex MTF, $m = |\underline{m}|$. Unfortunately the experimental determination of the modulation transfer function and the evaluation of the speech transmission index is a relatively time-consuming and complicated process. For this reason Houtgast and Steeneken[10] have developed a simplified version of the STI, called 'RApid Speech Transmission Index' (RASTI). It is obtained by measuring $m = |\underline{m}|$ for four modulation frequencies $\Omega/2\pi$ in the octave band centred at 500 Hz, and for five modulation frequencies in the 2000-Hz octave band. The applied modulation frequencies range from 0·7 to 11·2 Hz. Each of the nine values of m is converted into an 'apparent signal-to-noise ratio':

$$(S/N)_{app} = 10 \log_{10}\left(\frac{m}{1-m}\right) \qquad \text{(VIII.19)}$$

These figures are averaged after truncating any which exceeds the range of ± 15. The final parameter is obtained by normalising the average $\overline{(S/N)}_{app}$ into the range from 0 to 1:

$$RASTI = \tfrac{1}{30}[\overline{(S/N)}_{app} + 15] \qquad \text{(VIII.20)}$$

For practical RASTI measurements both octave bands are emitted simultaneously, each with a complex power envelope containing five modulation frequencies. Likewise, the automated analysis of the received sound signal is performed in parallel. With these provisions it is possible to keep the duration of one measurement as low as about 12 s. By extensive investigations on the validity of RASTI, carried out in several countries (i.e. languages), the abovementioned authors were able to show that there is good agreement between the results of RASTI and the more elaborate STI, and furthermore that the RASTI method is well suited to rate the speech intelligibility in auditoria. Table VIII.1 shows the relation between five classes of speech quality and certain intervals of RASTI values.

Table VIII.1
Relation between Scores of Speech
Transmission Quality and RASTI

Quality score	RASTI
Bad	<0·32
Poor	0·32–0·45
Fair	0·45–0·60
Good	0·60–0·75
Excellent	>0·75

VIII.5 MEASUREMENT OF REVERBERATION

For reasons which have been discussed earlier, Sabine's reverberation time is still the best known and most important quantity in room acoustics. This fact is the justification for describing the measurement of this important parameter in a separate section which includes that of its younger relative, the 'early decay time' (EDT).

Although both the reverberation time of a room as well as the 'early decay time' at a particular place in it can be derived from the corresponding impulse responses, we start by describing the more traditional methods which still maintain their place in everyday practice. They are usually based on the analysis of the decay process and hence on the evaluation of decay curves. Accordingly, the first step of a decay measurement is to record decay curves over a sufficiently large range of the decaying sound level.

The standard equipment for this purpose (which can be modified in many ways) is depicted schematically in Fig. VIII.10. A loudspeaker LS,

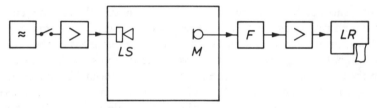

Fig. VIII.10.   Reverberation measurement by steady state excitation of the room.

driven by a signal generator, excites the room to steady state conditions. The output voltage of the microphone M is fed to an amplifier and filter F, and then to a logarithmic recorder LR, whose deflection is calibrated in decibels. At a given moment the excitation is interrupted by a switch and the recorder, whose paper transport is switched on simultaneously or shortly before, records the decay process starting at that moment.

The signal from the generator is generally a frequency modulated sinusoidal signal whose momentary frequency covers a narrow range. The modulation frequency chosen is usually about 10 Hz. A random noise generator followed by a filter which separates out a frequency band either of octave or third octave width is equally or possibly more suitable. Pure sinusoidal tones are applied only occasionally, as for example to excite individual modes and to measure the associated decay constants, a procedure which may be advantageous in very small rooms at low frequencies. The range of midfrequencies, for which reverberation measurements are usually taken, extends from about 50 to 10 000 Hz; most frequently, however, the range from 100 to 5000 Hz is considered to be sufficient.

The loudspeaker, or more generally the sound source, is usually placed at the same location where, during normal use of the room, the natural sound source is located. This applies not only to reverberation measurements but also to other measurements. Because of the validity of the reciprocity principle, however (*see* Section III.1), the location of sound source and microphone can be exchanged without altering the results, in cases where this is practical and provided that the sound source and the microphone have no directionality.

If the sound field were completely diffuse, the decay curves should be independent of the location of the sound source and the microphone. Since these ideal conditions hardly ever exist in normal rooms, it is advisable to carry out several measurements for each frequency at different microphone positions, as not only the reverberation time, which corresponds to the average slope of a decay curve, but also other details of the curve may be relevant to the acoustics of a hall or of a particular point in it.

One of the most interesting details of a decay curve is its initial slope represented by the 'early decay time', which is of importance to the subjective impression of reverberation and which may exhibit substantial variation from one seat to another (*see* Section VII.6). Hence, in larger halls, decay curves should be recorded at a number of representative places, for instance on the stage, on balconies and of course at various seats on the main floor.

The microphone is followed by a filter—usually an octave or third octave filter—largely to improve the signal-to-noise ratio, i.e. to reduce the disturbing effects of noise produced in the hall itself as well as that of the microphone and amplifier noise. Of course any non-linearity caused by too large signals must be avoided since this gives rise to erroneous decay curves.

For recording the decay curves a level recorder is utilised, which records the logarithm of the applied voltage on paper or something similar and which must be sufficiently inertia free. For correct evaluation of the curves the speed of the paper as well as the sensitivity has to be known exactly. Usually the usable paper width corresponds to a level range of 50 dB. For determination of the reverberation time the decay curve is approximated by a straight line as closely as possible by the use of a transparent ruler.

From its slope $\Delta L/\Delta t$, in dB/s, the reverberation time is obtained by

$$T = 60\left(\frac{\Delta L}{\Delta t}\right)^{-1} \qquad\qquad \text{(VIII.21)}$$

Frequently the slope of the decay curve is determined in the range from -5 to -35 dB relative to the steady state level. This procedure is intended to improve the comparability and reproducibility of the obtained reverberation times in such cases where the drop in level does not occur linearly. It is doubtful, however, whether the evaluation of an average slope from curves which are far from straight is very meaningful. We have already mentioned that the initial slope of a decay curve which leads to the 'early decay time' is probably more significant from a subjective point of view. The same applies to the determination of the absorption coefficient of a test material from reverberation measurements (Section VIII.8), since the initial slope is closely related to the average damping constant of all excited vibrational modes (*see* eqn (III.44)). The evaluation of the initial slope, using the abovementioned measuring techniques, is subject to considerable errors due to irregular level fluctuations, which are superimposed on the general fall in level and which can be considered to be complicated beats or to be the result of incomplete cancellation of the mixed terms in eqn (III.41). These fluctuations obscure the proper decay curve to a certain extent.

Furthermore, these fluctuations render automatic reverberation measurements relatively unreliable. In the course of time, various instruments and methods have been developed which dispense with the complete recording of decay curves; instead these instruments indicate the reverberation time directly. The feature common to these instruments is a switch, which starts and subsequently stops a timer when the momentary decay level passes two prescribed values. Alternatively, a certain time interval can be prescribed, at the beginning and the end of which the associated levels are measured and compared with each other. Since these instruments do not take into account the whole decay but only the level at two moments, accidental or random level fluctuations at the boundaries of the time interval can have considerable influence on the result.

These quasi-random fluctuations of decay level and the associated uncertainties about the true shape of a decay curve can be avoided, in principle, by averaging over a great number of individual reverberation curves, each of which was obtained by random noise excitation of the room. Fortunately this very time-consuming procedure will lead to the same result as another much more elegant method, called 'the method of integrated impulse response', which was proposed and first applied by Schroeder.[11] It is based on the following relationship between the ensemble average $\langle h^2(t) \rangle$ of all possible decay curves (for a certain place and bandwidth of exciting noise) and the corresponding impulse response $g(t)$:

$$\langle h^2(t) \rangle = \int_t^\infty [g(x)]^2 \, dx = \int_0^\infty [g(x)]^2 \, dx - \int_0^t [g(x)]^2 \, dx \quad (VIII.22)$$

$g(t)$ includes all linear distortions (of loudspeakers, for instance), the effect of band-limiting filters, and so on.

The proof of this relation is similar to that of eqn (VIII.11). Suppose the room is excited by white noise $r(t)$, which is switched off at the time $t = 0$. According to eqn (I.37), the sound decay is given by

$$h(t) = \int_{-\infty}^0 r(x)g(t - x) \, dx = \int_t^\infty g(x)r(t - x) \, dx \quad \text{for } t \geq 0$$

Squaring the latter expression yields a double integral, which after averaging reads

$$\langle h^2(t) \rangle = \int g(x) \, dx \int g(y)\langle r(t - x)r(t - y) \rangle \, dy$$

The brackets $\langle \ \rangle$ on the right-hand side indicate that an ensemble average is to be formed which is identical with the autocorrelation function of $r(t)$ with the argument $x - y$. Now the autocorrelation function of white noise is a delta function. Invoking eqn (I.36) shows immediately that the double integral is reduced to the single integral of eqn (VIII.22). This derivation is valid no matter whether the impulse response is that measured for the full frequency range or only of a part of it.

Equation (VIII.22) tells us that integrating the squared impulse response within the indicated limits is equivalent to averaging over all possible decay curves which can be obtained at the same place with white noise excitation. This shows very clearly that the method of 'integrated impulse response' is superior to all other methods of reverberation measurement, because it is free of any accidental circumstances of excitation.

The merits of this method may be underlined by the examples shown in Fig. VIII.11. The upper decay curves have been measured with the traditional method, i.e. with random noise excitation, according to Fig. VIII.10. They exhibit strong fluctuations of the decaying level which do not reflect any acoustical properties of the transmission path and hence of the

Room Acoustics

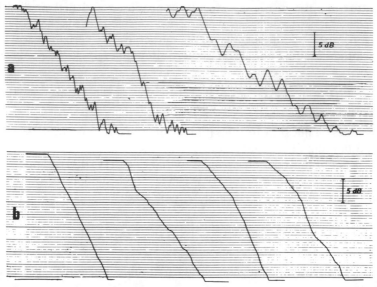

Fig. VIII.11. Examples of experimentally obtained reverberation curves: (a) recorded according to Fig. VIII.10; (b) recorded by application of eqn (VIII.22).

room, but are due to the random character of the exciting signal; if one of these recordings were repeated, each new decay curve would differ from the preceding one in many details. In contrast, the lower curves, obtained for different conditions by processing the impulse responses according to eqn (VIII.22), are free of such confusing fluctuations and hence contain only significant information. Repeated measurements for one situation yield identical results,[12] which is not too surprising since these decay curves are based on an exactly reproducible characteristic, namely the impulse response. It is clear that the reverberation time can be obtained from such curves with much greater accuracy than from those recorded in the traditional way, which is even more true for the 'early decay time'. Furthermore, any characteristic deviations of the sound decay from exponential behaviour are much more obvious (*see*, for instance, the third curve below in Fig. VIII.11).

Concerning practical application, it is certainly more convenient to carry out the operations prescribed by eqn (VIII.22) with a digital computer than with analogue equipment. In both cases, however, a problem of crucial importance arises, namely how to interpret the infinite upper limit of integration in eqn (VIII.22), since this formula does not account for the acoustical or electronic background noise which is present in every experimental setup. Therefore taking the ∞ sign literally would lead to a catastrophe. If a finite integration interval is chosen to be too long, the recorded decay curve will have a tail which limits the useful dynamic range. Too short an integration time, on the other hand, will cause a downward bend of the curve, which is also awkward. There seems to be no other way than to determine the integration time most appropriate to a certain experimental condition by a trial-and-error procedure.

We conclude this section by mentioning that the absorption of a room and hence its reverberation time could be obtained, at least in principle, from the steady state sound level or energy density according to eqn (V.36) or (V.37). Likewise, the modulation transfer function could be used to determine the reverberation time (*see* eqn (VII.17)). In practice, however, these methods do not offer any advantages compared to those described above, since they are certainly more time consuming and less accurate.

VIII.6 MEASUREMENT OF THE DIRECTIONAL COMPOSITION OF SOUND FIELDS

The directional distribution of sound waves arriving at a receiver (or at the human head) has physical implications as well as subjective ones. From the physical point of view it may be asked to what extent the sound field is diffuse, since this is the crucial condition for the validity of the relations which are most common and important in room acoustics, namely that for sound decay, reverberation time and steady state energy or level (*see* Sections V.3–V.5). The subjective aspect is related to our sensation of 'spaciousness' (*see* Section VII.5), which seems to be a major ingredient particularly of good concert hall acoustics.

It is evident that both aspects of directional composition should be covered by different experimental procedures, that means that methods should be at hand to indicate the objective directional distribution and others which are tailored for directional quantities relevant from the subjective standpoint. In the following discussion we start with the first kind of measuring procedures.

The directional distribution is characterised by the angular dependence of intensity $I(\varphi, \vartheta)$ in a sound field (*see* eqn (IV.14)). This quantity can be measured by scanning all directions with a directional microphone of sufficiently high resolution. Let $\Gamma(\varphi, \vartheta)$ be the directivity function, i.e. the relative sensitivity of the microphone as a function of angles φ and ϑ, from

which a plane wave reaches it, then the squared output voltage of the
microphone in a complicated sound field is

$$I'(\varphi, \vartheta) = \int \int I(\varphi', \vartheta') |\Gamma(\varphi - \varphi', \vartheta - \vartheta')|^2 \sin \vartheta' \, d\vartheta' \, d\varphi' \quad \text{(VIII.23)}$$

Only if the microphone has a high directionality, i.e. if $\Gamma(\varphi, \vartheta)$ has
substantial values only within a very limited solid angle, is there a virtual
agreement between the measured and the actual directional distribution; in
all other cases irregularities of the distribution are more or less smoothed
out.

The measurement is usually performed using a stationary sound source
which emits filtered random noise or warble tones (frequency modulated
sinusoidal tones). It is much more time consuming to determine
experimentally the directional distribution in a decaying sound field by
recording the same decay process at many different orientations of the
directional microphone and to compare subsequently the intensities
obtained at corresponding times relative to the arrival of the direct sound
or to the moment at which the sound source was interrupted.

Quantitatively, the degree of approximation to perfectly diffuse
conditions can be characterised by 'directional diffusion' defined according
to Thiele[13] in the following way. Let $\langle I' \rangle$ be the measured quantity
averaged over all directions and

$$m = \frac{1}{4\pi \langle I' \rangle} \int \int [I' - \langle I' \rangle] \, d\Omega \quad \text{(VIII.24}a\text{)}$$

the average of the absolute deviation from it. Furthermore, let m_0 be the
quantity formed analogously to m by replacing I' in eqn (VIII.23) by $|\Gamma|^2$.
Then the directional diffusion is

$$d = \left(1 - \frac{m}{m_0}\right) \cdot 100\% \quad \text{(VIII.24}b\text{)}$$

The introduction of m_0 effects a certain normalisation and consequently
$d = 100\%$ in a perfectly diffuse sound field, whereas in the sound field
consisting of one single plane wave the directional diffusion becomes zero.
This procedure, however, does not eliminate the fact that the result still
depends on the directional characteristics of the microphone. Therefore
such results can only be compared if they have been gained by means of

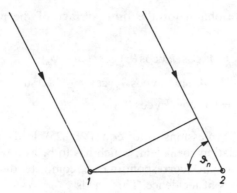

Fig. VIII.12.   Derivation of eqns (VIII.26).

similar microphones. Numerous results on the directional distribution measured in this way can be found in papers published by Meyer and Thiele[14] and by Junius.[15]

If one is not interested in all the details of the directional distribution but only in a measure for its uniformity, more indirect methods can be applied, i.e. one can measure a quantity whose value depends on diffusion. One of the most reliable procedures is the correlation of the steady state sound pressure at two different points, which yields characteristic values in a diffuse sound field. Or more precisely: we consider the correlation coefficient Ψ defined in eqn (VII.18) of the sound pressures p_1 and p_2 at two different points

$$\Psi = \frac{\overline{p_1 p_2}}{(\overline{p_1^2} \cdot \overline{p_2^2})^{1/2}} \qquad (VIII.25)$$

To calculate the correlation coefficient in the case of a diffuse sound field we assume that the room is excited by random noise with a very small bandwidth. The sound field can be considered to be composed of plane waves with equal amplitudes and randomly distributed phase angles ψ_n. The sound pressures due to one such wave at points 1 and 2, arriving under an angle ϑ_n (*see* Fig. VIII.12), is

$$p_1(t) = A \cos(\omega t - \psi_n) \qquad p_2(t) = A \cos(\omega t - \psi_n - kx \cos \vartheta_n)$$

Hence

$$\overline{p_1^2} = \overline{p_2^2} = \tfrac{1}{2}A^2$$

Furthermore, we obtain for the time average of the product of both pressures

$$\overline{p_1 p_2} = A^2 \cos{(kx \cos{\vartheta_n})} \overline{\cos^2{(\omega t - \psi_n)}}$$
$$+ A^2 \sin{(kx \cos{\vartheta_n})} \overline{\cos{(\omega t - \psi_n)} \sin{(\omega t - \psi_n)}}$$
$$= \tfrac{1}{2} A^2 \cos{(kx \cos{\vartheta_n})}$$

Inserting these expressions into eqn (VIII.25) leads to a direction-dependent correlation coefficient, which has to be averaged subsequently with constant weight (corresponding to complete diffusion) over all possible directions of incidence. This yields

$$\Psi(x) = \frac{\sin kx}{kx} \qquad\qquad (\text{VIII.26})$$

If, however, the directions of incident sound waves are not uniformly distributed over the entire solid angle but only in a plane containing both points, we obtain, instead of eqn (VIII.26),

$$\Psi(x) = J_0(kx) \qquad\qquad (\text{VIII.26}a)$$

(J_0 = Bessel function of order zero).

If the connection between both points is perpendicular to the plane of two-dimensional diffusion, the result is

$$\Psi(x) = 1 \qquad\qquad (\text{VIII.26}b)$$

The functions given by eqns (VIII.26) to (VIII.26b) are plotted in Fig. VIII.13. Thus the dependence of the correlation coefficient on the distance x gives an indication of the uniformity of the directional distribution. Evidently reliable diffusion measurements using this method can be carried out only by choosing several substantially different orientations of the axis connecting points 1 and 2 in Fig. VIII.12.

The derivation presented above is strictly valid only for signals with vanishing frequency bandwidths. Practically, however, its result can be applied with sufficient accuracy to signals with bandwidths of up to a third octave. For wider frequency bands an additional frequency averaging of the results is necessary.

For measuring the correlation coefficient, it should be noted that it is the value of the cross-correlation function at argument $\tau = 0$. The method of

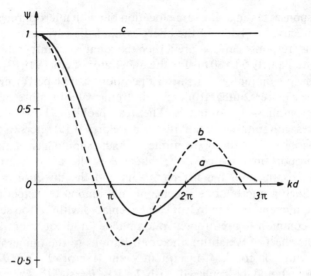

Fig. VIII.13. Theoretical dependence of correlation coefficient Ψ on the distance between both measuring points: (a) in a three-dimensional diffuse sound field; (b) in a two-dimensional diffuse sound field, measuring axis in plane of directions of sound incidence; (c) same as (b) but measuring axis perpendicular to sound propagation.

measuring must guarantee that the maximum of the cross-correlation function is safely observed even if there are unknown delays in one of the two signal paths.

Equation (VIII.26) has a remarkable similarity to eqn (II.34), which describes the pressure fluctuations in front of a rigid wall at random sound incidence. This similarity is not merely accidental, since these fluctuations are caused by interference of the incident and the reflected waves which become less distinct with increasing distance from the wall according to the decreasing coherence of those waves. On the other hand, it is just the correlation factor of eqn (VIII.25) which characterises the degree of coherence of two signals. The additional factor of 2 in the argument of eqn (II.34) is due to the fact that the distance of both observation points here is equivalent to the distance of the point from its image, the rigid wall being considered as a mirror.

Now we turn to the measurement of subjectively relevant directional parameters. One of them is the 'early lateral energy fraction' S, defined by eqn (VII.19). As discussed in Section VII.5, this quantity is closely related to the subjective impression of 'spaciousness'. It is determined from two impulse responses taken at the same location but with microphones having different directivities. To yield the energies E_i of the various components these impulse responses are squared, then the squares are integrated within proper limits, namely 5 to 80 ms for the numerator of eqn (VII.19) and 0 to 80 ms for the denominator. The latter operations can be performed either by analogue squarers, integrators and electronic gates or more easily by a properly programmed computer. The real problem, however, is the microphones with suitable directivities: since eqn (VII.19) refers to energies, the microphone for obtaining the numerator sum should have a directivity function proportional to $|\cos\theta|^{1/2}$, where θ is the angle between the horizontal axis through the listener's ears and the direction of sound incidence. Such a microphone is certainly not among the experimenter's standard equipment. Fortunately it can be replaced without too serious an error by a common figure-of-eight microphone (gradient microphone).[16] This has the effect of weighting the contributions to the numerator with $\cos^2\theta$ instead of $\cos\theta$. Consequently the factor $1 - \cos\theta$ in the denominator should be replaced with $1 - \cos^2\theta = \sin^2\theta$. Therefore the denominator can be obtained with the same figure-of-eight microphone as the nominator; between both measurements the microphone is just turned by 90° around a vertical axis. This is a great advantage because with two separate microphones the quality of the measurement could be impaired by different frequency responses.

As an alternative the 'interaural cross-correlation' (IACC) as defined by eqns (VII.21) and (VII.22) can be determined, which is also an indicator for the subjective 'spaciousness'. Again the determination of this quantity is based upon impulse responses, which now are measured at both ears of a listener. If such measurements are carried out only occasionally, the responses can be obtained with two small microphones fixed next to the entrance of both ear channels of a person whose only function is to scatter the sound waves properly. For routine work it is certainly more convenient to replace the human head by an artificial head with built-in microphones.

VIII.7 MEASUREMENT OF WALL ABSORPTION WITH THE IMPEDANCE TUBE

We conclude this chapter by describing in this and the subsequent section the measurement of a purely physical property, namely of sound absorption by boundaries (including that of chairs and audience). The knowledge of absorption is imperative for all tasks related to room acoustical design, i.e. for the prediction of the reverberation time, for planning model experiments (*see* Section IX.5), for computer simulation of the sound propagation in enclosures (Section IX.6), etc.

If it is sufficient to determine the absorption coefficient of a plane boundary for normal sound incidence only, this can be done by means of a simple device known as a 'standing wave tube' or 'impedance tube'. This is a pipe with rigid walls and with a rectangular or circular cross-section. To avoid resonances of the tube one of its two ends usually has a sound absorbing termination, but this is not essential for the principle of the method. At the other end the sample of the material under investigation is mounted in the same way as it is to be used in practice, for example at some distance in front of a rigid back plate, which takes the place of a rigid wall. A plane sound wave is generated in the tube and is partially reflected by the sample according to its acoustical impedance. As a result, a partially standing wave is formed in front of the sample in which the sound pressure is measured by a movable probe microphone, which must be small enough not to distort the sound field to any great extent. In Fig. VIII.14 the measuring setup is drawn schematically.

The tube should be long enough to permit the formation of at least one maximum and one minimum of the pressure distribution at the lowest frequency of interest. The lateral dimensions have to be chosen in such a way that at the highest measuring frequency they are still smaller than a certain fraction of the wavelength λ_{min}. Or, more exactly, the following requirements must be met:

$$\text{Dimension of the wider side} < 0.5\lambda_{min} \quad \text{for rectangular tubes}$$
$$\text{Diameter} < 0.586\lambda_{min} \quad \text{for circular tubes}$$
$$(VIII.27)$$

Otherwise, apart from the appearance of an essentially plane fundamental wave propagating at free field sound velocity of the medium, higher order wave types may occur with non-constant lateral pressure distributions and with different and frequency-dependent sound velocities. On the other hand, the cross-section of the tube must not be too small, since otherwise the wave attenuation due to losses at the wall surface would become too high. Generally at least two tubes of different dimensions are needed in order to cover the frequency range from about 100 to 5000 Hz.

For the determination of the absorption coefficient it is sufficient to

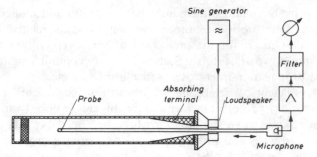

Fig. VIII.14. Impedance tube method, schematic representation.

measure the maximum and the minimum values of the sound pressure amplitudes, i.e. the pressures in the nodes and the anti-nodes of the standing wave. According to eqns (II.9) and (II.1), the absolute value of the reflection factor and the absorption coefficient are given by

$$|R| = \frac{\hat{p}_{max} - \hat{p}_{min}}{\hat{p}_{max} + \hat{p}_{min}} \qquad\qquad \text{(VIII.28)}$$

$$\alpha = \frac{4\hat{p}_{max}\hat{p}_{min}}{(\hat{p}_{max} + \hat{p}_{min})^2} \qquad\qquad \text{(VIII.29)}$$

Since the loudspeaker is not generally free from distortion and therefore also produces higher harmonics of the measuring frequency (overtones), particularly at those points where the sound pressure is at a minimum for the fundamental frequency, the use of a bandpass filter, tuned to the measuring frequency and following the microphone, is recommended. The scale of the indicating meter can be calibrated so as to indicate directly the absorption coefficient if the microphone is in the minimum pressure position and if the pointer has been adjusted earlier to a certain deflection when the microphone was in the maximum position. If possible, the maxima and minima closest to the test specimen should be used for the evaluation of R and α since these values are influenced least by the attenuation of the waves. It is possible, however, to eliminate this influence by interpolation or by calculation, but in most cases it is hardly worthwhile doing this.

The absorption coefficient is not the only quantity which can be obtained by probing the standing wave; additional information can be derived from the location of the pressure maximum (pressure node) which is next to the test specimen. According to eqn (II.9), the condition for the occurrence of a pressure node is $\cos(2kx + \chi) = -1$. If x_{min} is the distance of the nearest pressure node from the surface of the sample, this condition yields for the phase angle χ of the reflection factor

$$\chi = \pi\left(1 - \frac{4x_{min}}{\lambda}\right) \tag{VIII.30}$$

Once the complex reflection factor is known, the wall impedance Z or the specific impedance ζ of the material under test can be obtained by eqns (II.6) and (II.3), for instance by applying a graphical representation of these relations known as a 'Smith chart' (*see* Fig. VIII.15). Furthermore, the specific impedance of the sample can be used to determine its absorption coefficient α_{uni} for random sound incidence, either from Fig. II.11 or by applying eqn (II.38). In many practical situations this latter absorption coefficient is more relevant than that for normal sound incidence. However, the result of this procedure will be correct only if the material under test can be assumed to be of the 'locally reacting' type (*see* Sections II.1 and VI.6).

Several attempts have been made to replace the somewhat involved and

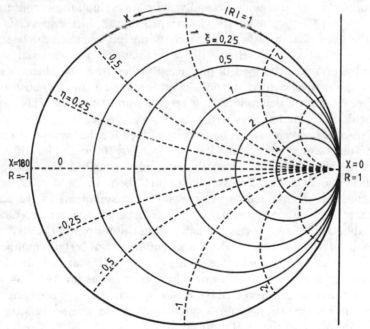

Fig. VIII.15. Smith chart (circles of constant real and imaginary part of ζ, represented in the complex R-plane).

time-consuming standing wave method by faster and more modern procedures. In fact, if a short impulse is applied to the test specimen, the reflected impulse (i.e. its impulse response) will contain in principle all information on its reflectivity, and the reflection factor can be obtained by Fourier transformation of the response. Moreover, the more sophisticated methods described in Section VIII.2 can be employed too. So far, however, no method has evolved from such attempts, which really could compete with the traditional tube method as far as simplicity, reliability and accuracy is concerned.

VIII.8 MEASUREMENT OF ABSORPTION WITH THE REVERBERATION CHAMBER

The reverberation method of absorption measurement is superior to the impedance tube method in several respects. First of all, the measurement is performed with a diffuse sound field, i.e. under conditions which are much more realistic for many practical applications than those encountered in a one-dimensional waveguide. Secondly, there are no limitations concerning the type and construction of the absorber, and furthermore, in the reverberation chamber, the arrangement of the test specimen can be set up to correspond very closely to the way in which the material under consideration is to be used in practice. Furthermore, the absorption of single absorbers, which cannot be characterised by an absorption coefficient, can be determined in a reverberation chamber. This applies particularly for audience as well as for unoccupied chairs.

A so-called reverberation chamber is required for the method discussed here. This is a small room with a volume of at least $100 \, \text{m}^3$, better still 200 to $300 \, \text{m}^3$, whose walls are as smooth and rigid as possible. The absorption coefficient α_0 of the bare walls, which should be uniform in construction and finish, is determined by reverberation measurements in the empty chamber and by application of one of the reverberation formulae. (Usually the Sabine formula, eqn (V.24), is sufficient for this purpose.) Then a certain amount of the material under investigation (or a certain number of absorbers) is brought into the chamber; the test material should be mounted in the same way as it would be applied in the practical case. The reverberation time is decreased by the test specimen and by applying once more the reverberation formula (preferably in the Eyring version, eqn (V.23), in this case) the total absorption

$$S_0 \bar{\alpha} = A = S\alpha + (S_0 - S)\alpha_0 \qquad \text{(VIII.31)}$$

is obtained, from which the absorption coefficient α of the test material can be calculated. In this equation S_0 is the total wall area of the chamber and S is the area of the test specimen. In the case of single absorbers, the first term on the right-hand side of eqn (VIII.31) is replaced by the number of absorbers times the absorption cross-section of one absorber (*see* Section VI.5).

When applying the reverberation formulae, the air absorption term $4mV$ can usually be neglected, since it is contained in the absorption of the empty chamber as well as in that of the chamber containing the test material and therefore will almost cancel out. Because the chamber has a small volume the effect of air attenuation is low anyway.

The techniques of reverberation measurement itself have been described in detail in Section VIII.2, and therefore no further discussion on this point is necessary.

The advantages of the reverberation method as mentioned at the beginning of this section are paid for by a considerable uncertainty concerning the reliability and accuracy of results obtained with it. In fact, several round robin tests[17,18] in which the same specimen of an absorbing material has been tested in different laboratories (and consequently with different reverberation chambers) have revealed a remarkable disagreement in the results. This must certainly be attributed to different degrees of sound field diffusion established in the various chambers and shows that increased attention must be paid to the methods of enforcing sufficient diffusion.

A first step towards higher sound field diffusion is to design the reverberation chamber without parallel pairs of walls and thus avoid sound waves which can be reflected repeatedly between two particular walls without being influenced by the acoustical properties of the remaining ones. The uniform distribution of absorption over at least three walls perpendicular to each other would principally serve the same purpose but cannot be applied practically because it conflicts with the very principle of this method.

Among all further methods to achieve a diffuse sound field the introduction of volume scatterers as described in Section V.1 seems to be most adequate for reverberation chambers, since an existing arrangement of scatterers can easily be changed if it does not prove satisfactory. Practically, such scatterers can be realised as bent shells of wood, plastics or metal which are suspended from the ceiling by cables in an irregular arrangement (*see*, for instance, Fig. VIII.16). If necessary, bending resonances of these shells should be damped by applying layers of lossy

Fig. VIII.16. Reverberation chamber fitted out with 25 diffusers of perspex (volume 324 m³, dimensions of one shell 1·54 m × 1·28 m).

material onto them. It should be noted, however, that too many diffusers may also affect the validity of the usual reverberation formulae and that therefore the density of scatterers has a certain optimum.[19] If H is the distance of the test specimen from the wall opposite to it, this optimum range is about

$$0.5 < \langle n \rangle Q_s H < 2 \qquad \text{(VIII.32)}$$

with $\langle n \rangle$ and Q_s denoting the density and the scattering cross-section of the diffusers introduced at the end of Section V.1. This condition has also been proven experimentally.[20] For not too low frequencies the scattering cross-section Q_s is roughly half the geometrical area of one side of a shell.

Systematic errors of the reverberation method may also be caused by the so-called 'edge effect' of absorbing materials. If an absorbing area has free edges, it will absorb more sound energy per second than is proportional to its geometrical area, the difference being caused by diffraction of sound into the absorbing area. Formally, this effect can be accounted for by introducing an 'effective absorption coefficient':[21]

$$\alpha_{\text{eff}} = \alpha_\infty + \beta L' \qquad \text{(VIII.33)}$$

α_∞ is the absorption coefficient of the unbounded test material and L' denotes the total length of the edges divided by the area of the actual sample. The factor β depends on the frequency and the type of material. It may be as high as 0.2 m or more and can be determined experimentally using test pieces of different sizes and shapes. A comprehensive treatment of the edge effect can be found in Ref. 1 of Chapter VI.

The best way to avoid this kind of edge effect in absorption measurements is to cover one wall of the reverberation chamber completely with the material to be tested, since then there will be no free edges. However, the adjacent rigid or nearly rigid walls cause another, although less serious, edge effect, sometimes referred to as 'Waterhouse effect'.[22] According to eqn (II.34) (see also Fig. II.9), the square of the sound pressure amplitude in front of a rigid wall exceeds its value far from the wall, and the same holds for the energy absorbed per unit time and area by the test specimen which is perpendicular to that wall. This effect can be corrected for by replacing the geometrical area S of the test specimen with

$$S_{\text{eff}} = S(1 + \tfrac{1}{8} L' \lambda) \qquad \text{(VIII.34)}$$

Finally, a remark may be appropriate on the frequency range in which a given reverberation chamber can be used. If the linear chamber dimensions are equal to a few wavelengths only, then statistical reverberation theories can no longer be applied to the decay process and hence to the process of sound absorption. Likewise, a diffuse sound field cannot be established when the number and density of eigenfrequencies (*see* Section III.2) are small. It has been found experimentally that absorption measurements employing reverberation chambers are only possible for frequencies higher than the following limiting frequency:

$$f_g \approx \frac{1000}{(V)^{1/3}} \tag{VIII.35}$$

where the room volume V has to be expressed in m^3 and the frequency in Hz.

REFERENCES

1. Klug, H. & Radek, U., in *Fortschr. d. Akustik—DAGA '87*. Bad Honnef, DPG-GmbH, 1987.
2. Fasbender, J. & Günzel, D., *Acustica*, **45** (1980) 151.
3. Golomb, S. W., *Shift Register Sequences*. Holden Day, San Francisco, 1967.
4. Alrutz, H. & Schroeder, M. R., Proceedings of the 11th International Congress on Acoustics, Paris, 1983, Vol. 6, p. 235.
5. Borish, J. & Angell, J. B., *J. Audio Eng. Soc.*, **31** (1983) 478.
6. Kuttruff, H., *Acustica*, **13** (1963) 120; *ibid.*, **16** (1965/66) 166.
7. Bilsen, F. A., *Acustica*, **19** (1967/68) 27.
8. Kuttruff, H., Proceedings of the Sixth International Congress on Acoustics, Tokyo, 1968, paper GP-4-1.
9. Schroeder, M. R., *Acustica*, **49** (1981) 179.
10. Houtgast, T. & Steeneken, H. J. M., *Acustica*, **54** (1984) 186.
11. Schroeder, M. R., *J. Acoust. Soc. America*, **37** (1965) 409.
12. Kuttruff, H., *Acustica*, **13** (1963) 120; *ibid.*, **16** (1965/66) 166.
13. Thiele, R., *Acustica*, **3** (1953) 291.
14. Meyer, E. & Thiele, R., *Acustica*, **6** (1956) 425.
15. Junius, W., *Acustica*, **9** (1959) 289.
16. Fasbender, J., *Appl. Acoust.*, **16** (1983) 11.
17. Kosten, C. W., *Acustica*, **10** (1960) 400.
18. Myncke, H., Cops, A. & de Vries, D., Proc. 3rd Symp. of FASE on Building Acoustics, Dubrovnik, 1979, p. 259.
19. Kuttruff, K. H., *J. Acoust. Soc. America*, **69** (1981) 1716.
20. Kuhl, W. & Kuttruff, H., *Acustica*, **54** (1983) 41.
21. de Bruijn, A., Calculation of the edge effect of sound absorbing structures. Dissertation, Delft (Netherlands), 1967.
22. Waterhouse, R. V., *J. Acoust. Soc. America*, **27** (1955) 247.

IX

Design Considerations and Design Procedures

The purpose of this chapter is to describe and to discuss some more practical aspects of room acoustics, namely the acoustical design of auditoria in which some kind of performance (lectures, music, theatre, etc.) is to be presented to an audience, or of spaces in which the reduction of noise levels is of most interest. Its contents are not just an extension of fundamental laws and scientific insights towards the practical world, nor are they a collection of guidelines and rules deduced from them. In fact, the reader should be aware that the art of room acoustical design is only partially based on theoretical considerations, and that it cannot be learned from this or any other book but that successful work in this field requires considerable practical experience. On the other hand, mere experience without at least some insight into the physics of sound fields and without certain knowledge of psychoacoustic facts is of little worth, or is even dangerous in that it may lead to unacceptable generalisations.

Usually the practical work of an acoustic consultant starts with drawings being presented to him which show the details of a hall or some other room which is at the planning stage or under construction, or even one which is already in existence and in full use. First of all, he must ascertain the purpose for which the hall is to be used, i.e. which type of performances or presentations are to take place in it. This is more difficult than appears at first sight, as the economic necessities sometimes clash with the original ideas of the owner or the architects. Secondly, he must gain some idea of the objective structure of the sound field to be expected, for instance the values of the parameters characterising the acoustical behaviour of the room. Thirdly, he must decide whether or not the result of his investigations favours the intended use of the room; and finally, if necessary, he must work out proposals for changes or measures which are aimed at improving the acoustics, keeping in mind that these may be very costly or may

257

substantially modify the architect's original ideas and therefore have to be given very careful consideration.

In order to solve these tasks there is so far no generally accepted procedure which would lead with absolute certainty to a good result. Perhaps it is too much to expect there ever to be the possibility of such a 'recipe', since one project is usually different from the next due to the efforts of architects and owners to create something quite new and original in each theatre or concert hall.

Nevertheless, a few standard methods of acoustical design have been evolved which have proven useful and which can be applied in virtually every case. The importance which the acoustic consultant will attribute to one or the other, the practical consequences which he will draw from his examination, whether he favours reverberation calculations more than geometrical considerations or vice versa—all this is left entirely to him, to his skill and to his experience. It is a fact, however, that an excellent result requires close and trustful cooperation with the architect—and a certain amount of luck too.

As we have seen in preceding chapters, there are a few objective sound field properties which are beyond question regarding their importance for what we call good or poor acoustics of a hall, namely the strength of the direct sound, the temporal and directional distribution of the early sound energy, and the duration of reverberation processes. These properties depend on constructional data, in particular on the

(a) shape and
(b) volume of the room;
(c) the number of seats and their arrangement;
(d) the materials of walls, ceiling, floor, seats, etc.

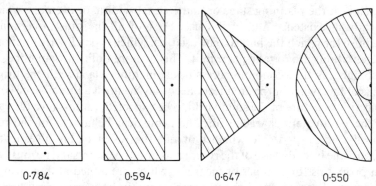

0·784   0·594   0·647   0·550

Fig. IX.1. Normalised average distance from listeners to source for various room shapes.

While the reverberation time is determined by factors (b) to (d) but not remarkably by the room shape, the latter influences strongly the number, directions, delays and strengths of the early reflections received at a given position or seat. The strength of the direct sound depends on the distances to be covered, and also on the shape of the areas which are occupied by the audience.

In the following discussion we shall start with the last point, namely with factors which determine the strength of the direct sound in a hall.

IX.1 EXAMINATION OF THE ROOM SHAPE WITH REGARD TO THE DIRECT SOUND

The direct sound signal arriving from the sound source to a listener along a straight line is not influenced at all by the walls or the ceiling of a room. Nevertheless, its strength depends on the geometrical data of the hall, namely on the (average) length of paths which it has to travel, and on the height at which it propagates over the audience until it reaches a particular listener.

Of course the direct sound intensity under otherwise constant conditions is the higher, the closer the listener is seated to the sound source. Different plans of halls can be compared in this respect by a dimensionless figure of merit, which is the average distance of all listeners from the sound source divided by the square root of the area occupied by audience. For illustration, in Fig. IX.1 a few floor plans are shown; the numbers indicate this normalised average distance. The audience areas are shaded and the sound source is denoted by a point.

It is seen that a long rectangular room with the sound source on its short side seats the listeners relatively far from the source, whereas a room with a semicircular floor plan provides particularly short direct sound paths. This is probably the reason why most ancient amphitheatres have been given this shape by their builders. For a closed room this shape is affected with specific acoustical risks in that it concentrates the sound reflected from the rear wall toward certain regions. Generally considerations of this sort should not be given too much weight since they are only concerned with one aspect of acoustics which may conflict with other ones.

Attenuation of the direct sound due to grazing propagation over the heads of the audience (*see* Section VI.7) can be reduced or avoided by sloping the audience area upwardly instead of arranging the seats on a horizontal floor. This holds also for the attenuation of side or front wall reflections. A constant slope (*see* Fig. IX.2(a)) is less favourable than an

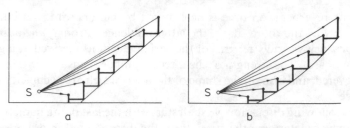

Fig. IX.2. Reduction of direct sound attenuation by sloping the seating area: (a) constant slope; (b) increasing slope.

increasing ascent of the audience area. The optimum slope (which is optimal as well with respect to the listeners' visual contact with the stage) is reached if all sound rays originating from the sound source S strike the audience area at the same incidence angle ϑ (*see* Fig. IX.2(b)). The mathematical expression for this condition, which can be strictly fulfilled only for one particular source position, is

$$r(\varphi) = r_0 \exp(\varphi \tan \vartheta) \qquad (IX.1)$$

In this formula $r(\varphi)$ is the length of the sound ray leaving the source under an elevation angle φ and r_0 is a constant. The curve it describes is a logarithmic spiral. The requirement of constant angle of incidence is roughly equivalent to that of constant 'sight-line distance', by which term we mean the vertical distance of a ray from the end of the ray beneath it. A reasonable value for this distance is about 10 cm, of course higher values are even more favourable. However, a gradually increasing slope of the seating area has certain practical disadvantages. They can be circumvented by approximating the sloping function of eqn (IX.1) by a few straight sections, i.e. by subdividing the audience area in a few blocks with uniform seating rake within each of them.

Front seats on galleries or balconies are generally well supplied with direct sound since they do not suffer at all from sound attenuation due to listeners sitting immediately in front. This is one of the reasons why seats on galleries or in elevated boxes are often known for excellent listening conditions.

IX.2 EXAMINATION OF THE ROOM SHAPE WITH REGARD TO REFLECTIONS

As already mentioned, the delay times, the strengths and the directions of incidence of the reflections—and in particular of early reflections—are

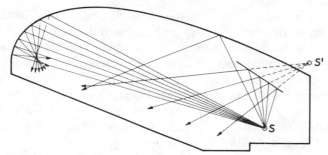

Fig. IX.3. Construction of sound ray paths in the longitudinal section of a hall.

determined by the position and the orientation of reflecting areas, i.e. by the shape of a room. Since these properties of reflected sound portions are to a high degree responsible for good or poor acoustics, it is indispensable to investigate the shape of a room carefully in order to get a survey on the reflections produced by the enclosure.

A simple way to obtain this survey is to trace the paths of sound rays which emerge from an assumed sound source, using drawings of the room under consideration. In most cases the assumption of specular reflections is more or less justified.

The sound rays after reflection from a wall portion can be found very easily if the enclosure is made up of plane boundaries; then the concept of image sound sources as described in Chapter IV can be applied with advantage. This procedure, however, is feasible for first-order or at best for second-order reflections only, which on the other hand is often sufficient.

For curved walls the method of image sources cannot be applied. Here we have to determine the tangential plane (or the normal) of each elementary area of interest and to consider the reflection from this plane. This procedure is relatively simple if a sufficiently large portion of the wall or ceiling has a circular shape in the sectional drawing, or can be approximated by a circle. A schematic example of sound ray construction is presented in Fig. IX.3.

From the constructed sound paths one can usually establish very quickly whether the reflected sound rays are being concentrated on some point or in a limited region, and where the focus or caustic curve is to be expected. Furthermore, the directions of incidence onto various seats can be seen immediately, whereas the delay time between a reflection with respect to the direct sound is determined from the difference in path lengths after dividing the latter by the sound velocity.

The decision whether a particular reflection will be perceivable at all, whether it will contribute to speech intelligibility, to 'clarity' or to 'spaciousness', or whether it will be heard as a disturbing echo requires knowledge of its relative intensity (*see* Chapter VII). Unfortunately the determination of the intensities of reflected signals is affected with greater uncertainties than that of their time delays. If the reflection occurs on a plane boundary with dimensions large compared to acoustical wavelengths, the $1/r$ law of spherical wave propagation can be applied. Let r_0 and r_i be the path lengths of the direct sound ray and that of a particular reflection, measured from the sound source to the listener, then

$$\Delta L = 20 \log_{10} (r_0/r_i) \quad \text{dB}$$

is the pressure level of that reflection relative to the direct sound pressure. If the reflecting boundary has an absorption coefficient α, the level of first-order reflections is lower by another $10 \log(1/\alpha)$ decibels. Irregularities on walls and ceiling can be neglected as long as their dimensions are small compared to the wavelength; this requirement may impose restrictions on the frequency range for which the results obtained with the formula above are valid. The strengths or intensities of reflections from a curved wall section can be estimated by comparing the density of the reflected rays in the observation point with the ray density which would be obtained if that wall section were plane.

The techniques of ray tracing with pencil and ruler takes into account only such sound paths which are situated in the plane of the drawing to hand. Sound paths in different planes can be found by applying the methods of constructive geometry. This, of course, involves a considerably greater amount of time and labour, and it is questionable whether this expenditure is justified in every case considering the rather qualitative character of the information gained by it. For rooms of more complicated geometry it may be more advantageous to investigate the reflections experimentally using a room model at a reduced scale (*see* Section IX.4) or by applying computerised ray tracing techniques (*see* Section IX.5).

So far we have described methods to investigate the effects of a given enclosure upon sound reflections. Beyond the particular case, there are some general conclusions which can be drawn from geometrical considerations, and experiences collected from existing halls or from basic investigations. They shall be summarised briefly below.

If a room is to be used for speech, it is an advantage to support the direct sound by as many strong reflections as possible with delay times not exceeding about 50 ms. Reflecting areas (wall portions, screens) placed very close to the sound source are especially favourable, since they can collect a great deal of the emitted sound energy and reflect it in the direction of the audience. For this reason it is wrong to have heavy curtains of fabric behind the speaker. On the contrary, the speaker should be surrounded by hard and properly orientated surfaces, which can even be in the form of portable screens, for instance. Similarly, reflecting surfaces above the speaker have a favourable effect. If the ceiling over the speaker is too high to produce strong and early reflections, the installation of suspended and suitably tilted reflectors should be taken into consideration. An old and familiar example of a special sound reflector is the canopy above the pulpits in churches. The acoustical advantage of these canopies can be observed very clearly when it is removed during modern restoration.

Unfortunately these principles can only be applied to a limited extent to theatres, where such measures could in fact be particularly useful. This is because the stage is the realm of the stage designer, of the stage manager and of the actors; in short, of people who sometimes complain bitterly about the acoustics but who are not ready to sacrifice one iota of their artistic intentions in favour of acoustical requirements. It is all the more important to shape the wall and ceiling portions which are close to the stage in such a way as to direct the incident sound immediately onto the audience.

In conference rooms, school classrooms, lecture halls, etc., at least the front and central parts of the ceiling should be made reflecting since, in most cases, the ceiling is low enough to produce reflections which support the direct sound. Absorbent materials required for the reduction of the reverberation time can thus only be mounted on more remote ceiling portions (and on the rear wall).

In the design of concert halls, it is advisable to make only moderate use of areas projecting the sound energy immediately towards the audience. This would result in a high fraction of early energy and—in severe cases—to subjective masking of the sound decay in the hall. The effect would be dry acoustics even if the objective reverberation time has correct values. As with lecture halls, etc., the sound sources on the stage should be surrounded by reflecting areas which collect the sound without directing it towards special locations and directions. As we have seen in Section VII.5, it is the fraction of lateral reflections in the early energy which is responsible for the 'spatial impression' or 'spaciousness' in a concert hall. For this reason particular attention must be given to the design of the side walls, especially to their distance and to the angle which they include with the longitudinal axis of the plan.

This may be illustrated by Fig. IX.4, which shows the spatial distribution of early lateral energy computed for three differently shaped two-

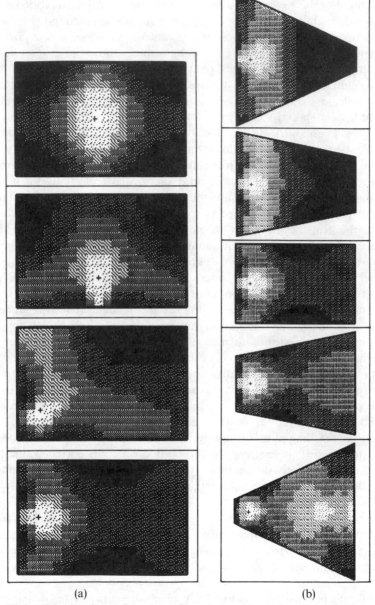

(a)   (b)

Fig. IX.4. Distribution of early reflected sound energy in different two-dimensional enclosures of 600 m^2: (a) rectangular, different source positions; (b) fan-shaped.

dimensional enclosures,[1] the area of which was assumed to be 1000 m^2. The position of the sound source is marked by a cross; the densities of shading of the various areas correspond to the following intervals of the 'early lateral energy fraction' S (*see* eqn VII.19): 0–0·06, 0·06–0·12, 0·12–0·25, 0·25–0·5 and >0·5. In all examples the quantity S is very low at locations next to the sound source, but it is highest in the vicinity of the side walls. Accordingly the largest areas with high S and hence with satisfactory 'spaciousness' are to be expected in long and narrow rectangular halls. On the other hand, particular large areas with low 'early lateral energy fraction' appear in fan-shaped halls, a fact which can easily be verified by a simple construction of the first-order image sources. These findings explain—at least partially—why so many concert halls with excellent acoustics (for instance Boston Symphony Hall or Großer Musikvereinssaal in Vienna; *see* Table VII.3) have rectangular floor plans with relatively narrow side walls. It may be noted, by the way, that the requirement of strong lateral sound reflections favours quite different room shapes than the requirement of strong direct sound (*see* Section IX.1).

In real, i.e. in three-dimensional halls, additional lateral energy is provided by the double reflection from the edges formed by a side wall and horizontal surfaces such as the ceiling or the underfaces of galleries or balconies (Fig. IX.5). These contributions are especially useful since they are less attenuated by the audience below than reflections from the side walls alone. If no balconies are planned the beneficial effect of underfaces can be achieved as well by properly arranged surfaces or bodies protruding from the side walls.

With regard to the performance of orchestral music one should remember that various instruments have quite different directivity of sound

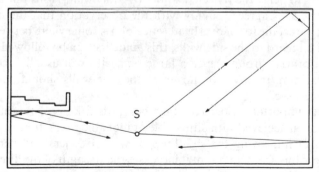

Fig. IX.5. Simplified cross-section of a hall showing the origin of lateral reflections.

radiation which depends also on the frequency. Accordingly sounds from certain instruments or groups of instruments are predominantly reflected by particular wall or ceiling portions. Since every concert hall is expected to house orchestras of varying composition and arrangement, only some general conclusions can be drawn from this fact, however. Thus the high frequency components, especially from string instruments, which are responsible for the brilliance of the sound, are reflected mainly from the ceiling overhead and in front of the stage, whereas the side walls are very important for the reflection of components in the range of about 1000 Hz and hence for the volume and sonority of the orchestral sounds.[2]

Some further comments may be appropriate on the acoustical design of the stage of concert halls, which has been a neglected subject for many years but recently has attracted the attention of several researchers. From the acoustical point of view, the stage enclosure of a concert hall has the purpose of collecting sounds produced by the musical instruments, to blend them and finally to project them towards the auditorium, but also to reflect part of the sound energy back to the performers. This is necessary to establish the mutual auditory contact they need to maintain ensemble, i.e. proper intonation and synchronism.

At first glance platforms arranged in a recess of the hall seem to serve these purposes better in that their walls can be designed in such a way as to direct the sound in the desired way. As a matter of fact, however, several famous concert halls have more exposed stages which form just one end of the hall. From this it may be concluded that the height and inclination of the ceiling over the platform deserves particular attention.

Marshall et al.[3] have found by systematic experimental work that the surfaces of a stage enclosure should be far enough away from the performers to delay the reflected sound by more than 15 ms but not more than 35 ms. This agrees roughly with the observation that the optimum height of the ceiling (or of overhead reflectors) is somewhere between 5 and 10 m. With regard to the side walls, this guideline can be followed only for small performing groups, since a large orchestra will usually occupy the whole platform. In any case, however, the side walls should be surfaces which reflect well.

Another important aspect of stage design is raking of the platform,[4] which is often achieved with adjustable or movable risers. It has, of course, the effect of improving the sightlines between listeners and performers. From the acoustical standpoint it increases the strength of the direct sound and reduces the obstruction of sound propagation by intervening players. It seems, however, that this kind of exposure can be carried too far;

probably the optimum rake has to be determined by some experimentation.

The inspection of room geometry can lead to the result that some wall areas, particularly if they are curved, will give rise to very delayed reflections with relatively high energy, which will neither support the direct sound nor will they be masked by other reflections, but instead these reflections will be heard as echoes. The simplest way of avoiding such effects is to cover these wall portions with highly absorbent material. If this precaution causes an intolerable drop in reverberation time or is impossible for other reasons, a reorientation of those surfaces could be suggested or they could be split up into irregularly shaped surfaces so that the sound is scattered in all directions. Of course the size of these irregularities must at least be comparable with the wavelength in order to be effective. If desired, any treatment of these walls can be concealed behind acoustically transparent screens, consisting of grids, nets or perforated panels, whose transmission properties were discussed in Section VI.3.

IX.3 REVERBERATION TIME

In principle, all information on the transient acoustical behaviour of a room could be deduced from the examination of sound ray paths as was described in the preceding section and in Section IV.2. This, however, would be a very laborious and time-consuming procedure and would yield much more information than is actually required. This is the reason why, in practice, the complex transient response of a room is often characterised by a single quantity only, based on the average fate of sound rays: the reverberation time, which is related to constructional data of the room and to the absorptivity of its walls by relatively reliable and tractable formulae. Their application permits us to lay down practical procedures, provided we have certain ideas on the desired values of the reverberation times at various frequencies, which in turn requires knowledge of the purposes for which the room is intended.

For an exact prediction of the reverberation time quite a few room data are needed: the volume of the room, the materials and the surface treatment of the walls and of the ceiling, the number, the arrangement and the type of seats. Many of these details are often only finally settled at a later stage. This is an advantage as it enables the acoustician to exercise his influence to a considerable extent in the direction he desires. On the other hand, he must at first be content with a rough assumption about the properties of the walls. Therefore it is sound reasoning not to carry out a detailed

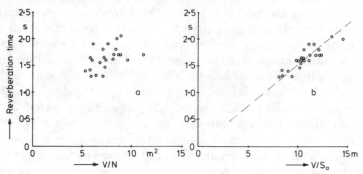

Fig. IX.6. Reverberation times of occupied concert halls related to (a) volume per seat and (b) volume divided by effective audience area.

reverberation calculation at this first stage but instead to predict or estimate the reverberation approximately.

An upper limit of the attainable reverberation time can be obtained from Sabine's formula (V.24) with $m = 0$, by attributing an absorption coefficient of 1 to the areas covered by an audience and an absorption coefficient of 0·05–0·1 to the remaining areas, which need not be known too exactly for this purpose.

Alternatively, the reverberation time can be estimated using data of existing halls. For concert halls a survey is presented in Fig. IX.6 which plots the reverberation times of a number of occupied halls as a function of the room volume per seat and as a function of the ratio of room volume to the effective audience area S_a. Most of these data are taken from Beranek's extensive collection (*see* Ref. 34 of Chapter VII). The indicated

Table IX.1
Equivalent Absorption Coefficient

Centre frequency of octave band (Hz)	Occupied hall	Unoccupied hall
63	0·85	0·68
125	0·96	0·76
250	1·00	0·81
500	1·05	0·81
1 000	1·09	0·82
2 000	1·15	0·86
4 000	1·29	1·01
6 000	1·51	1·27

reverberation times are average values over the frequency range 500–1000 Hz. The quantity S_a includes the area occupied by the audience, the orchestra and the chorus, and is furthermore increased by a strip 1 m wide around the seating areas. Aisles are added *in toto* to S_a if they are narrower than 2 m.[5] (These extra areas account for the sound diffraction at the edge of absorbing areas.)

In Fig. IX.6a the points representing different concert halls show considerable scatter, thus the volume per seat is not well suited for estimating the reverberation time to be expected. The only conclusion we can draw from Fig. IX.6a is that the reverberation time of a hall with less than $7 \, \text{m}^3$/seat is unlikely to reach 1·8 s or more. On the contrary, Fig. IX.6b reveals a rather close relation between the reverberation time and the volume per $1 \, \text{m}^2$ of audience area, which is expressed by

$$T \approx 0.15 \frac{V}{S_a} \qquad \qquad \text{(IX.2)}$$

(T in seconds, V in m^3, S_a in m^2).

Still another method for an approximate calculation of the reverberation time of a concert hall was proposed by Kosten and de Lange.[6,7] It is based upon the assumption that in most halls the ratio between heavily absorbent (audience, etc.) and slightly absorbent areas is about the same. Then the wall absorption, the audience absorption and the attenuation effected by the medium can be collected in an 'equivalent absorption coefficient α_e' of the audience area, as is listed in Table IX.1.

From it the reverberation time is calculated by the formula

$$T = 0.163 \frac{V}{\alpha_e S_a} \qquad \qquad \text{(IX.3)}$$

Although the results of the methods of preliminary decay time estimation are usually not too bad, a more detailed reverberation calculation should definitely be carried out at a more advanced phase of planning, during which it is still possible to make changes in the interior finish of the hall without incurring extra expense. The most critical aspect is the absorption by the audience. The factors which influence this phenomenon have already been discussed in Section VI.7. The uncertainties caused by audience absorption are so great that it is almost meaningless to try to decide whether Sabine's formula (V.24) would be sufficient or whether the more accurate Eyring equation (V.23) should be applied. Therefore the simpler Sabine formula is preferable with the term $4mV$ taking into account the sound attenuation in air.

It is frequently observed that the actual reverberation time of a hall is found to be lower than predicted. This fact is usually attributed to the impossibility of taking into account all possible causes of absorption. The variation will, however, scarcely exceed 0·1 s, provided that there are no substantial errors in the applied absorption data and in the evaluation of the reverberation time.

As regards the absorption coefficients of the various materials and wall linings, use can be made of compilations which have been published by several authors. Extensive tables of absorption coefficients can be found in a brochure edited by the Deutscher Normenausschuß,[8] and in a book by H. Schmidt.[9] It should be emphasised that the actual absorption, especially of highly absorptive materials, may vary considerably from one sample to the other and depends strongly on the particular way in which they are mounted. Likewise, the coefficients presented below in Table IX.2 are to be considered as average values only. In many cases it will be necessary to test actual materials and the influence of their mounting by *ad hoc* measurements of their absorption coefficient which can be carried out in the impedance tube (*see* Section VIII.7) or, more reliably, in a reverberation chamber (*see* Section VIII.8). This applies particularly to chairs whose acoustical properties can vary considerably depending on the material and the quantity and quality of the fabric used for the upholstery. If possible the

Table IX.2

Typical Absorption Coefficients of Various Types of Walls

Material	Centre frequency of octave band (Hz)					
	125	250	500	1 000	2 000	4 000
Hard surfaces (brick walls, plaster, hard floors, etc.)	0·02	0·02	0·03	0·03	0·04	0·05
Slightly vibrating walls (suspended ceilings, etc.)	0·10	0·07	0·05	0·04	0·04	0·05
Strongly vibrating surfaces (wooden panelling over air space, etc.)	0·40	0·20	0·12	0·07	0·05	0·05
Carpet, 5 mm thick, on hard floor	0·02	0·03	0·05	0·10	0·30	0·50
Plush curtain, flow resistance 450 Ns/m³, deeply folded	0·15	0·45	0·90	0·92	0·95	0·95
Polyurethane foam, 27 kg/m³, 15 mm thick	0·08	0·22	0·55	0·70	0·85	0·75
Acoustic plaster, 10 mm thick, sprayed on solid wall	0·08	0·15	0·30	0·50	0·60	0·70

chair should be constructed in such a way that, when it is unoccupied, its absorption is not substantially lower than when it is occupied. This has the favourable effect that the reverberation time of the hall does not depend too strongly on the degree of occupation. With tip-up chairs this can be achieved by perforating the underside of the plywood or hardboard seats and backing them with rock wool. Likewise, an absorbent treatment of the rear of the backrests could be advantageous. In any event the effectiveness of such treatment should be checked by absorption measurements.

Similarly, it is recommended that reverberation measurements in the hall itself be performed during several stages of the hall's construction. This allows the reverberation calculations to be checked and to be corrected if necessary. Even during later stages in the construction there is often an opportunity of proposing corrective measures to the interior of the building.

In practice it is not uncommon to find that a room actually consists of several partial rooms which are coupled to each other. Examples of coupled rooms are theatres with boxes which communicate with the main room through relatively small apertures only, or the stage of a theatre or opera house which is coupled to the auditorium by the proscenium, or churches with several naves or chapels. Cremer was the first to point out the necessity of considering coupling effects when calculating the reverberation time of such a room. This necessity arises if eqn (V.53) is fulfilled, i.e. if the area of the coupling aperture is substantially smaller than the total wall area of a partial room.

Let us denote the partial room in which the listener finds himself by number 1 and the other partial room by 2. Now we must distinguish between two different cases, depending on whether room 1 on its own has a longer or a shorter reverberation time than room 2. In the first case the reverberation of room 2 will not be noticed in room 1 as the coupling area acts merely as an 'open window' with respect to room 1 and can be taken as having an absorption coefficient 1. Therefore, whenever an auditorium has deep balcony overhangs, it is advisable to carry out an alternative calculation of decay time in this way, i.e. by treating the 'mouths' of the overhangs as completely absorbing wall portions.

Matters are more complicated if room 2 has the longer decay time. The listener can hear this longer reverberation through the coupling aperture, but will not perceive it as a part of the decay of the room which he is occupying. How strongly this 'separate reverberation' will be perceived depends on how the room is excited and on the location of the listener. If the sound source excites room 1 predominantly, then the longer decay from room 2 will only be heard, if at all, with impulsive sound signals (loud cries, isolated chords of a piece of music, etc.) or if the listener is close to the coupling aperture. If, on the contrary, the location of the sound source is such that it excites both rooms almost equally well, as may be the case with actors performing on the stage of a theatre, then the longer reverberation from room 2 is heard continually or it may even be the only reverberation to appear. In any event it is useful to calculate the reverberation times of both partial rooms separately. Strictly speaking, for this purpose the eigenvalues δ_i' of Section V.7 should be known. For practical purposes, however, it is sufficient to increase the total absorption $\sum S_i \alpha_i$ for each partial room by the coupling area and to insert the result into Sabine's reverberation formula.

There is some relation between the sound decay of coupled rooms and the reverberation of rooms in which there is a lack of diffusion. In the latter case, the application of the usual reverberation formulae would also lead to erroneous results. Lack of diffusion can happen in rooms having simple geometrical shapes and extremely non-uniform distribution of absorption on the walls. A rectangular room, for instance, whose ceiling is not too low and which has smooth and reflecting side walls will, when the room is fully occupied, often build up a two-dimensional reverberating sound field in the upper part with a substantially longer decay time than corresponds to the average absorption coefficient. The sound field consists of horizontal or nearly horizontal sound paths and is influenced only slightly by the audience absorption. Similarly, an absorbent or scattering ceiling treatment will not have much effect. This effect may also occur with other ground plans. Whether the listeners will perceive this separate reverberation at all again depends on the strength of its excitation.

For lecture halls, theatre foyers, etc., this relatively long reverberation is of course undesirable. In a concert hall, however, it can lead to a badly needed increase in reverberation time beyond the Sabine or Eyring value, namely in those cases where the volume containing a given number of listeners is too small to yield a sufficiently long decay time in diffuse conditions. An example of this is the Stadthalle in Göttingen, which has an exactly hexagonal ground plan and in fact has a reverberation time of about 2 s, although calculations had predicted a value of 1·6–1·7 s only (both for medium frequencies and for the fully occupied hall). Model experiments carried out afterwards had demonstrated very clearly that it was a sound field of the described type which was responsible for this unexpected, but highly desirable, increase in reverberation time. This particular lack of diffusion in itself does not cause specific acoustical deficiencies; actually it can only be detected by thorough experimental investigations.

But even if the enclosure of a hall can be assumed to mix and thus to redistribute the impinging sound by diffuse reflections, the diffusion of the sound field and hence the validity of the simple reverberation formulae may be impaired merely by non-uniform distribution of the absorption. Since this is typical for occupied auditoria, it may be advisable to check the reliability of reverberation prediction by tentatively applying the more exact eqn (V.48).

Sometimes the acoustical consultant is faced with the task of designing a room which is capable of presenting different kinds of performances, such as speech and music. This is typical for multipurpose halls; the same thing is frequently demanded of broadcasting or television studios. As far as the reverberation time is concerned, some variability can be achieved by installing movable or revolving walls or ceiling elements which produce some acoustical variability by exhibiting reflecting surfaces in one position (long reverberation time) and absorbent ones in the other (short reverberation time). The resulting difference in reverberation time depends on the fraction of area treated in this way and on the difference in absorption coefficients of those elements. Installations of this type are usually quite costly and sometimes give rise to considerable mechanical problems. A relatively simple way of changing the reverberation time in the abovementioned manner was described by Kath.[10] In a broadcasting studio with a volume of 726 m^3 the walls were fitted with strips of glass wool tissue which can be rolled up and unrolled electrically. Behind the fabric there is an air space with an average depth of 20 cm, subdivided laterally in 'boxes' of 0·5 m × 0·6 m. The reverberation time of the studio for the two

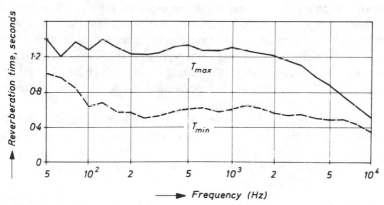

Fig. IX.7. Maximum and minimum reverberation times in a broadcasting studio with changeable acoustics.

extreme situations (glass wool rolled up and glass wool completely unrolled) are shown in Fig. IX.7 as a function of the frequency. It is clearly seen that the reverberation time at medium frequencies can be changed from 0·6 to 1·25 s and that a considerable degree of variability in reverberation time has also been achieved at other frequencies. Other methods which make use of electroacoustical installations will be described in Chapter X.

IX.4 NOISE LEVELS—PREDICTION AND REDUCTION

There are many spaces which are not intended for any acoustical presentations but where some acoustical treatment is nevertheless desirable or necessary. Although they show wide variations in character and structural details, they all fall into the category of rooms in which people are present and in which noise is produced, for instance by noisy machinery or by the people themselves. Examples of this are staircases, concourses of railway stations and airports, entrance halls and foyers of concert halls and theatres, etc. Most important, however, are working spaces such as open-plan offices, workshops and factories. Here room acoustics has the relatively prosaic task of reducing the noise level.

Traditionally acoustics does not play any important role in the design of a factory or an open-plan office, to say the least; usually quite different aspects, as for instance those of efficient organisation, of the economical use of space or of safety, are predominant. Therefore the term 'acoustics' applied to such spaces does not have the meaning it has with respect to a lecture room or a theatre. Nevertheless, it is obvious that the way in which the noise produced by any kind of machinery propagates in such a room and hence the noise level in it depends highly on the acoustical properties even of such a room, and further that any measures which are to be taken to reduce the noise exposure of the personnel must take into regard the acoustical conditions of the room.

A first idea of the steady state sound pressure level a sound source with power output P produces in a room with wall area S and average absorption coefficient $\bar{\alpha}$ is obtained from eqn (V.37). Converting it in a logarithmic scale with PL denoting the sound power level (*see* eqn (I.41)) yields

$$SPL = PL - 10\log_{10}\left(\frac{\bar{\alpha}S}{1m^2}\right) + 6\,\text{dB} \qquad \text{(IX.4)}$$

This relation holds for distances from the sound source which are significantly larger than the 'reverberation distance' as given by eqn (V.38) or (V.38a). It is valid under the assumption that the sound field in the room is diffuse.

Numerous measurements in real spaces have shown, however, that the actual sound pressure level decreases more or less with increasing distance, in contrast to eqn (IX.4). Obviously sound fields in such spaces are not completely diffuse, and the lack of diffusion seems to affect the validity of eqn (IX.4) much more than that of reverberation formulae. This lack of diffusion may be accounted for in several ways. Often one dimension of a working space is much larger (very long rooms) or smaller (very flat rooms) than the remaining ones. Another possible reason is non-uniform distribution of absorption. In all these cases a different approach is needed to calculate the sound pressure level.

For enclosures made up of plane walls the method of image sources could be employed, which has been discussed at some length in Section IV.2. It must be noted, however, that real working spaces are not empty, and that there are machines, piles of material, furniture, benches, etc., in them; in short, numerous obstacles which scatter the sound and may also partially absorb it. This requires at least some modification of the image source concept.

One way to account for the scattering of sound in fitted working spaces is to replace the sound propagation in the free space by that in an 'opaque' medium as explained at the end of Section V.1. Such a medium is characterised by a free path length $\bar{r} = 1/\langle n \rangle Q_s$ between successive collisions of a hypothetical sound particle with scatterers, with $\langle n \rangle$ denoting their number density and Q_s their average scattering cross-section. Then the scattering objects will attenuate an original sound wave according to a factor $\exp(-r/\bar{r})$ while the sound particles removed from the original wave will perform what is sometimes called a 'random walk' through the opaque medium. Accordingly, without any walls, the energetic impulse response of the medium at the distance r from a unidirectional source would consist of two parts,[11] namely that of the unscattered component

$$u_0(r, t) = \frac{E_0}{4\pi c r^2} \exp(-r/\bar{r})\delta(t - r/c) \qquad \text{(IX.5a)}$$

and that of the scattered sound

$$u_s(r, t) = E_0 \left[\frac{3}{4\pi \bar{r} c t} \right]^{3/2} \exp\left(-\frac{3r^2}{4\bar{r}ct} \right) \qquad \text{(IX.5b)}$$

with E_0 denoting the energy released from the sound source at $t = 0$. The latter expression is an approximation derived from the theory of diffusion, valid only for $ct \gg \bar{r}$, strictly speaking. Considered as a function of time t, it describes the (non-exponential) reverberation of the medium itself. The effects of absorbing scatterers or of air absorption can easily be included if necessary.

Now we are ready to account for the walls of the enclosure by combining this model of sound propagation with the principle of image sources. One problem is how to deal with the absorption of the walls, since the rate at which a sound particle will be weakened by wall absorption does not only depend on the geometry of the room but also on the free path length $\bar{r}$. For the infinite flat room, which was already considered in Section IV.2, Jovicic has calculated a 'loss exponent' which accounts for this fact, and on this basis he has derived a closed expression for the steady state energy density in this type of enclosure. More details can be found in the comprehensive work of Hodgson,[12] which contains also numerous experimental data collected in empty factories as well as in fitted ones, including measurements taken in models.

However, there remains an uncertainty on the values of the scattering cross-sections of machines or other pieces of equipment; obviously there is no way to calculate them reliably from geometric data. This difficulty can be circumvented by a quite different approach. In it the scatterers are projected onto the walls, so to speak, i.e. it is assumed that the walls produce diffuse reflections rather than specular ones. Then the problem can be treated by application of the integral equation (V.42). As already mentioned in Section V.6, this equation has a closed solution for the infinite flat room which can be approximated by a simple formula (*see* eqn (V.43)). Figure IX.8 shows how the sound pressure level, obtained with this formula, depends on the distance from an omnidirectional sound source for various values of the (average) absorption coefficient α of the walls. The shape of these curves is typical for sound propagation in spaces with wall or volume scattering. At small distances the sound pressure level drops significantly more slowly than at free propagation, but in a somewhat more remote region the level decreases at a larger rate. This general behaviour was also observed in Hodgson's measurements mentioned before.

Both aforementioned methods are well suited to predicting noise levels in working spaces and estimating the reduction which can be achieved by an absorbing treatment of the ceiling, for instance. Other possible methods are measurements in a scale model of the space under investigation (Section IX.5) or computer simulation as described in Section IX.6.

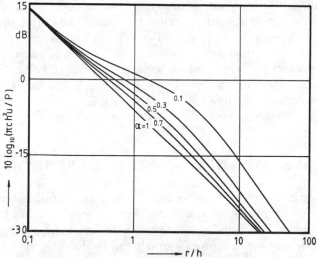

Fig. IX.8. Sound pressure level in an infinite flat room as a function of the ratio r/h. (The parameter of the curves is the (average) absorption coefficient of the wall, h is the height of the room.)

Absorbing treatment of walls or the ceiling has a beneficial effect, not only in working spaces such as factories or large offices but also in many other rooms where many people gather together, e.g. in theatre foyers. A noise level reduction of only a few decibels can increase the acoustical comfort to an amazing degree. If the sound level is too high due to insufficient boundary absorption, people will talk more loudly than in a quieter environment. This in turn again increases the general noise level and so it continues until finally people must shout and still do not achieve satisfactory intelligibility. In contrast, an acoustically damped environment usually makes people behave in a 'damped' manner too—for reasons which are not primarily acoustical—and it makes them talk no louder than necessary.

There is still another psychologically favourable effect of an acoustically damped theatre or concert hall foyer: when a visitor leaves the foyer and enters the hall, he will suddenly find himself in a more reverberating environment, which gives him the impression of solemnity and raises his expectations.

The extensive application of absorbing materials in a room, however, is accompanied by an oppressive atmosphere, an effect which can be observed quite clearly when entering an anechoic room. Furthermore, since the level of the background noise is reduced too by the absorbing areas, a conversation held in a low voice can be understood at relatively great distances and can be irritating to unintentional listeners. Since this is more or less the opposite of what should be achieved in an open-plan office, masking by background noise is sometimes increased in a controlled way by loudspeakers fed with random white or 'coloured' noise, i.e. with a 'signal' which has no time or spectral structure. The level of this noise should not exceed 50 dB(A). Even so it is still contested whether the advantages of such methods surpass their disadvantages.

IX.5 ACOUSTICAL MODEL MEASUREMENTS

A well tried method which has been used over a long period of time for the acoustical design of large halls is to build a smaller model of the hall under consideration which is similar to the original room, at least geometrically, and to study the propagation of sound in this model. This method has the advantage that, with little expenditure, a great number of variations can be tried out: from the choice of various wall materials to major changes in the shape of the room.

Since several properties of propagation are common to all sorts of waves, it is not absolutely necessary to use sound waves for the model measurements. This principle was used particularly during earlier times when acoustical measuring techniques were not yet at the advanced stage they have reached nowadays. So waves on water surfaces were sometimes applied in 'ripple tanks'. The propagation of these waves can be studied visually with great ease. The use of them, however, is restricted to an examination of plane sections of the hall. More profitable is the use of light as a substitute for sound. Since wavelengths of light are very small compared with all room dimensions, the use of optical models corresponds to the limit of very high frequencies, which is nevertheless of great importance. In this case absorbent areas are painted black or covered with black paper or fabric, whereas reflecting areas are made of polished sheet metal. Likewise, diffusely reflecting areas can be quite well simulated by white matt paper. The detection of the energy distribution can be carried out by photocells or by using frosted glass for the auditorium and photographing from the rear.[13] The directional distribution can be measured by the use of pinhole cameras[14] or by a photocell which is fitted with a suitable tube in front of it.

While the investigation of the gross energy distribution is carried out with an omnidirectional light source, single ray paths can be studied with a narrow light beam which is generated most conveniently by a small neon–helium laser and can be directed towards the desired directions. If the model is filled with smoke, the ray paths can be followed conveniently through several reflections.

Thus optical model measurements yield useful information on the steady state distribution of energy in a room, on concentrations of energy or on areas where there is either an insufficient or no supply of energy at all. Furthermore, these optical measurements indicate the wall or ceiling portions which are responsible for certain reflections. The model scale can be as high as 1:50 or 1:100. It does not tell us anything about the time intervals at which several energy portions will reach a listener, however; the duration of the decay processes are not shown either. Hence questions which are even more important to the acoustics of a room than its steady state behaviour are not answered by optical model measurements.

To demonstrate this more clearly we denote all quantities referring to the model by a prime and introduce the scale factor σ by

$$l' = \frac{l}{\sigma} \qquad \text{(IX.6)}$$

where l and l' are corresponding lengths. For the time intervals in which waves with velocities c or c' travel along corresponding distances we obtain

$$t' = \frac{l'}{c'} = \frac{l}{c'\sigma} = \frac{c}{c'}\frac{t}{\sigma} \qquad \text{(IX.7)}$$

The ratios between the wavelengths and frequencies are

$$\lambda' = \frac{\lambda}{\sigma} \qquad \text{(IX.8)}$$

and

$$f' = \sigma \frac{c'}{c} f \qquad \text{(IX.9)}$$

With optical models the ratio of propagation velocities c/c' is of the order of magnitude of 10^{-6}; therefore with a model scale 1:10, i.e. $\sigma = 10$, a travelling time difference of 0·01 s in the real enclosure corresponds to a transit time of 1 ns (10^{-9} s) in the model. The reverberation time will be decreased by the same ratio compared with those of the original room and will amount to fractions of a microsecond. Although such very short times can be handled nowadays by means of modern laser technology and the associated measuring techniques, it is not very likely that these methods will be accepted by laboratories dealing with room acoustics.

It is much more feasible to use sound waves in the model too, whereby $c = c'$, i.e. all occurring times (delay times and reverberation times) will be shorter by a factor σ compared with the original room. According to eqn (IX.9) the sound frequencies must be larger by a factor σ than the corresponding original ones. The level differences are not subject to any scaling. Hence we obtain for the law of energy decrease in a decaying sound field

$$\exp\left\{-\left[m'c - n'\ln(1-\alpha')\right]t'\right\} = \exp\left\{-\left[mc - n\ln(1-\alpha)\right]t\right\}$$

(*see* eqn (IV.6)), where as before m is the attenuation constant of the air and n is the average number of wall reflections of a sound ray per second. Since $t' = t/\sigma$ and $n' = \sigma n$, the frequency dependence of the absorption coefficients and of air attenuation can only be accounted for if we put

$$\alpha = \alpha' \tag{IX.10}$$

and

$$m' = \sigma m \tag{IX.11}$$

at corresponding frequencies.

Of course these requirements can be fulfilled only approximately, and the required degree of approximation depends on the kind of information we wish to obtain from the model experiment. If only the initial part of the impulse response or 'reflectogram' is to be studied (over, say, the first 100 or 200 ms in the original time scale), it is sufficient to provide for only two different kinds of surfaces in the model, namely reflecting ones (made of metal, glass, gypsum, etc.) and absorbing ones (for instance felt or plastic foam). The air absorption can be neglected in this case.

Matters are different if much longer reflectograms are to be observed, for instance, for evaluating the reverberation time from them. Then the absorption coefficients of corresponding surfaces in both the model and the full-scale room should agree quite well. This can only be achieved if the absorptive properties of the model materials at model frequencies are known. They may be obtained from free field measurements, but it seems doubtful whether this expenditure is worthwhile just to determine the reverberation time which is obtained more easily and with sufficient accuracy by calculation.

The requirements concerning the acoustical similarity between an original room and its model are still more stringent if a technique is to be applied which was originally proposed by Spandöck.[15] According to this idea music or speech signals which have been recorded without any reverberation are replayed in the model at frequencies elevated by the factor given in eqn (IX.9). At a point under investigation within the model, the sound signal is picked up with a miniaturised artificial head which has the same directionality and transfer function at the model frequencies as the human head in the normal audio range. After transforming the re-recorded signals back to the original time and frequency domain it can be presented directly to a listener who can judge subjectively the 'acoustics' of the hall and the effects of any modifications to be studied.

The practical execution of this method is hampered by several difficulties. This does not hold for the twofold frequency transformation needed for this process, which can be achieved with a tape recorder with variable speeds or by means of a digital transient recorder. Much more difficult, however, is the realisation of electroacoustic transducers with the required properties, in particular of the artificial head, and also the correct modelling of wall and audience absorption including their frequency dependence. A special problem is the absorption of the gas with which the model is filled, since eqn (IX.11) requires that it should have the same complicated frequency dependence as that of air at audio frequencies. Several groups[16,17] have tried to meet this requirement by filling the model either with dried air or with nitrogen, and also to design suitable miniaturised transducers with the required properties. Nevertheless, it seems that still more effort is needed to develop this fascinating idea into a practical tool for the acoustical design.

Concerning the instrumentation for measuring the impulse response in scale models, the omnidirectional impulse excitation of the model is more difficult the higher the scale factor and hence the frequency range to be covered. Small spark gaps can be successfully used for this purpose, but in any case it is advisable to check their directivity and frequency spectrum beforehand. Furthermore, electrostatic[17] or piezoelectric[18] transducers have been developed for this purpose; they have the advantage that they can be fed with any desired electrical signal and therefore allow the application of the more sophisticated methods described in Section VIII.2. Since it is virtually impossible to combine in such transducers high efficiency with very small dimensions, they must have (at least approximate) spherical symmetry. For piezoelectric transducers this can be achieved with foils of certain high polymers which can be formed in spherical shape and which can be made piezoelectric by special treatment.

Likewise, the microphone should be non-directional. Fortunately sufficiently small condensor microphones are commercially available ($\frac{1}{4}$- or $\frac{1}{8}$-in microphones). Concerning further processing of the received signals, the presentation of the impulse responses and their judgement, we refer to the discussions of Chapters VII and VIII.

IX.6 COMPUTER SIMULATION

Although physical models of enclosures have proven to be a very useful tool for the acoustical design of large halls they are being superseded gradually by a cheaper, faster and more efficient method, namely by digital simulation of sound propagation in enclosures. The introduction of the digital computer into room acoustics is probably due to M. R. Schroeder[19] and his co-workers. Since then this method has been employed by many authors to investigate various problems in room acoustics; examples have been presented in Sections V.6 and IX.2 of this book. The first authors who have applied digital simulation to concert hall acoustics were Krokstad *et al.*,[20] who have evaluated a variety of parameters from impulse responses obtained by digital ray tracing techniques.

The principle of digital ray tracing is illustrated in Fig. IX.9. A sound source at a given position is imagined to release numerous sound particles in all directions at time $t = 0$. Each sound particle travels on a straight path until it hits a wall which we assume to be plane for the sake of simplicity. The point where this occurs is obtained by first calculating the intersections of the particle path with all planes in which the walls are contained, and then selecting the nearest of them in the forward direction. Provided this intersection is located within the real wall, it is the point where the particle will be reflected, either specularly or diffusely. In the first case its new direction is calculated from the law of geometrical reflection; however, if diffuse reflection is assumed to occur, the computer generates two random numbers from which the azimuth angle φ and the polar angle ϑ of the new direction is calculated in such a way that the latter angle is distributed according to eqn (V.9). (The angle σ with respect to the wall normal as a polar axis.) After its reflection the particle continues on its way along the new direction towards the next wall, etc. The absorption coefficient of a wall can be accounted for in two ways: either by reducing the energy of the particle by a factor of $1 - \alpha$ after each reflection or by interpreting α as 'absorption probability', i.e. by generating another

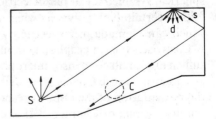

Fig. IX.9. Principle of ray tracing.

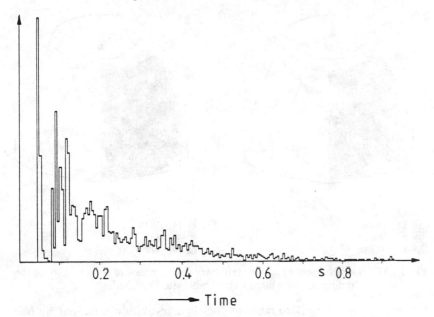

Fig. IX.10.   Time histogram of received particle energy (the interval width is 5 ms).

random number which decides whether the particle will proceed or whether it has been absorbed. In a similar way the effect of air attenuation can be taken into regard. As soon as the energy of the particle has fallen below a prescribed value or the particle has been absorbed, the path of another particle will be 'traced'. This procedure is repeated until all the particles emitted by the sound source at $t = 0$ have been followed up.

The results of this procedure are collected by means of 'counters', i.e. of counting areas or counting volumes which must be assigned previously. Whenever a particle crosses such a counter its energy and arrival time are stored, if needed also the direction from which it arrived. After the process has finished, i.e. the last particle has been followed up, the energies of all particles received in a certain counter within prescribed time intervals are added; the result is a histogram (*see* Fig. IX.10), which can be considered as a short-time averaged energetic impulse response. The selection of these intervals is not uncritical: if they are chosen to be too long, the histogram will be only a crude approximation to the true impulse response since significant details are lost by averaging; too short intervals, on the other hand, will afflict the results by strong random fluctuations superimposed on them. As a practical rule, the interval should be in the range 5–10 ms, since

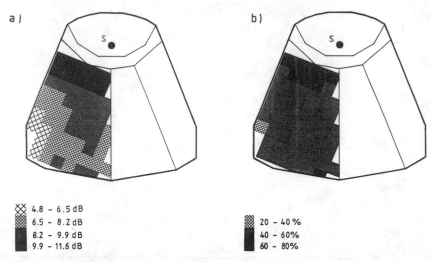

a)   b)

XX 4.8 – 6.5 dB
▓   6.5 – 8.2 dB   ▓   20 – 40 %
    8.2 – 9.9 dB   40 – 60%
■   9.9 – 11.6 dB   ■   60 – 80%

Fig. IX.11.   Distribution (a) of the stationary sound pressure level and (b) of the 'definition' in a large lecture hall (after Vorländer[21]).

this figure corresponds roughly to the time resolution achieved by our hearing.

The problem of properly selecting the time intervals in which the arrival times are classified does not apply if only one of the parameters introduced in Chapter VII, for instance the 'definition' D (eqn (VII.8)), the 'centre of gravity time' t_s (eqn (VII.6) with $\tau = \infty$) or the 'early lateral energy fraction' S (eqn (VII.19)), is to be determined, since the calculation of these parameters involves integrations over the whole impulse response or parts of it. The same holds for the 'early decay time' evaluated with the method of integrated impulse response (*see* Section VIII.5) or the steady state energy density which is just proportional to the integral over the whole energetic impulse response (*see* eqn (VII.25)). As an example, Fig. IX.11 depicts the distribution of the stationary sound pressure level and definition obtained by application of ray tracing techniques to a lecture hall with a volume of $3750\,\text{m}^3$ and 775 seats.[21]

In any case, however, the achieved accuracy of the results depends on the number of single events, i.e. on the number of sound particles counted with a particular counter. For this reason the counting area or volume must be chosen so that it is not too small; furthermore, the total number of particles which the original sound impulse is thought to consist of must be sufficiently large. As a practical guideline, a total of 10^4–10^5 sound particles will yield sufficiently precise results if the dimensions of the counters are of the order 1 m. With a good personal computer the time required for one run is somewhere between one and several hours, depending on the number of counters, the complexity of the room to be investigated and the efficiency of the algorithm employed.

The most tedious and time consuming part of the whole process is the collection and input of room data such as the positions and orientations of the walls and their acoustic properties. If the enclosure contains curved portions these must be approximated by planes unless their shape is very simple, for instance spherical or cylindrical. The degree of approximation is left to the intuition and experience of the operator.

The process described can be modified and refined in many ways. Thus the sound radiation need not necessarily be omnidirectional, instead the sound source can be given any desired directionality. Likewise, one can study the combined effect of more than one sound source, for instance of a real speaker and several loudspeakers with specified directional characteristics, amplifications and delays. This permits the designer to determine the optimal configuration of an electroacoustic installation in a hall. Furthermore, any mixture of purely specular or ideally diffuse wall reflections can be taken into consideration; the same holds for the directional dependence of absorption coefficients.

It is inherent in this method that the sound propagation is assumed to follow strictly geometrical laws, which justifies the name 'ray tracing'. As a consequence, interference effects and in particular diffraction cannot be accounted for, in contrast to the examination of a physical model, and it is still an open question whether this is a severe limitation of the method or not. This remark holds also for a different method of simulating sound propagation in rooms which is based on the old concept of image sources as described in Sections IV.1 and IV.2. The computer is used to construct all image sources which can be expected to contribute significantly to the energy density in a receiving point, and to collect all their contributions taking into account their strengths and their delays with respect to the direct sound.

In this simple form, however, the application of the image source model would require impractically long computing time because of the tremendous number of image sources needed. This may be illustrated by a simple example. Consider a hall made up of eight plane walls with a total area of $3800 \, m^2$; the volume of the hall would be $12\,000 \, m^3$. According to eqn (IV.8), a sound ray or sound particle would undergo about 27 reflections per second on the average. Consequently, to compute only the first 400 ms of the impulse response, image sources of up to the 11th order (at least!) must be considered. With this figure and with $N = 8$, eqn (IV.2) tells us that about 2.6×10^9(!) image sources must be constructed. But even worse: as pointed out in Section IV.1, only a small fraction of these image sources are 'visible' from a given receiver position because the walls are not infinite planes but have finite dimensions, and the 'visibility' or validity of each image source must be checked separately by means of a relatively time-consuming algorithm.

Fortunately Vian and van Maercke[22] and independently Vorländer[23] have found a way to determine the locations exactly of the valid image sources neglecting the invalid ones. This is done by an abbreviated ray tracing process which precedes the actual simulation: whenever a particle arrives at a counter it must have passed a certain sequence of image sources, which can be determined by backward tracing the fate of the particle. The next particle which hits the same counter at the same time can be omitted, since it would yield no new image sources. After running the ray tracing for a certain period one can be sure that all significant image sources have been found, including their relative strengths which depend on the absorption coefficients of the walls involved in the mirroring process. For the actual simulation of the sound propagation from the original sound source to the assumed receiving point the enclosure is no longer needed since its effect is contained in the contributions of the image sources. In contrast to the ray tracing techniques, they yield the exact energy impulse response. However, only specularly reflecting walls can be modelled with this method since the image source model fails for diffuse wall reflections.

On the other hand, this combined ray tracing–image source model offers possibilities which are far beyond the evaluation of objective sound field parameters from which the expected listening conditions can be inferred. Probably most fascinating is the idea of designing digital filters which influence speech or music signals in exactly the same way as the room under investigation would do (see Refs 2 and 3 of Chapter VII). Then a listener could hear the sound signal as if he were sitting in the hall, and he would get an immediate impression of its acoustics. This is a modern version of Spandöck's old conception, originally meant for application in physical room models (see preceding section).

For this purpose we need the true (amplitude) impulse response of the room rather than its energetic response. To obtain it the acoustic properties of the walls are not accounted for just by their absorption coefficients but by their complex and frequency-dependent reflection factors or by what corresponds to them in the time domain. In another approach the simulation is carried out for several frequency bands, each time with the correct set of absorption coefficients. The results are properly combined into the ultimate impulse response. Furthermore, it is imperative that the processed sound signals are presented binaurally, otherwise the listener will not receive a realistic spatial impression of the sound field. Therefore the impulse response must be modified so as to include the listener's individual ear transfer functions (*see* Section I.6). Since these functions depend on the direction of sound incidence, rapid measuring routines for their determination are needed, for instance by employing maximum length sequences as test signals in combination with the fast Hadamard transform (*see* Section VIII.2). When all these operations have been performed, we are ready to process 'dry' sound signals in the same way the real hall would do and to present them to a listener, either through earphones or with the free field reproduction techniques described at the end of the introduction to Chapter VII.

It is evident that this technique by which an old dream of the acoustician is going to come true will be extremely helpful, not only for the practical design of halls of any kind but also for getting more insight into the way geometric details of a hall, the properties of its walls, the arrangement of the audience, etc., influence listening conditions at any desired position.

REFERENCES

1. Vorländer, M. & Kuttruff, H., *Acustica*, **58** (1985) 118.
2. Meyer, J., *Acustica*, **36** (1976) 147.
3. Marshall, A. H., Gottlob, D. & Alrutz, H., *J. Acoust. Soc. America*, **64** (1978) 1428.
4. Allen, W. A., *J. Sound Vibr.*, **69** (1980) 143.
5. Beranek, L. L., *J. Acoust. Soc. America*, **32** (1960) 66.
6. Kosten, C. W. & de Lange, P. A., Proceedings of the Fifth International Congress on Acoustics, Liège, 1965, paper G43.
7. Kosten, C. W., *Acustica*, **16** (1965/66) 325.
8. Deutscher Normenausschuß, *Schallabsorptionsgrad-Tabelle*. Beuth-Vertrieb, Berlin–Köln Frankfurt, 1968.
9. Schmidt, H., *Schalltechnisches Taschenbuch* (2nd edn). VDI-Verlag, Düsseldorf, 1976.
10. Kath, U., Proceedings of the Seventh International Congress on Acoustics, Budapest, 1961.
11. Kuttruff, H., *Acustica*, **18** (1967) 131.
12. Hodgson, M., Theoretical and physical models as tools for the study of factory sound fields. PhD thesis, University of Southampton, 1983.
13. Vermeulen, R. & De Boer, V., *Philips Techn. Rundschau*, **1** (1936) 46.
14. Vermeulen, R., *Philips Techn. Rundschau*, **5** (1940) 329.

15. Spandöck, F., *Ann. d. Physik V.*, **20** (1934) 345.
16. Brebeck, P., Bücklein, R., Krauth, E. & Spandöck, F., *Acustica*, **18** (1967) 213.
17. Els, H. & Blauert, J., Proc. Vancouver Symposium, 12th International Congress on Acoustics, 1986, p. 65.
18. Kuttruff, H., *Appl. Acoust.*, **27** (1989) 27.
19. Schroeder, M. R., Atal, B. S. & Bird, C., Proceedings of the Fourth International Congress on Acoustics, Copenhagen, 1962, paper M21.
20. Krokstad, A., Strøm, S. & Sørsdal, S., *J. Sound Vibr.*, **8** (1968) 118.
21. Vorländer, M., *Acustica*, **65** (1988) 138.
22. Vian, S. P. & van Maercke, D., Proc. Vancouver Symposium, 12th International Congress on Acoustics, 1986, p. 74.
23. Vorländer, M., *J. Acoust. Soc. America*, **86** (1989) 172.

X

Electroacoustic Installations in Rooms

Nowadays there are many points of contact between room acoustics and electroacoustics even if we neglect the fact that modern measuring techniques in room acoustics could not exist without the aid of electroacoustics (loudspeakers, microphones, tape recorders). Thus we shall hardly ever find a meeting room of medium or large size which is not provided with a public address system for speech amplification; it matters not whether such a room is a church, a council chamber or a multi-purpose hall. We could dispute whether such an acoustical 'prothesis' is really necessary for all these cases or whether sometimes they are more a misuse of technical aids; it is a fact that many speakers and singers are not only unable but also unwilling to exert themselves to such an extent and to articulate so distinctly that they can make themselves clearly heard even in a hall of moderate size. Instead they prefer to rely on the microphone which is readily offered to them. But the listeners are also demanding, to an increasing extent, a loudness which will make listening as effortless as it is in broadcasting, television or cinemas. Acousticians have to come to terms with this trend and they are well advised to try to make the best of it and to contribute to an optimum design of such installations.

The loudness as well as the quality of the electroacoustically amplified sound signals depend to a large extent on the acoustical qualities of the room in which a public address system operates. Therefore, the use of such a system does not mean that we can dispense with careful planning of the acoustics of the room. Furthermore, without knowledge of the acoustical factors responsible for speech intelligibility and of the way in which these factors are influenced by the construction as well as of the interaction between the room and the electrical system, it would hardly be possible to plan, to install and to operate electroacoustical systems with optimal performance.

Beyond this, room acoustics has its own particular interest in loudspeaker installations. This results from the increasing sizes of the halls and the increasing number of listeners and spectators who personally wish to witness cultural or sports events or be entertained; hence it is fundamentally impossible to achieve the necessary loudness required by the listener by means of conventional room acoustics only. Furthermore, very large halls are used—largely for economic reasons—frequently for very different kinds of presentations: sometimes the range of presentations extends from boxing matches or bicycle racing to theatrical productions, from the performance by a large orchestra and chorus to fashion shows, political meetings, cabarets and chamber music evenings. A compromise must be reached in the design of these halls, even though such a compromise is quite naturally not the optimum for most of the uses of the hall.

In this situation it is a great advantage to have an electroacoustic installation which is designed optimally for speech and which has a directivity matched to the particular hall. Such an installation can provide for satisfactory speech intelligibility at reverberation times which are longer than the optimum for speech, and hence the latter can be appropriately adapted to musical events. The reverse way is even more versatile, but also more difficult technically: to render the natural reverberation of the hall relatively short in order to match the needs of optimum speech transmission. For the performance of music, the reverberation is lengthened by electroacoustical means to a suitable and adjustable value. The particular circumstances will decide which of the two possibilities is more favourable. In any case, well trained and reliable personnel are required for the operation, a fact which is frequently overlooked.

Using an installation which lengthens the reverberation electro-acoustically—as one has with some electronic musical instruments—we can try to attain a true simulation of 'natural acoustics' and we also try to produce quite new artificial acoustical effects which cannot be obtained in any other way. In the latter respect, we are only at the beginning of a development whose progress cannot yet be predicted.

X.1 DIRECTIVITY OF LOUDSPEAKERS

In this and the next section we consider commonly used public address systems consisting of a microphone for picking up a speaker's voice, an amplifier, and one or several loudspeakers which re-radiate the amplified speech sounds. Frequently the dimensions of the loudspeakers are not small compared with the wavelengths of interest and therefore have some directivity which can be employed to project the sound preferentially towards the audience or parts of it. This holds especially for regular arrays of loudspeakers which are fed by identical electrical signals. A frequently used combination of loudspeakers is the linear array consisting of several equal loudspeaker systems arranged along a straight line with equal spacing.

In the following a few facts on such linear arrays, which are sometimes simply referred to as 'loudspeaker columns', are presented. For the sake of simplicity it is assumed that the elements of the column, which are spaced at distances d, have no directivity themselves.

The directivity function as defined by eqn (I.25) of a linear array is given by

$$\Gamma(\vartheta) = \frac{\sin\left(\tfrac{1}{2}Nkd\sin\vartheta\right)}{N\sin\left(\tfrac{1}{2}kd\sin\vartheta\right)} \tag{X.1}$$

where N is the number of elementary systems and ϑ is the angle which the considered direction of radiation includes with the normal of the array. This is illustrated in Fig. X.1 which plots $|\Gamma(\vartheta)|$ as a polar diagram for $kd = \pi/2$ and $N = 8$. The three-dimensional directivity can be imagined by rotating this diagram around the (vertical) axis of the column. There is a main lobe which is the narrower the larger the quantity $kd = 2\pi f d/c$ at constant N. Furthermore, directional diagrams of loudspeaker columns

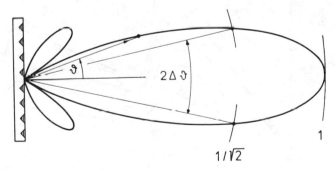

Fig. X.1. Directivity function $|\Gamma(\vartheta)|$ of a linear loudspeaker array with $N = 8$ elements for $kd = \pi/2$.

contain smaller side lobes, the number of which depends on N and on kd, i.e. on the frequency. The largest of these side lobes is at least 10 decibels lower (for $N > 3$) than the maximum of the main lobe.

The width of the main lobe can be characterised by the angular distance $2\Delta\vartheta$ of the points in the polar diagram for which $|\Gamma^2| = 0.5$ (*see* Fig. X.1). For linear arrays of the assumed kind this quantity is approximately

$$2\Delta\vartheta \approx \frac{15}{fL} \quad \text{degrees} \tag{X.2}$$

Here f is the frequency in kilohertz and $L = (N - 1)d$ is the total length of the array. This relation, however, is applicable only if the resulting $2\Delta\vartheta$ is less than $30°$.

Another important quantity is the directivity factor or gain G of a linear array as generally defined in eqn (I.26). It is plotted in Fig. X.2 as a function of $d/\lambda = kd/2\pi$ and for various numbers N of elements. On the average over a large frequency range and in the limit of very high frequencies, $G \approx N$.

Although the directivity of loudspeaker columns is frequency dependent it can be taken into account with advantage. The dimensions of a loudspeaker array should be chosen in such a way that at least for medium frequencies an optimum portion of the audience receive amplified sound. Furthermore, the directivity of loudspeakers can help to suppress acoustical feedback to the microphone (*see* Section X.4).

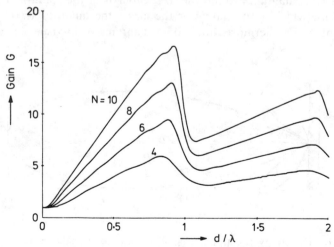

Fig. X.2. Gain G of linear loudspeaker arrays as a function of d/λ.

Another type of loudspeaker which is commonly used in public address systems is the horn loudspeaker. It consists of a tube with steadily increasing cross-sectional area, called a horn, and of an electrodynamically driven membrane at the narrow end (the throat) of the horn. Its main advantage is its high efficiency because the horn improves the acoustical match between the membrane and the free field. Furthermore, by combining several horns a wide variety of directional characteristics can be obtained. For these reasons, horn loudspeakers are often employed for large-scale sound reproduction. The most common horn shapes are the conical and particularly the exponential horn. The latter has a marked cutoff frequency which depends on the flare of the horn and below which no efficient sound radiation is possible.

The directional characteristics of a horn loudspeaker depends on the shape and the opening area of the horn and, of course, on the frequency. As long as the acoustical wavelength is larger than all lateral dimensions of the opening, i.e. at relatively low frequencies, its directivity pattern is similar to that of a plane piston with the same shape. For a circular piston mounted in an infinite baffle the directivity function reads

$$\Gamma(\vartheta) = \frac{2J_1(ka \sin \vartheta)}{ka \sin \vartheta}$$

where a denotes the radius of the piston and J_1 is the Bessel function of first order. Its directional pattern has rotational symmetry about the normal of the piston plane. At higher frequencies, the directional characteristics of horn loudspeakers are broader than those of the corresponding piston. Since they do not depend only on the size and shape of the opening but also on the shape of the whole horn, they cannot be expressed in simple terms, instead the reader is referred, for instance, to Olson's book.[1]

As mentioned, the directivity pattern can be shaped in a desired way by combining several or many horn loudspeakers. The most straightforward solution of this kind is the multi-cellular horn consisting of many single horns the openings of which approximate a portion of a sphere and yield nearly uniform radiation into the solid angle subtended by this portion.

X.2 DESIGN OF ELECTROACOUSTIC INSTALLATIONS FOR SPEECH TRANSMISSION

This section deals with factors influencing the performance of public address systems, namely with the acoustical power to be supplied by the

loudspeakers, with their directionality and with the reverberation time of
the room where the system is operated.

If speech intelligibility were a function merely of the loudness, i.e. of the
average energy density w at a listener's position, we could use eqn (V.37) for
estimating the necessary acoustical power of the loudspeaker:

$$P = \frac{c}{4} A w = 13 \cdot 8 \frac{V}{T} w \tag{X.3}$$

with

$$A = \sum_i S_i \alpha_i$$

denoting the total absorbing area in the room.

We know, however, from the discussions in Chapter VII, that the
intelligibility of speech depends not only on its loudness but even more on
the structure of the impulse response characterising the sound transmission
from a sound source to a listener. In particular, the classification of the total
energy conveyed by the impulse response into useful and detrimental
energy is of great importance.

To derive practical conclusions from this latter fact, we idealise the
impulse responses of individual transmission paths by an exponential
decay of sound energy with a decay constant δ:

$$E(t) = E_0 \exp(-2\delta t)$$

Now suppose we have a sound source supplying an average power P to
the room under consideration. We regard as detrimental those contributions to the resulting energy which are conveyed by the 'tail' of the
energetic impulse response and which are due to reflections being delayed by
more than 100 ms with respect to the direct sound. The corresponding
modification of eqn (V.34) (second version) reads

$$E = P \int_{0 \cdot 1\,\text{s}}^{\infty} \exp(-2\delta t)\, dt$$

and leads to the detrimental part of the reverberant energy density

$$w_r = \frac{P}{2V\delta} \exp(-0 \cdot 2\delta) \tag{X.4}$$

On the other hand, the direct sound energy supplied by the loudspeaker is
regarded as useful energy, taking into account, however, the directivity of
the loudspeaker and eventually including the contributions made by

reflecting surfaces close to the loudspeaker. We assume that the loudspeaker or the loudspeaker array has a gain G and points with its main
lobe towards the most remote parts of the audience which are at a distance
r_{max} from it. Then the density of the useful energy in that most critical
region is, according to eqns (I.15) and (I.26):

$$w_d = \frac{GP}{4\pi c r_{max}^2} \qquad (X.5)$$

On the assumption that the level L_d of the speech signal, undistorted by
decaying sound energy, is about 70 to 80 dB, satisfactory intelligibility is
achieved (*see* Fig. VII.12) if

$$w_d \approx w_r$$

or, after insertion of eqns (X.4) and (X.5):

$$\frac{G}{2\pi r_{max}^2} \approx \frac{c}{V\delta} \cdot \exp(-0.2\delta)$$

By introducing the reverberation time $T = 3 \ln 10/\delta$ and solving for r_{max}, we
obtain an expression for the range which can be supplied with amplified
speech at good intelligibility

$$r_{max} \approx 0.057\left(\frac{GV}{T}\right)^{1/2} 2^{1/T} \qquad (X.6)$$

(r_{max} in metres, V in cubic metres).

This critical distance is plotted in Fig. X.3 as a function of the
reverberation time; the product GV of the loudspeaker gain and the room
volume is the parameter of the curves.

In the most important range of reverberation times $1 < T < 2$ the
complicated T-dependence of eqn (X.6) can be approximated by $2/T$ which
leads to

$$r_{max} \approx 0.11\frac{(GV)^{1/2}}{T} \qquad (X.6a)$$

It should be noted that eqns (X.6) and (X.6a) indicate rather the order of
magnitude of the allowed r_{max} than an exact limit. They predict that
listeners seated at distances from the loudspeaker which are noticeably
larger than r_{max} cannot be supplied with amplified sound in a satisfactory
manner. Obviously, the reach of the loudspeaker cannot be extended by
increasing the power since this would augment not only the useful but also

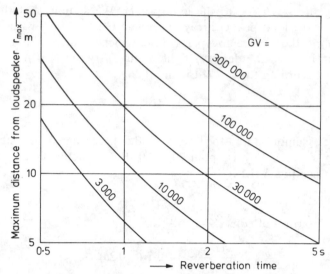

Fig. X.3. Allowed maximum distance of listeners from loudspeaker as a function of the reverberation time for various values of GV (V in m^3).

the detrimental energy. An improvement can be achieved, however, by increasing the directivity of the loudspeaker, by reducing the reverberation time or by operating several loudspeakers at separate locations each of which supplies its own part of the audience (*see* next section).

The acoustical power to be emitted by the loudspeaker is determined by the requirement that the directly transmitted sound portion leads to a sufficiently high sound pressure p_d or pressure level L_d even at the most remote seats:

$$P = \frac{4\pi r_{max}^2}{\rho_0 c G} \cdot \overline{p_d^2} \approx \frac{12}{G} r_{max}^2 \cdot 10^{0.1 L_d - 12} \quad \text{watts} \tag{X.7}$$

This is the same formula as that to be applied to outdoor sound amplification since it does not include any room properties.

For a better illustration, we shall consider a numerical example. In a hall with a volume of $15\,000\,m^3$, let the largest distance to be covered by the loudspeaker be $r_{max} = 30\,m$. The loudspeaker combination is assumed to have a gain of 5. If a speech level of 80 dB is required, according to eqn (X.7) we need an acoustical power of $0.22\,W$. Assuming an electroacoustical efficiency of 5%, this means that an electrical power of $4.4\,W$ must be supplied to the loudspeaker. This is in contrast to the prediction of eqn (X.3) which would demand an acoustical power of 20 mW or an electrical power of 0·4 W for an assumed reverberation time of 3 s. Even more serious than this discrepancy in the power is the fact that under the given circumstances eqn (X.6) would be nowhere near satisfied. In order to achieve equality, G would have to be selected as high as 35, which is nearly impossible for practical loudspeaker combinations. If, however, the reverberation time of the hall is decreased to 1 s by an absorbent treatment, eqn (X.6) could be fulfilled with $G = 5$, which is not an unrealistic figure.

In a large hall there is usually a certain noise level, which is due to a restless audience, to the air-conditioning system or to insufficient insulation against exterior noise sources. If this level is 40 dB or less it can be left out of consideration as far as the required loudspeaker power is concerned. This is not so at higher noise levels, of course. To be prepared for all eventualities it is advisable to increase the acoustical power given by eqn (X.7) by a substantial safety factor. In any case, it is obvious that good speech intelligibility is not achieved just with sheer power.

X.3 REMARKS ON THE SELECTION OF LOUDSPEAKER POSITIONS

Sound radiated electroacoustically in a room can be effected by one central loudspeaker, but equally by several or many loudspeakers distributed throughout the room. (The term 'central loudspeaker' includes of course the possibility of combining several loudspeakers closely together in order to achieve a suitable directivity, for instance in a linear array.) This section will deal with several factors which should be considered when a suitable loudspeaker location is to be selected in a room.

In each case the loudspeakers should ensure that all the listeners receive a uniform supply of sound energy; furthermore, for speech installations, a satisfactory speech intelligibility is required. We have already seen in the preceding section that this is not only a matter of applied acoustical power but also a question of a suitable loudspeaker arrangement and directionality.

In addition a public address system should, in most cases, yield a natural sound impression. In the ideal case (possibly with the exception of the presentation of electronic music) the listener would be unable to notice the electroacoustical aids at all. To achieve this, it would at least be necessary, apart from using high quality microphones, loudspeakers and amplifiers, for the sound radiated by the loudspeakers to reach, or appear to reach, the listener from the same direction from which he either sees or hears the actual speaker or natural sound source.

In most cases, the sound signal emitted by the loudspeaker is picked up by a microphone close to the natural sound source. If loudspeakers as well as the microphone are in the same hall, the microphone will inevitably pick up sound arriving from the loudspeaker as well. This phenomenon, known as 'acoustical feedback', can result in instability of the whole equipment and can lead to howling or whistling sounds. However, even with stable operation, the quality of the amplified sound signals can be reduced substantially by acoustical feedback. A suitably selected loudspeaker location can minimise this effect. We shall discuss acoustical feedback in a more detailed manner in the next section.

With a central loudspeaker installation, the irradiation of the room is achieved by a single loudspeaker or loudspeaker combination with the desired directionality, and if necessary there is additional support from subsidiary loudspeakers in the more remote parts of the room (boxes, balconies, spaces behind corners, etc.). A simple central installation is depicted schematically in Fig. X.4. The location of the loudspeaker, its directionality and its orientation have to be chosen in such a way that the audience is supplied with direct sound as uniformly as possible. This can be checked experimentally, not by stationary measurements, but by impulse measurements or using correlation techniques. In most cases, the loudspeaker will be mounted above the natural sound source; its actual position must be so chosen that feedback becomes as little as possible. This way of mounting has the advantage that the direct sound, coming from the loudspeaker, will always arrive from roughly the same direction (with regard to a horizontal plane) as the sound arriving directly from the sound source. The vertical deviation of directions is not very critical, since our

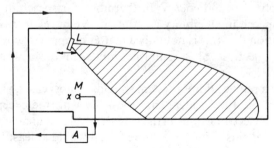

Fig. X.4. Central loudspeaker system (schematic representation). L = loud-speaker, M = microphone, A = amplifier, x = source.

ability to discriminate sound directions is not as sensitive in a vertical plane as in a horizontal one. The subjective impression is even more natural if care is taken that the loudspeaker sound reaches the listener simultaneously with the natural sound or a bit later. In the latter case there is a possibility, according to the law of the first wavefront, of raising the illusion in the listener, that all the sound he hears is produced by the natural sound source, i.e. that no electroacoustic system is in operation. This illusion can be maintained even if the level of the loudspeaker signal at the listener's position surpasses that produced by the natural source by 5 to 10 dB, provided the latter precedes the loudspeaker signal by about 10 to 15 ms (Haas effect, *see* Section VII.3).

The exact conditions under which the increase of loudness, achieved in this way, will also contribute to speech intelligibility have been investigated by Lochner & Burger.[2] According to their results, an increase in speech intelligibility will occur if the energy emitted by the loudspeaker does not substantially excite the reverberation of the room but instead reaches the listener virtually unreverberated. This in turn requires that the loudspeaker is either positioned close to the listeners and hence the distance between it and the listeners is smaller than the reverberation distance, or that the loudspeaker, due to its directionality, produces only a few wall reflections, and instead radiates its energy predominantly towards the (absorbent) audience or other absorbent areas. This finding once more underlines our earlier statement that speech intelligibility achieved by a loudspeaker installation is not only a matter of amplification, but depends to much the same extent on the treatment of the walls of the room, on the location and orientation of the loudspeakers, etc.

The simultaneous or delayed arrival of the loudspeaker's signals at the listener's seat can be achieved by increasing the distance between the loudspeaker and the audience (*see* Fig. X.4). The application of this simple measure is limited, however, by the fact that it will generally increase the danger of acoustical feedback, since the microphone will lie more and more in the range of the main lobe of the loudspeaker's directional characteristics. Thus, a compromise must be found. Another way is to employ electrical methods for effecting the desired time delay. They are described below.

Very good results in sound amplification, even in large halls, are obtained by using a speaker's desk which has loudspeakers built into the front facing panel; these loudspeakers should be arranged in properly inclined, vertical columns with suitable directionality. With this arrangement, the sound from the loudspeakers will take almost the same direction as the sound from the speaker himself. It reduces problems due to feedback provided that we prevent the propagation of structure-born sound by resiliently mounting the loudspeakers and the microphone.

In very large or long halls, or in halls consisting of several sections, the supply of sound energy by one single loudspeaker only will usually not be possible, for one thing because condition (X.6) cannot be met without unreasonable expenditure. The use of several loudspeakers at different positions has the consequence that each loudspeaker must only reach a smaller maximum distance r_{max} which makes it easier to satisfy eqn (X.6). Simple examples are shown in Fig. X.5. If all loudspeakers are fed with identical electrical signals, however, areas will be created in which the listeners feel irritated in that they consciously hear sound from more than one source. In these areas it is not only the natural localisation of the sound source which is impaired but the intelligibility will also be significantly diminished. Therefore it is quite useful for the electrical signals, which are applied to the subsidiary speakers, to be delayed electrically at least by a time interval which will ensure that the sound signal coming from the subsidiary loudspeakers will not reach any listener's seat before the sound

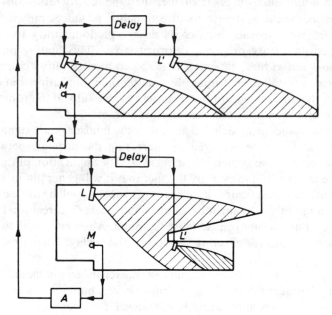

Fig. X.5. Public address systems with more than one loudspeaker unit. L, L' = loudspeakers, M = microphone, A = amplifier.

from the main loudspeaker. Furthermore, the power of the subsidiary loudspeakers must not be too high since this again would make the listener aware of it and hence destroy his illusion that all the sound he receives is arriving from the stage.

The delay times needed in public address systems are typically in the range 10–100 ms, sometimes even more. In the past, tape recorders with endless magnetic tapes or wheels with a magnetic track on their periphery have been used for this purpose. They were equipped with one recording head and several playback heads at distances proportional to the desired delay times. Nowadays these electromechanical devices have been superseded by purely electronic delay units, either of the analogue type (for instance so-called 'charge transfer devices') or digital circuits. In the latter case, the electrical audio signal must first be converted into digital information, which—after passing a shift register—is reconverted into an analogue signal.

In halls where a high noise level is to be expected, but where nevertheless announcements or other information must be clearly understood by those present, it can be an advantage to sacrifice the ideal of a natural-sounding sound transmission, which preserves or simulates the original direction of sound propagation, and to work with many loudspeakers which are distributed fairly uniformly and are fed by identical electrical signals. In this case it is important to ensure that all the loudspeakers which can be mounted on the ceiling or suspended from it are supplied with equally phased signals. The listeners are then, so to speak, in the near field of a vibrating piston. Sound signals of opposite phases are noticed in the region of superposition in a very peculiar and unpleasant manner.

If the sound irradiation is effected by directional loudspeakers from the stage towards the back of the room, the main lobe of one loudspeaker will inevitably project sound towards the rear wall of the room, as we particularly wish to reach those listeners who are seated the furthest away immediately in front of the rear wall. Thus, a substantial fraction of the sound energy is reflected from the rear wall and can cause echoes in other parts of the room, which can irritate or disturb listeners as well as speakers. For this reason it is recommended that the remote portions of wall being irradiated by the loudspeakers are rendered highly absorbent. In principle, an echo could also be avoided by a diffusely reflecting wall treatment which scatters the sound in all possible directions. But then the scattered sound would excite the reverberation of the room, which, as was explained earlier, is not favoured for speech intelligibility.

The preceding discussions refer mainly to the transmission of speech.

The electroacoustical amplification of music—apart from entertainment or dance music—is firmly rejected by many musicians and music lovers for irrational reasons and also because they have suffered at the hands of poor loudspeaker installations. If, in spite of objections, electroacoustical amplification is mandatory in very large halls, the installation must be carefully designed and constructed with first class components and it must preserve, under all circumstances, the natural direction of sound incidence. Care must be taken to avoid linear as well as non-linear distortions and the amplification should be kept at a moderate level only. For entertainment music, the requirements are not as stringent; in this case people have long been accustomed to the fact that a singer has a microphone in his or her hand and the audience will more readily accept that it will be conscious of the sound amplification.

These remarks have no significance whatsoever for the presentation of electronic music; here the acoustician can safely leave the arrangement of loudspeakers and the operation of the whole equipment to the performers.

X.4 ACOUSTICAL FEEDBACK AND ITS SUPPRESSION

Acoustical feedback of loudspeaker installations in rooms has already been mentioned in the last section. In principle, feedback will occur whenever the loudspeaker is in the same room as the microphone which inevitably will pick up a portion of the loudspeaker signal. Only if this portion is sufficiently small are the effects of feedback negligibly faint; in other cases, it may cause substantial linear distortions, ringing effects and finally self-sustained oscillations of the whole installation which are heard as howling or whistling.

Before discussing measures for the reduction or suppression of feedback effects, we shall deal with its mechanism in a somewhat more detailed manner.

We assume that the original sound source, for instance a speaker, will produce at the microphone a sound signal whose spectrum is denoted by $S(\omega)$ (see Fig. X.6.). Its output voltage is amplified with a frequency independent amplifier gain q and is fed to the loudspeaker. The loudspeaker signal will reach the listener by passing along a transmission path in the room with a complex transfer function $\bar{p}_\omega$ (see Section III.4); at the same time, it will reach the microphone by a path with the transmission function p_ω. The latter path, together with the microphone, the amplifier and the loudspeaker, constitutes a closed loop through which the signal passes repeatedly.

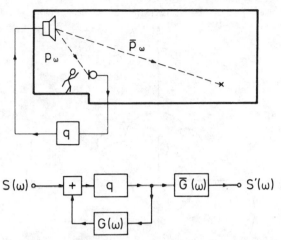

Fig. X.6. Acoustical feedback in a room. In the lower part of the transmission paths in the room and the loudspeakers are represented by 'black boxes'.

The lower part of Fig. X.6 shows the mechanism of acoustical feedback in a more schematic form. Here p_ω has been replaced by $G(\omega)$, which includes the transfer function of the loudspeaker. The same holds for $\bar{p}_\omega$ and $\bar{G}(\omega)$. The complex amplitude spectrum of the output signal (i.e. of the signal at the listener's seat) is given by

$$S'(\omega) = q\bar{G}(\omega)\left[S(\omega) + G(\omega)\frac{S'(\omega)}{\bar{G}(\omega)} \right]$$

From this expression we calculate the transfer function of the whole system including the effects of acoustical feedback, $G'(\omega) = S'(\omega)/S(\omega)$:

$$G'(\omega) = \frac{q\bar{G}(\omega)}{1 - qG(\omega)} = q\bar{G}(\omega) \sum_{n=0}^{\infty} [qG(\omega)]^n \qquad (\text{X}.8)$$

The latter expression clearly shows that acoustical feedback is brought about by the signal repeatedly passing through the same loop. The factor $qG(\omega)$ which is characteristic for the amount of feedback is called the 'open loop gain' of the system. Depending on its magnitude, the spectrum $S'(\omega)$ of the received signal and hence the signal itself may be quite different from the original signal with the spectrum $S(\omega)$.

A general idea of the properties of the 'effective transfer function' G' can easily be given by means of the Nyquist diagram in which the locus of the complex open loop gain is represented in the complex plane (*see* Fig. X.7).

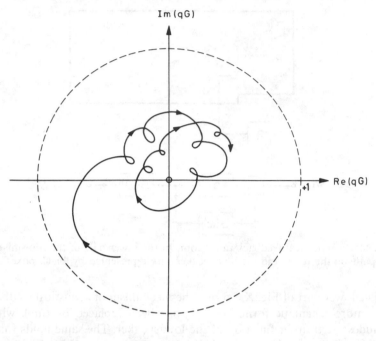

Fig. X.7. Nyquist diagram illustrating stability of acoustical feedback.

Each point of this curve corresponds to a particular frequency, abscissa and ordinate are the real part and the imaginary part of qG respectively. The whole system will remain stable if this curve does not include the point $+1$, which is certainly not the case if $|qG| < 1$ is true for all frequencies.

Now let us suppose that the amplifier gain and thus qG is at first very small. If we increase the gain gradually, the curve in Fig. X.7 is inflated, keeping its shape. In the course of this process, the distance between the curve and the point $+1$, i.e. the quantity $|1 - qG|$, could become very small for certain frequencies. At these frequencies, the absolute value of the transfer function G' will consequently become very large. Then the signal received by the listener will sound 'coloured' or, if the system is excited by an impulsive signal, ringing effects are heard. With a further increase of q, $|qG|$ will exceed unity somewhere, namely for a frequency close to that of the absolute maximum of $|G(\omega)|$. Then the system becomes unstable and performs self-excited oscillation at that frequency.

The effect of feedback on the performance of a public address system can also be illustrated by plotting $|G'(\omega)|$ on a logarithmic scale as a function of

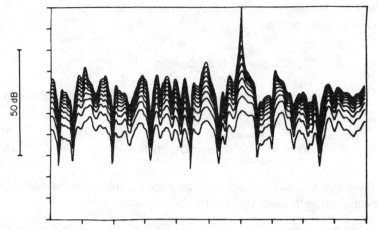

Fig. X.8. Simulated frequency curves of a public address system operated in a hall at various amplifier gains. The latter range from $-20\,\text{dB}$ to $0\,\text{dB}$ with respect to the critical gain q_0. The total frequency range is $90/T\,\text{Hz}$.

the frequency. This leads to 'frequency curves' similar to that shown in Fig. III.8). Figure X.8 represents several of such curves for various values of the open loop gain qG, obtained by simulation with a digital computer.[3] With increasing gain one particular maximum starts growing more rapidly than the other maxima and becomes more and more dominating. This is the condition of audible colouration. When a critical value q_0 of the amplifier gain is reached, this leading maximum becomes infinite which means that the system carries out self-sustained oscillations. (In real systems, the amplitude of these oscillations remains finite because of inevitable non-linearities of its components.)

A question of great practical importance concerns the amplifier gain q which must not be exceeded if colouration is to be avoided or to be kept in tolerable limits. According to listening tests as well as to theoretical considerations[3] colouration remains imperceptible as long as

$$20\log(q/q_0) \lesssim -12\,\text{dB} \qquad\qquad (\text{X.9})$$

For speech transmission, this quality may be raised up to about $-5\,\text{dB}$ without the risk of intolerable deterioration of the speech quality by colouration.

Another effect of acoustical feedback is the increase of reverberance which is again restricted to those frequencies for which $G'(\omega)$ is particularly high. To show this, we simplify eqn (X.8) by putting $\bar{G} = G$. Then the second version of this equation reads

$$G'(\omega) = \sum_{n=1}^{\infty} [qG(\omega)]^n \qquad (X.8a)$$

The corresponding impulse response is obtained as the (inverse) Fourier transform of that expression (*see* eqn (I.28a)):

$$g'(t) = \frac{1}{2\pi} \int_{-\infty}^{+\infty} G'(\omega) \exp(i\omega t) \, d\omega = \sum_{n=1}^{\infty} q^n g^{(n)}(t) \qquad (X.10)$$

In the latter formula $g^{(n)}$ denotes the n-fold convolution of the impulse response $g(t)$ with itself, defined by the recursion

$$g^{(n+1)}(t) = \int_0^t g^{(n)}(t')g(t - t') \, dt'$$

and

$$g^{(1)}(t) = g(t)$$

For our present purpose it is sufficient to use $g(t) = A \exp(-\delta t)$ as a model response. It yields $g^{(n)}(t) = t^n \exp(-\delta t)/n!$. If this is inserted into eqn (X.10), the sum turns out to be the series expansion of the exponential function, hence

$$g'(t) = Aqt \exp[-(\delta - Aq)] \qquad (X.11)$$

Evidently, the decay constant of the exponential is reduced to $\delta' = \delta - Aq$, and the reverberation time is increased by a factor

$$\frac{T'}{T} = \frac{\delta}{\delta'} = \frac{1}{1 - Aq/\delta} \qquad (X.12)$$

When q approaches the critical value δ/A, the reverberation time becomes infinite. On account of our oversimplified assumption of $g(t)$, eqns (X.11) and (X.12) do not show that the lengthening of the decay process and of the reverberation time occurs noticeably only at one or a few discrete frequencies, and that therefore the reverberation sounds coloured as does a steady state signal of wide bandwidth.

Acoustical feedback can be avoided by selecting a sufficiently small amplifier gain. This, however, makes the loudness of the loudspeaker signal at the listener's seat so low that eventually the system will become virtually useless. The loudspeaker system can be rendered much more effective, however, by making the mean absolute value of $\bar{G}(\omega)$ in the frequency range of interest as high as possible, but that of $G(\omega)$ as low as possible. This in turn is achieved by using highly directional loudspeakers whose main lobes point towards the listeners, whilst the microphone is in a direction of very low radiated intensity. Furthermore, the microphone can also be given a suitable directional characteristic which favours the original signal produced by the natural sound source, but not the signal which arrives from the loudspeaker. The most convenient means of achieving this is a gradient or a cardioid microphone with the direction of minimum sensitivity pointing towards the loudspeaker. With these rather simple methods, which are very effective when applied carefully, acoustical feedback cannot be completely eliminated, but the point of instability can be shifted far enough away so that it will never be reached during normal operation.

The self-excitation of the system could be completely avoided at a given mean value of the transfer function, if the open loop gain qG could be made absolutely independent of the frequency. Then it could be given a value which lies so close to unity that it makes G' as high as desired for a relatively broad frequency band, according to eqn (X.8) (first expression on the right-hand side), without enhancing only one or a few spectral components. In this way, we could achieve a very high loudness at the listener's seat. A corresponding increase in speech intelligibility, however, would not be obtained, since, according to eqn (X.12), the reverberation time would also be increased. The additional reverberation created by feedback would certainly not sound coloured, but would nevertheless diminish intelligibility. The effect of such a system would be the same as that of an extremely undamped room (a reverberation chamber for instance), where a high sound intensity or overall loudness, without any sort of instability, can be obtained at moderate or even low power output of the source, but where speech intelligibility is low due to the long reverberation time. We can conclude from this comparison that a loudspeaker system with an open loop gain which has a perfectly flat response would be ideal for lengthening the reverberation time and for controlling it easily but not for speech amplification.

Nevertheless a limited increase in the tolerable amplifier gain and hence in the loudness perceived by the listeners can be achieved by methods which aim in this direction. Such an increase may be extremely valuable in cases where the intelligibility is marginal due to insufficient loudness or else due to a relatively high noise level in a hall. In principle flattening out or averaging the frequency curve of a room could be achieved by moving the microphone along a circular path during its operation.[4] Since each point of the path has its own transmission characteristics, the maximum and minimum or the phase relation between several components which make up the resulting sound pressure at the microphone, are averaged out to some degree provided that the diameter of the circle is substantially larger than all the wavelengths of interest. The use of a gradient microphone rotating around an axis which is perpendicular to the direction of maximum sensitivity has also been proposed and this has an effect which is similar to a moving microphone. These methods have the disadvantage that they require mechanical movements and they also produce some amplitude modulation which can be detected subjectively.

It should be remarked that the required averaging cannot be achieved merely by using several loudspeakers or several microphones connected in parallel or in series. This is because the resultant frequency curve is the vector sum of the single frequency curves and hence has the same general properties as a single frequency curve which itself is the vector sum of numerous components superimposed with random phases (see Section III.4). In particular its absolute values are again distributed according to Rayleigh's law (eqn (III.32)) with a relative mean standard deviation of 0·523 independent of the number of added frequency curves.

According to Franssen,[5] the combination of several frequency curves will only result in an advantage as regards acoustical feedback if many mutually independent channels are used, each consisting of a microphone, a loudspeaker and an amplifier. Since such a loudspeaker system is rather costly, its application will probably only be justified for artificial reverberation lengthening and not for normal public address systems. For this reason, we postpone its discussion to the next section.

Another method of virtually flattening the frequency characteristics of the open loop gain has been proposed and applied in practice by Schroeder.[6,7] As we saw, acoustical feedback is brought about by particular spectral components which always experience the same 'favourable' phase conditions when circulating along the closed loop. If, however, at the beginning of each roundtrip, the frequencies of all spectral components are shifted by a small amount, then a particular component will experience favourable as well as unfavourable phase conditions, which, in effect, is the same as averaging the frequency curve. Let us suppose a sinusoidal signal has originally the angular frequency ω. After each roundtrip in the feedback loop its angular frequency has been increased by $\Delta\omega$, whereas its level has been increased or diminished by $L = 20\log_{10}|qG(\omega')|$ with ω' denoting the actual frequency. Hence, after having performed N roundtrips, the angular frequency of the signal is $\omega + N\Delta\omega$ and its total change in level is

$$L(\omega + \Delta\omega) + L(\omega + 2\Delta\omega) + \cdots + L(+N\Delta\omega) \approx N\langle L\rangle$$

where $\langle L\rangle$ is the average of the logarithmic frequency curve from ω to $\omega + N\Delta\omega$. The system will remain stable if $N\langle L\rangle \to -\infty$ as N approaches infinity, i.e. if $\langle L\rangle$ is negative. In any event, it is no longer the absolute maximum of the frequency curve which determines the onset of instability, but a certain average value. Since the difference between the absolute maximum and the mean value is about 10–12 dB for most large rooms, as we saw in Section III.4, it is this level difference by which the amplifier gain theoretically may be increased without the danger of instability, compared with the operation without frequency shifting. $\Delta\omega$ must be small enough on the one hand so that the frequency shift will not be heard and on the other hand, it must be high enough to yield an effective averaging after a few roundtrips. The latter will be the case if $\Delta\omega$ corresponds roughly to the mean spacing of frequency curve maxima, i.e. if according to eqn (III.33) the frequency shift is chosen to be

$$\Delta\omega > 2\pi(\Delta f)_{max} = \frac{8\pi}{T}. \tag{X.13}$$

Both conditions can be fulfilled quite well in the case of speech; with music, however, even very small frequency shifts are audible, since they change the musical intervals. Therefore, this method is applicable to speech only. In practice the total increase in amplification of about 10 or 12 dB, which is possible theoretically, cannot be used; if the increase exceeds 5–6 dB, speech begins to sound unnatural and finally becomes unintelligible, even with stable conditions. In practice, the frequency shift is achieved by inserting a suitable electronic device into the amplifier branch.

A similar method of reducing the danger of acoustical feedback was proposed by Guelke & Broadhurst[8] who replaced the frequency shifting device by a phase modulator. The effect of phase modulation is to add side lines to each spectral line lying symmetrically with respect to the centre line. At a suitable modulation index, the latter can be removed altogether. In this case, the authors were able to obtain an additional gain of 4 dB. They stated that the modulation was not noticeable even in music if the modulation frequency was as low as 1 Hz.

X.5 ELECTROACOUSTIC CONTROL OF REVERBERATION

As pointed out earlier in this book, there is an increasing demand for rooms and halls which can be used for many different kinds of performances such as those involving speech as well as music. Designing the room so that one obtains a compromise as regards the reverberation time, cannot of course satisfy the acoustical needs of each kind of sound signal. In order to create nearly optimum acoustical conditions for any kind of performance, we must at least provide means for varying the reverberation time.

This can be achieved, within certain limits at least, by purely acoustical, i.e. mechanical means, as we saw in Section IX.3. In principle a more versatile and perhaps less costly method is the application of certain electroacoustical systems which will render the acoustics of a hall variable. It is the objective of this final section to discuss possible systems for this purpose and to report on experiences which have been made to date with such installations.

A normal public address system designed carefully for optimum speech intelligibility, already represents the first step in this direction. If the loudspeaker sounds are projected mainly towards the audience, i.e. towards absorbent areas, if care is taken to avoid acoustical feedback during normal operation, and if the low frequency components which are not very important to the intelligibility of speech are suppressed rather than enhanced by the amplifier, then the system will perform satisfactorily even if the reverberation time of the room is longer than is optimum for speech. This is because the reverberating sound field is only slightly excited by the loudspeakers. Hence a fairly good intelligibility can be obtained in a hall which was originally designed for musical events.

According to Fig. IX.6, the long reverberation time needed for orchestral music generally requires a high specific volume of a hall, i.e. high volume per seat, or, more clearly, high volume per square metre of audience. Since, on the other hand, volume is expensive, clients and designers have a natural tendency to cut costs by reducing the enclosed volume, and sometimes the acoustical consultant will find it hard to win through against this tendency. Another common situation is that of an existing hall which is to be used for orchestral performances although it was originally intended for other purposes and therefore has relatively short reverberation. In any event, a consultant is sometimes faced with the problem of too short a reverberation time which is more difficult to handle than the reverse problem.

The 'natural' solution to this problem, namely to increase the volume

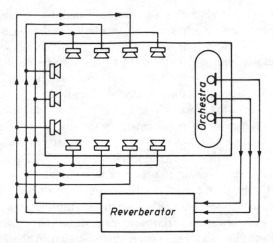

Fig. X.9. Principle of electroacoustic reverberation system employing separate reverberator.

of the hall, is almost impossible because the costs of this measure are prohibitive. Therefore, it is not unreasonable to ask whether the same goal could be reached at less expense by employing electroacoustical aids. In fact, several types of electroacoustical systems for raising the reverberation time have been developed and applied.

The principle of one of them is depicted in Fig. X.9. The sounds produced by the orchestra are picked up by microphones which are as close as possible to the musicians. The electrical signals are fed into a so-called 'reverberator'. This is a linear system with an impulse response which is more or less similar to that of an enclosure and which therefore adds reverberation to the signals. After this modification, they are re-radiated in the original room by loudspeakers. In addition, delaying devices must usually be inserted into the electrical circuit in order to ensure that the reverberated loudspeaker signals will not reach any listener's place earlier than the direct sound signal from the natural sound source, at the same time taking into account the various sound paths in the room.

It should be noted that the location of the loudspeakers has a great influence on the effectiveness of the system and on the quality of the reverberated sound. The obvious supposition that a great number of loudspeakers are required is not necessarily correct. The reverberating sound field must indeed be diffuse, not in an objective sense but in a subjective one, i.e. the listener should have the impression of 'spaciousness'.

According to Section VII.5, this is not a question of numerous directions of sound incidence but a question of incoherence between the various components. Therefore, the reverberator should have several output terminals yielding mutually incoherent signals which are all derived from the same input signal. In order to provide each listener with sound incidence from several substantially different directions, it may be necessary to use far more loudspeakers than incoherent signals. Nevertheless, the primary requirement is the use of incoherent signals, whereas the number of loudspeakers is a secondary question.

It is quite obvious that all the loudspeakers must be sufficiently distant from all the listeners in order to prevent one particular loudspeaker being heard much louder than the others. Finally, care must be taken to prevent significant acoustical feedback. Even when the amplification is low enough to exclude self-excitation, feedback can impair the quality of the loudspeaker sounds, since reiteration of the signal in the feedback loop causes the exaggeration of certain spectral components and the suppression of others. This was discussed in Section X.4. The resulting colouration of the sound can be intolerable for music at a gain at which it would still be unnoticeable for speech. For this reason, the use of directional loudspeakers for emitting reverberated signals is to be recommended.

A system of this type was installed for permanent use with music in the 'Jahrhunderthalle' of the Farbwerke Hoechst AG at Hoechst near Frankfurt.[9] This hall, the volume of which is $75\,000\,\text{m}^3$, has a cylindrical side wall with a diameter of 76 m, its roof is a spherical dome. In order to avoid echoes, the dome as well as the side wall are treated with highly absorbing materials. In this state it has a natural reverberation time of about one second. To increase the reverberation time, the sound signals are picked up by several microphones on the stage, passed through a reverberator and finally fed to a total of 90 loudspeakers which are distributed in a suspended ceiling and along the cylindrical side and rear wall. With this system, which underwent several modifications in the course of time, the reverberation time can be raised to about 2 s.

Adding reverberation to an electrical signal by a 'reverberator' can be effected in various ways. The most natural is to apply the microphone signal(s) to one or several loudspeakers in a separate reverberation chamber which has the desired reverberation time including the proper frequency dependence. The sound signal in the chamber is again picked up by microphones which are far apart from each other to guarantee the incoherence of the output signals (*see* Section VIII.6). The reverberation chamber should be free of flutter echoes and may be as small as about $200\,m^3$.

Another type of reverberator which had found widespread application mainly in broadcasting is the reverberation plate as first described by Kuhl.[10] It can be considered as a two-dimensional 'room' and consists of a thin and flat sheet of steel with typical dimensions of $1\,m \times 2\,m$ suspended in a frame. By a suitable transducer, the electrical signal is converted into a bending wave which is repeatedly reflected from the free edges of the plate. Thus reverberation is brought about in much the same way as in a three-dimensional enclosure: due to the low velocity of bending waves the obtained decay time may be quite considerable. The reverberated sound signal is re-converted into an electrical signal by a second transducer. A miniaturised version of this device has been described by van Leeuwen.[11]

By further reducing the number of dimensions we arrive at acoustical or mechanical waveguides with reflecting terminations. A device of this kind which was frequently used in the past consisted of a helical spring equipped with torsional transducers at one or both of its ends, and again the decay time may be quite long because of the low velocities of torsional waves on springs. However, because of the regular succession of the reflections, the result is rather a kind of flutter echo than naturally sounding reverberation.

The essential thing about this device is the finite travelling time between successive reflections. Therefore, in order to produce something like reverberation, we only require, in principle, a delaying device and a suitable feedback path by which the delayed signal is transferred again and again from the output to the input of the delay unit (see Fig. X.10a). If q denotes the open loop gain in the feedback loop, which must be smaller than unity for stable conditions, and t_0 denotes the delay time, the impulse response of the circuit is the same as that given by eqn (VII.4). With each roundtrip, the signal is attenuated by $-20 \log q$ dB, and hence after $-60/(20 \log q)$ roundtrips, the level has fallen by 60 dB. The associated total delay is the reverberation time of the reverberator and is given by

$$T = -\frac{3t_0}{\log q} \qquad (X.14)$$

It can be controlled by varying the open loop gain or the delay time t_0.

In order to reach a realistic reverberation time, either q must be fairly close to unity, which makes the adjustment of the open loop gain very critical, or t_0 must have a relatively large value. In both cases, the reverberation has an undesirable tonal quality. A reverberator built in this way has a transfer function with maxima and minima as shown in Fig. VII.8

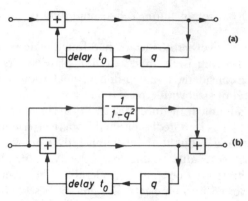

Fig. X.10.   Reverberators employing one delay unit only. (a) Comb filter type
reverberator, (b) all-pass type reverberator.

(central part, right-hand side), which become more prominent the closer q is
to unity. Quantitatively the ratio of maximum to minimum absolute values
of the transfer function is $(1+q)/(1-q)$. Open loop gains close to unity
therefore cause colourations, whereas long delay times t_0 are heard as a
flutter.

   The quality of the reverberation can be improved to a certain degree[12,13]
by subtracting from the output signal of the reverberator, the fraction
$1/(1-q)^2$ (*see* Fig. X.10b). The impulse response of the modified
reverberator is

$$g(t) = -\frac{\delta(t)}{1-q^2} + \sum_{n=0}^{\infty} q^n \delta(t - nt_0) \qquad (X.15)$$

Its Fourier transform, i.e. the transfer function of the reverberator is given
by

$$G(f) = \frac{1}{1 - q\exp(-2\pi i f t)} - \frac{1}{1-q^2}$$

$$= \frac{q\exp(-2\pi i f t)}{1-q^2} \cdot \frac{1 - q\exp(2\pi i f t)}{1 - q\exp(-2\pi i f t)} \qquad (X.16)$$

   Since the second factor in eqn (X.16) has the absolute value 1, the absolute
value of $G(f)$ is completely independent of frequency; there are no longer
maxima and minima. Subjectively, however, the undesirable properties of
the reverberation produced in this way have not completely disappeared
at all, since our ear does not perform a Fourier analysis in the mathematical

sense, but rather a 'short-time frequency analysis', thus also being sensitive to the temporal structure of a signal. A substantial improvement can only be effected by a combination of several reverberation units with different delay times, connected partly in parallel, partly in series. Schroeder describes the properties of several such combinations which he had simulated on a digital computer. Of course it is important to avoid simple ratios between the various delay times as well as long pronounced fundamental repetition periods in the impulse response. A thorough investigation of the structure of the reverberation, and hence of its quality, can be carried out by autocorrelation measurements as described in Section VIII.3, since these measurements give evidence of periodicities which will eventually occur.

By adding further refinements to these circuits, it is possible to impose a prescribed frequency dependence on the open loop gain and hence on the reverberation time obtained, without abandoning the all-pass character of the reverberator.[14]

Concerning the practical implementation of such reverberators, we can refer to Section (X.3) where several methods of producing time delays of 10 ms and more have been described.

If, as a delaying device, one tries to use a sound path in the room whose reverberation time is to be increased, one arrives at the other possibility of creating reverberation, as already mentioned in the preceding section. It makes use of the regeneration of a signal in an acoustical feedback loop whose gain is smaller than, but not small compared with unity. The most straightforward attempt at constructing such a system was carried out by Guelke & Broadhurst[8] who used two feedback circuits, each essentially consisting of a horn loudspeaker and a highly directional microphone installed at opposite corners of a 2000 m³ theatre and pointing towards the associated loudspeaker. The undesirable colourations of reverberation were eliminated by a phase modulating device (see page 309). With this system, the reverberation time of the theatre at medium frequencies reportedly can be continuously increased from about 1 s to 1·8 s.

In general, it is believed, however, that only a multi-channel system is suited to take advantage of reverberation lengthening by acoustical feedback without the risk of poor tonal quality due to ringing effects. In Fig. X.11, the system invented by Franssen,[5] mentioned in the preceding section, is depicted schematically. It consists of N ($\gg 1$) independent transmission channels with each microphone arranged outside the reverberation distance (see eqn V.38) of any loudspeaker. Electrically, the kth microphone is connected to the kth loudspeaker via an amplifier with

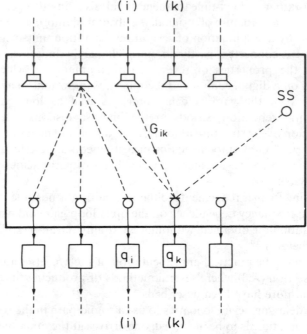

Fig. X.11. Multi-channel system after Franssen.[5]

gain q_k. Its output voltage contains the contribution $S_0(\omega)$ made by the sound source SS as well as the contributions of all loudspeakers. Therefore, its amplitude spectrum is given by

$$S_k(\omega) = S_0(\omega) + \sum_{i=1}^{N} q_i G_{ik}(\omega) S_i(\omega) \qquad (\text{X.17})$$

where G_{ik} characterises the acoustic transmission path from the ith loudspeaker to the kth microphone, including the properties of both transducers.

The expression above represents a system of N linear equations from which the unknown signal spectra $S_k(\omega)$ can be determined, at least in principle. To get a basic idea of what the solution of this system is like we can neglect all phase relations and hence replace all complex quantities by their squared magnitudes averaged over a small frequency range, i.e. S_k by the real quantity s_k and likewise G_{ik} by g_{ik} and S_0 by s_0. This is tantamount to superimposing energies instead of complex amplitudes and seems to be justified if the number N of channels is sufficiently high. Furthermore, we assume all amplifier gains and also $g_{ik} \equiv g$ for all i and k. Then we obtain immediately from eqn (X.17):

$$s_k = s = \frac{s_0}{1 - Nq^2g} \quad \text{for all } k \qquad \text{(X.18)}$$

The ratio s/s_0 characterises the increase of the energy density at a particular microphone caused by the electroacoustic system. On the other hand, under certain assumptions the reverberation time may be taken proportional to the steady state energy density in a reverberant space (*see* Section V.5). Therefore the ratio of reverberation times with and without the system is

$$\frac{T'}{T} = \frac{1}{1 - Nq^2g} \qquad \text{(X.19)}$$

This formula is similar to eqn (X.12), but in the present case, one can afford to keep the open loop gain of each channel low enough to exclude the risk of sound colouration by feedback, due to the large number N of channels. Franssen[5] recommended making q^2g as low as 0·01; then 50 independent channels would be needed to double the reverberation time.

However, more recent investigations into the properties of such multi-channel systems have shown that eqn (X.19) is too optimistic in that the actual gain of reverberation time is lower. This has been shown by computer simulation (Behler[15]) and also by a mathematically rigorous treatment of this problem (Ohsmann[16]). According to the latter author, a system consisting of 100 amplifier channels will increase the reverberation time by slightly more than 50% if all channels are operated with gains 3 dB below instability.

For the performance of a multi-channel system of this type it is of crucial importance that all open loop gains are virtually frequency independent within a wide frequency range. To a certain degree, this can be achieved by carefully adjusted equalisers which are inserted into the electrical paths. In any case there remains the problem that such a system comprises N^2 feedback channels, but only N amplifiers gains and equalisers to influence them.

Nevertheless, systems of this kind have been successfully installed and operated at several places, for instance in the Concert House at Stockholm.[17] This hall has a volume of 16 000 m³ and seats 2000 listeners. The electroacoustical system consists of 54 dynamic microphones and 104 loudspeakers. That means there are microphones which are connected to more than one loudspeaker. It increases the reverberation time from 2·1 s (without audience) to about 2·9 s. The tonal quality is reportedly so good that unbiased listeners do not become aware of the fact that an electroacoustical system is in operation.

An electroacoustical multi-channel system of quite a different kind, but to be used for the same purpose, has been developed by Parkin & Morgan[18] and has become known as 'assisted resonance system'. But unlike Franssen's system, each channel has to handle only a very narrow frequency band. Since the amplification and the phase shift occurring in each channel can be adjusted independently (or almost independently), all unpleasant colouration effects can be avoided. Furthermore, electroacoustical components, i.e. the microphones and loudspeakers need not meet high fidelity standards.

The 'assisted resonance system' was originally developed for the Royal Festival Hall in London. This hall, which was designed and constructed to be used solely as a concert hall, has a volume of 22 000 m^3 and a seating capacity of 3000 persons. It has been felt, since its opening in 1951, that the reverberation time is not as long as it should have been for optimum conditions, especially at low frequencies.[19] For this reason, the electroacoustical system for increasing the reverberation time was installed in 1964; at first this was on an experimental basis, but in the ensuing years several aspects of the installation have been improved and it has been made a permanent fixture.

In the final state of the system, each channel consists of a condenser microphone, tuned by an acoustical resonator to a certain narrow frequency band, a phase shifter, a very stable 20W amplifier, a broad band frequency filter and a 10- or 12-inch loudspeaker, which is tuned by a quarter wavelength tube to its particular operating frequency at frequencies lower than 100 Hz. (For higher frequencies, each loudspeaker must be used for two different frequency bands in order to save space and therefore has to be left untuned.) The feedback loop is closed by the acoustical path between the loudspeaker and the microphone, which is also in the ceiling. For tuning the microphone, Helmholtz resonators with a Q factor of 30 are used for frequencies up to 300 Hz; at higher frequencies they are replaced by quarter wave tubes. The loudspeaker and the microphone of each channel are positioned in the ceiling in such a way that they are situated at the antinodes of a particular room mode.

There are 172 channels altogether, covering a frequency range 58–700 Hz. The spacing of operating frequencies is 2 Hz from 58 Hz to 150 Hz, 3 Hz for the range 150–180 Hz, 4 Hz up to 300 Hz, and 5 Hz for all higher frequencies.

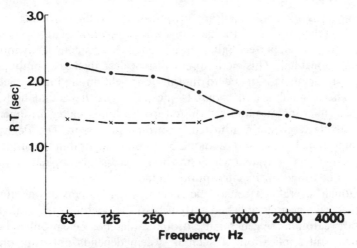

Fig. X.12. Reverberation time of occupied Royal Festival Hall, London as a function of frequency both with and without 'assisted resonance system'.[20]

In Fig. X.12 the reverberation time of the occupied hall is plotted as a function of frequency, again with both system on and system off. These results were obtained by evaluating recordings of suitable pieces of music which were taken in the hall. The difference in reverberation time below 700 Hz is quite obvious. Apart from this, the system has the very desirable effect of increasing the overall loudness of the sounds perceived by the listeners and of increasing the diffusion, i.e. the number of directions from which sound reaches the listeners' ears. In fact, from a subjective point of view, the acoustics of the hall seems to be greatly improved by the system and well-known musicians have commented enthusiastically on the achievements.[20]

During the past years, assisted resonance systems have been installed successfully in several other places. These more recent experiences seem to indicate that the number of independent channels need not be as high as was chosen for the Royal Festival Hall.[21]

Yet another electroacoustic system for increasing the reverberation of a hall, named Acoustic Control System (ACS)[23] is based on the old idea of wavefront reconstruction. In fact, this system reconstructs the wavefronts of the direct sound as well as those originating from image sources (*see* Section IV.2). However, the image sources are not those of the real hall, their positions correspond to the geometry of an idealized rectangular room. The same holds for the strengths of the image sources which are determined by the prescribed absorption of the walls and hence by the desired reverberation time. In this way, the reverberation of an acoustically satisfactory or even perfect hall is transplanted electroacoustically into the real, less perfect hall. This method may also be described as a combination of an electroacoustic system with digital sound field simulation (*see* Section IX.6). The original sound signal is picked up in the actual hall with numerous microphones and reradiated from a loudspeaker arrangement after passing a properly adjusted electronic processor. The degrading effect of feedback can also be avoided by accounting for it in the processor. More details on this system which has been successfully applied in several halls can be found in the cited publication.

Although several electroacoustic reverberation systems of one kind or the other have been established and successfully operated, these methods have not yet found the general attention they deserve. One problem is that the successful application of such a system depends not only on the technical perfection of its components but also on the skill and experience of the person who operates it. In the future, however, the 'human factor' will certainly be reduced by more sophisticated systems, allowing application also in places where no specially trained personnel is available.

REFERENCES

1. Olson, H. F., *Acoustical Engineering*. D. van Nostrand, Princeton, 1960.
2. Lochner, J. P. A. & Burger, J. H., *Acustica*, **9** (1959) 31.
3. Kuttruff, H. & Hesselmann, N., *Acustica*, **36** (1976) 105.
4. Zwikker, C., French Patent No. 712 588.
5. Franssen, N. V., *Acustica*, **20** (1968) 315.
6. Schroeder, M. R. Proceedings of the Third International Congress on Acoustics, Stuttgart. Elsevier, Amsterdam, 1959, p. 897.
7. Schroeder, M. R., *J. Acoust. Soc. America*, **36** (1964) 1718.
8. Guelke, R. W. & Broadhurst, A. D., *Acustica*, **24** (1971) 33.
9. Meyer, E. & Kuttruff, H., *Acustica*, **14** (1964) 138.
10. Kuhl, W., *Rundfunktechn. Mitteilungen*, **2** (1958) 111.
11. van Leeuwen, F. J., Proceedings of the Fifth International Congress on Acoustics, Liège, 1965, Paper H 68.
12. Schroeder, M. R., *J. Acoust. Soc. America*, **33** (1961) 1064.
13. Schroeder, M. R. & Logan, B. F., *J. Audio Eng. Soc.*, **9** (1961) 192.
14. Date, H., Uzihara, Z. & Tozuka, Y., *NHK Laboratories Note* No. 110, March, Tokyo, 1967.
15. Behler, G., *Acustica*, **69** (1989) 95.
16. Ohsmann, M., *Acustica*, **70** (1990) 233.
17. Dahlstedt, S., *J. Audio Eng. Soc.*, **22** (1974) 626.

18. Parkin, P. H. & Morgan, K., *J. Sound Vibr.*, **2** (1965) 74; *J. Acoust. Soc. America*, **48** (1970) 1025.
19. Parkin, P. H., Allen, W. A., Purkis, H. J. & Scholes, W. E., *Acustica*, **3** (1953) 1.
20. Parkin, P. H. & Morgan, K., *J. Acoust. Soc. America*, **48** (1970) 1025.
21. Berry, G. & Crouse, G. L., 52nd Convention of the Audio Eng. Soc., 1975, Preprint No. 1070.
22. Berkhourt, A. J., *J. Audio Eng. Soc.*, **36** (1988) 977.

Index

Absorbent materials, 255, 263, 277
Absorption. *See* Sound absorption
Absorption coefficient, 29, 32, 36, 39, 42, 43, 48, 49, 84, 87, 97, 115, 117, 119, 124, 139, 141, 142, 145, 146, 151, 155, 156, 158 60, 163, 167, 240, 249–51, 255, 262, 270, 271, 276, 280, 286, 287
Absorption constant, 137
Absorption measurement, 252–6
Acoustic admittance, 30
Acoustic Control System (ACS), 319
Acoustic properties of materials, 218
Acoustical behaviour, 3, 218, 257, 267
Acoustical deficiencies, 5, 6
Acoustical design, 257
Acoustical diagnosis, 4
Acoustical feedback, 292, 298, 302–9
Acoustical measurements. *See* Measuring techniques
Acoustical models, measurements on, 278–81
Acoustical power, 296, 297
Acoustical qualities, 1–6, 210–16, 289
Acoustical quantities, 7–9, 14
Acoustical waveguides, 313
Acoustically rough walls, 102
Air attenuation, 280
Air conditioning, 7
Amplifier gain, 304, 305, 307
Amplitude spectrum, 316
Anechoic room 166–70, 176, 277
Angular frequency, 66–7, 308–9
Angular resonance frequency, 149

Apparent signal-to-noise ratio, 237
Arbitrary shape rooms, 61
Artificial reverberation, 208
Assisted resonance system, 318, 319
Attenuation constant, 136
Audience absorption, 162–6
Audience areas, 259, 260, 268–9
Autocorrelation analysis, 235
Autocorrelation function, 16, 17, 26, 223–5, 228–31, 236
Autocorrelogram, 230, 231
Average number of wall reflections per second, 110–14
Axial mode, 59, 62

Background noise, 277–8
Bandpass filtering, 221
Barker coded impulse sequences, 224
Bessel function, 293
Binary impulse sequences, 223
Binaural impulse response, 173, 221
Binomial distribution, 115
Binomial theorem, 116
Bipolar rating scales, 211, 212
Boston Symphony Hall, 166
Boundary conditions, 50, 52–4, 56, 58, 62, 63
Broadcasting, 171, 207, 273
Butterfly algorithm, 227

Canopy, 263
Cardioid microphone, 307